States of Emergency

STATES OF EMERGENCY

Essays on Culture and Politics

PATRICK BRANTLINGER

INDIANA UNIVERSITY PRESS

Bloomington *and* Indianapolis

This book is a publication of

Indiana University Press
Office of Scholarly Publishing
Herman B Wells Library 350
1320 East 10th Street
Bloomington, Indiana 47405 USA

iupress.indiana.edu

Telephone orders   800-842-6796
Fax orders   812-855-7931

© 2013 by Patrick M. Brantlinger

∞ The paper used in this publication
meets the minimum requirements of
the American National Standard for
Information Sciences—Permanence
of Paper for Printed Library Materials,
ANSI Z39.48-1992.

*Manufactured in the
United States of America*

Brantlinger, Patrick, [date]
  States of emergency : essays on culture
and politics / Patrick Brantlinger.
    pages cm
  Includes bibliographical references and
index.
  ISBN 978-0-253-01015-5 (cl : alk. paper)
— ISBN 978-0-253-01019-3 (pb : alk. paper) — ISBN 978-0-253-01196-1 (ebook)
  1. United States—Social conditions—
21st century. 2. United States—Social
life and customs—21st century. 3. Social
history—21st century. I. Title.
  HN59.2.B73 2013
  306.0973—dc23
                                        2013008539
1 2 3 4 5   18 17 16 15 14 13

The tradition of the oppressed teaches us that the "state of emergency" in which we live is not the exception but the rule.

—WALTER BENJAMIN, "Theses on the Philosophy of History"

But we continue sailing on our *Titanic* as it tilts slowly into the darkened sea. The deckhands panic. Those with cheaper tickets have begun to be washed away. But in the banquet halls, the music plays on. The only signs of trouble are slightly slanting waiters, the kabobs and canapés sliding to one side of their silver trays, the somewhat exaggerated sloshing of the wine in the crystal wineglasses. The rich are comforted by the knowledge that the lifeboats on the deck are reserved for club-class passengers. The tragedy is that they are probably right.

—ARUNDHATI ROY, *An Ordinary Person's Guide to Empire*

CONTENTS

PREFACE

In his big book of the Apocalypse, *Living in the End Times* (2010), Slavoj Žižek, dubbed by *The New Republic* "the most dangerous philosopher in the West," declares that his "underlying premise . . . is a simple one: the global capitalist system is approaching an apocalyptic zero-point."[1] I agree with that premise. Žižek adds that the "'four riders of the apocalypse' are comprised by the ecological crisis, the consequences of the biogenetic revolution, imbalances within the system itself (problems with intellectual property; forthcoming struggles over raw materials, food, and water), and the explosive growth of social exclusions and divisions" (19). The essays in *States of Emergency* deal with these and other related crises.

Of the four "riders" named by Žižek, the one that I mention only in passing—the ecological crisis—may well be the leading factor that causes the ultimate collapse of "the global capitalist system." Last year was the hottest on record for planet earth. In February and March 2012, much of the United States, including Indiana where I live, experienced nearly a month of 80-degree temperatures, over 30 degrees above normal. Heat waves and drought have afflicted large swathes of the nation, causing record-setting forest fires in Colorado and Utah. The year 2012 also witnessed a record number of tornados, including the outbreak that demolished most of as Joplin, Missouri. And then there was Hurricane Sandy. "Extreme weather events," as the expression has it, will only get worse as the heating of the planet accelerates.

The two sections of *States of Emergency*, "Class Conflicts" and "Postmodern Conditions," are meant to suggest some of the connections among the diverse themes of the essays that may not otherwise be apparent. Five of the essays were invited contributions for anthologies and journals and have been published in earlier forms, now revised to bring them up to date. The other seven appear here for the first time. The essays vary in approach from journalistic to theoretical to satiric, but all fit my conception of cultural studies: interdisciplinary analysis combining humanistic and social science approaches and open to many theories and influences. Several of my earlier books and articles deal with the history and practice of cultural studies, including *Crusoe's Footprints: Cultural Studies in Britain and America* (1990) and *Who Killed Shakespeare? What's Happened to English since the Radical Sixties* (2001).

The first chapter of *States of Emergency* stresses that the cultural studies movement, developing out of labor history and the culture and society tradition in Britain, has served as a counter-discourse to orthodox (capitalist) economics. Cultural studies focused at first on issues of social justice, especially class struggle; I hope that will continue to be its main emphasis, although media studies and "cultural populism"[2] are leading cultural studies in other, less political and perhaps less polemical directions. I also examine today's top-down class warfare in the United States and around the world. The second chapter offers a critique of neoliberal economics and the ideology of "free markets." Among other issues, I note the inability of orthodox economists such as Alan Greenspan and N. Gregory Mankiw either to predict or to explain the 2007–8 crash. Along with Joseph Stiglitz, Thomas Frank, and many others, I stress the obvious: markets are not perfect mechanisms: they often fail. I follow this chapter with a partly satiric and theatrical examination of the Tea Party movement. Its adherents worship at the altar of free markets and of everything else they identify with freedom, like the freedom to carry concealed weapons. I note the inaccuracies and lies of several Tea Party gurus, including Glenn Beck, Rush Limbaugh, and Sarah Palin. I also glance at the Republican presidential primary of 2011 and the likely impact of the Citizens United Supreme Court decision on the November 2012 election.

Chapter 4, on the Virginia Tech tragedy, analyzes the writings and videos that Seung-hui Cho left. These express rage about the social, racial, and gender exclusions Seung experienced. U.S. gun culture also made it easy for Seung to commit his massacre, as it did for the Columbine High killers and for Jared Lee Loughner, who on January 8, 2011, shot Congresswoman Gabby Giffords and eighteen others in Tucson, Arizona.

I was asked by the editors of South Korean online journal *Situations* to write about the Virginia Tech massacre for its inaugural issue. Chapter 5, "What Is the Matter with Mexico?" turns to the history of U.S. military and economic involvement in Mexico, and to the current immigration crisis. I review John Kenneth Turner's reasons, in his 1910 exposé *Barbarous Mexico*, for calling Mexico a "slave colony" of the United States. Today's advocates of deporting all "illegals" and militarizing the border fail to understand that Mexico is still enslaved to the U.S. economy. The sixth essay in this section, coauthored by Dr. Richard Higgins, analyzes how capitalism has caused "waste" and "value" to become increasingly interchangeable in modern and now postmodern societies. Thorstein Veblen and H. G. Wells are our main examples, but we deal with ideas about waste and value from John Locke to Don DeLillo. Because this essay suggests that capitalism produces "superfluous" or "waste" people, it points ahead to "Army Surplus" in section two.

In the second section, "Postmodern Conditions," the chapters on the rhetoric of "the war on terror" and on "the state of Iraq" are twins. Apart from that, the essays take up seemingly unrelated topics. All of them, however, stress aspects of postmodernity that suggest possible futures. "The war on terror," we have often been told, may be endless. The Bushites liked to call it a war against "evil." And "state building" in Iraq is likely to mean that American involvement in that unfortunate country will last well into the future. Geographically, at least, the chapter on Aboriginal authors and postmodern Australia could not be farther removed from Iraq. Yet inauthenticity is often said to be a defining characteristic of postmodernity, while nothing seems more antithetical to copies, fakes, and simulacra than authentic Aboriginality. Frequent hoaxes and revelations of inauthenticity, combined with the emergence of Aboriginal arts and literature, have given Australian culture an exemplary postmodern status. The futures of indigenous peoples everywhere, moreover, seem to depend on their ability to preserve Aboriginality (read: traditional lifestyles) while also adapting to (post)modernization. The chapter on Marshall McLuhan, "crash theory," and "nanobots" focuses on science and technology, which obviously affect notions of postmodernity and possible futures—or "ends of history." As the crash theorists and many science fiction writers have recognized, the question of technological determinism that McLuhan foregrounded is crucial for understanding what futures may be in store for planet earth. The last two chapters, "Army Surplus" and "World Social Forum," offer contrasting possibilities about the future, one dismal and the other hopeful. "Army Surplus" is my attempt to answer the question, raised in "What's the Matter with Mexico?" and "Waste and Value," about how and why societies produce "surplus" or "rubbish" people. It is also my attempt to explain the causes of state-sponsored genocides, a topic I have dealt with in my studies of race and the British Empire. The final essay, based on a trip to Brazil and the 2005 World Social Forum (WSF) in Porto Alegre, expresses my hope that the alter-globalization movement will open the way to a more just, inclusive, democratic, prosperous, nonviolent, and environmentally sustainable future for humanity and for the planet that we share with all other species. Although the WSF itself may be losing steam, the U.S. Social Forum and regional forums around the globe are continuing its work, as are many other movements for social and environmental justice such as Occupy Wall Street. After all, aren't all forms of political engagement based on the belief that, as the motto of the WSF has it, "Another world is possible"? One condition of postmodernity is the recognition among increasing "multitudes" that another world had better be possible, or else.

ACKNOWLEDGMENTS

I have many people, journals, and organizations to thank for helping me write these essays. As noted earlier, my friend and former student Richard Higgins coauthored the essay on waste and value. The editors of *Situations* invited me to write about the Virginia Tech tragedy, and Professor Suk-koo Rhee followed up that invitation by asking me to come to Yonsei University to discuss cultural studies with his colleagues and students. Thanks, too, to Professor Sang-ki Park, who helped make my stay in Seoul a pleasant one. I am grateful as well to Professors Cynthia Fuchs and Joe Lockard for inviting me to write "Shopping on Red Alert" for their anthology, *Iraq War Cultures.*

Professor Paul Grosswiler long ago asked me to contribute to an anthology reassessing the ideas and influence of Marshall McLuhan, which led to the essay on crash theory and nanobots, first published in *Transforming McLuhan.* Another friend and former student, Professor Todd Avery, filled me in on recent work dealing with culture and nanotechnology. I also thank the editors of *Criticism* for permission to reprint "Waste and Value" from that journal. Regarding the essay on Aboriginal writers, Dr. Simon Caterson, author of *Hoax Nation,* generously sent me a copy of that book when I first learned about it but was unable to obtain a copy in the United States. I hope he and my other friends and colleagues in Australia will agree with my assessment of fakery in their country's cultural history.

I am grateful as well to many students and colleagues at Indiana University, including Professor Jim Naremore and the other participants in the faculty seminar on cultural studies that led to the creation of our

Cultural Studies Program, now expertly directed by Professor Purnima Bose. And I thank my wife Ellen, to whose memory *States of Emergency* is dedicated. Together with our friends and colleagues Milton Fisk and Mike Gasser, Ellen and I traveled the World Social Forum in 2005. And may all of my other activist friends in Jobs with Justice, Occupy Bloomington, and the Progressive Faculty and Staff Coalition at Indiana University keep up the good work of helping to create another, better world.

PART ONE

CLASS CONFLICTS

ONE

Class Warfare and Cultural Studies

Wherever you find injustice, the proper form of politeness is attack.

—T. BONE SLIM OF THE IWW

Cultural studies examines how people are classified (or "classed") and how they classify the world around them. In its initial phase in Britain in the 1960s, it focused on the relations between social class and cultural value; its emphasis on justice was unmistakable and remained so as it added both race and gender to its New Left agenda. From the outset, moreover, cultural studies has served as a counterdiscourse to the modern "science of value"—that is, to economics in its dominant, capitalist mode.

The seminal texts of the cultural studies movement—Raymond Williams's *Culture and Society,* Richard Hoggart's *The Uses of Literacy,* and E. P. Thompson's *The Making of the English Working Class*—all treat culture as classed and all stress the active role of workers in its production and consumption, even as they also stress the rise of industrialized mass culture. After the establishment of the Birmingham Centre for Cultural Studies in the early 1960s, these concerns remained central in, for example, the analysis of "subcultures."[1] This was a variation on the themes of "class fractions" and mass culture, from which emerged the interminable debate over whether the mass media can be genuinely "popular" in the sense of democratic or are merely "mass"—conformist, ideological, and antidemocratic.[2]

Hoggart's and Thompson's books belong to a lengthy tradition of labor history in Britain; they are both versions of "history from below."[3] Williams's *Culture and Society* takes a different tack; it is a literary study dealing mainly with canonical nineteenth- and early twentieth-century writers, and to that extent it pursues a top-down approach. But Williams stresses the many ways in which the writers he examines turned "culture" into a critical tool for analyzing and challenging social-class inequality and economic orthodoxy, as in Charles Dickens's *Hard Times* and Elizabeth Gaskell's *Mary Barton*. In the tradition Williams surveys—itself a principal source of cultural studies—culture was typically viewed as transcendent, rising above what Matthew Arnold saw as the "anarchy" of material competition and class conflict. For Arnold, high culture—at once aesthetic and ethical—was to be the modern substitute for religion and the arbiter of all values, including economic ones.

Needless to say, Arnold's faith in high culture seems naïve today. Nevertheless, from our postmodern standpoint, seemingly characterized by what Fredric Jameson calls "the disappearance of class,"[4] it is possible to look back with an ironic nostalgia to nineteenth-century Britain or France, when social-class boundaries were clear and when all cultural values were arranged in hierarchies marked by class—aristocratic, bourgeois, proletarian. In *The Origins of Postmodernity,* Perry Anderson notes that, starting in the nineteenth century, cultural modernism in its confrontation with capitalism and economics "could appeal to two alternative value-worlds, both hostile to the commercial logic of the market and the bourgeois cult of the family." An aristocratic perspective "offered one set of ideals against which to measure the dictates of profit and prudery." In contrast, the "emergent labour movement" also opposed bourgeois hegemony and unregulated capitalism, seeking "its solution in an egalitarian future rather than hierarchical past" (103). Both Anderson and Jameson are well aware that class has not really disappeared in postmodern societies. Nevertheless, the hereditary aristocracy is nonexistent in the United States and has almost disappeared in Europe. Much of the American working class, from the 1950s into the 1980s, saw itself as middle class. And especially since the economic collapse of 2007–8, sizable portions of both the middle and the working classes have fallen into poverty. Moreover, the postmodern condition involves a significant degree of "social homogenization" which, Jameson notes, has often been explained in terms of "the embourgeoisement of the worker, or better still, the transformation of both bourgeois and worker into that new grey organization person known as the consumer" (*Signatures*, 36). After the 2007–8 economic crisis, however, instead of upward mobility, the middle and working classes are experiencing an accelerating "race to the bottom." Meanwhile, what has become of that very Victorian and Marxist notion of class conflict?

POSTMODERNISM AS A DECLASSED AND DECONSTRUCTED CONDITION

Jameson's homogenized, "new grey organization person" is not so new. He or she was as much a modern or even a Victorian person as a postmodern one. Between the 1870s and World War I, the old Marxist threat of the revolutionary "masses" acquired a very different meaning. No longer threatening revolution or even economic redistribution, the new idea of the "masses" referred to petit-bourgeois or even classless conformists, the empty-headed individuals who were steered into lives of mediocrity and acquiescence in their lot partly by prosperity (consumption) and partly by ideology (advertising, religion, education—Louis Althusser's ISAs).[5] Instead of revolutionary values, the new masses were the bearers of no values whatsoever—José Ortega y Gassett's mindless millions in *Revolt of the Masses*, T. S. Eliot's "hollow men," Karl Čapek's "robots."[6] These valueless (in two senses) "masses" are no different from Herbert Marcuse's "one-dimensional men" of the 1960s or Jean Baudrillard's postmodern "silent majorities." While the earlier discourse about the robot-like masses points ahead to theories of the postmodern, both versions either implicitly or explicitly blame large-scale economic factors on producing nonindividuals who are all "mass" or mass produced because they cannot think for themselves. It hardly matters, moreover, whether the economic factors involve communism, socialism, or capitalism. In all three versions of modernization, patterns of intellectual and cultural "distinction" or "values" are eviscerated or disappear altogether through the collapse of older structuring principles—or at least through the new "mass" inability to recognize the operation of those structuring principles. From a Marxist perspective, for the mindlessness of the new gray masses you can substitute the view that they have no class consciousness, which is close to Thomas Frank's conclusion in *What's The Matter with Kansas?* Conservative Kansans, Frank writes, even blue-collar, low-income ones, believe that you choose what class you belong to just as you choose "hairstyles or TV shows" (26). So what if you're broke or homeless? Seven years later, in *Pity the Billionaire,* Frank finds his diagnosis confirmed by the Tea Party movement and the ability of billionaires such as the Koch brothers to influence both politicians and the general public (partly by funding the Tea Party movement).

In many dystopian visions of modern and now postmodern society, people herd together in gray gulags where they rot until, perhaps, slaughtered in future wars. This dismal picture of what the lives of ordinary (mass) individuals are like in modern or postmodern society perhaps expresses little more than intellectual disdain and stereotyping.[7] Yet it was also a picture that helped Hannah Arendt, Theodor Adorno, and many others understand how emergent democracies gave way to totalitarianism, as in the case of the Weimar Republic.[8] That recent theories of the postmodern often echo this dystopian view is an indication of the power of the mass media to overwhelm processes of cultural "distinction," dumbing down the masses; but it is perhaps also due to the willingness of many intellectuals to abandon questions of social justice in favor of the very discourse about "the masses" that allows them seemingly to transcend (or escape) the cultures they purport to analyze (see Niethammer). In short, while "the masses"—in the United States, at least—may be both anti-intellectual and lacking in intellectual sophistication, postmodern theorists are often equally and perversely anti-intellectual, in part because they fail to grapple with the problem of how cultural "distinction" is organized and operative in today's societies, in part because they underestimate their fellow citizens including workers, and in part because they do not believe that class warfare is happening.

Capitalist economics helped produce Jameson's "new grey organization person known as the consumer." Social-class categories are based on production, not consumption. This is historically the case, although Pierre Bourdieu has demonstrated how patterns of consumption are closely related to class and even class fractions. But starting in the 1870s, with the economists' turn away from labor theories of value and to the theory of marginal utility (or price theory emphasizing consumption rather than production), economics has promoted the notion that all actors in the marketplace operate on equal terms. This is perhaps the key version of the illusion of classlessness under capitalism, which has its echoes in several prominent theories of postmodernism, including Baudrillard's. Yet given this apparently hegemonic view, how can anyone explain the now wide-spread notion that, as media pundit Lou Dobbs claims, there is "a war on the middle class"?[9] If there is only one happy class of united, prosperous, middle-class consumers, who or what could possibly be waging class war? There is no aristocracy, and it surely cannot be the working class, which seems to have nearly disappeared from the myriad flat screens of post-modern American culture. When was the class war that eliminated the working class? But the main threat of the war against the middle class is that it will drive its bourgeois members straight into the working class or worse—into a "jobless future" when work itself disappears, as has been happening at a great rate since 2007. Given the subprime mortgage crisis, people's homes are also disappearing. Presto-change-o, the alleged class-less condition in which we all belong to the middle class has devolved into a condition of classlessness in which increasingly large numbers of people, except CEOs and hedge-fund managers, are jobless and homeless.

Besides the modernist and now postmodern theme of the mindless masses and besides the shift in orthodox economics from production to price theory and consumption, a third source of the illusion that class has vanished from postmodern culture is postmodern culture itself. The pop art of Andy Warhol and Roy Lichtenstein presented us with images of commodified images, including movie stars and soup cans, cartoons and ads. Once again, what is stressed is consumption, available for everybody. Further, various theories of the postmodern condition celebrate or at least announce the downfall of cultural hierarchies, the complete relativization of values, and the vanishing of class conflict into Baudrillard's "silent majorities"—that is to say, into the indiscriminate and apolitical masses. According to Baudrillard, there is no longer any "reality," only "hyperreal-ity" consisting of "simulacra," or image-copies without originals (*Simula-tions*). His postmodern conception of value as sheer contingency mirrors, perhaps intentionally, what neoliberal economics has to say: "The entire strategy of the system lies in this hyperreality of floating values," writes Baudrillard; "It is the same for money and theory as for the unconscious. Value rules according to an ungraspable order: the generation of models, the indefinite chaining of simulation."[10] This is similar to what Gianni

Vattimo, in *The End of Modernity*, calls the postmodern "dissolution of truth into value": "Truth . . . reveals itself to be 'a value which dissolves into itself,' or, in other words, no more and no less than a belief without foundation."[11]

In *The Postmodern Condition*, Jean-François Lyotard famously argued that today all metanarratives of emancipation, including both liberalism and the Marxist metanarrative of emancipation from social-class exploitation and inequality, are no longer credible; postmodern culture instead consists of micronarratives and a global swirl of incommensurate language games. No doubt poststructuralist theory helped give birth to Lyotard's version of the postmodern condition. On the one hand, there is Lyotard's metanarrative about the untenability of all metanarratives; on the other, there is Foucault's poststructuralist metanarrative about the modern, disciplinary diffusion of power—it is everywhere, it apparently needs no ruling class or headquarters or economic base, and it both creates and distributes value and serves as its own tautological explanation.

For Jacques Derrida, too, the question of value is indeterminable. In *The Politics of Friendship*, Derrida writes: "darkness is falling on the value of value" (81). Derrida's analyses of value are, he would have been the first to admit, "spectral," because all values are "spectral." This point of view is rendered all the more spectral because, in *Specters of Marx*, Derrida quite implausibly claims that "deconstruction" is an "attempted radicalization of Marxism" (92). Derrida, nevertheless, insists that, even though Francis Fukuyama might in the 1990s declare "the end of history" via the triumph of capitalism and liberal democracy, neither the need for social critique nor the goal of social justice has disappeared. Derrida echoes the Frankfurt theorists when he asserts that, like Marxism, deconstruction is "heir to a spirit of the Enlightenment which must not be renounced" (ibid., 88). His deconstructive understanding of the "spectral" rootlessness or indeterminacy of value is, however, little different from that of neoliberal economics, and therefore from Baudrillard's and Fukuyama's ends-of-history notions.

Like neoliberal economics, by downplaying or ignoring actual social classes and class conflict, poststructuralism and some versions of postmodernism leave the question of value up to market forces. This mirroring of the neoliberal embrace of global capitalism renders it difficult if not impossible for poststructuralism to be the "radicalization of Marxism" that Derrida hoped for, and both Lyotard and Baudrillard abandoned Marxism long ago for "the ecstasy of communication." Nevertheless, some other theorists of postmodernism have not abandoned Marx and his central problematic of social class and class conflict. I have in mind Jameson, Perry Anderson, David Harvey, Ellen Meiskins Wood, Terry Eagleton, Nancy Fraser, and Slavoj Žižek, among others. Jameson's analyses of postmodernity view it as "the logic of late capitalism"; Harvey is in agreement when he relates postmodernism to the transition from the Fordist mode of production and the Keynesian welfare state to the mode of "flexible accumulation" or transnational corporate capitalism and neoliberal, "free market" economics.

Neither Jameson nor Harvey is under any illusion that workers today form a potentially revolutionary class. For a Marxist, Jameson has little to say about social class, although that is in part a reflection of the postmodern condition. When Jameson does address social class as a category, it is to indicate how "groups" like ethnic minorities or even the homeless have replaced class in others' social analyses and, more importantly, to indicate how postmodern culture occludes class divisions and class conflict. Postmodern culture typically flattens cultural values into a faux-populist mishmash—a version of what Jameson refers to as deliberate depthlessness—a commodified, mass-mediated grab bag with something for everyone (if you can pay for it). For Jameson, moreover, if postmodern culture expresses class interests, it is as "the 'consciousness' of a whole new class fraction," one "variously labeled as a new petit bourgeoisie, a professional-managerial class, or more succinctly as 'the yuppies.'"[12] Anderson similarly argues that the historical bourgeoisie, just like the historical proletariat, has now been complicated, fragmented, and decentered nearly out of existence, so that there is nothing any longer for an antibourgeois aesthetic or political avant-garde to target. And, arming himself with thorough analyses of both capitalism and traditional Marxism, David Harvey writes about the downsizing and deskilling of the labor force, along with the weakening of trade unionism from the recession of 1973 forward.

These analysts of the postmodern condition understand that neither the capitalist class nor the working class, either nationally or internationally, has or will disappear in the foreseeable future. According to Terry Eagleton, "If it is a mistake of some Neanderthal Marxists to imagine that there is a single agent of social transformation (the working class), it is equally an error of new-fangled postmodernists to imagine that this agent has now been outdated by the 'new political movements.'"[13] Eagleton has in mind the claim that Ernesto Laclau and Chantal Mouffe make in *Hegemony and Socialist Strategy* that "the new social movements" seeking environmental sustainability and justice for racial minorities, women, and gays have displaced the industrial proletariat as the agents of historical progress. Except for environmentalism, which involves a different form of economic redistribution than does addressing social-class inequality, the other "new social movements" appear to demand adequate cultural recognition as their version of social justice. However, as Nancy Fraser contends, "justice today requires both redistribution and recognition" (2).[14] Even though it has slipped out of view in mainstream American culture, the growing ranks of the new working class also demand both recognition and redistribution, as evident in the Wisconsin uprising in early 2011 and similar demonstrations at statehouses in Ohio, Indiana, and elsewhere.

A key role of "populist" or "yuppified" postmodern, mass-mediated culture has been to occlude both the working class as a potential agent of social and cultural change and the ownership class as its opposition and, in doing so, to put a smiling face on that all-pervasive source of contemporary power—capitalism, or as its true believers like to call it, "the free market." As I have just done, Eagleton also notes that some varieties of supposedly radical current theory help with this mystification:

> We now find ourselves confronted with the mildly farcical situation of a cultural left which maintains an indifferent or embarrassed silence about that power which is the invisible colour of everyday life itself, which determines our very existence [and] decides in large measure the destiny of nations. . . . It is as though almost every other form of oppressive system—state, media, patriarchy, racism, neo-colonialism—can be readily debated, but not the one which so often sets the long-term agenda for all of these matters," namely capitalism. (*Illusions of Postmodernism*, 22–23)

That is at least partly because, as Anderson contends, while "late capitalism [has] remained a class society," the configuration of the classes has drastically changed, both in their internal and in their external relations. "On a world scale—in the postmodern epoch," Anderson writes, "no stable class structure, comparable to that of an earlier capitalism, has yet crystallized. Those above [in the class hierarchy] have the coherence of privilege; those below lack unity and solidarity. A new 'collective labourer' has yet to emerge. These are the conditions," Anderson concludes, "of a certain vertical indefinition" (*Origins of Postmodernity*, 62). In other words, there is still a hierarchy of social classes, now globalized, though it is less well defined than it used to be.

Although social classes have arranged themselves in many different ways throughout history, there has never been and never will be a classless society. Class, caste, or status systems are themselves both cultural value hierarchies and sites of class struggle, operative even in those societies— the United States or the People's Republic of China, for instance—that claim to be relatively classless or egalitarian. Even the simple societies that Marx and Engels identified as practicing "primitive communism" have structures of authority and value based on age, gender, kinship, and often wealth or property. Indeed, as anthropologists have repeatedly demonstrated, the value hierarchies of so-called primitive societies are frequently highly elaborate. Moreover, all versions of cultural value and classification become incoherent when detached from the economic factors, including class conflict, that shape them.

To return to the notion of "the war on the middle class," in the nineteenth century, the European bourgeoisie gradually overtook the traditional aristocracy. By the end of that century, and especially in the United States, "the triumph of the bourgeoisie" seemed complete. So who or what is driving members of today's bourgeoisie into the working class or perhaps eliminating both classes altogether? And if you eliminate both of these major classes, who will then be the consumers who flock to the markets to buy the goods produced by an apparently totally automated, jobless, globalized, and classless capitalism? Will the ultimate triumph of capitalism indeed be the end of history? Or will Charlie Chaplin escape from the gears of the gigantic machine of capitalist, industrial production and rediscover himself as a rebellious worker—or anyway, as a sweet and sentimental albeit unemployed and homeless, hungry, wannabe consumer, with little wherewithal to buy or consume anything? I will try to answer these questions in the second part of this essay, in which, however, instead of the modern Little Tramp, enters from stage right wing the postmodern Chicken Little—W (or as the late Molly Ivins liked to call him, "Shrub").

CLASS WARFARE? THAT'S NOT HOW WE THINK

During a press conference in January 2003, a reporter asked W about his plan for boosting the economy by a tax cut "weighted toward helping the wealthiest Americans." W replied, "I understand the politics of economic stimulus, that some would like to turn this into class warfare. That's not how I think."[15] Apparently, that is not how millions of Americans think either. Even when class warfare is clobbering us, we do not know what it is. According to the pundits, watching the news about Hurricane Katrina's devastation of New Orleans in 2005 awakened Americans to the poverty in our midst. If it takes the catastrophic drowning of a major city to alert us to something as obvious as poverty, then we really have been asleep at the switch. And if we are not aware of poverty, then "class warfare" cannot be how we think.

It is true that a lot of the poor are literally invisible: out of sight, out of mind. With the highest incarceration rate in the world, the United States disappears a huge number of its citizens. Over 2.6 million Americans, most of them poor and about half of them black, are behind bars (another 18 percent are Hispanic). Further, it does not seem likely that most prisoners think that way either. People arrested for drug dealing or other petty street crimes do not typically see themselves as waging class warfare. Many Americans besides Thomas Frank's Kansans appear to believe that wealth and poverty are natural, God given, and earned. If you are rich, you deserve your money; if you are poor, you deserve your poverty. Government, in any case, cannot, will not, or should not do anything about it. And besides, aren't almost all Americans (excluding prisoners) middle class? That is what the reporter who questioned W suggested: the tax cut would help "the wealthiest" but not "middle-income" Americans. He did not mention the working class, the poor, or prisoners, perhaps because these huge populations have become almost invisible to the rest of us.

But if "class warfare" is unthinkable in American culture, why did W choose that phrase to respond to the reporter? Among ways to spin his response, three seem obvious. First, W wished to paint the opponents of his tax cuts into a corner identified as leftwing, extremist, perhaps even communist. Second, he is a pseudoegalitarian, faithful to trickle-down Reaganomics: he believes that whatever benefits the rich and the corporations will (eventually) benefit the "middle-income" people and maybe even the poor. (But supposedly the poor are poor because they deserve or choose to be so.) And third, "class warfare" names a type of turmoil that W believes America, in contrast to other parts of the world, has outgrown or never even experienced. These meanings all resurfaced around the issue of tax cuts during the presidential campaign of 2012.

There is also a fourth, less obvious way to interpret W's comment: "class warfare" has never gone away; it is now everywhere evident in American culture and society, as in Lou Dobbs's version—"war on the middle class." In short, Bush's statement was a denial of the obvious. The first three spins—the ones W probably believes—are thinkable only because of ideological mystification. That a president of the United States could express all three of them in one sentence, confident that millions would agree with him, suggests how thoroughly the concept of class warfare has been rendered un-American and unthinkable in postmodern America.

Recently, however, both the Tea Party movement and Occupy Wall Street have brought the obvious to the fore. The Tea Party wages class warfare indirectly and in large measure unconsciously (see chapter 3). Its adherents vent their anger against President Obama, the federal government, liberals, and the "elites" in Washington. But its billionaire funders such as the Koch brothers arouse the populist masses at their peril. With the emergence of the Occupy movement in September 2011, Tea Partiers now have the opportunity to vent their wrath also against Wall Street, billionaires, and growing inequality. Occupy's version of the class divide in the United States is both dramatic and inclusive: "We are the 99%" versus "the 1%." The Occupy movement seemed to spring up instantaneously, like the revolutions of the "Arab spring" of 2011, but today's class warfare was begun by the 1 percent in the 1970s.[16]

Of course, the concept of class war carries a lot of European, and specifically Marxist, baggage. *The Communist Manifesto* begins with the claim that "the history of all hitherto existing society is the history of class struggles"[17] and ends with the famous revolutionary battle-cry, "Workers of the world, unite! You have nothing to lose but your chains!" Whether W knows this is not important: he knows how to use "class warfare" to tar and feather his critics as un-American, if not explicitly communist. Waging "preemptive warfare" in Iraq is okay. But "class warfare" is "not how I think" because it is just not American to think that way.[18]

Even if it is not how W thinks, what does he think "class warfare" is or was? Was he thinking of Robin Hood, perhaps, who stole from the rich and gave to the poor—long ago and in an un-American country? Probably not, but as Senator Paul Wellstone used to say, W behaved like Robin Hood in reverse by stealing from the poor and giving to the rich.[19] Although he did not use the phrase "class warfare" (W did), the reporter was right: W's tax cuts amount to top-down class warfare. Between 2001 and 2010, the wealthiest 20 percent of the nation received 68.5 percent of the Bush tax rebate; the rest—80 percent of us—received 31.5 percent. Over the decade, the poorest 20 percent got $21.9 billion, which sounds pretty good until contrasted to the amount the richest 20 percent have raked in: $1,303.9 billion—that is, more than a trillion dollars. Of that staggering amount, more than half—$715.2 billion—went to the wealthiest 1 percent of the nation. The wealthiest 1 percent already owns over 33 percent of the nation's wealth, and the richest 20 percent owns 83 percent of it, while the poorest 18 percent are, well, worthless—they own zero or negative wealth.[20]

After all, what is the benefit of a tax cut to those who pay no taxes? It is not zero, but negative, because cutting taxes ultimately means cutting programs that benefit the poor. The tax cuts mushroomed W's record-breaking deficit, which then became the excuse to gut social programs. Funds for student loans, Medicaid, food stamps, childcare, and low-income housing were all axed in the budget passed by Congress on December 21, 2005. "That Republicans had the nerve to ram through such a budget a week before Christmas," wrote Eyal Press in *The Nation*, "vividly illustrates that when it comes to so-called class warfare, it is the right that is on the offensive" (4). And then there is the assault on Social Security. The Congressional Budget Office reports that Social Security will be solvent until 2052 and that it can easily be stabilized long after that. But W preemptively proclaimed its bankruptcy by 2027. This is just one more instance of what Paul Krugman has called the Bush administration's "world-class mendacity" (xxxvi). Social Security is apt to go broke only because, if enacted, any privatization scheme will keep billions from going into the trust fund, thus compounding the currently nonexistent crisis.[21]

Today's class warfare of the rich against the poor, devastating much of the middle class in the process, started well before President Reagan busted PATCO, the air-traffic controllers' union, in 1981. But from that date forward, organized labor has been in a tailspin. In 1973, 24 percent of the workforce was unionized; in 2001, the number had fallen to 13.5 percent.[22] As Robert Perrucci and Earl Wysong put it in *The New Class Society*, the gains in social welfare and civil rights made in the 1960s and '70s caused "panic among the U.S. capitalist class," which fought back: "The superclass response was a concerted, large-scale mobilization for total class war" (70). They quote Reagan's budget director David Stockman: "'The Reagan Revolution required a frontal assault on the American welfare state'" (71). Or as Bill Moyers puts it, "Our business and political class . . . declared class war [over] twenty years ago, and it was they who won. They're on top" (12).

W, of course, would have none of this: as far as he could think, to accuse the rich of class warfare is to foment class warfare where none exists. Nevertheless, he knew who buttered his bread. At a fund raiser in 2000, W said, "This is an impressive crowd, the haves, and the have-mores. Some people call you the elite. I call you my base." From time to time, W displayed his economic expertise by uttering versions of the number-one axiom of latter-day economics—that is, of Reaganomics: growth is good and, ultimately, good for everyone. So what if growth can sometimes be cancerous? Who disputes that sacrosanct law of economics espoused by such powerful figures as Alan Greenspan and the late Milton Friedman? Here is one of W's versions of it: "We ought to make the pie higher." W uttered that gem, worthy of Little Jack Horner, on February 15, 2000. Two years later, regarding his energy policy, he declared, "We need an energy bill that encourages consumption." Growth is good: keep the engines humming, the oilrigs gushing, and the bombers bombing. But who does higher pie benefit the most? Those at the top of the pie, of course.[23]

Besides the seemingly self-evident goodness of economic growth, there is also the notion that whatever is good for corporations is good for everyone. And there is a corollary: the product of a corporation may not be made in postmodern America (and probably is not), but if it is bought in America, it is still good for America. True, the pundits occasionally fret about the mushrooming trade deficit with China. Also true, scandals like the Enron blow-out put a dent in the notion that corporations are good for us, but what is the alternative? After Wal-Mart has driven the little guys out of business in your hometown, what next? Shopping at Wal-Mart, of course. And shopping, we know, is good for the economy—even, since 9/11, a patriotic duty (see chapter 9). Further, after General Motors and General Electric and all the rest have downsized and outsourced American jobs, where are new jobs popping up? Why, of course, Wal-Mart to the rescue! Writing about Wal-Mart's role in today's "corporate race to the bottom," Barbara Ehrenreich notes how it has helped swell "the ranks of the thirty million Americans—nearly one worker in four—who work full-time for less than a poverty-level wage" ("Earth to Wal-Mars," 51).

The excuse for all the union busting, downsizing, and outsourcing is always some version of "It's the economy, stupid!" The pressure on corporations exerted by globalization and competition is so great, say their hucksters, that they cannot behave in any other way—even as CEO salaries and bonuses skyrocket and many of the megacorporations outstrip the economies of entire nations. (Wal-Mart is currently the nineteenth largest economic power in the world.) This is just how competition works under "free-market" capitalism, we are told. When corporations win, everyone wins. Doesn't every American schoolchild learn that "free" in "free market" or "free trade" means democracy? In *Capitalism and Freedom*, Milton Friedman, Reagan's favorite economist, taught us that "the organization of the bulk of economic activity through private enterprise operating in a free market" is "a necessary condition for political freedom" (4). Apart from a bare minimum of defense and law enforcement, government should stay its hand—otherwise, it is interfering with both economic and political freedom. This has been the simplistic view of the Tea Party and, apparently, of the vast majority of Americans (see chapters 2 and 3). After all, in a society that views corporations as persons and in which personal freedom is the paramount value, Wal-Mart should be just as free as you or me, only—because it has a lot of money and clout—a lot more so.

According to economic orthodoxy, in a free society, corporations should at least be free of government "interference" (a.k.a. "regulation"). This is how W thinks, just like Milton Friedman, only without the math. As W put it shortly before he became president, "Entrepreneurship equals freedom." Every man his own CEO. And, of course, if you are going to give tax cuts to individuals, then you ought to give tax cuts to corporations. As presidential candidate Mitt Romney explained to an incredulous crowd, corporations are defined by American law as "persons"—and very deserving persons, at that, just like Mitt Romney. So, federal and local governments have been giving them billions in tax rebates to help them out, even though many of them pay no taxes whatsoever. According to Vijay Prashad, "Even though Enron [paid no] taxes from 1996 to 2000, it received a net tax rebate of $381 million—$278 million alone thanks to GWB's tax cut" (*Fat Cats and Running Dogs*, 51). Some forty major corporations paid no taxes in 2010, yet they paid $465,000,000 to lobbyists. And according to Lawrence Lessig, through lobbying, campaign donations, and the privatization of once-public jobs, corporations have virtually bought up what remains of government. Molly Ivins comments that W "is a wholly owned subsidiary of corporate America" (*Shrub*, xvi). So is Mitt Romney, child of Bain Capital.

Are most Americans concerned about any of this? Perhaps more so than we were a decade ago when, reviewing a number of opinion polls, Everett Ladd and Karlyn Bowman reported in *USA Today* that "the nation says NO to class warfare." According to Ladd and Bowman, "With the bulk of society describing itself . . . as middle-class, polarization is not pronounced." Obviously, class warfare cannot occur if we all belong to one big, happy class. Another reason cited by Ladd and Bowman is "Americans tolerate great differences in wealth" because we "believe that opportunity is broadly present." But if opportunity means the chance to move out of poverty or out of the working class into the middle or upper classes, there is much less of it today than there was at the end of World War II. On the contrary, many Americans are now realizing that, for them, downward rather than upward mobility is what they are experiencing.

The notion that almost everyone belongs to the middle class was fueled by 1950s and 1960s prosperity. During those decades, many with working-class jobs could self-identify as middle class on the basis of income, ownership (homes, cars), pensions (including Social Security), and the prospect of sending their kids to college. Besides, it is comforting to believe that we are just like everyone else—at home in the heartland. But since the mid-1970s, that version of the American dream—everyone able to join the great middle class—has steadily eroded. In a 1998 poll by the National Opinion Research Center, 45 percent of the respondents identified as working class and 5 percent as "lower" class. The vast majority of Americans—roughly 80 percent—now belong to what Perucci and Wysong in 2003 called "the new working class" (*New Class Society*,

29). Still, the belief persists, even after the 2007–8 crash, that Americans should all belong to the middle class, even though we no longer do.

The belief also persists that, compared to all other countries, the United States has the most dynamic economy and the greatest prosperity. That may be true if the comparison is with countries in Latin America, Africa, and parts of Asia, but not in regard to other "developed" countries. The nation-states of Western Europe and also Japan, Canada, Australia, and New Zealand now all enjoy living standards as high, or higher, than ours.[24]

China is also rapidly overtaking us. Take health care: Canada, Japan, and the European countries with "interventionist economies" all have national health insurance plans. But as of 2011, approximately fifty million Americans had no health insurance. Even after passage of the Affordable Health Care Act and its approval, on July 28, 2012, by the Supreme Court, twenty million may still not be covered. This was a key problem the act was supposed to fix. But along the way, Obama and Congress knuckled under to the insurance and pharmaceutical companies, so that today very few Americans—least of all Tea Partiers—are happy with the result. Speaker of the House John Boehner, who would like nothing better than to repeal "Obamacare," claims that "America has the best health care system in the world," a belief many rightwingers share (see chapter 3). America has the most expensive healthcare system in the world but does not rank in the top twenty among nations in either life expectancy or infant mortality rates. Michael Moore's 2007 film *Sicko* tells it like it is.

During the cold war and the era of McCarthyite red-baiting, it became difficult or impossible for anyone to discuss class warfare unless it was how W did it in 2003—as a way of attacking his opponents.[25] Otherwise, "That's not how I think." Today politicians regularly accuse each other of engaging in class war, while downplaying the actual class warfare of the rich and corporations against labor and the attempts by unions and Occupy Wall Street to fight back. If W were ever to think about it, however, he might wonder if Marx was right to claim that class struggle is the main engine of history? When have there ever *not* been conflicts between classes over power, money, scarce resources, and cultural values? What is exceptional about America today is not that it lacks classes or class conflict; it is instead that the corporate mass media downplay or erase social class as a major factor in determining American values, including economic and governmental policy. This has been the main ideological victory in America's class warfare so far—the success of the media, bolstered by orthodox economics, in convincing the public of the relative insignificance of social class. If cultural studies is going to continuing to make social justice a main item on its agenda, then it must both expose and resist the ideology of classlessness, which has historically been based on the illusion that capitalism is an even-handed, democratic provider for everyone.

Marx's prediction that the ultimate outcome of class warfare would be a classless utopia was wrong, but that does not mean he misinterpreted the past. The communist regimes of Eastern Europe and the Soviet Union failed not just because they were totalitarian and inefficient but also because they continued to be wracked by class conflict—think of Solidarity in Poland, for example, which began as a trade-union movement among dockworkers in Gdansk. If all "hitherto" history can be understood in terms of "class struggles," on what basis can anyone assume that such struggles are not occurring in the United States? No one, not even Glenn Beck, would ever be crazy enough to claim that the United States is, in fact, the classless society that the Soviet Union failed to become.

Bush unwittingly (what else is not news?) illustrated rightwing discourse about top-down "class warfare" because "That's not how I think." Turning Bush's denial around, all the Republican candidates in the 2011 presidential primary illustrated that discourse by claiming that any attempt by the Obama administration or by other Democrats to raise taxes on the superrich and corporations, even if only by failing to make permanent Bush's tax cuts for the wealthy, is "class warfare." According to Mitt Romney, "all the carping about greed and excess in America is 'about envy. It's about class warfare'" (quoted in Powers, "To Romney, . . ."). He might have been better off saying, "Class warfare? That's not how I think."

Yes, there is class warfare at this moment in the United States, very aggressively being waged by the Tea Party, the Republican Party, and billionaires like the Koch brothers against the poor and the working and middle classes. Passage of so-called right to work laws in Wisconsin, Indiana, and elsewhere is just one aspect of this top-down version of class warfare. Attempts to pass voter ID laws; to dismantle the Affordable Health Care Act; to undermine Social Security; to privatize public schools, prisons, toll roads, and everything else on the planet are all part of the rightwing putsch to, in Tea Party lingo, "take back our country." And there are many other instances of today's class warfare.

Despite the obfuscations of the mass media, of neoliberal economists, and of some theorists of the postmodern condition, class struggle continues to shape American culture, a fact that the 2007–8 crash has made glaringly obvious. With the 2011 labor rebellion in Wisconsin, Ohio, and other states against rightwing antilabor legislation, and with the emergence of both the Tea Party and Occupy Wall Street, class war has reappeared as a highly visible factor in the United States. But it has always been through class struggle that the values of everyday life are organized and from which the hope for social justice arises—the hope, that is, of rearranging our common life together in less unequal, more democratic ways. Besides the Occupy movement, among the many signs that American workers and progressive members of the middle class are now challenging the powers-that-be, trade unionists teamed up with environmentalists, feminists, Native Americans, and many other activist organizations in the Battle of Seattle in 1999, signaling the beginning of the "alter-globalization" movement. Many workers' organizations have participated in the meetings of the World Social Forum, the U.S. Social Forum, and regional forums in America and elsewhere (see chapter 12). Many of them are also aligning themselves with the immigrants' rights movement (see chapter 5). Efforts to unionize the factories of the *maquiladora* are now being made on both sides of the border, according to Kari Lydersen. The reinvigoration of the labor movement now depends on its articulation, at both the national and the international levels, with many other activist movements in the fight against transnational corporate power. The Tea Party has alerted many Americans that all is not well in the republic. Tea Partiers get a lot of their facts wrong (see chapter 3), but at least they are angry about whatever is going on.[26] Occupy Wall Street has put many of the facts into clearer focus, especially skyrocketing economic inequality and the role of banks and big corporations in producing that inequality. What happens next is anybody's guess, but Americans are beginning to recognize that, as the motto of the World Social Forum has it, "Another world is possible."

TWO

"It's the Economy, Stupid!"

We ought to make the pie higher.

—GEORGE W. BUSH

When it comes to economics, most noneconomists, myself included, are idiots. We cannot do the math. At least President Bush, while running the U.S. economy into the ditch, had the advice of experts. The version of Economics 10 that I took in college may have been over my head. I found it boring because it did not address any of the issues I was interested in at the time: girls, poetry, the civil rights movement, and the war in Vietnam. I did not expect Ec10 to deal with girls and poetry, but why not with racism and war? After all, it was supposed to be a social science. I remember "supply and demand," "marginal utility," and a few other phrases and concepts from that class. My economics professor believed that free trade and political freedom were inseparable, though he did not explain why. He also believed that economics is a science whose subject is wealth. Poverty—like girls, poetry, racism, and war—is not one of its primary concerns.

FREE MARKETS FOR IDIOTS

If economics is a science, it is the only one I can think of that deals with the workings of a perfect mechanism—"the market"—in an imperfect world where there are wars, racism, and a lot of poverty. "Typical eco-

nomics courses," write the editors of *Field Guide to the U.S. Economy,*
"confine much of their attention to the theory of competitive markets
and treat the economy as a self-regulating system." Interference by governments is, well, interference. There may be bumps and bubbles, but,
via "free markets," the "self-regulating system" soon returns to "equilibrium." This is the work of Adam Smith's "Invisible Hand." In Ec10, I
wondered whose hand it was. Economics via the Invisible Hand struck
me as a quasi-religion (the phrase "voodoo economics" had not yet been
coined).[1] I wondered if the Invisible Hand also corrects or at least mod-
erates inequality. But today's economists also "often teach students that
there is an inevitable trade-off between economic equality and efficiency.
The message . . . is that social justice is just too expensive."[2] At least my
professor recognized that there were alternative modes of producing and
distributing wealth: he mentioned socialism and communism, only to assert that they were failures. I wondered: don't economists in socialist and
communist countries also regard themselves as scientists?

Why, moreover, did Thomas Carlyle call economics "the dismal science" (a phrase I picked up in a literature class)? For Carlyle, economics
seemed to be the science of poverty, not of wealth. Or at least it was an
impoverished science that failed to explain poverty. Particularly anger-
ing Carlyle was the Reverend Thomas Malthus's theory of population
because it treated poverty as inevitable and identified vast numbers of
people as superfluous (for more on Malthus, see chapter 11). Besides Carlyle, we read some Charles Dickens, who also worried about poverty and
took a dim view of Malthus and economics. Dickens believed that the
economists of his time blamed the poor for poverty (they were lazy, plus
they overpopulated); he recognized that the rich like Ebenezer Scrooge
had something to do with it (they were stingy and treated their employees
like dirt).

We also read *The Communist Manifesto* in a history class, and I decided that, like Carlyle and Dickens, Karl Marx and Friedrich Engels
had some good ideas. They, too, championed the working class and social
justice. Was poverty really the fault of the poor? What was the connection
between poverty and revolution? If capitalism worked so well, why was
its history marred by crises, recessions, and depressions, as well as, apparently, revolutions? Why were trade unions necessary? How could any
social science treat vast numbers of people as "surplus population"? Why

was there so much poverty in the midst of Victorian prosperity—or for that matter, in the United States in the 1960s?

After college, most of my reading about the economy came from newspaper articles about "indicators" that "the perfect mechanism" of the marketplace is not so perfect—even that it is crisis prone. I was, therefore, interested to discover that, contrary to my experience in Ec10 and to troublesome economic news, "economics is really fun." Harvard economist N. Gregory Mankiw says so (perhaps this should be called "Mankiw's Law"). Mankiw's happy locution, if not law, was quoted by Alison Schneider in a 1997 article titled "A Harvard Economist Hits the Jackpot." Schneider reported that Mankiw had just received a record $1.4 million advance for his textbook *Principles of Economics*. No doubt that helps explain why he thinks "economics is really fun."

For students required to take Ec10 at any college or university, the purchase of Mankiw's textbook—or any textbook, for that matter—will not illustrate how a free market works. I have no idea how much Mankiw has made in royalties, though his is said to be the leading economics textbook worldwide. To buy the fifth edition of his *Principles* means shelling out $231. There is a "study guide" for another $41.95, as well as other spinoffs (*Brief Principles,* for example—$157.95—might be even more fun than the 800-page grand tome). Economics is probably also fun for Mankiw because periodically he revises his textbooks so that students have to buy the new editions at even higher prices. Yet according to Mankiw's *Principles,* the "principles of economics" do not change from year to year or even age to age. Textbooks change frequently, but the laws of economics are eternal.[3]

Schneider goes on to say that Mankiw's tome could become "the next Samuelson." Paul Samuelson wrote the textbook assigned in my Ec10. Samuelson won the Nobel Prize in Economics in 1970, but "his most enduring legacy may be the introductory textbook that he published in 1948," Schneider states. By 1997, his book had "sold 3.5 million copies and ha[d] been translated into 46 languages. It topped the textbook market for almost 30 years, and it's still being published." Compared to Mankiw's, Samuelson's book did not cost much when I bought it in 1961—about $25—though the most recent version costs $154.93. Correct for inflation.

Samuelson offered a Keynesian approach to economics. In contrast, by most accounts, Mankiw is a neoliberal economist. Nevertheless,

Mankiw claims that he is "viewed as a neo-Keynesian, so in no sense am I trying to take Keynes out of the classroom."[4] He even declares that he named his pet dog "Keynes." Yet as chair of President George W. Bush's Council of Economic Advisors, Mankiw supported "nearly all of the Bush conservative agenda, including tax cuts for the rich, deregulation, and reduced government spending" (Maier, "From Classroom to the White House")—hardly a Keynesian agenda. "Mankiw proudly claims that his Harvard students couldn't guess his political viewpoint," writes Mark Maier, yet he has published articles "supporting school vouchers, privatization of Social Security, [and] an end to inheritance taxes," and he opposes minimum wage legislation while advocating "right-to-work"—that is, antiunion—legislation.

Mankiw's attempted obfuscation of his conservatism was belied when, in 2001, a number of students joined Harvard workers to demand a living wage at the university. Mankiw told *Harvard Magazine* that it was a mistake to pay the workers more than the market rate: "To do so would compromise the University's commitment to the creation and dissemination of knowledge."[5] The Invisible Hand must be holding these apples and oranges together. Mankiw views the labor market as no different from any other market, apparently including the knowledge market. Trade unions, unemployment compensation, and minimum wage legislation are all interferences with the "free" workings of the labor market. This is apparent from his *Principles,* in which he asserts that policies like welfare and unemployment insurance "reduce efficiency":

> When the government redistributes income from the rich to the poor, it reduces the reward for working hard; as a result, people work less and produce fewer goods and services. In other words, when the government tries to cut the economic pie into more equal slices, the pie gets smaller.[6]

And that was exactly what President Bush said we should not do with our pie. *Principles* does not mention that many of the world's wealthiest individuals do not work at all. Their wealth typically comes from investments including "blind trusts" like Mitt Romney's and often also from inheritance, which is pretty much how Bush got his pie.[7]

In 2003, more than seven hundred undergraduates signed a petition requesting that Harvard offer some alternative to its Ec10, which uses Mankiw's textbook and is required of economics and social science majors (DiMaggio). An article in *The Harvard Crimson* reported that "students have known for nearly two decades that Ec10 is flagrantly biased."[8] The petitioners did not get their way. Classes by economists who offer alternative views, such as Stephen Marglin, are not required—hardly a free market in intellectual wares. Michael Perelman quotes the 1992 complaint by four Nobel Prize economists about "intellectual monopoly" in their field: "Economists will advocate free competition, but will not practice it in the marketplace of ideas."[9] Most recently, on November 2, 2011, during the Occupy Wall Street movement, some seventy students in Mankiw's Ec10 staged a walkout to "express our discontent with the bias inherent in this introductory economics course." In the letter they handed to Mankiw, they wrote, "Since the biased nature of Economics 10 contributes to and symbolizes the increasing economic inequality in America, we are walking out of your class today both to protest your inadequate discussion of basic economic theory and to lend our support to a movement that is changing American discourse on economic injustice."[10]

This is not the first time that there has been resistance to economic dogma in the Harvard Economics Department. In an essay for the 1989 anthology *How Harvard Rules: Reason in the Service of Empire,* Lawrence Lifschultz reports that, at the 1973 convention of the American Economics Association, John Kenneth Galbraith, then president of the association and a professor of economics at Harvard, called on his colleagues throughout the profession to "reassociate with reality." Current economic orthodoxy, he declared, "offers no useful handle for grasping the economic problems that now beset society."[11] Galbraith was upset partly because his Harvard colleague, Associate Professor Samuel Bowles, was being denied tenure for advocating unorthodox, leftwing views. And Bowles himself had the temerity to criticize his orthodox colleagues for going "into the lucrative and gratifying business of directly advising corporations, government bureaus and presidents,"[12] which is just how Mankiw adds to the millions he is raking in from royalties.

The situation at Harvard has been mirrored by events at the University of Notre Dame. Until recently, many of the faculty in its Economics Department were critics of neoliberal orthodoxy. Because of its critical stance, the national ratings of the Notre Dame Economics Department were low (the ratings are based mainly on the opinions of neoliberal economists like Mankiw). So, in 2010, the administration shunted the critical

group into an interdisciplinary program and hired a new cadre of orthodox economists. David Ruccio, one of the heterodox economists, refused
to be reassigned to the new program. Yet he is not listed on Notre Dame's
website among the economics faculty. Ruccio emailed me recently to
explain that he is the only "at large" faculty member at his university.[13]

UTOPIAN CAPITALISM

French sociologist Pierre Bourdieu writes of a "utopian capitalism,"
which he attributes in large measure to "a certain scientistic madness currently triumphant in Chicago today."[14] This is the neoliberal or "Chicago
School" economics established by Milton Friedman and his followers,
which Bourdieu also calls an intellectual "scourge" (vii). Similarly, heterodox economist Michael Hudson claims that the field of economics "has
been sterilized by more than a generation of Chicago School intolerance.
The economics profession does not seem to be amenable to reform along
the lines that would get you interested in it. It has become mainly a rhetorical gloss to depict financial oligarchy as if it were populist economic
democracy." He adds that neoliberal economists "preferred to put on
blinders when it came to looking at wealth distribution and the classical
distinction between 'earned' and 'unearned' (that is, parasitic) income."[15]

Regarding utopianism, according to Mankiw and other neoliberal
economists, capitalism may not be the best of all possible worlds, but
it is nearly so and could easily be improved if governments would stop
meddling with it. Even if there are occasional rough spots (recessions,
depressions) in the dough (so to speak), the pie is always rising higher.
Obeying the supposedly natural laws of economics, society is constantly
progressing for the benefit of everyone—a view that does not, however,
account for increasing inequality and poverty at home and around the
world. Nor does it matter, writes Ronaldo Munck, that this perspective
transforms the world into "one giant marketplace where everything and
everybody can be bought and sold" (*Globalization and Contestation*, 16).[16]

In the rosy neoliberal view, a free market economy is inseparable
from political freedom and democracy. They are, if not exactly identical,
Siamese twins. In *Capitalism and Freedom*, Milton Friedman, President
Reagan's favorite economist, famously contended that "competitive capitalism," or "the organization of the bulk of economic activity through

private enterprise operating in a free market," is "a necessary condition for political freedom" (4). He claimed that there are only two types of economic arrangement—"free" and "coerced." If a government interferes with the workings of the free market, it is setting forth down the dark road to communism and totalitarianism. Not all present-day economists go quite as far as Friedman, but the identification between free markets and political freedom is at least implicit in virtually every introduction to economics textbooks I have dipped into, including Mankiw's. Of course, Friedman also famously declared that "there is no such thing as a free lunch," but (apparently) that's another story.[17]

Neoliberal economists also flatter us by telling us we are all rational agents acting in our free markets to maximize utility or value for ourselves. We may be idiots when it comes to economics, but we know what we are doing; the customer is always right. It is true that, when grocery shopping, some of us look for the best products at the cheapest prices; some of us even use coupons. But how does that explain why all those inferior products at higher prices also get sold?[18] People frequently behave in irrational ways; fortunes have been squandered; the economists have apparently never heard of psychoanalysis or of Emile Durkheim's analyses of anomie and suicide. The classic image of a bankrupt stockbroker leaping out of a skyscraper window is not reassuring.[19] By assuming that everyone is rational within a free market economy, however, the economists also affirm the rationality of capitalism. Other sorts of economic arrangements—socialist, communist, cooperative, feminist, green, mercantilist, anarchist—are apparently all irrational.

What, moreover, is a market, which is supposed to work so magically for all of us? The stock market, even neoliberal economists acknowledge, is significantly different from the labor market. Trying to find work also bears little resemblance to grocery shopping. The economist may view an unemployed worker as a seller in the labor market, with employers as potential buyers. But the worker may be just as helpless as a grapefruit in a grocery store. She is the seller, but she is also the commodity—or, at any rate, her labor is the commodity. When far more people are sellers than buyers in the labor market, it is not a situation of "perfect competition" or of "freedom" in the sense either of democratic parity or of free choice. What does the word *free* mean in that case? You are "free" to sell your labor to Wal-Mart or McDonalds, if you are lucky?

Before slavery was abolished, what was free about the market for slaves? It, too, was a labor market that for much of its history operated under the rules of capitalism.[20] In contrast to either slave labor or wage labor, many other kinds of productive activities—work of various sorts—are not governed by money and market exchanges. Feminist economists—and there are some—complain that mainstream economics treats the labor of housewives as nonlabor, of no accountable value in the money economy. "The exclusion of women's work from national income accounts," writes Diana Strassmann in "Not a Free Market," "has had particularly pernicious effects for women in developing nations" (60). She points also to child rearing as typically a labor of love that both mothers and fathers, including economists, ordinarily do not assess in monetary terms. And she notes that the economics profession—academic, corporate, and governmental—has always been male dominated. Strassmann cites another feminist economist, Julie Nelson, who argues that mainstream economics "marginalizes phenomena characterized by connection, tradition, and domination, and is likely to create 'a feeling of distortion, a feeling that that which is most important has been left out'"—family, friendship, community, religion . . . whatever is not a market (62).[21]

In *Railroading Economics*, Perelman points out that, after Marx published *Capital* in 1867, capitalist economists busily depoliticized and made mathematical what had previously been called "political economy" into the modern, academic science of economics, more or less as we have it today.[22] The new science of marginal utility and price theory shifted class conflict to the back burner. "In this new form of economics," writes Perelman, "capitalists and workers alike no longer appeared as members of distinct classes, but as part of a homogeneous group of individuals. Whether the 'individual' is Wal-Mart selling toilet paper or a worker selling labor makes little difference."[23] It is conceivable that Wal-Mart could run out of toilet paper, but, according to many economists, there is a natural rate of unemployment that will never go away, so the supply of cheap labor is inexhaustible. The labor market is, hence, forever tilted in favor of the employer or, as both Malthus and the Bible claim, "the poor ye shall always have with you."

A good test of an economist's politics is what he or she says or does not say about unemployment and poverty. A neoliberal economist like Mankiw has very little to say about them. Economists focus on how to increase productivity—how to make the pie higher, in Bush's lingo. But many heterodox economists stress that, without governmental or societal regulation of some sort, increased productivity on the capitalist, free market model also increases poverty. How does this apparent contradiction come about? One reason is that the more efficient a business or factory becomes, the less labor it will need to sustain its productivity.

Putting slavery, housework, and unemployment aside, neither a grocery store nor a labor market much resembles the global, electronic, trillion-dollar derivatives market in which only megabuck banks, insurance companies, hedge funds, and billionaires participate. What is being bought and sold in that sort of market is money, including your money whether you like it or not, in the form of hundreds of thousands of debts (mortgages, for example) bundled together and sold as speculative commodities. Whether any of the individual debts ever get paid does not matter to the big-time investors—unless they get stuck, as many of them did in the 2007–8 crash, which turned a lot of derivatives into "toxic assets." The banks and insurance giants that held these bad assets were then bailed out by none other than the government, again using your money (that is, taxpayers' money). The fallout from reckless financial speculation matters to you not just as a taxpayer but also if you go bankrupt, lose your home, or lose your job. Where is the freedom in that sort of supposedly free market? Yet neoliberal economists consider it a free market if government does not try to regulate it.

Wasn't the bank bailout contrary to Mankiw's *Principles*? Of course it was, but, in an emergency, free market economics is likely to fly out windows along with bankrupt stockbrokers. Given its ideological dominance, however, it will soon fly back in again on the economists' magical free market carpet. Since the 1980s, faith in "free enterprise" has become so dominant in the United States that it is difficult even to question it. The market is today supposedly "the guarantor of freedom," James Galbraith complains, "while the state is its nemesis: markets good, government bad" (*Predator State,* 21). In 2011, any attempt by the state to enact economic reform, such as the recent feeble effort to overhaul the banks and Wall Street, is attacked by conservatives as "socialism."

Galbraith also has in mind the widely held opinion that private enterprise gets things done more efficiently and less expensively than government ownership, control, or regulation. One outcome has been the rush to privatize as much public business as possible—prisons, schools, toll roads, espionage, water, you name it. The advocates of privatization downplay the fact that privately run businesses make profits.[24] Their usual claim is that the profits come from greater efficiency. But all greater efficiency often amounts to is hiring fewer workers, paying them less, and providing no benefits. Since the start of the "Reagan revolution" in 1980, "the prison-industrial complex," to take just one example, has helped the United States become the world's leader in incarceration. As of 2009, nearly two and a half million were in American prisons. Many are being held for nonviolent drug offenses. Whatever the figures, "prison corporations have not lived up to their promises," write the editors of *Capitalist Punishment*. "They have not saved governments substantial amounts of money, nor have they proven to be more secure." Instead, they have diminished training, standards, and safety for prison guards, and they "have contributed to an unacceptable level of neglect and violence against inmates."[25]

Privatizing in other arenas has also proven to be costlier and less efficient than many government-run operations. When its Republican governor privatized much of Indiana's welfare system, turning it over to IBM, he was soon forced to rescind its contract because of inadequate performance. He also privatized the Indiana Toll Road, which is in worse condition than it has ever been. And what about the billions squandered, missing, or stolen through various forms of corporate fraud and embezzlement in Iraq? Of course, a lot of the work or nonwork in Iraq was farmed out on the basis of no-bid contracts, so blame the government, too. Even when they are functioning honorably and efficiently, large, multinational corporations throw several monkey wrenches into the perfect machinery of free market capitalism. They obviously exercise far more power over economies throughout the world than do the vast majority of individuals or even many governments. A 1997 comparison of corporations and nations revealed that over half the top one hundred economic powers were corporations.[26]

It is, therefore, surprising that Mankiw's *Principles* pays very little attention to corporations. In a half-page insert on "Corporate Management," Mankiw says that corporations are differently managed from small firms—no surprise there. He also mentions that corporate crime became "big news" in 2005, with the Enron, Tyco, and WorldCom scandals, but then adds this misleading claim: "Fortunately, criminal activity by corporate managers is rare" (486). Just a few bad apples? A 1982 study of the five hundred largest corporations in the United States found that 23 percent of them had been convicted of criminal activity over the past decade.[27] Given their vast resources, it is extremely difficult to get convictions against corporations, so 23 percent is probably a drastic underestimate of the amount of corporate crime. Yet it is evident that "corporate crime and violence inflicts far more damage on society than all street crime combined."[28] In *Thieves in High Places* (2003), Jim Hightower writes, "Today most corporations are Enron—booking phantom assets, hiding losses, manipulating prices, looting pensions," and the list continues (62). No corporation steals wages from workers at a greater clip than Wal-Mart, which hires many of its employees as "contract workers" —that is, as self-employed—so it can pay them less than the legal minimum wage.

Mankiw acknowledges that there is a range from perfect competition to monopoly control in many areas of the economy, but "monopoly power is a matter of degree" and is "usually limited," he claims, so that "we will not go far wrong assuming that firms operate in competitive markets, even if that is not precisely the case" (*Principles,* 340).[29] On what planet does Mankiw live? In his alternative universe, transnational corporations' overwhelming power to dominate markets, fix prices, ship jobs overseas, evade regulations, conceal information, influence consumers, buy politicians, mislead shareholders, cook their books, and dodge taxation are not major problems.[30] According to Mankiw, "the main reason for rising healthcare costs" has nothing to do with the price gouging of insurance and pharmaceutical corporations but is instead caused by "medical advances that provide new, better, but often expensive ways to extend and improve our lives" (247). But these medical advances are also expensive in Canada, Denmark, and Great Britain, whose citizens have universal health insurance and who, despite the taxes they pay for this privilege, spend per capita only about half of what privately insured Americans pay. And roughly fifty million Americans are not insured.[31]

Privatization, which means turning increasing amounts of public property and more and more public business over to corporations, also entails the relentless "proletarianization" of millions.[32] From the standpoint of free market zealotry, we are all just "human capital." But capitalism needs fewer and fewer workers to produce the goods it takes to market, although it must have consumers to purchase those goods. The consumers do not have to be anywhere near to the point of production, however. It does not matter to General Motors that the unemployment rate in Detroit is above 40 percent; it now sells more cars in China than in the United States. Capitalism needs workers, of course, but it also needs what Marx called "a reserve army" of the unemployed to keep wages down. From the free market standpoint, the size of this army of redundant workers is irrelevant; if anything, the larger the better. Those who can neither find employment nor consume anything are, from the capitalist standpoint, worthless (see chapter 11).[33]

CRISIS MANAGEMENT

In *One Market under God*, Thomas Frank writes that "American leaders in the nineties came to believe that markets were a popular system, a far more democratic form of organization than (democratically elected) governments" (xiv). E-trading over the Internet seemed to make getting rich via the stock market available to everyone. According to e-trade boosters, Wall Street suddenly became the friend rather than the enemy of the little guy. Computers had finalized the marriage of free markets and the freedom of the individual. Frank quotes banker Walter Wriston: "Markets are voting machines; they function by taking referenda" (55). In performing even more democratically than political democracy, according to Wriston, markets give "power to the People." The crash of the dot-com market in 2000 seems hardly to have dimmed this utopian view of capitalism and computers spreading prosperity throughout the world. If you or your company did not go bankrupt, economics really was a lot of fun. The 2007–8 crash, however, has been much harder to downplay as just another unfortunate but minor bump on the highroad to riches for all. Try telling the unemployed guys freezing in vacant lots all over 2011 America, or, for that matter, Mexican peasants thrown off their land by NAFTA, that thanks to the Internet, globalization, and free markets we will soon all be rich.

An accurate label for a realistic rather than utopian economics might be "crisis management." But neoliberal economists have seemed incapable either of predicting or of explaining crises when they happen. The market machinery appears to be running smoothly, just as they predict. Then out of nowhere, bang! A crisis. Where did that come from? Some "externality"? The economists draw a blank. Testifying before Congress after the crash, Allan Greenspan, then chairman of the Federal Reserve, confessed that he did "not fully understand what went wrong in what he thought were self-governing markets." Greenspan declared he was "very distressed" to find "a flaw" in his economic reasoning: "Those of us who have looked to the self-interest of lending institutions to protect shareholders' equity . . . are in a state of shocked disbelief." As he told Congress, "This crisis has turned out to be much broader than anything I could have imagined."[34]

Apparently, Greenspan was unaware that capitalism has always produced crises just as regularly as it produces goods.[35] He seems not to have realized that markets return to equilibrium not through some Invisible Hand but through crises. Noting that "markets evidently fail—and fail very frequently," Joseph Stiglitz adds that they are "self-correcting," but only because the "bubbles" they produce burst, causing misery and a certain amount of economic realism (*Freefall*, 12, 18). Similarly, Richard Posner, in *A Failure of Capitalism* (2009), writes that the new "depression" was not caused by government but by markets. Citing "the disappointing performance of the economics profession," Posner adds that in regard to 2007–8, "economists have become a lagging indicator of our economic troubles" (xiv, vii).

Government, however, also failed, to the extent that it followed the bidding of neoliberal economists and deregulated financial investments. The editors of *The Economic Crisis Reader* write, "Anyone could have seen that a boom fueled by rising debt, issued by an increasingly leveraged and unregulated financial market, could not be sustained and would end in a crisis. Anyone, that is, except an economist trained in neoclassical orthodoxy" (2). In the same anthology, David Kotz states what should be one of the first lessons in Ec10: "Every form of capitalism has contradictions that eventually bring about a structural crisis of that form of capitalism" (35). Earlier crises, from the Great Depression to the rise and collapse of Enron, should have provided Greenspan and other neoliberals with some clues, at least.[36] In *Low-Wage Capitalism*, Fred Goldstein contends that, regarding crises, nothing has changed since the early days of the Industrial Revolution:

> The capitalist system at the dawn of the twenty-first century behaves in the same fundamental way that it did in 1825, during the first capitalist crisis of overproduction. Profits pile up. Fortunes are made. Then markets collapse. Profits shrink. Workplaces shut down. Workers are thrown out and left on their own. This in a nutshell is the bare bones of every capitalist crisis. Except that this time [2007–8], as in the 1930s, it is not just a cyclical crisis, but a crisis of the system.[37]

Now "the system" has been globalized, and workers in the United States and everywhere else have been plunged into "a great worldwide race to the bottom."[38]

When has capitalism ever been a smooth road to prosperity for everyone? When has it ever been either fair or free? Writing about the Enron crisis, Vijay Prashad argues that that debacle may have been extreme but was not exceptional in the history of corporate capitalism. The rise and fall of Enron's colossal Ponzi scheme reveals "precisely the nature of 'free markets,'" at least when they take the form of enormous financial investments.[39] Far from moving in the direction of economic "equilibrium" and "perfect competition," Enron moved in exactly the opposite direction. Prashad continues:

> Big players get help from politicians to design a system where they can win. When the system is implemented, the big guys quickly monopolize supply. This is the logical outcome of completely unfettered competition. Eventually, only a small handful of competitors survive, making it possible for them to reduce or eliminate the "free market" so that profits for the few can sky-rocket.[40]

It appears to be the case that the freer a market is from government regulation or oversight, the more crisis prone it becomes and the more costly—definitely not free—for the average citizen.[41]

Large, well-developed economies like those of the United States and the European Union are no doubt better able to weather crises than are smaller, weaker economies. The bonanza that "free trade" was supposed to bring to the poorer countries of the world has entailed "shock therapy" and not always a whole lot more than that (Klein, *Shock Doctrine*). NAFTA has not been a bonanza for Mexico—far from it.[42] "The number of failed states in the world," writes William Tabb, "and the deteriorated condition of others, who despite following IMF-sanctioned policies have not found their economies growing, attest to the limits of the [free trade, neoliberal] model" (86). The Center for Popular Economics points out that the "neoliberal era (beginning in the 1980s) has been characterized by the near continuous outbreak of financial crises. One is hard-pressed to think of a part of the world that has not been adversely impacted by one in the past two decades, with the recent crisis in Asia affecting the only developmental success story of the past 50 years." The Center cites Martin Wolff commenting in the *Financial Times* on a 1998 World Bank report about the Asian financial crisis that started in 1997: "Three crucial lessons can be drawn from the report. It is surprisingly difficult for countries embarking on financial liberalization to avoid disasters. When they succumb, it is no less difficult to escape economic depressions. If short-term capital flows are not tamed, such crises are certain to reoccur."

Have the countries of "the developing world" jumped voluntarily on the international "free trade" bandwagon? More often than not, they have been coerced to accept the neoliberal policies of the IMF, World Bank, and WTO. As Naomi Klein demonstrates in *The Shock Doctrine: The Rise of Disaster Capitalism,* political crises like the overthrow of democratically elected Salvador Allende in Chile in 1973 have prepared the way both for dictatorships and for the imposition of neoliberal economic policies, which seem always to lead to economic crises.[43] Milton Friedman and "the Chicago boys" were only too happy to serve as economic advisors to General Augusto Pinochet and his ilk. Klein challenges "the official story—that the triumph of deregulated capitalism has been born of freedom, that unfettered free markets go hand in hand with democracy." On the contrary, neoliberal economic policies have "consistently been midwifed by the most brutal forms of coercion."[44]

Capitalist globalization and free trade were supposed to usher in an era of peace and prosperity, "the end of history." While it has brought prosperity to some, it has brought increasing poverty and even catastrophe to many others.[45] The number of those who, worldwide, now live or try to live on less than $1 per day has mushroomed. And even in the United States, the poor have gotten a lot poorer since the 1980s: over forty-seven million people in the United States are currently living in poverty. "The defenders of today's predatory capitalism have to contort themselves to make the claim that the system they advocate is the best way to meet the needs and aspirations of humanity," writes James Laxer. "Capitalism works best for a small minority of the world's people, condemns hundreds of millions to exploitation and a stunted existence, and leaves billions, particularly in the Third World, in a state of poverty."[46]

These are lessons college students are not likely to learn in Ec10, and certainly not from Mankiw's *Principles*. They will also not learn that economic globalization in its current form will not lift all boats—boat people often drown. They are even less likely to learn, according to Pierre Bourdieu, that economic globalization "is not a mechanical effect of the laws of technology or the economy, but the product of a policy implemented by a set of agents and institutions, and the result of the application of rules deliberately created for specific ends, namely, trade liberalization (that is, the elimination of all national regulations restricting companies and their investments)." Bourdieu thus stresses that current national and international economic arrangements are the result of political decision making, not of impersonal market forces. Though the decision making is underwritten by neoliberal economics, politics creates "the conditions for domination by starkly confronting agents and firms hitherto confined within national limits with competition from more powerful and more efficient forces and modes of production." In the so-called developing world, the abolition of trade barriers "spells ruin for national enterprises and . . . leads to the collapse of local enterprises, which are bought up, often at ridiculously low prices, by the multinationals." Bourdieu adds, "We know that, as a general rule, formal equality in a situation of real inequality favours the dominant" (*Acts of Resistance*, 225).

As critics like Bourdieu insist, the current regime of international "free trade," dominated by the IMF, the World Bank, the WTO, and the wealthiest countries, especially the United States, is hugely lopsided, tilted in favor of the multinational corporations usually headquartered and bankrolled in those countries. Nevertheless, the 2007–8 crisis may have tilted the balance away from the United States. Its economy will remain the largest in the world "for a while longer," John Gray predicts, "but it will be other countries that, once the crisis is over, buy up what remains intact in the wreckage of America's financial system."[47]

AMERICA: THE NEW LAND OF DEBT PEONAGE

"They hate us for our freedoms." So President Bush, to his satisfaction at least, explained 9/11. What "freedoms" did he have in mind? "Free trade" or the "free market" are probably at the top of his list. Meanwhile, thanks in large measure to Bush's economic agenda—or lack of one— the indebtedness of millions of Americans and also the indebtedness of the U.S. government have mushroomed. The unanticipated invasions of Afghanistan and Iraq account for much of that increase. So do Bush's tax cuts for the wealthy. According to Jan Nederveen Pieterse,

> In 2005 the national debt stood at $13.5 trillion, 115 percent of GDP. In 2007 the current account deficit was $800 billion per year and the US borrowed $70 billion per month and $3 billion each trading day. In 2006 alone the US borrowed 60 percent of all global credit. The interest on the debt is $7 billion per week. This means that poorer countries are funding American overconsumption. It also means increasing foreign ownership of American assets.[48]

Assessing American imperial and military hegemony in light of these facts, Pieterse adds, "It is a fiction of state that the U.S. can have guns and butter, tax cuts and war, that it is possible to do empire on the basis of a world-historic deficit. Neoconservatives have been long on power and short on economics" (141). They are "short on economics" precisely because they have chosen to listen to neoliberal economists—or not, as the case may be. They do not appear to listen to any other type of economist. And the upshot is a nation rapidly entering a phase of imperial and economic decline—a phase that could also be described as one of international debt peonage.[49]

By now, millions of Americans have become debt peons. Pieterse notes that Lyndon Johnson's "war on poverty turned into a war on the poor" (*Is There Hope for Uncle Sam?* 144), which has lasted from the early 1980s to the present and is now also widely understood as a war on the middle class. As the post–World War II era of prosperity started to wind down in the 1970s, American workers began to rely more and more on credit. Both the working and the middle classes went on "the greatest binge of borrowing" in history. "Members of the business community," writes Richard Wolff, "began to realize that they had a fantastic double opportunity." He continues:

> They could get the profits from flat wages and rising productivity, and then they could turn to the working class traumatized by the inability to have rising consumption, and give them the means to consume more.

> So instead of paying your workers a wage, you're going to lend them the
> money—so they have to pay it back to you! With interest!⁵⁰

This is the old ruse of the company store on a much grander scale. "Ten percent of Americans, those in the lowest income bracket, spend 40 percent of their income on debt," notes Pieterse (*Is There Hope for Uncle Sam?* 133). According to Sherle Schwenninger, "household debt as a percentage of disposable income rose from 90 percent in the late 1990s to 133 percent in 2007" ("Redoing Globalization," 31). By 2008, approximately two million people had lost their homes, and perhaps twice that number was threatened with foreclosure.⁵¹ As a result, economic growth in the United States has come to what Schwenninger calls "a screeching halt."⁵²

In "Dress Rehearsal for Debt Peonage," Michael Hudson stresses that "Wall Street's product is debt" and that, in the current crisis, the market has become inundated with that negative product. "The negative equity we are seeing today is a key component of debt peonage," he claims. "It forces debt peons to spend their lives trying to work their way out of debt. The more desperate they get, the more risks they take, and the deeper they end up." Hudson is thinking mainly of people who default on their mortgages and lose their homes, or are at any rate struggling to keep them. "The distinguishing feature about [debt] peonage is its *lack of choice*," Hudson notes; "It is the antithesis of free markets." He adds,

> many families today find themselves locked into homes that have *negative equity*. Their mortgage debt exceeds the market price. These homes can't be sold—unless the family can pay the difference to the banker who has made the bad mortgage loan. The gap may exceed all the income the family earns in an entire year—just as it was making on paper a price gain larger than its annual take-home pay.

There are many other forms of debt peonage, and many Americans, who may or may not hold mortgages, are over their heads in trying to pay for cars or for purchases on their credit cards. In terms of income, the bottom 20 percent in the United States have negative wealth—that is, they owe more than they take in, sometimes substantially more. Lack of health insurance accounts for the largest number of individual bankruptcies in the United States. Students and former students often have decades to go before they can finally pay off their college loans. And so on.

Nobel Prize winning economist Paul Krugman wrote that billionaire Warren Buffett "recently made headlines by saying America is more likely to turn into a 'sharecroppers' society' than an 'ownership society.' But I think the right term is a 'debt peonage' society—after the system, prevalent in the post–Civil War South, in which debtors were forced to work for their creditors."[53] This is exactly what Mexico and much of the rest of Latin America have been for centuries. Harvey, Ehrenreich, Pieterse, Hudson, and Krugman are all saying the United States is rapidly achieving, through its national version of "the race to the bottom," the same level of inequality and poverty that characterizes Mexico or Guatemala. Along the way to Mexico's current condition, the United States has done everything in its power to force that unlucky country into extreme inequality, poverty, political instability, and economic dysfunctionality.[54]

A REALISTIC EC10?

Economists who teach EC10 typically present the notions that capitalism is the only system that works and that political and social freedoms depend on free markets. These notions are presented as unassailable axioms. The economists can get away with it in part because their students are eager to learn the supposedly scientific wisdom that has made America and most of their parents prosper. And neither the economists nor the students are likely to get any alternative messages from advertising, the movies, or television, much less from their textbooks. They certainly will not get it from Mankiw's *Principles*.

What would an EC10 textbook look like, however, if it contained chapters on debt peonage and the flaws in capitalist globalization? Suppose it addressed issues like the relationship between multinational corporations, neoimperialism, war, and third world poverty? What if it stressed that the history of capitalism is characterized by frequent economic crises and crashes? What if it also stressed that technological innovation increases unemployment as machines replace workers? Suppose it insisted that there are valuable forms of labor outside the money economy, like parenting and volunteer work for charities? Suppose it further insisted that communities are at least as important as markets? Maybe it should have a chapter on the benefits of socialism in the places where socialism has worked, as in Scandinavia? It should certainly have a chapter on environmental sustainability, and also one on the commons, or those resources such as water, air, wildlife, forests, parks, beaches, and other public lands that should not be privatized or commodified.[55] A chapter on public ownership, including the importance of public education, public safety, and public utilities, would be essential. Finally, suppose this textbook ditched the phony claim that paying for social justice and greater economic equality undermines efficiency? If economics is the science of wealth, shouldn't its aim be wealth for everyone—that is, common-wealth—instead of corporate and imperial domination?

An ideal—that is, a realistic and honest—Ec10 textbook might end by citing Joe Hill. If he were alive today, he would probably include neo-liberal economists like Alan Greenspan and N. Gregory Mankiw among the "long-haired preachers" who respond to the pleas for sustenance by the poor, the unemployed, and the dispossessed:

> You will eat, bye and bye,
> In that glorious land above the sky;
> Work and pray, live on hay,
> You'll get pie in the sky when you die.

THREE

Tea Party Brewhaha

I say on the air all the time, "if you take what
I say as gospel, you're an idiot."

—GLENN BECK

*Lurking in the shadows of our fair Republic, its tentacles reaching
secretly in all directions, a Vast Conspiracy threatens our liberty and
our prosperity. No, this is not a conspiracy directed by the Islamic
terrorists and suiciders who also would like to destroy America.
They have their own foul conspiracy. The far more insidious and
dangerous conspiracy comes from Americans themselves. These
homegrown conspirators claim to be patriots, but they are the
Republic's greatest enemies. They are* THE PROGRESSIVES,
*starting with that arch-progressive Woodrow Wilson, and lead-
ing on through the machinations of FDR, Frances Fox Piven,
ACORN, and Barack Hussein Obama.*

To learn all about this "Vast Conspiracy," one could tune in to Glenn
Beck, Tea Party guru, on the Fox News Channel—at least, while his show
was still being aired by Fox.[1] The "progressive movement," according to
Beck, is "the lunatic fringe of the left. It is the home of everything that
you despise. It is the home of income tax." The progressives are next of
kin to Nazis, socialists, communists, and Islamicists. And Obama is the
progressive socialist closet Muslim conspirator-in-chief. It is so easy to

call him "Osama." How many of Beck's three-million-plus devotees buy into his conspiracy theory, and how many of them are also Tea Partiers, is unclear. But for Beck as well as for many Tea Partiers, history itself is a conspiracy (what you do not study might swallow you alive), and at the dark heart of that conspiracy are not merely "the progressives" but nothing less than the federal government of the United States, which for the last century and more has fallen into the clutches of the progressives.

The federal government is the trillion-dollar gorilla in the closet!

On their web site, the Tea Party Patriots announce that their "mission is to restore America's founding principles of Fiscal Responsibility, Constitutionally Limited Government, and Free Markets." These sound like noble goals, if you do not ask what exactly they mean. "Fiscal responsibility" means do not spend our tax money on aspects of government we do not like, such as "Obamacare," viewed by many Tea Partiers as a conspiracy to exercise tyrannical control over their health and bodies. It does not appear to mean reining in defense spending. "Constitutionally Limited Government" means get the federal government out of our lives and stop taxing us. And "Free Markets" means eliminate governmental regulations on business and leave the economy entirely up to private enterprise—although since the crash of 2007–8, some Tea Partiers may not want to include banks, mortgage companies, hedge funds, and Wall Street in the category of "free markets." So these noble goals have, to put it mildly, some limitations. Also, most Tea Partiers are not about to admit that their movement, which sprang to life after the 2007 election of Barack Obama, has been in any way motivated by racism: their hatred of "Osama Obama" has, they claim, nothing to do with the fact that he is the nation's first African American president.

Shortly after the 2010 midterm election, I sent a letter to the editor of our local newspaper comparing the Tea Party to the Know-Nothings of the 1850s. I noted that some Tea Party candidates had lost their races partly because of their ignorance. My chief example was Christine O'Donnell's not knowing that the Constitution mandates separation of church and state. (Ex-witch and Tea Party candidate O'Donnell, running for Senate from Delaware, claimed to know all about the Constitution.) I also mentioned Congressman John Boehner's assertion that "America has the best health care system in the world." Boehner is not a Tea Partier, but his assertion is widely shared among Tea Party opponents of Obamacare or indeed health insurance reform in general. I cited the 2000 World Health Organization (WHO) ranking of the U.S. health care system as thirty-seventh in the world. I noted as well that WHO gives the United States first place in one category: per capita cost for health care.

My letter provoked two counter letters to the editor. Both correctly asserted that the Constitution does not contain the words "separation of church and state." And both also incorrectly asserted that "America has the best health care system in the world." Here is one of the responses:

> Show us in the Constitution the words "separation of church and state," not your interpretation. The actual words are not there.... But if Jesse Jackson, Bill and Hillary Clinton or Barack Obama want to speak from the pulpit of a church that's OK with people like you, but don't let a Republican walk within a block of a church. And when some world leader wants health care where do they go for it—France, Spain, Cuba, Great Britain? No way; they head straight for America, where we have the best health care in the world.

In a second letter to the editor, I pointed out that, although the Constitution does not contain the words "separation of church and state," the first amendment begins, "Congress shall make no law respecting an establishment of religion, or prohibiting the free exercise thereof." I noted that it was not me but Thomas Jefferson who first interpreted that language as mandating "the separation of church and state."

My second letter also added some new statistics about health care from the 2009 CIA Fact Book: infant mortality in the United States is 6.26 per 1,000 live births, compared to 5.04 in Canada, 5.82 in Cuba, and 2.31 in Singapore. Life expectancy in the United States is 78.11, versus 81.23 (Canada) and 82.12 (Japan)—the United States ranks forty-ninth in the world in this category. In another study, only 40 percent of Americans said they were satisfied with our health care system, compared to 46 percent (Canada), 57 percent (U.K.), 65 percent (France), and 91 percent (Denmark). I doubt that I convinced my critics. But perhaps they are not among the complete boneheads now cropping up on the political landscape (including most of the Republican candidates for president in 2012). At least the critics read our local newspaper. I do not know if they are Tea Partiers. At the same time, approximately 15 percent of American voters are Tea Partiers, and perhaps another 25 percent are attracted to Tea Party ideology.[2] What does it all mean? Or unmean?

PAST AND PRESENT POLITICAL BONEHEADISM

I thought my comparison between the Tea Party and the Know-Nothings was clever and original, but I soon learned that a number of other commentators had already made that comparison. A *New York Times* "opinionator" blog for August 25, 2010, is titled "Building a Nation of Know-Nothings." Its author, Timothy Egan, discusses "the flat-earth wing" of the Republican Party and excoriates both Rush Limbaugh and Glenn Beck for spewing forth half-truths, outright lies, and ignorance, including the notions that President Obama is a Muslim and that he was not born in the United States. The Wikipedia article on the Know-Nothing movement of the 1850s also cites a *Times* editorial for May 20, 2007, on immigration legislation that refers to "this generation's Know-Nothings" and a 2006 editorial in *The Weekly Standard,* in which conservative William Kristol attacks "populist Republicans" who threaten to turn the GOP into "an anti-immigration, Know-Nothing party."

It is not clear that the original Know-Nothings were complete ignoramuses. The name derives from the password—"I know nothing"—that was used to gain admission to the secret lodges some of them established. What the Know-Nothings believed they knew was that the United States was being overwhelmed by German and Irish immigrants, most of them Roman Catholics. And at least some of them believed the immigrants were being urged on by the pope and the Catholic priesthood to undermine Protestantism and undo the American republic. In "The Paranoid Style in American Politics," Richard Hofstadter quotes an 1855 article from a Texas newspaper: "It is a notorious fact that the Monarchs of Europe and the Pope of Rome are at this very moment plotting our destruction and threatening the extinction of our political, civil, and religious institutions" (8). According to the Know-Nothings, the agents of this conspiracy were multiplying daily through lax immigration laws, allowing German Catholics and the Irish, with Jesuits circulating secretly and freely among them, to inundate the United States.

Whatever the original Know-Nothings may or may not have known, their anti-immigration paranoia is similar to that expressed by many Tea

Partiers. Immigration has not been the major Tea Party focus, which has instead aimed most of its wrath at Obama, Obamacare, the national debt, and what it sees as an out-of-control and invasive federal government. Why the Tea Party did not arise when President George W. Bush was authorizing torture and warrantless wiretapping, invading Iraq under false pretenses, and spending the country into the economic hole it is currently struggling to climb out of is an interesting question. In any event, some Tea Partiers appear to recognize, with Sarah Palin, that the United States has historically been "so welcoming" to immigrants. Dick Armey's FreedomWorks, for example, supports a guest worker program to permit businesses to hire Mexicans and other foreigners, like the earlier Bracero program. The guest workers would apply for visas and other identification papers; they would go back to Mexico after their work was done, and there would be no "amnesty" for anyone who entered the country illegally.[3]

The keynote speaker at the February 2010 Tea Party convention in Nashville, Tom Tancredo of Colorado, advocates the total militarization of the U.S. border with Mexico. "Plenty of people coming across that border want to do very bad things to us," Tancredo claims; "we know it's been an entry point for terrorists."[4] As if Mexican "illegals" were not bad enough (Tancredo thinks they should all be rounded up and deported), Muslim immigrants are coming to the United States in droves to subvert American freedoms and install Shari'a law. Goodbye, fair Republic! Like Tancredo, many Tea Partiers believe that most immigrants do not understand or share American values, that there should be no "amnesty" for "illegals," and that English should be declared the official language of the United States. At an August 2010 town hall meeting in North Carolina, Ada Smith, Republican national committeewoman, proclaimed to much applause, "You cannot be one nation under God when everyone's speaking something different."[5] How, then, has Switzerland held together with its four official languages? How many different languages are spoken in India? Is it a major problem for Canada to have signs in both English and French? Why the punitive attitude toward those whose first language is Spanish? Furthermore, Smith's English-only stance suggests that God speaks English, which may be politically correct from the Tea Party perspective, but is both historically and theologically incorrect.

Most Tea Partiers supported the attempt by Arizona Republicans and Governor Jan Brewer to pass an immigration law that would make it mandatory for police to ask for proof of citizenship from anyone they suspected of being in the United States illegally. In an April 2010 broadcast, Tea Party guru Rush Limbaugh told his listeners,

> But notice here . . . how the Democrats, the [Obama] regime, the media, the Left are calling Arizona's new immigration bill an outrageous usurpation of power. Meanwhile, that same regime is moving to take away our salt, our light bulbs, reaching down into every nook and cranny of our lives and they don't bat an eye, and yet they have the audacity to accuse Arizona's immigration bill of being an outrageous usurpation of power.[6]

The Feds are going to come knocking at your door to take away your salt and your light bulbs?

The FDA was merely considering whether to require producers of processed foods to inform consumers about the amount of salt in their products. And while the Energy Independence and Security Act of 2007, approved by President Bush and not President Obama, requires all 100-watt bulbs to be 30 percent more efficient by 2012, nowhere does it say that, if you have old 100-watt bulbs, you cannot use them. Limbaugh's conspiracy-minded craziness, here and on many other occasions, expresses contemporary know-nothingism at its worst.

In my first letter to the editor, I pointed out that the earlier Know-Nothing movement was short lived, lasting no more than a decade and a half, and I said, probably too optimistically, that the Tea Party would also soon fade away.[7] In my desire to believe that ignorance cannot support a political movement for very long, I overlooked many contrary examples—for instance, the anti-Catholicism of the first Know-Nothings has been around ever since the Reformation. Moreover, I had just completed a book concerning the (pseudo)scientific racism, including Social Darwinism, that pervaded intellectual discourse among both Europeans and North Americans from the Enlightenment up to World War II and that still crops up from time to time.[8]

With ignorance in charge, there is perhaps no need for any very sophisticated ideology to dupe people. Patriotism is enough. The power of ignorance to stimulate political movements, moreover, probably depends on a wide range of factors, including the influence of those promoting the ignorance and also the quality and degree of the paranoia that stokes it. Beck, Limbaugh, Tancredo, Armey, Palin, and the Tea Party are receiving huge amounts of media attention these days. They are backed by huge amounts of right-wing foundation and corporate money, including money from the Koch brothers, which is not likely to dry up soon. The influence of these contemporary disseminators of conspiracy theories and reactionary boneheadism is far greater than anything the original Know-Nothings could muster, although nineteenth-century "nativism" and anti-Catholicism were quite influential.

Hofstadter notes that probably all political ideologies and movements are afflicted by paranoia, albeit some much more seriously than others. Has the anti-Catholicism of the original Know-Nothings completely died out? Although it seems weak today, it has certainly been a force in American politics since the Puritans. The "take-back-our-country" desire expressed by the Tea Party has perhaps always been with us. Given the "birther" flap over where President Obama was born, that Tea Party aim has an evident though not explicitly stated racist meaning. Citing sociologist Daniel Bell on the feeling of "dispossession" expressed by "the modern right wing" in the United States, Hofstadter in 1965 could be describing the Tea Party today:

> The old American virtues have already been eaten away by cosmopolitans and intellectuals; the old competitive capitalism has been gradually undermined by socialist and communist schemers; the old national security and independence have been destroyed by treasonous plots, having as their most powerful agents not merely outsiders and foreigners but major statesmen seated at the very centers of American power.[9]

If this sounds like Limbaugh or Beck on President Obama with his alleged nefarious ties to ACORN, or the Tides Foundation, or even Islamic terrorism, that should not be surprising: if history does not always repeat itself, political paranoia does. Among other examples, Hofstadter cites both Joseph McCarthy and Robert H. Welch Jr., founder of the John Birch Society. McCarthy suspected anybody and everybody of being a communist or at least a "fellow-traveler." Welch also believed that "Communist influences are now in almost complete control of our Federal Government." He thought that John Foster Dulles was "a Communist agent." And even Dwight Eisenhower was, according to Welch, "a dedicated, conscious agent of the Communist conspiracy."[10]

What is the relationship, if any, between the political paranoia that typically sees the world in conspiratorial terms and the boneheadism of Beck, Limbaugh, or Palin, who among other gaffs declared that the United States is at war with Iran and that America has a staunch ally in North Korea? Perhaps these gaffs were just slips of her tongue. But probably not. While visiting Kodiak Island, Palin said, "As we work and sightsee on America's largest island, we'll get to view more majestic bears," apparently forgetting about Hawaii. She also asserted that she was able to keep track of Russian skullduggery (and, hence, that she knows something about foreign policy) by watching the Russians from Alaska. And in regard to her malapropisms like "refudiate," she declared that Shakespeare, too, "liked to coin new words." (Waxing mavericky, Palin has also claimed that "only dead fish go with the flow.")

Smart, well-educated people can and often do believe in conspiracy theories, even when these have been roundly debunked. But a weak grasp of politics, history, and the general complexities of human interactions is surely fertile ground for the spread of such theories. Of course, some conspiracies are real enough—Al-Qaeda, for example. And members of the Aryan Nation and other white supremacist groups, many of whom may also be Tea Partiers, are conspiring to "take back the country" from blacks, Latinos, gays, and liberals (Beck's "progressives"). A mixture of weak knowledge and a lot of ignorance has often led to understanding history itself as a conspiracy, as Hofstadter notes:

> The distinguishing thing about the paranoid style is not that its exponents see conspiracies or plots here and there in history, but that they regard a "vast" or "gigantic" conspiracy as *the motive force* in historical events. History *is* a conspiracy, set in motion by demonic forces of almost transcendent power, and what is felt to be needed to defeat it is not the usual methods of political give-and-take, but an all-out crusade. The paranoid spokesman sees the fate of this conspiracy in apocalyptic terms.[11]

For many Tea Partiers, the election of President Obama was just the tip of the iceberg of the vast conspiracy that is threatening to undermine everything the Founding Fathers created, including Fiscal Responsibility, Constitutionally Limited Government, and Free Markets.

The Tea Party has been motivated in part by a racism its supporters deny and sometimes try to tamp down.[12] The racism is evident, however, in the birther movement and claims that Obama grew up in Indonesia or Kenya, or in the favorite joke among Tea Partiers: "The zoo has African lions, but the White House has a lyin' African." Their wish to "take back our country" implies getting rid of the black closet Muslim in the White House and installing a white Christian instead. Mark Williams, spokesman for the Tea Party Express, has called the NAACP a racist organization and has also called Obama an "Indonesian Muslim turned welfare thug." As Tancredo, Dinesh D'Souza, and Newt Gingrich all have it, Obama is loyal to his Kenyan father's "tribal" values. The 2008 presidential candidate Mike Huckabee echoed this patent falsehood, claiming that Obama's Kenyan upbringing explains why he is "anti-British" and why his foreign policy is completely at odds with that of his predecessors: "If you think about it, his perspective as growing up in Kenya with a Kenyan father and grandfather, he probably grew up hearing that the British were a bunch of imperialists who persecuted his grandfather" for participating in the Mau Mau rebellion. Quite apart from the false Kenyan claim, does Huckabee really believe that the British were not imperialists?

None of these reactionaries admits that his or her opinions about Obama are tinged by racism. But why are the overwhelming majority of Tea Partiers angry white people, many of whom Obama himself once accurately described as clinging to their guns and their religion? The election of a black president seems to have sent many white Americans a signal that they will soon be outnumbered by nonwhite voters. Racist resentment is often expressed at Tea Party rallies—for example, by assertions that Obama's "regime" means "white slavery." Palin disavows racism, yet, during the 2008 presidential campaign, she declared that Obama "is not one of us." She also came to the defense of Dr. Laura Schlessinger, who was roundly condemned when, on her talk show program, she used the "n-word" nearly a dozen times. "Dr. Laura," Palin advised, "don't retreat—reload!" (Guns often crop up in Palin's imagination. She also insists that the Constitution is a Christian document, based on the Bible.[13])

Perhaps Beck's most infamous statement, a bizarre reversal of reverse racism, was his claim that Obama has "a deep-seated hatred for white people, or the white culture." Later he seemed to retract this remark, but then again asserted, "I think the President is a racist." Far more dangerously, our "racist" president is at the center—whether as leader or as pawn—of the conspiracy or the "revolution" that is undoing what the Founding Fathers established. (Beck likes to compare himself to the Founding Fathers—Franklin, Tom Paine, Jefferson, Paul Revere—except that he is all about halting the "revolution" caused by "progressives" like Obama.) "There is a coup going on," Beck has asserted; "There is a stealing of America." This robbery has come about through elections, but no matter. "They have their hands around the neck of this republic," Beck believes, "and they are about to snap it, if we don't wake up." Comedian Jon Stewart was perhaps engaging in understatement when he said about Beck, "Finally, a guy who says what people who aren't thinking are thinking."

<h2 style="text-align:center">MORE TEA PARTY TRIPE</h2>

If Beck likes to compare himself to Tom Paine or Paul Revere, he also likes to compare Obama to Hitler. Limbaugh, too, has told his radio listeners that "Obama's got a health care logo that's right out of Adolf Hitler's playbook. . . . Adolf Hitler, like Barack Obama, also ruled by dictate." It appears the Tea Partiers are big on Hitler lore, a veritable "Tourette's syndrome" version of Nazism, as *The Daily Show* has it. Everything they do not like is tarred with the Hitler brush, including Obama's face in signs at Tea Party rallies. Of course, Limbaugh like Beck believes Obama is a "racist" who is secretly pursuing "reparations" for black slavery, while working to establish a new, white slavery through the entire overthrow of the "free world."

But, according to Beck, "the vampires" who are "sucking the blood out of the republic" are more than just Nazis and our Hitler-like black president. They are communists, socialists, Muslims, and above all "progressives." Beck claims that the Nazis "were using early American progressive tactics. And that is not my opinion, that's historic fact." According to Beck,

> See, when you take a little bit of truth, and then you mix it with untruth, or your theory, that's where you get people to believe. You know? It's like Hitler. Hitler said a little bit of truth, and then he mixed in "and it's the Jews' fault." That's when things got troublesome, and that's exactly what's happening [today].

If one substitutes "and it's the progressives' fault" for the Jews in that statement, it echoes Beck's main theme.

Hitler comparisons have been commonplace in the controversy over health care and insurance reform. The Tea Partiers call health care reform a "government take-over" and "socialized medicine." They refer to it as "Obamacare" and "Obammunism," even though, after Congress dropped the public option, the bill that was passed largely caved in to the insurance companies and "big pharma." Having just been declared constitutional by the Supreme Court and Chief Justice John Roberts, there is an additional traitor in the Tea Party's view—and that is Roberts himself. No matter, Tea Partiers and their Republican tag-alongs demand its immediate repeal, apparently without considering its benefits to themselves and their families. Presidential candidate Mitt Romney said he will repeal it (before he started to waffle about it), even though the Affordable Health Care Act was modeled on the health care legislation Romney supported when he was governor of Massachusetts. Its rabid opponents often falsely claim "Obamacare" will pay for abortions and for the health care of "illegal aliens." And many of them seem still to believe Palin's assertion that it will lead to the establishment of "death panels." That phrase suggested a holocaust of the elderly. Many also seem not to recognize that Medicare and Medicaid, on which they rely, are government programs.

The wholesale rejection of health care reform by the Tea Party goes hand in hand with its rejection of global warming and other scientific hogwash. Of course, Obama is chief among Beck's versions of the present-day *Führer*, but Al Gore is not far behind. On one occasion, Beck told his audience, "Al Gore's not going to be rounding up Jews and exterminating them. It is the same tactic, however . . . you must silence all dissenting voices. That's what Hitler did. That's what Al Gore, the U.N., and everybody on the global warming bandwagon" are doing. Whether or not all Tea Partiers reject global warming as some sort of lie, much less believe that the lie is part of a vast conspiracy aiming to overthrow America and capitalism, it is certain that many of them do. Palin has called the hundreds of studies that have now demonstrated global warming "a bunch of snake oil science" and has tried to get polar bears removed from the endangered species list. Limbaugh has said that "despite the hysterics of a few pseudo-scientists, there is no reason to believe in global warming." And Michele Bachmann, presidential candidate and Tea Party darling from Minnesota, is certain that "global warming is a hoax." Sure of her science, Bachmann has claimed that, although "carbon dioxide is portrayed as harmful . . . there isn't even one study that can be produced that shows that carbon dioxide is a harmful gas." This chemically enlightened opinion supports her stance on energy legislation, about which she is prepared to fight, using, just as Sharron Angle of Nevada advised her followers to do, "Second Amendment remedies":

> I want people in Minnesota armed and dangerous on this issue of the energy tax because we need to fight back. Thomas Jefferson told us "having a revolution every now and then is a good thing," and the people—we the people—are going to have to fight back hard if we're not going to lose our country.

Bachmann in her scientific wisdom has also asserted that there are "hundreds and hundreds of scientists, many of them holding Nobel Prizes, who believe in intelligent design," which is similar to Beck's view that "I don't think we came from monkeys. I think that's ridiculous. I haven't seen a half-monkey/half-person yet." And Christine O'Donnell agrees with Beck: "You know what, evolution is a myth. Why aren't monkeys still evolving into humans?"[14]

Limbaugh's familiarity with science allowed him to speak expertly about the causes and consequences of the 2010 Gulf oil disaster. The main cause of the spill was not negligence or malfeasance by BP, Halliburton, and TransOcean, but more likely environmentalists, including the Sierra Club. He suspected that "environmental wackos" blew up the oil rig to put an end to offshore drilling. What is more, according to Limbaugh, the oil spill would not do any serious damage to the Gulf, because "the ocean will take care of this on its own if it [the oil spill] was left alone and left out there. It's natural. It's as natural as the ocean water is." So a man-made disaster is just Mother Nature doing her harmless thing.

Probably most Tea Partiers agreed when Bachmann called on the media to take a close look "at the views of the people in Congress and find out: are they pro-America or anti-America?" The general opinion seems to be that liberals or "progressives," as Beck calls them, are "anti-America." This is consistent with Bachmann's claim that the outbreak of swine flu during Jimmy Carter's presidency was "an interesting coincidence," insinuating that Carter and the Democrats were to blame for that disease. The outbreak occurred, however, when Gerald Ford was president. But what did the average Tea Partier make of Bachmann's statement apropos of the economy and the government stimulus that "I don't know where they're going to get all this money because we're running out of rich people in this country"? Rich people like herself?

As to Second Amendment "remedies" or "rights," the Tea Party rallies, at least in the early going, attracted a lot of gun-toting dudes, exercising those rights. Tea Party candidate Angle, who lost her bid to unseat Senator Harry Reid, may have failed in part because she championed those rights too vociferously. Resorting to guns, she suggested, might be the only way to deal with the Obama and Reid "tyranny":

> You know, our Founding Fathers, they put that Second Amendment in there for a good reason and that was for the people to protect themselves against a tyrannical government. And in fact Thomas Jefferson said, it's good for a country to have a revolution every 20 years. I hope that's not where we're going, but, you know, if this Congress keeps going the way it is, people are really looking toward those Second Amendment remedies and saying, my goodness, what can we do to turn this country around? I'll tell you, the first thing we need to do is take Harry Reid out.

Angle later said she meant take Harry Reid out of office, not shoot him— in her mind, perhaps just a minor qualification.

Angle probably lost to Reid because of her ignorance and her many extreme views. She wants to scrap the Education Department and eliminate Social Security. She believes that "illegal aliens" are victimizing (white) Americans. Meeting with a group of Latino high schoolers, she told them that some of them looked like Asians to her, although she added, "I don't know." No, she does not. Perhaps some Tea Partiers would not go so far as Angle in claiming that the unemployed are "spoiled"—at least, not unemployed Tea Partiers:

> You can make more money on unemployment than you can going down and getting one of those jobs that is an honest job, but it doesn't pay as much. And so that's what's happened to us is that we have put in so much entitlement into our government that we really have spoiled our citizenry and said you don't want the jobs that are available.

This interesting opinion is on a par with Bachmann's comment about the country running out of rich people.

As to "Second Amendment" remedies and rights, Palin, who likes to go moose hunting, grossly overreached when a map on her web site placed certain congressional districts in gun sight crosshairs, targeting them for defeat in 2010. One of those districts was that of Congresswoman Gabby Giffords, who was shot by Jared Loughner in Tuscon, Arizona, on January 8, 2011. Loughner killed six people and wounded, including Giffords, thirteen. When criticized for her use of gunslinging rhetoric and imagery, Palin retaliated: "Especially within hours of a tragedy unfolding, journalists and pundits should not manufacture a blood libel that serves only to incite the very hatred and violence they purport to condemn. That is reprehensible." A "blood libel"? What was she thinking, if anything, when she used that bizarre phrase?

And what are Tea Party women in general thinking when, like Palin, Bachmann, O'Donnell, and Angle, they express views that are both prolife and antifeminist? Of course, Tea Party men are also prolife and antifeminist. According to Palin, the feminist movement is just "a cackle of rads who want [to] crucify other women." However, she says her attempt to rally "mama grizzlies" is also a call for an alternative, conservative feminism. Limbaugh agrees with her about left-wing feminism, which he says "was established so as to allow unattractive women easier access to the mainstream of society." Rush is, however, fond of women, perhaps overly so (though he is notoriously not fond of Michele Obama, the black dictator's black wife). Is there any limit to Tea Party boneheadism? Lost in the swamps of the Vast Conspiracy.

ALICE AT THE TEA PARTY

Including the 2010 election of many of its sympathizers to the House of Representatives, and then their blocking everything Obama and the Democrats have proposed over the last two years, the Tea Party has provided so much recent political drama that it seems appropriate to end this essay with a drama. Some of the authors in Laura Flanders's anthology *At the Tea Party* refer to *Alice in Wonderland;* the most extended analogy occurs in Richard Kim's "The Mad Tea Party." It has not been easy to get Lewis Carroll's characters to match the vitriol and paranoia expressed by some Tea Party gurus, but the curtain of this essay now rises on

The Tea Party: A Play in One Act (And We Hope That's All)

CAST: *Alice, Mad Hatter, March Hare, Dormouse.*

The Setting: *Wonderland; a rickety table with teapot, tea cups, etc.; the back drop is a tattered version of the American flag, crookedly hung. The Mad Hatter wears a battered Uncle Sam hat.*

ALICE (*entering*). Is this the Tea Party?

MARCH HARE. You're late! You'll soon be unemployed! (*Takes out enormous pocket watch on large gold chain.*) According to my watch, it's 1776! All the rest of it until now has been a waste of time and taxpayers' money!

MAD HATTER (*and the apparently asleep dormouse*). Fiscal responsibility! Fiscal responsibility!

MARCH HARE. Once there were Kings who had crowns, and now there are Presidents who don't have birth certificates.

ALICE. Doesn't he have one from Hawaii?

MARCH HARE. A fake birth certificate from an offshore island doesn't count!

MAD HATTER. Once there were Elephants and Donkeys, and now there are Delephants and Honkies! New species, spawning together with the lobsters—er, lobbyists!—and paid for by our favorite corporations.

DORMOUSE (*wakes up*). A tale I could tell! (*Falls asleep again.*)

MARCH HARE. It's the downfall of everything! It's the triumph of the tittlebats!

MAD HATTER (*flourishes a Glock-19 pistol, which goes off accidentally, startling the Dormouse and Alice*). Off with their heads! Off with their heads! Take back the country!

ALICE (*calming down when she sees the Mad Hatter put the gun on the table and cover it with his Uncle Sam hat*). I want to hear the Dormouse's tale.

DORMOUSE (*drowsily*). Once upon a time—

MAD HATTER. The Founding Fathers! Tell us the tale about the Founding Fathers and the finding of the Constitution!

DORMOUSE. Once upon a time there were twelve million illegal aliens living high off the hog—

MAD HATTER. Seven cheers for free markets!

MARCH HARE. Start at the beginning! 1776 and all that!

DORMOUSE. I wasn't alive at that time.

MAD HATTER. Then I'll tell it! Once upon a time George Washington chopped down a cherry tree and threw a silver dollar over the Delaware—

MARCH HARE. Alas, the very first bail out! The tittlebats were in an uproar—

ALICE. Pray tell, what is a tittlebat?

MAD HATTER. You don't know your Constitution, do you? Or your Declaration of Insolence. A tittlebat, my dear, is what makes this great nation the great nation that its greatness makes.

DORMOUSE. Never heard of a tittlebat? Pour some more tea for her. By the way, what *is* a tittlebat?

MAD HATTER (*reaches under his hat for the pistol*). There will be no questions without representation! The King saw to it that there was no representation for tittlebats, so they poured the tea into the harbor, making treacle—

MARCH HARE. Whose story are you telling? I won't recognize it unless I've seen it on Fox News.

ALICE. Treacle?

MAD HATTER. Treacle for one and all! A treacle well in every tittlebat's back yard! Let's end our dependence on foreign treacle—!

MARCH HARE. Glenn, Rush, Turd Blossom, and all the rest of the gang always sweeten their tea with artificial treacle. And they all say it's the liberals who are the downfall of this great nation of ours. Are you a liberal, my dear? If so, you're unconstitutional!

ALICE. I'm not sure what I am. I suppose I'm an independent.

MARCH HARE. Independents be diddled! Now you're with the Tea Party!

MAD HATTER. Long live Queen Sarah! She shoots the moose, she clubs the flounder, and she watches Russia from her front porch.

DORMOUSE. —The King got mighty angry and ordered up the heads of the Founding Fathers on a platter, because they would not drink their treacle without tea—

MARCH HARE. What does treacle have to do with constitutionally limited government, or tea either for that matter?

MAD HATTER (*to Alice*). Why is a ding-a-ling like a Democrat? Or a raving like a Republican?

ALICE. I'm not very good at riddles.

MAD HATTER. No, you're not.

DORMOUSE. —The King got mighty angry, and so there was an awful hubbub in which many teetotalers lost their heads—

MARCH HARE. Pshaw! They were already lost.

DORMOUSE (*yawns*). Speaking of constitutions, mine is inclined to hibernation (*dozes off*).

MAD HATTER (*puts his hat back on and waves pistol*). Then the tale I will tell, the tale of this glorious nation! They hate us for our freedoms! And now, my dear, are you of voting age? If so, I have some prospective tittlebats for you—

MARCH HARE. Don't leave out the Bible! (*To Alice*): How is the Bible like the Constitution?

ALICE. I said I'm not good at riddles.

MARCH HARE. Because it *is* the Constitution! This nation of ours is a *Christian* nation, or it is no nation at all.

MAD HATTER. There'll be no representation without the sort of representation that represents what we want to have represented! And what we want is representation without taxation! Free government for everyone! Free everyone from the government! Freedom forever!

DORMOUSE (*wakes up shrieking*). Death panels! Everywhere death panels! They're killing the grandmothers and the babies!

MAD HATTER. Hurrah for the Tea Party! There'll be no gays in the military and no socialized medicine! And no marriages!

ALICE. No marriages?

MAD HATTER. I mean no marriages except between taxpayers and tittlebats.

DORMOUSE (*yawning*). As I was saying, once upon a time there was a Big Bang—

MAD HATTER (points pistol at Dormouse without firing). You mean, like this?

MARCH HARE. It sounds to me like that blasted theory of evolution of his. (*Looking at his watch*): But I'm afraid it's too late! We've got to protect what little we have left of our precious freedoms and liberties! Off with their heads!

ALICE. Isn't that what the King of Hearts is supposed to say?

MAD HATTER. He was the Queen of Hearts.

MARCH HARE. My dear, you have no idea what this country is coming to! They say the man is actually a Kenyan.

ALICE. No, I don't suppose I do know what this country is coming to.

DORMOUSE. Pour her some more tea.

MAD HATTER (*takes tea pot, pours it over the Dormouse*). Here you go!

DORMOUSE (*sings*): Twinkle, twinkle little star— And so, good night, my dears! (*Falls asleep.*)

ALICE. He didn't finish his tale.

MARCH HARE. He never does.

MAD HATTER. 'Tis a tale that will come to no good end—

MARCH HARE (*looking at watch*). They never do.

MAD HATTER (*flourishing the gun*). Pow, pow, pow!

DORMOUSE. Here we go again! He's about to exercise his Second Amendment rights!

All of the characters including Alice dive under the table.

(The End)

FOUR

Shooters: Cultural Contexts of
the Virginia Tech Tragedy

A well-regulated militia being necessary to the security of a free state, the right of the people to keep and bear arms shall not be infringed.

—SECOND AMENDMENT TO THE CONSTITUTION

After the massacre at Virginia Tech University on April 16, 2007, if Seung-Hui Cho had not shot himself, would a jury have found him innocent because of insanity? Perhaps. Seung was clearly deranged; he may have been autistic, or paranoid, or schizophrenic; he was a sociopath; he didn't relate well to other people.[1] Maybe the conviction that he was insane helps to explain the forgiveness expressed by many in the Virginia Tech community, which has been extraordinary. His older sister, Sun-Kyung, graduated from Princeton University in economics in 2004 and now works for the U.S. State Department. She too is extraordinary. But sadly, though she should not feel guilt for her brother's deeds, she may always feel guilt for her brother's deeds: "He has made the world weep. We are living a nightmare." She is a successful woman, but has been "humbled by this darkness." So have we all. "We have always been a close, peaceful and loving family. . . . We never could have envisioned that he was capable of so much violence."[2]

From a cultural studies standpoint, the exact diagnosis of Seung's insanity, even if it could be established, is almost irrelevant.[3] On the contrary, what cultural studies can help to explain or at least explore are the *reasons* behind his rampage. In particular, what cultural factors contributed to his state of mind and may have prompted the massacre? I will examine four factors: race, class, gender, and America's "gun culture" or, simply, "gunism."[4] Regarding race, class, and gender, it seems obvious that Seung, a 23-year-old English major at Virginia Tech, felt trapped. According to Sun-Kyung, even in childhood Seung "struggled to fit in." The mass media have relentlessly, and it appears accurately, described him as a "loner" and a "loser." He may have been deranged, but he was also rational enough to recognize that, despite getting a college education, he had little "cultural capital" at his disposal.

In Pierre Bourdieu's terms, the value of cultural capital is determined by both the "social field" and "the habitus" common to those within the field. The field is the set of social positions more or less available for individuals to compete for, occupy, or avoid, mapped by hierarchies of value. What Bourdieu calls "the habitus" is the set of "dispositions" individuals have for valuing one position over another, and for striving to move in one direction or another within the social field. When I say that from a cultural studies perspective what must be explained are the *reasons* Seung acted as he did, I am using a deliberately ambiguous term: *reasons* can refer to the rules governing the social field; *reasons* can also refer to "the habitus," or to Seung's "dispositions" or "motivations" for his behavior—his personal justifications, whether conscious or otherwise, for his rampage. "Reasons" may or may not be rational by normal standards; "reasons" in a general sense refers to the causes of events.

"It follows as a point of method," writes Bourdieu, "that one cannot give a full account of the relationship obtaining at a given moment between the space of positions and the space of dispositions, and, therefore, of the set of *social trajectories* (or constructed biographies)" of individuals (65). In other words, there is no strict determinism whereby the social field and the habitus cause individuals to behave in specific ways; there are instead tendencies in this or that direction—always steerings and strivings, never absolute destinies (except death). A story told from this perspective is a narrative about positions in the social field and about dispositions—individuals' desires to attain or avoid certain situations. Fundamental to all cultures is the desire "to fit in," to be fully integrated in the group or groups that occupy the most valued positions in the social field, including in the American context to be fully American—to be what I will call "all-American."

In all cultures, it is good to be a "winner" rather than a "loser" or a "loner." Regarding race, Seung, as a Korean-American, was a member of a "model minority."[5] And yet that position in the social field may have posed problems for him that came to seem insurmountable. Regarding social class, Seung's immigrant parents, working in dry cleaning establishments, were able to send their daughter to Princeton and their son to Virginia Tech. It is extremely difficult to gain admission to Princeton; Virginia Tech is also a selective institution, so Seung must have done reasonably well in high school and on the SATs to gain admission there. Sun-Kyung majored in economics and is currently well-employed, living the "American dream" of upward class mobility. Majoring in English, Seung must have wondered what he was going to do after graduating? Assuming he worried about it, he cannot have felt himself well-positioned to succeed professionally or economically. And regarding gender, much has been made of his "stalking" women students. Their negative reactions to him contributed to his suicidal disposition. In all three categories—race, class, gender—it appears likely that Seung had come to view himself as badly positioned in the social field, a "loser." In one of the video clips Seung sent to NBC, he says: "you forced me into a corner and gave me only one option. . . . Now you have blood on your hands that will never wash off."[6] "Gunism" offered Seung vengeance against those he blamed for his bad positioning—his not "fitting in," his feeling "cornered"—and an escape route from the American social field that, in his case, he experienced as entrapment and not as "a land of opportunity." Whatever sort of insanity that afflicted him, Seung had his more or less rational dispositions—his "reasons"—to behave as he did.

RACE

Anyone belonging to a racial, ethnic, cultural, or religious minority, whether in the United States or elsewhere, is unlikely to be well positioned in the social field in comparison to the majority population—relatively powerless instead of empowered. This is especially true in a society that, no matter how devoted to freedom, once practiced slavery and also genocide (exterminating Native Americans) and in which racism has always played a major role. Even members of "model minorities" experience racism in the United States, which is one reason that many strive all the more self-consciously to be "model" immigrants and citizens. Unlike his sister, Seung failed to be a "model" anything—except in the context of the pathological realm of "gunism." It is difficult to feel any sympathy for Seung, but everyone can feel sympathy for the sorrow and pain of his family. And for all the grieving students, faculty, and friends of Virginia Tech. And for Koreans and Korean Americans. And for everyone who belongs to a "minority." And perhaps even for the majority population of the United States, white Americans, who, like Seung, are also struggling and failing to be all-Americans.

Seung "was trapped in a generational warp," speculates Evan Thomas in *Newsweek;* he was "neither quite Korean like his parents nor American like his peers" (24). If that is so, then perhaps he felt like the hyphen in "Korean American," neither one thing nor the other, no more than a punctuation mark: one name he gave himself was "Question Mark." As a nation of immigrants, America—so the standard assumption has it—is a "melting pot," the land where everyone wants to assimilate and be free and equal with everyone else. But belonging in an absolute sense—being all-American—is an impossibility. No one is ever fully assimilated; everyone is only striving for that utopian ideal. All-Americanness is a position beyond positionality, the fetishized status of complete and final national identification—always aspired to, never attained.[7] I am obviously not defining "all-American" as the designation of a great college athlete, but as a total, unqualified harmonization of self with nation. It is possible for someone to say, "I am more American than you"; a white American may feel that way toward a Korean American or an African American. But it is not possible for anyone to say, "I am the ultimate all-American."

National and racial belonging—positioning oneself in those terms in a way that is at least self-satisfying, if never ideally so—is often a difficult process. It is obviously more difficult for immigrants and members of minorities, both because of racism and because of economic factors. However, Professor Richard Kim, who teaches American Studies at Skidmore College, points out that race seems not to have been a major motivating factor—or disposition—behind Seung's rampage. Yet, in high school, Seung was bullied and racially taunted. One former classmate reported that "Seung was mocked . . . for reciting an assignment in an oddly guttural accent. 'As soon as he started reading, the whole class started laughing and pointing and saying, "Go back to China."'"[8] The students did not even get the Korean part of Seung's hyphenated national and ethnic identity correct.

Seung's classmates claim he "got picked on every day at school." He was "an easy target and everyone aimed at him. And, of course, the more he withdrew, the more he was picked on." He was "the kid everyone bullied." After the massacre, police investigated possible connections between "the bullying and those he killed." As still another student put it, "There were people who were mean to him. They would push him down and laugh at him. He didn't speak English well. They made fun of him." Seung started to keep a "hit list of people who bullied him." Everybody knew about the list but considered it, like Seung himself, "a joke."[9] According to sociologist Katherine Newman, "Bullying at school is probably the most commonly accepted explanation for school shootings, and for good reason."[10] Seung repressed his anger until he was a senior at Virginia Tech, about to graduate; but bullying, with racist overtones, was part of the story.

How much racial harassment did Seung's family encounter after emigrating from South Korea to the United States when he was eight years old? How much of the bullying he endured in elementary, middle, and high school was due to racism instead of other factors? We will never know. At least at Virginia Tech, Seung encountered a racially, nationally, and culturally diverse student body, a racially tolerant faculty and administration, and a few individual students who tried to befriend him. He also found a couple of caring and concerned professors, Nikki Giovanni and Lucinda Roy, who tried to get him the psychological help he clearly needed. The university did not follow through with appeals from professors or students to do something about Seung, including insisting that he seek further counseling, in part because of the view that doing so would interfere with his rights as an individual—and an adult individual, at that. Whether university officials could have done more to prevent the massacre is a question that no investigation is likely to answer in any definitive manner.

Korean American commentators on the Virginia Tech tragedy have worried about possible racist repercussions: would the fact that Seung came from South Korea cause a reaction against all Koreans and Korean Americans? Professor Edward Park, who teaches at Loyola Marymount University, writes that, on hearing the first news from Virginia Tech, members of various racial minorities hoped that the shooter would not turn out to be African American or Latino or . . . When they learned that the shooter was Asian, then people of Asian origin hoped that he would not turn out to be Vietnamese or Chinese or Filipino or . . . And when Park and others learned that Seung was Korean, that fact became "all-consuming" as "fears of a backlash gripped the Korean-American community."[11] But what happened? It may be, as *Newsweek* reported, that talk-show radio and Internet chat rooms "'throbbed with hate.'"[12] Seung's parents reportedly were placed under police protection. A major backlash, however, did not materialize. Why not?[13]

One factor is surely that mass murders and serial killings, both real and fictional, are staples of contemporary American mass culture. Because homicides are committed by all sorts and conditions of people on a daily basis, there is the general feeling that the Virginia Tech shooter could have been anybody at all. The white boys who committed the Columbine slayings came from middle-class, fairly affluent families. Jared Loughner, the Tuscon shooter, and James Holmes, the Aurora shooter, were also white and middle class. Sadly, Seung's committing mass murder seems, in the words of African American activist H. Rap Brown, "as American as cherry pie." As much as anything else he might have done, Seung's shooting rampage made him seem perversely very American, if not all-American. Richard Kim notes that "the media's relentless coverage has been largely free of the worst racial and ethnic stereotypes." Yet "race still colors perceptions of events." But, he adds, Seung's victims were racially various and included Asian students. If Seung had shot only white students, then there might have been a stronger anti-Korean reaction. In any event, Kim says, Seung's statements express "class rage" more clearly than "racial antipathy."

CLASS

In South Korea, Seung's parents lived in a low-rent basement apartment, while running a used-book store that, according to one report, "just eked out a profit."[14] The father, Sung-Tae Cho, "came from a poor rural area." Seung was born in 1984, two years after Sun-Kyung, and came to America with his parents in 1992. Other members of the family had already immigrated to the United States. After a "difficult" time in Detroit, they moved to the Washington, D.C., area, at the encouragement of the father's younger brother.[15] Although one news source says that they were able to buy a "row house" in Centerville, Virginia, for $400,000,[16] another account asserts that they paid $145,000 for it in "one of scores of cookie-cutter developments in the area. They were so proud of their new home that they sent photos to loved ones in South Korea."[17]

Seung's parents worked for different dry-cleaning businesses. The father "pressed pants six days a week at a dry cleaner in Manassas, VA, west of Washington. Seung's mother worked at another Korean-run dry-cleaning business in nearby Haymarket." She, too, worked six days a week. The owner of the second business declared, "I knew life was hard for her. Her health was not good, and her husband suffered from a back problem." Yet only once did she ever ask for time off, and that "was to attend her daughter's graduation from Princeton and to take her son to Virginia Tech."[18] After 2004, both parents retired for health reasons.

Whether or not Seung appreciated his parents' struggle to make a better life for him and his sister, theirs is a typical immigrant story. Even though he has often been described as incommunicative and almost speechless, a police search revealed that he "phoned his family nearly every Sunday night."[19] Sun-Kyung did so well in school and on exams that she was able to go to Princeton; she was also admitted to Harvard but turned it down because Princeton offered her a better scholarship. Seung also did well enough in school to gain admission to Virginia Tech and almost to graduate (he was a senior).[20] He is said to have been a good student and particularly good in math.

Seung began at Virginia Tech majoring in business information technology (BIT). According to *The Washington Post*, "BIT is one of Virginia Tech's most challenging undergraduate disciplines—and No. 6 on the university's list of majors with the highest median starting salary after graduation."[21] But somewhere along the line, the seemingly inarticulate young man switched majors to English and took several creative-writing courses, rather than pursuing more career-oriented objectives. This is not to say that English majors in American universities cannot go on to enjoy successful careers; but they often do so by double-majoring in journalism or education or by pursuing graduate degrees in law, business, or some other field. Without hearing from them, it is impossible to know what Seung's parents thought of his change in majors—if he told them about it.

Sun-Kyung was able to move from her parents' position on the American social-class ladder—the working class—into the middle class. At Princeton, she was a quiet but also sociable, active, hard-working student, respected for being "deeply spiritual." She "spent much of her spare time at prayer meetings and Friday night Bible studies with the Princeton Evangelical Fellowship."[22] Her interest in global economics led her to travel to Thailand as an intern, where she examined sweatshop conditions in textile factories near the Thai-Myanmar border. She wrote in the *Princeton Weekly Bulletin* that those "were the most amazing three months of my life."[23]

The materials Seung sent to NBC constitute what Thomas calls a "rancid manifesto" against "Christian Criminals" who have "raped and sodomized, humiliated and crucified him and others he describes as the 'Weak and Defenseless.'" I will consider the sexual content of this "rancid manifesto" in the next section. Thomas continues:

> He seems to blame the wealthy for his suffering. "You had everything you wanted," he taunts. "Your Mercedes wasn't enough, you brats? Your golden necklaces weren't enough, you snobs? Your trust fund wasn't enough? Your vodka and cognac weren't enough?"[24]

To assess class resentment as a factor in Seung's reasons for the massacre, it might help to know more about the economic difficulties his parents encountered in sending him to Virginia Tech. Also, though a fine university, that school is not Princeton, not Ivy League. Not all Virginia Tech students—"Hokies"—drive around in Mercedes (neither do all Princeton students). Demographically, Hokies are similar to students at other state universities: some from very wealthy backgrounds, many more from the middle class, some from the working class. Were there social class factors, perhaps including resentment, involved in Seung's relationship with his sister, the successful economics major from Princeton? Did Seung's parents stress and perhaps overstress the economic sacrifice they were making for him? Without more evidence, it is impossible to answer these questions, though they indicate possibilities.

In the two extant plays that Seung wrote for a creative-writing class, apart from their evident anger, foul language, and sexual content, the most surprising passage occurs in "Richard McBeef." The thirteen-year-old John accuses his new stepfather (the title character) of various crimes, including trying to molest him and murdering his real dad. Calling McBeef both "a piece of shit" and "DAD" (ironically, because McBeef insists that John use that name for him), John adds to his enraged accusations:

> Guess what, Dick? . . . You wanna know why I don't like you? Because you can't provide for my mom. You barely make the minimum wage, man. . . . You piece of shit! You were a janitor one time. You're a onetime truck driver. You taught pre-school kids for two months. And now you're what you call a chef, what the rest of the world calls hamburger flipper.[25]

For three weeks also, the "fat and lazy" Richard McBeef failed as a pro football player. It is tempting to interpret "DAD" and John's murderous rage at his stepfather as expressing how Seung felt about his father, but that may be both unfair and unwarranted. Nevertheless, John expresses total contempt for "barely mak[ing] the minimum wage" and for working-class jobs. It seems likely that Seung felt contempt or shame toward his father's and mother's jobs. Perhaps Seung was also expressing depression and anger about the sort of job he might be able to find after he graduated from Virginia Tech as an English major (on the basis of the two plays, a poor English major at that) with no specific occupational or professional credentials.

Even in the supposedly free-and-equal United States, schools are not so much "melting pots" as they are, for many students, boiling points of various sorts of anger and resentment, often involving inequalities of race, class, and sexuality. In a study examining why even "winners" in school settings express frustration and anger, Ellen Brantlinger notes that many school shootings like the one at Columbine High School in 1999 have occurred in white, affluent, suburban locations. Schools operate by grading and tracking, sorting children into successful and unsuccessful categories, which eventually turn into occupational, income, and social-class positions. Besides outright bullying, kids constantly grade and sort each other, creating pecking orders of winners and losers. By constructing and reinforcing social inequalities, all schools—even universities such as Princeton and Virginia Tech—"inflict symbolic violence . . . a potent source of anger and acting out. Rooted in frustration and depression, violence reveals the deeply emotional dimensions of classroom life. . . . The institutional reaction, however, is to identify 'misbehaviors' as personal pathology and label the culprits 'emotionally disturbed.'"[26]

Whatever the exact relationship between social-class resentment and the Virginia Tech massacre, Seung had the wherewithal to buy his weapons and ammunition: "At Roanoke Firearms, he used a credit card to purchase a Glock 19 and a box of 50 cartridges—for $571."[27] Were Seung's parents aware of how he used that credit card? It is, at any rate, possible that "class rage" in Seung's statements stands in for and/or helps bolster other aspects of his motivations, and the most likely candidate is gender relations or issues of sexuality.

GENDER

"Richard McBeef" and "Mr. Brownstone" deal with "racially undefined characters," as Kim puts it; the focus of both is on "sexual trauma rather than racial alienation." They express homophobia, among other revulsions. In the NBC materials, Seung claims to have been "raped and sodomized" by "Christian Criminals," strong metaphors for his sense of victimization. Whether Seung was ever sexually abused or engaged in any homosexual activity will probably never be known. His other fantasies seem both adolescent and straightforwardly heterosexual. For example, according to Evan Thomas in his *Newsweek* article, "He imagined a supermodel girlfriend named Jelly, and as her fantasy lover called himself Spanky" (23).

On CNN, reporter Jason Carroll said to news anchor Wolf Blitzer, "I have to tell you some of the material [in Seung's plays] is so disturbing we simply cannot read it to you. Some of the language . . . is so graphic that we are unable to even show you some of the material." Partially contradicting this self-censorship, Carroll proceeded to describe the two plays that "contain graphic passages about plans to kill a main character." In "Richard McBeef," "the young character accuses his stepfather of molesting him, saying, 'Get your hands off me, you sicko. Damn you.' The mother in the play brandishes a chainsaw. The young man tries choking his stepfather with a cereal bar" (CNN). Instead, Richard McBeef kills the young man.

In "Mr. Brownstone," a high-school math teacher also engages in sexually molesting as well as robbing his students. The three teenage characters agree that Mr. Brownstone "ass-rapes us all. Isn't that what high school teachers do?" Jason Carroll did not use the term "ass-rape" on CNN. Nor did he cite the Guns N' Roses song that Seung quotes for about a page and a half in his short play:

> But that old man he's a real muthafucker
> Gonna kick him on down the line.

Despite the murderous anger of the kids, like Richard McBeef, Mr. Brownstone comes out on top. After one of the boys wins $5,000,000 at a casino, Brownstone has the security guards kick the other teenagers out of the place and collects the money for himself.

Seung was accused of intimidating women at Virginia Tech "by sneaking photographs of them (he aimed his cell phone camera at women from underneath his desk, reportedly)" (Thomas, "Making of a Massacre," 26). He also "stalked" at least two women:

> First, the otherwise stone-silent Cho began chatting up one woman by instant message. Then he went to pay her a visit. In a rare, revealing conversation with a roommate . . . Cho explained that the reason he went to see the girl was "to look in her eyes to see how cool she was." "When he looked in her eyes," the roommate recounted . . . "he saw promiscuity."[28]

Seung told the woman his name was "Question Mark." According to the roommate, that "really freaked the girl out"; she notified the police, though without pressing charges. In a second episode, Seung pestered another woman, and she, too, called the police, who apparently viewed Seung's behavior as "mild" and as not constituting "stalking."[29] For the police to intervene, "stalking" has to be more overtly threatening. Seung's interest in both young women was perhaps innocently romantic, yet his response—"promiscuity"—suggests a misogynistic revulsion that matches the homophobia he expressed in the plays and the NBC materials. Perhaps fearing—and courting—rejection, he rejected those he accused of engaging in abhorrent sexual behaviors.

After the second incident, Seung told one of his roommates that "he might as well kill himself," which prompted a third call to the police. Seung was then sent to the Carillion St. Albans Behavioral Health Center as "'an imminent danger to self or others as a result of mental illness' —the boilerplate language a judge uses for temporary involuntary commitment."[30] According to the psychologist's report from the center, Seung seemed depressed but otherwise "normal" and, therefore, not "an imminent danger" to anyone. After he obtained legal assistance, Seung was quickly released. The judge continued to believe that he was "an imminent danger" at least to himself, but because there were "alternatives to involuntary hospitalization," he ordered Seung to receive outpatient therapy. There is no record of Seung's having obeyed that order.[31] If Seung had reported this brief confinement for mental illness on the gun-permit form, he would not have been able to purchase weapons or ammunition in Virginia retail outlets.

Seung's behavior toward women at Virginia Tech "freaked them out" rather than causing them to find him attractive and interesting. Seung's feeling suicidal after the second "stalking" episode suggests that his failure to make himself appealing may have been the most important of the three cultural factors I have reviewed here. Shooting is one (perverse) way to assert masculinity. In her important study of massacres in public schools, Newman writes, "In the months and weeks leading up to rampages, most shooters feel trapped and in need of a 'manly' exit."[32] But besides issues involving sexuality and sexual identity, racial and social-class factors also contributed to Seung's alienation and anger. If all desirable positions in the social field seem closed to a young man, what options are left? In Seung's case, the answer was the very American one of buying guns and using them to commit mass murder and suicide.

GUNISM

The Virginia Tech massacre was horrific but hardly unique. School and campus shootings have occurred in many countries. However, starting with the August 1, 1966, sniping by Charles Whitman from the University of Texas clock tower, in which he killed thirteen and wounded thirty-one, America has led the way, accounting for most of the massacres.[33] In *The New Yorker*, Adam Gopnik writes that, in the four decades between Whitman's and Seung's massacres, "not enough was done . . . to make weapons of mass killing harder to obtain" in the United States. That is an understatement. Gopnik proceeds:

> In fact, while campus killings continued—Columbine being the most notorious, the shooting in the one-room Amish schoolhouse the most recent—weapons have got more lethal, and, in states like Virginia, where the N.R.A. [National Rifle Association] is powerful, no harder to buy.[34]

Even the peaceful campus where I taught for thirty-six years, Indiana University, has had its share of violence. During my four-year term as chair of the English Department (1990–94), I had to deal with the aftermath of a double homicide and suicide. On America's Independence Day, July 4, 1999, under the influence of white supremacist Matthew Hale, Benjamin Smith went on a shooting rampage in Illinois and Indiana, killing eleven people. One of his victims was Northwestern University basketball coach Ricky Birdsong, an African American; another was Indiana University graduate student Won-Joon Yoon, shot down outside the Korean Methodist Church next to campus. In these and many other tragic episodes, guns have played a leading role: firepower is star power.

The gun is the ultimate fetish in American mass culture.[35] At least temporarily, it gives the illusion of solving all problems by negating the boundaries of the social field—as the expression has it, a gun can "level the playing field." If a man (or sometimes woman) feels powerless, with phallic similitude the gun fills the void by adding to the void in what many have come to see as "an ugly, uncaring society," in the words of Brooks Brown, with "a violent culture in and of itself."[36] In 1999, Brown was at first suspected of being one of the Columbine High School shooters. Brown's *No Easy Answers*, written with Rob Merritt, provides an insightful analysis, according to its subtitle, of "the truth behind death at Columbine."

In an issue of *The Chronicle of Higher Education* devoted to the Virginia Tech massacre, Harvard psychiatrist Robert J. Lifton notes,

> a gun is not just a lethal device but a psychological actor in this terrible drama. Guns and ammunition were at the heart of Seung-Hui Cho's elaborate orchestration of the event and of his Rambo-like self-presentation to the world. When you look at those pictures [Seung's videos], you understand how a gun can merge so fully with a person that a man who makes regular use of it could (in the historical West and in Hollywood) become known as a "gun." ("An Ideology of 'Gunism,'" B11)

The issue of *Newsweek* containing Evan Thomas's report also contains "The Story of a Gun" by Jerry Adler, all about Seung's main "lethal weapon," his 9mm Glock 19 automatic pistol. The story features an in-your-face, full-page photograph of the gun listing its exact dimensions and giving its "brief history." The gun itself, it seems, deserves almost as much journalistic attention as does Seung.

The Glock 19 has its own "story" to tell, which—in contrast to Seung's—is a highly successful one.[37] Much of Adler's report reads like advertising copy: "It's sleek, light and frighteningly lethal. . . . It's a lethal gun, but then all guns are" (37). However, it is more lethal than most. The story concerns "how the 9mm became the weapon of choice for cops and criminals, civilians and soldiers. . . ." The "9" has what Seung, with his glasses, odd speech, and acne lacked: sex appeal. When it appeared on the scene, writes Adler, the "9" "had glamour; cinematographers [just like Adler and the editors of *Newsweek*] fell in love with the automatic's sleek, sinister profile, in contrast to the almost feminine bulge of the revolver." Noting that it is "an icon of rap culture," Adler quotes Ice Cube: "'Cock my nine, and separate yo' head from yo' spine.'" In prose that sprays statistics around like so many bullets, he adds, "Of the 188 shots fired in the Columbine High School massacre, which until Virginia Tech set the standard for depraved mass schoolroom slaughter, 55 came from Dylan Klebold's Tec-9." What does "set the standard" mean in that sentence? More advertising copy? Seung was well aware of the Columbine High shootings, modeling his behavior in part on that of Klebold and his fellow shooter, Eric Harris. In one of the video clips he sent to NBC, Seung speaks of "martyrs like Eric and Dylan."[38]

As do most accounts about the Virginia Tech massacre, Adler's "Story of a Gun" cites movies featuring the "glamour" of guns. Adler mentions *Boyz n the Hood* and *New Jack City*. He is not suggesting that Seung saw these specific films and was copycatting them; it's just that the "9" plays a starring role in them. But other authors name films, television shows, and video games that *may* have influenced Seung—and the titles are legion. To what extent Seung's mental state was affected by violence in the mass media will never be known, of course. He did not come to the United States until he was eight; perhaps in South Korea he was insulated from violence on TV and in the movies. However, in 1993, the American Psychological Association concluded, "There is absolutely no doubt that higher levels of viewing violence on television are correlated with increased acceptance of aggressive attitudes and increased aggressive behavior. . . . Children's exposure to violence in the mass media, particularly at young ages, can have harmful lifelong consequences."[39]

In the London *Sunday Times,* Sarah Baxter notes that the videos Seung sent to NBC "showed him posing like the star of a Quentin Tarantino film or Lara Croft," the gun-toting "tomb raider" played by Angelina Jolie. Baxter also mentions the films *Taxi Driver* and *Rambo*. The title of her article is "American Psycho," referencing both Alfred Hitchcock's famous slasher film *Psycho* and the 1991 novel about serial killing by Bret Easton Ellis, *American Psycho*. Other authors name *Natural-Born Killers* (which has apparently set the record for inspiring copy-cat crimes), *Old Boy, Scream, High Plains Drifter, Pulp Fiction, Texas Chainsaw Massacre, Lethal Weapon*, and on and on. As well, Seung seems to be striking the pose of a terrorist—another specialist in mass murder with star power in the mass media. By sending his videos to NBC, Seung courted and won media attention in America and around the world.[40] Seung's statements, play scripts, and videos invite us to see his life and death precisely in relation to the mass media's fascination with terror and mass murder—"the pathological public sphere" of America's "wound culture."[41] It is a pathology evident, writes Mark Seltzer, in "that peculiar mixture of moral and feral intentions that seems to animate the media fascination with serial murder" (*Serial Killers*, 39).[42] Such a "peculiar mixture"—shocked horror, sadomasochistic attraction—was evident in all the early television reports on the Virginia Tech massacre.

On April 17, 2007, CNN's *Situation Room* offered the "portrait of a mass killer," with various correspondents piecing the "details" together like clues in a police investigation. As nearly as possible, Wolf Blitzer promised, the show would take viewers inside the mind of "Cho Seung-Hui"; indeed, "in the footsteps of a killer, we're going to walk you across the sprawling university and retrace the nightmare that unfolded right here." You the viewer might imagine yourself in the role of detective or reporter; you could also imagine yourself as Seung by following in his "footsteps"—the "footsteps of the killer." As Sisela Bok notes in *Mayhem* (37), this procedure is improved upon in countless superviolent video games such as *Doom, Mortal Kombat,* and *Grand Theft Auto:* you do not just follow in "the footsteps of the killer," you are the killer. The player is positioned as the "first-person shooter," and winning consists of slaughtering every enemy who comes into view.

Two weeks before Seung's killing spree, David Denby reviewed the movie *Shooter* for *The New Yorker*. Starring Mark Wahlberg and directed by Antoine Fuqua, *Shooter* depicts a hired gun, Bob Lee Swagger, who is betrayed by the undercover agents who hire him. The agents in turn are obeying the orders of an "oil-mad" senator from Montana resembling Vice President Dick Cheney (played by Ned Beatty). After Swagger discovers the betrayal, "he takes vengeance on the swine who tried to do him in" by mowing them down.

> For two hours, chase follows shoot-out as Swagger fires at men who, like movie targets from time immemorial, obligingly refused to take cover. Swagger never misses—he could hunt mosquitoes for a living—and the extras, both live and digital, do their job; they fall down.[43]

Denby notes that the film is tiresomely repetitious—it is a "standard industrial product"—and is not as effective as Fuqua's 2001 "fiery and memorable" action film *Training Day*. Denby approves, however, of *Shooter*'s "liberal ideological sentiments"—against "oil interests," against Abu Ghraib, against Dick Cheney. Yet, he says, *Shooter* "places these sentiments within a matrix of gun culture and lonely-man-of-honor myths."

Seung evidently saw himself as a lonely "man-of-honor," standing up for the "weak" and "defenseless" as did "Jesus Christ."[44] At any rate, it is highly ironic that Denby goes on to mention how easy it is for Swagger to acquire "an astounding amount of what can only be called ordnance at a Virginia shopping mall" (88–89). Seung also found it easy to purchase his weapons and ammo in Virginia, "a state with a strong gun-loving population."[45] Denby apparently approves—with qualifications—of a film in which, while "the government may be rotten . . . American honor is saved by the lone killer" (88). He notes that *Shooter* is one of countless American novels and films in which, betrayed by the powers-that-be, the heroes become heroic by shooting virtually everyone who gets in their way. The massacre at Virginia Tech followed this plot, except that nobody believes Seung was justified or that his victims were traitorous "swine."

American culture is rife with examples of valorizing serial killers, mass murderers, and their weapons: there are entire genres that do so, including video games, gangster films, police shows, spy movies, and horror films. At least, in the horror films, the killers are villains, not good guys. In the other genres, the good-guy killers are busily exterminating the bad guys who are frequently also mass murderers. The common denominator is mass murder for as long as the novel or film or video game lasts. I am not claiming that Seung was merely acting out films like *Shooter*, though his own playwriting and the videos that he sent to NBC suggest that possibility. The play scripts are jejune, to say the least; but "Richard McBeef" belongs in the same category of tales of homicidal mayhem to which *Shooter* belongs. And so, in a sense, do most of the news reports on the Virginia Tech tragedy, including CNN's April 17 broadcast of *The Situation Room* and the April 30 issue of *Newsweek*, both representatives of mainstream journalistic accounts.

What country besides the United States can boast of having a vice president who has, while in office, accidentally shot a friend in the face? It was, of course, an accident, but a very American one. The United States has a high incidence of hunting accidents, as well as the highest homicide rate among so-called developed, industrialized nations.[46] Bill O'Reilly may rant on Fox News about the un-Americanness of those who blame America's gun culture for school shootings like the one at Virginia Tech, but the United States is leading in that fatal statistic as well—over twenty major school shootings between 1988 and today, not counting shootings at colleges and universities. For every one hundred American citizens, there are ninety firearms in their possession. Ranking second in that statistic is Yemen, with sixty-one weapons per one hundred Yemenis. It seems Iraqis possess even fewer weapons per capita than the Yemenis.[47]

I am not aware of any other country whose constitution or legal system guarantees the right for all citizens to bear arms. And no other country has a lobby so influential on politicians of all persuasions as the NRA, which has rendered effective gun control in the United States virtually impossible. Gun ownership and gunfire are tragically entangled with American notions of individualism and freedom. Individualism entails explaining events in terms of what individuals do, rather than in collective, cultural, or sociological terms. "If history is any guide," writes Kristin Goss in *The Chronicle of Higher Education*, "the nation is about to embark on a collective search for a narrative to explain what happened at Virginia Tech. And if history is any guide, those narratives will revolve around the private story of the killer, Seung-Hui Cho; his mental-health status; his parents; and his upbringing." Goss comments that "the privatization of our very public problem of gun violence," which "was apparent after the Columbine massacre in 1999," increases the difficulty of finding public policy solutions.

Apparently, many otherwise rational Americans believe, with Newt Gingrich, that the solution to school violence is to arm all students—

those old enough to bear arms, anyway. On the campuses of Utah's universities, students now have the right to carry concealed weapons into classrooms, and some seem to feel safer because of that misguided policy. Psychologist James Gabarino points to the lunacy of the idea that guns can save us from guns. He notes the shock expressed by people from other societies when they learn that a therapist actually recommended that Kip Kinkel's father "buy him a gun so they could have something to do together."[48] Kinkel proceeded to kill his parents, two students, and wound twenty-two others in his high school in Springfield, Oregon, in 1998. Guns do not protect people; they destroy people.

Despite or rather partly because of holding the record for exporting guns to other countries, the United States is helping make the world a more dangerous place than it was before 9/11. Most of the weapons used in the drug wars in Mexico come from the United States. Contrary to the Bush administration's "preemptive war" policy, guns, war, and military occupation cannot bring about peace and democracy in Iraq or anywhere else. Playing to the media, Donald Rumsfeld's "shock-and-awe" bombardment in Iraq did not end "the war on terror"; it fomented it. For millions around the world, at the time of the Virginia Tech massacre, the world's leading terrorist was not Osama bin Laden, but George Bush, with Rumsfeld and Dick Cheney not far behind.

Just as "Richard McBeef" and "Mr. Brownstone" are apparently white, all-American names, so the story of Seung's life and death is also thoroughly and familiarly American. He may have been Korean American, but he takes his place in the Gothic pantheon of American psychos, mass murderers, and serial killers who achieve celebrity. In their journals, the Columbine killers Eric Harris and Dylan Klebold wrote that they hoped to reach a high enough death toll to gain "movie status."[49] Though it was probably not the movie of Harris and Klebold's nightmares, they do figure importantly in Michael Moore's Oscar award-winning 2002 documentary *Bowling for Columbine*. The events of 9/11 achieved worldwide media attention for Osama bin Laden and Al-Qaeda; Rumsfeld's shock-and-awe campaign did the same for himself, George Bush, Dick Cheney, and their "war on terror."

Although there have been mass homicides in South Korea as in every other major country in the world today, the good news is that they are rare. Apart from geography, population, and other factors, a major difference between South Korea and the United States is that the private ownership of assault weapons is outlawed in one, permitted in the other. The general problem for the United States is how to get the guns out of the hands of crazed young men like Seung-Hui Cho, Kinkel, Harris, and Klebold and also out of the hands of gangsters, terrorists, and politicians.

In conclusion, race, class, and gender were all factors, or cultural and social *reasons,* that help explain the Virginia Tech massacre. Seung-hui Cho's inability to find hopeful, upwardly aspiring positions for himself in the American social field may have exacerbated some irrational, perhaps insane streak in his individual makeup. But racism, classism, and sexism, coupled with American gunism, provide a cultural-studies explanation of a tragedy that has had its unfortunate antecedents and that will, no doubt, have many successors. The ways to limit the number of future mass killings seem obvious, if difficult to achieve: combating racism and the different varieties of sexism (including homophobia); reducing social-class inequalities; and ending America's insane love affair with guns.

FIVE

What Is the Matter with Mexico?

Imprisoned country. . . . It's the children who play with skeletons.

—JUAN BAÑUELOS

Every morning around two hundred Mexican and Central American immigrants gather outside a Home Depot in Washington, D.C., waiting for a house painter or carpenter or plumber to hire them for a few hours or, if they are lucky, for a few days. Many—perhaps most—are "undocumented aliens" or "illegals." This is a scene repeated in every major city in the United States. If the average gringo does not jump to the conclusion that something is the matter with these "illegals" (besides their being "illegal"), then he or she probably wonders, "What's wrong with Mexico?"

Why can't the Mexican economy provide enough jobs to prevent thousands of Mexicans from spilling over the border in search of work, especially when the United States is also struggling with high unemployment? Securing the border and deporting the "illegals" will not help, in part because many U.S. businesses are eager to hire undocumented workers. The jobs they take are supposedly ones that U.S. citizens will not take. Or is it the case that some businesses prefer to hire undocumented workers because they can pay them less and exploit them more easily than they can U.S. citizens?

Then there are the headlines about the violence of the drug cartels in Ciudad Juàrez and elsewhere in Mexico. Again, the question arises, what is the matter with Mexico? But can Mexico end the narcotics epidemic in the United States? And most of the guns used by the Mexican drug gangs come from north of the border. Besides the gun trade, to what extent are other legal U.S. businesses dependent on illegal narcotics trafficking? To ask what is wrong with Mexico means asking as well what is wrong with the United States.

BARBAROUS MEXICO

One person who tried to find out what was the matter with Mexico was John Kenneth Turner. Early in 1908, as a reporter for the *Los Angeles Express,* Turner interviewed a group of Mexican prisoners arrested for "planning to invade a friendly nation—Mexico—with an armed force from American soil." Turner wanted to know why "four educated, intelligent Mexicans, college men, all of them," were attempting to overthrow the government of President Porfirio Díaz, whom many Americans understood to be a duly elected head of state.[1] Díaz, however, had managed to get himself fraudulently elected for six terms, which a miniscule number of U.S. observers criticized as undemocratic. Díaz had many supporters—cronies, in effect—among American businessmen and government officials, so the mainstream press ignored his corrupt practices.

What the prisoners told Turner piqued his curiosity about "political Mexico." Above all, their claim that slavery was still practiced south of the border led him to travel several times to Yucatan and other parts of Mexico to investigate. In 1910, the year the great Mexican Revolution broke out, Turner collected his various reports and published them as a muckraking bestseller, *Barbarous Mexico.* Out of prison by 1911, the four Mexicans Turner had interviewed invaded their country with a small band of rebels. Turner secretly supplied the group, led by Flores Magón, with fifty rifles and ammunition. The rebels captured Mexicali early in 1911. Although Turner did not engage in the fighting, the Mexican government asked U.S. authorities to arrest him. That did not happen, however, and Turner continued reporting on the revolution.

In *Barbarous Mexico,* Turner writes, "Mexico is a people starved, a nation prostrate. What is the reason? Who is to blame?" (119). Turner's immediate answer was "the 'system' of General Porfirio Díaz" (120), whom he exposed as a ruthless dictator. But a full answer includes the entire history of Mexico, from colonial times to the present. And it includes U.S. imperialism and the financial interests of many wealthy Americans and American corporations.

On his first trip to Mexico in 1908, Turner pretended to be a rich gringo, looking to invest in a henequen plantation in Yucatan. The Mexican prisoners had told him that slavery provided the labor for henequen production. He had also learned that slavery was one explanation for the rapid disappearance of the Yaqui Indians from Sonora, in northwestern Mexico. The Yaquis were being subjected to a deliberate campaign of extermination, ordered by Díaz—genocide, as it would today be called. The Yaquis had resisted conquest since the earliest colonial times. They are the first group of indigenous rebels John Gibler mentions in *Unconquered Mexico:* they "fiercely repelled Spanish land invasions for over 100 years" (28) in the early stages of conquest and colonization. Gibler mentions the Yaquis later, when he writes that they resisted "the Spanish nonstop, fought the newly independent Mexican state right up to the Revolution [of 1910], and have resisted the economic imperialism of the post-revolutionary state up to the present" (293). The Mexican army during Díaz's dictatorship killed many Yaquis, while many others died in slave gangs on their way to Yucatan. Many also escaped into the United States. A small population of Yaquis—perhaps thirty thousand—still lives in Sonora, so they were not completely liquidated by the Mexican state. "The extermination of the Yaquis began in war," Turner reported; "its finish is being accomplished in deportation and slavery" (*Barbarous Mexico,* 37). The person in charge of rounding them up and either killing or capturing them, Col. Francisco Cruz, was getting rich through "the appropriation of [Yaqui] property" and through "the sale of their bodies" into slavery (ibid., 47).

In Yucatan, Turner learned that the henequen plantations were owned by fifty "henequen kings," some of them gringos. Even though Mexico had officially outlawed slavery in 1829, four years before the British abolished it, its practice continued under other names, including "enforced service for debt" (*Barbarous Mexico,* 16). Of course the eight thousand or so Yaqui slaves on the plantations were not in debt to the henequen kings; neither were most of the one hundred thousand Mayas engaged in henequen production (ibid., 15). They were slaves, plain and simple:

> In Yucatan I soon learned what became of the Yaqui exiles. They are sent
> to the henequen plantations as slaves, slaves on almost exactly the same
> basis as are the 100,000 Mayas whom I found on the plantations. They are
> held as chattels, they are bought and sold, they receive no wages, but are
> fed on beans, tortillas and putrid fish. They are beaten, sometimes beaten
> to death.[2]

The "dormitories" in which the slaves were kept were no better than
crude, closely guarded jails. Escape was impossible because everyone who
was not a slave was on the lookout to cash in on the rewards for capturing
escapees. Both the army and the *rurales,* or mounted police who roamed
the countryside to put down unrest, enforced the practice of slavery by
guarding slave caravans and capturing escapees.

If the condition of the slaves in Yucatan was terrible, it was even
worse, Turner discovered, for the slaves in the Valle Nacional, which he
dubbed "the Valley of Death" (*Barbarous Mexico,* 83). Most of the slaves
on the tobacco plantations there were not indigenous rebels or "Indians," according to Turner, but "Mexicans"—that is, mestizos (ibid., 68).
Many of these had been lured into servitude or simply kidnapped by
engachadores or "snatchers" of labor:

> Valle Nacional is probably the worst slave hole in Mexico. Probably it is
> the worst in the world. . . . In Yucatan the Maya slaves die off faster than
> they are born and two-thirds of the Yaqui slaves are killed during the first
> year after their importation into the country. In Valle Nacional all of the
> slaves, all but a very few—perhaps five percent—pass back to earth within
> a space of seven or eight months.[3]

The slaves in the southern United States, Turner declared, may have been
treated like cattle, but compared to the slaves of Yucatan and Valle Nacional, they were also "treated as well as cattle" (*Barbarous Mexico,* 35).
They were valuable property, whereas the Yaquis, Mayas, and many other
impoverished and landless Mexicans were treated like dirt. It was cheaper
to pay for new slaves than to feed and house the dying ones adequately.

Mexican landowners also employed African slaves. When the Spanish colonizers found it difficult to enslave "Indians," both because they
were rebellious and because they were not immune to diseases brought
from Europe, they began importing slaves from Africa; and, by the early
1800s, "Africans and Afro-Mestizos numbered . . . more than ten percent

of the population."[4] Adding Africans to the brew of Mexico's many indigenous communities and rapidly growing mestizo population, together with the practice of slavery and wars of extermination, produced a racist order similar to apartheid in South Africa. John Ross writes,

> To combat miscegenation and keep the coloreds in their place, the Colony's Spanish and Creole rulers constructed the most rigid racial barriers in all of the Americas—an apartheid that encompassed 16 separate castes with accompanying derogatory nomenclature—"mulattos," "zambos," "zambaigos," "castizos," "moroscos," "lobos," "coyotes" and "cambujos," amongst others—that precisely described the subject's parental mix.[5]

This rigid racial order served to keep *"los de abajo"*—nonwhite Mexicans—at the bottom of the social pyramid, far below the Spanish-born and white Creole population. However, the *casta* system expressed the instability of a society based on slavery and the oppression of the vast majority by a small minority. Besides the violence necessary to maintain order, the more complicated a racial hierarchy becomes, the harder it is to police. Mexican racism sometimes tried to distinguish among as many as forty different races and racial mixtures.[6] The upshot has been, more often than not, chaotic, with the general notion of *mestizaje* or racial mixing eventually predominating for the majority of Mexicans and Mexican Americans or Chicanos.

Throughout Central and South America, moreover, land was divided among the colonists in a manner that left the indigenous and mestizo majorities landless and impoverished. When landless peasants and Indians were not directly enslaved, they were often forced into debt peonage, working perpetually for their masters in an impossible effort to repay what the masters claimed they owed. Though debt peonage involved a sort of negative financial transaction, it was not much different from slavery.[7] The *encomiendas* or lands entrusted by the Spanish Crown to Spanish colonists supposedly came with the obligation to provide protection and Christianity for the indigenous peoples within their boundaries. In exchange, the *encomenderos* were granted rights to their labor and produce. That they ruthlessly exploited the natives is certain. In Mexico "the *encomienda* system evolved into debt peonage, semi-free forced labor," writes Gibler. "While the Spaniards drove the indigenous off their land and into forced labor, Mexico became the first colony to develop millionaires."[8]

As Turner points out, the *enganchadores,* with the connivance of landowners, officials, the army, and police, practiced kidnapping, but it was sometimes kidnapping through the use of bait. A labor recruiter might offer a poor man an advance on the wages he would earn if he came to work on a particular hacienda. Once the poor man accepted the advance, he was immediately in debt to his employer, and he was likely soon to discover that he would forever be in his employer's debt. "Debts are handed down from father to son," Turner writes, "and on down through the generations":

> Though the constitution does not recognize the right of the creditor to take and hold the body of the debtor, the rural authorities everywhere recognize such a right and the result is that probably 5,000,000 people, or one-third the entire population [of Mexico], are today living in a state of helpless peonage.[9]

Turner also estimated that "probably not fewer than eighty per cent of all the farm and plantation laborers in Mexico are either slaves or are bound to the land as peons" (*Barbarous Mexico,* 111).

As already noted, Turner blamed the "system" of Porfirio Díaz for the wretched poverty and slavery he witnessed: "It was under . . . Díaz that slavery and peonage were re-established in Mexico" (*Barbarous Mexico,* 121). That statement suggests that "slavery and peonage" had been abolished or at least abated during the "reform era" under Benito Juárez, a possibility that Turner comes close to affirming (ibid., 163). Although reform legislation—specifically, the Lerdo Law of 1856—was an attempt at land redistribution that aimed to "facilitate the emergence of a class of numerous and active small proprietors," it was not successful.[10] The big haciendas and plantations such as those that Turner visited were not broken up under Juárez. Instead, his regime targeted church lands and the communal lands of indigenous villages, and these, in turn, were rapidly bought up by large landowners.

Under the Porfiriato, capitalist "accumulation by dispossession" continued apace.[11] Although the amount of "the confiscation of the lands of the common people" such as the Yaquis and Mayas increased from the 1880s to 1910, it was the old story of the formation of enormous landed estates or *latifundios* that occurred all over Central and South America.[12] Turner concluded that robbing the peasants, including indigenous communities, of their land explained why "the typical Mexican farm is the million-acre farm" (*Barbarous Mexico*, 127). Díaz enriched himself, his family, his collaborators, and "his foreign favorites" (ibid., 126) through land confiscations.

The "foreign favorites" were mainly wealthy gringos, which helped explain why there was little or no accurate information about Mexico's condition in the United States. In *Harvest of Empire*, Juan Gonzalez writes,

> By the time Díaz was overthrown, U.S. investment in Mexico totaled $2 billion. Led by the Rockefellers, Guggenheim, E. H. Harriman, and J. P. Morgan, North Americans ended up controlling all the country's oil, 76 percent of its corporations, and 96 percent of its agriculture. The Hearst family, whose newspapers and magazines routinely lauded Díaz, owned a ranch with a million cattle in Chihuahua.[13]

While Díaz garnered praise, the Mexican people were widely maligned in the American press. The reason for this stereotyping—a version of blaming the victim—Turner explained as "a defense against indefensible conditions whereby the defenders are profiting" (*Barbarous Mexico*, 330). That is to say, many wealthy Americans and big businesses had major stakes in the Porfiriato, which included keeping the vast majority of Mexicans poor and on a short leash, while also keeping most Americans in the dark. Blaming poor Mexicans for their poverty helped.

Díaz's modernization program, widely praised by U.S. officials and capitalists, involved the general attempt to eradicate Mexico's many indigenous communities, including the Yaquis and Mayas. American investors facilitated a huge expansion of Mexico's railways, which, in turn, caused the dispossession of indigenous communities and forced thousands of small farmers into peonage and often, as Turner discovered, outright slavery. Land consolidation under Díaz's regime led to an enormous concentration of ownership by the wealthy at the expense of the poor. "By 1906," Gibler notes, "the government-associated oligarchy had taken possession of nearly . . . a quarter of the arable land in the country. By 1910, the Díaz government had expropriated 95 percent of village communal lands" (*Mexico Unconquered*, 36). Although such expropriation had occurred throughout Mexican history, the Porfiriato paved the way for the gaping inequality between rich and poor that exists today. "The prime distinguishing characteristic of the Mexican economy is inequality. Mexico contains one of the greatest, most obscene, gulfs between its wealthiest and most destitute citizens of all the nations on the planet."[14] (Since the 1980s, in terms of poverty and inequality, the United States has been catching up to Mexico and other "third world" countries.)[15]

The fact that "American capital" was cashing in on Díaz's version of modernization, Turner argued, meant that it was "not at present in favor of [the] political annexation of Mexico. This is because the slavery by which it profits can be maintained with greater safety under the Mexican flag than under the American flag" (*Barbarous Mexico*, 268). Without officially colonizing it, the United States had helped turn Mexico "into a slave colony" for the benefit of business and governing elites in both countries (ibid., 254). Turner's thirteenth chapter details American complicity in supporting the Díaz dictatorship, including maintaining the pretense that it was a popular, democratic regime; and chapter fourteen is titled "The American Partners of Díaz." "Most effectively has the police power" of the United States, Turner declared, "been used to destroy a movement of Mexicans for the abolition of Mexican slavery and to keep the chief slave-driver of Barbarous Mexico, Porfirio Díaz, upon his throne" (ibid., 254). But in 1910, the revolution led by Emiliano Zapata and Pancho Villa was just beginning, and Díaz would soon go into exile in France.

TO THE HALLS OF MONTEZUMA

What is the matter with Mexico today may be that the United States did not seize all of it in 1848. What the United States did seize—half of Mexico's territory—amounted to a gargantuan amputation. The alleged surgeon was "Manifest Destiny." Anyone familiar with the war Uncle Sam waged against Mexico in the years 1846–48 will recognize that the prospect of "American capital" colonizing all of Mexico, as Turner suggested, was and still is hardly far-fetched. Both the official and the unofficial annexation of Mexico by its northern neighbor started at least as soon as Mexico gained its independence from Spain in 1821. If annexation means more than just an imperialist land grab and includes economic exploitation, then it is still going on.

A mere twenty-five years after Mexico freed itself, American troops marched into it and defeated its army under Santa Anna. By the 1848 Treaty of Guadalupe Hidalgo, the Mexican government ceded the vast territory that eventually became the states of the American southwest: Texas, New Mexico, Arizona, Utah, California, and parts of Colorado, Nevada, and Oklahoma. In the decades after the war, many of the farms and ranches north of the Rio Grande that were owned by Mexicans were confiscated. "The land established by the [1848] treaty as belonging to Mexicans" living north of the new border, Gloria Anzaldúa writes, was "soon swindled away from its owners" (*Borderlands/La Frontera*, 7). From owning a farm, her father was himself reduced to being a sharecropper; in the 1930s, "agribusiness corporations cheated" the remaining "small Chicano landowners" out of their property, creating huge, well-irrigated, mechanized farms (ibid., 9). The population of Mexicans living in the United States prior to the 1840s war was sparse, so relieving them of their property, together with that of a few thousand Apaches and other assorted Indians, did not pose much difficulty for the advocates of the Manifest Destiny of the United States to expand all the way to the Pacific.

After the U.S. victory in 1848, why didn't President James Polk order Generals Zachary Taylor and Winfield Scott to take over all of Mexico? In 1847, the *New York Herald* called "the annexation of all Mexico" a "gorgeous prospect," and continued,

> It were more desirable that she should come to us voluntarily; but as we shall have no peace until she be annexed, let it come, even though force be necessary at first to bring her. Like the Sabine virgins, she will soon learn to love her ravishers.[16]

A number of other newspapers and several major politicians agreed with this view. As late as 1860, the *New York Times* insisted that "the Mexicans, ignorant and degraded as they are," would welcome becoming a colony of the United States, so that "after a few years of pupilage, the Mexican state would be incorporated into the Union under the same conditions as the original colonies."[17]

Although he had manipulated both countries into the war, Polk chose not to go as far as total annexation. Perhaps he believed that acquiring the northern half of Mexico and reaching the Pacific was more than enough empire building—for the time being, at least. However, racism provided a key sticking point for many Americans. According to Mae Ngai, "Euro-Americans never considered Mexicans their racial equals."[18] Racism helped justify the brutalities and massacres of civilians committed during the war, but it also prevented the United States from seizing the entire country.[19] "The annexation of [all of Mexico] would be a calamity," declared the *Democratic Review,* because it would mean acquiring a population of "ignorant and indolent half-civilized Indians," plus "free negroes and mulattoes." Quoting this remark, the authors of one standard American history textbook state, "The virulent racism of American leaders allowed the Mexicans to retain part of their nation"—the part that is today's Mexico.[20] Congressman Columbus Delano of Ohio, an antislavery Whig, feared that white Americans would mingle with the inferior races of Mexico—races that "embrace all shades of color . . . a sad compound of Spanish, English, Indian, and negro bloods . . . and resulting . . . in the production of a slothful, ignorant race of beings."[21] The Whig press generally "emphasized that it wanted neither Mexican soil nor the 'wretched population' that went with it."[22]

There were, of course, those who, like Abraham Lincoln, opposed the war against Mexico on principle. Henry David Thoreau refused to pay taxes, spent a night in jail, and wrote his essay on civil disobedience in opposition to the war. Some feared that Polk and the Democrats were looking to extend slavery beyond Texas, which had earlier been amputated from Mexico and had become a new state of the Union in 1845. Others were outraged at the lies and deceptions of Polk and his supporters that prompted the war. The agreed-upon border between Texas and Mexico had been the Nueces River. But Polk ordered General Taylor to move his troops into position farther south to the Rio Grande, across from Matamoros. This led, in turn, to the skirmishes that triggered the full-scale war. In his diary, Col. Ethan Allen Hitchcock wrote, "We have outraged the Mexican government and people by an arrogance and presumption that deserve to be punished. For ten years we have been encroaching on Mexico and insulting her." He added, "Her people I consider a simple, well disposed, pastoral race, no way inclined to savage usages."[23]

After 1848, "Mexico's demolished economy was a symptom of its wrecked government, which struggled with the humiliation of losing the war."[24] Santa Anna's return to power in 1853 showed how bankrupt the government was. Two years later, the revolution of Ayutla toppled him from power. The war increased the number and intensity of peasant and indigenous rebellions that have characterized Mexican history down to the present.[25] For example, the "Caste War of the Yucatan," beginning in 1847, "pitted the native Maya against whites and mestizos." Many Mayas fled; their population dropped by 30 percent in six years. "Sugar plantations were devastated, and survivors ran from the region en masse, which impaired Mexico's ability to regenerate a healthy economy in the years following the war."[26]

From the mid-1850s, the liberal reform movement led by Benito Juárez promised to bring some stability to Mexico, but, as noted earlier, its successes were limited. The French invasion of 1861 and the installation of Maximilian as "emperor," who ruled from 1863 until he was dethroned and executed in 1867, impeded the reform movement. President again from 1867 to 1876, Juárez was himself ousted by the rebellion of Tuxtepec. General Porfirio Díaz seized power and ruled as "president" from then until 1911, with one brief interval when one of his henchmen served as president to maintain the facade of democratic elections.

During the Porfiarato, though Díaz managed to attract a great deal of foreign, especially U.S., investment, that only exacerbated inequality and class conflict. The Heidlers write that large landowners "enhanced their holdings at the expense of Mexico's chronic poor. As the landless population . . . grew, many fell into hopeless debt peonage . . . [which was] very much like slavery in practice if not name." By the end of the Díaz era, "as much as nine-tenths of the population in certain regions were landless peasants. It was not a good way to start the twentieth century" (*The Mexican War*, 147). According to Eduardo Galeano, at the beginning of the revolution, "workers' wages had not risen by a centavo since the historic rising of the priest Miguel Hidalgo in 1810. In 1910 eight hundred-odd *latifundistos*, many of them foreigners, owned almost all the national territory" (*Open Veins of Latin America*, 135). During the revolution, an estimated one to one and a half million Mexicans crossed the northern border to escape the violence, though many later returned.

The revolution ended Díaz's dictatorship, but it did little to change poverty for the vast majority of Mexicans. If many of them were the virtual slaves of the *latifundistos*, Mexico itself had become enslaved by U.S. capitalism. For the most part, Mexico remains a slave colony of the United States today. Actual slavery south of the border, as Turner contended, could be kept out of sight from the American public. When in the twenty-first century Mexican poverty—slavery in all but name—

spills over the border in the form of "illegal aliens," it once again stirs the hornet's nest of American racism and anti-immigrant sentiment, even though many U.S. businesses profit from low-wage or sometimes no-wage Mexican labor. It is good for the U.S. economy in general to have so much cheap labor readily available—the next best thing to slavery. When in 2011, in response to anti-immigration legislation in Alabama and Georgia, Mexican farm workers fled those states, their former employers suddenly learned the high value of their cheap labor as crops rotted in fields and orchards.

NARCOS AND ZAPATISTAS

One hundred years ago, Turner called Mexico the slave colony of the United States. If Mexico has not been economically decolonized since that time, what differences are there between then and now? One difference is that, in the United States, the Latino population, a large percentage of which is Mexican American, is today enormous and rapidly growing. As citizens and voters, Latinos now constitute a major force, able to influence presidential elections, as happened in 2012.[27] But the number of impoverished, undocumented workers, despite renewed efforts to secure the border, is also increasing. In technical terms, they are not slaves, but many of them may feel that they might as well be slaves. Since 9/11, moreover, the anti-immigrant backlash has been compounded by fears that brown-skinned border crossers may be terrorists pretending to be Mexicans; they may also be, it is claimed, members of the drug cartels, bringing their guns and narcotics with them.

The mass demonstrations for immigrant rights by Latinos and their supporters in many American cities in 2006 might have led to sensible legislative reforms. President George W. Bush seemed to understand the wisdom of creating a path to citizenship for undocumented immigrants, while also advocating stricter border enforcement. But the backlash so far has made it difficult for either major political party to do anything except build higher walls and bring on the military. The problem for the Obama administration, which has promised reform, is that doing anything sensible is likely to be condemned by the Right as being soft on "illegals" or even as giving them "amnesty." While doing little or nothing may not please the majority of Latino voters, it is currently the safe position: most Latinos will continue to support the administration, knowing the alternative is far worse.

An anti-immigration fanatic like Tom Tancredo, former Republican congressman from Colorado, believes that the American border with Mexico should be militarized and that all illegal immigrants should be rounded up and deported—an impossible task because there are at least twelve million (nobody knows the exact figure, of course). In the preface to *In Mortal Danger,* Tancredo writes, "I want to do what I can to defend the West in the clash of civilizations that threatens humanity with a return to the Dark Ages" (see chapter 3). Apparently, Mexico is not part of "the West." Currently, over five thousand children of undocumented immigrants are in foster care; their parents have been detained or deported, but the children are U.S. citizens because they were born here.[28] And during the Obama administration, deportations have reached an all-time high at more than four hundred thousand.

Besides Mexicans, there are many undocumented immigrants from other countries—all worrisome to those who insist they pose a threat to national security. Tancredo links illegal immigration to post-9/11 terrorism. But the 9/11 terrorists had entered the country legally. Besides, the patiently hopeful laborers at the Home Depot carry tools, not bombs. Some who advocate tighter border security, moreover, also acknowledge the demand for Mexican workers. Thus, Dick Armey's conservative Freedom Works supports more policing of the borders and of "illegals" but also advocates a guest-worker program, like the Bracero program that began in the midst of World War II. Of course, this is a way to continue to supply many U.S. employers with cheap labor without swelling the number of Latino citizens of the United States.[29]

Between 1942 and 1964, thousands of Mexicans were brought into the United States as duly registered, temporary guest workers to harvest crops and do other forms of manual labor.[30] Their temporary status and low wages guaranteed that they would not bring their families with them. And the "braceros"—*brazos* means arms—had to pay for health care and other social services. These and other factors militated against union organization and also against the workers becoming citizens. The *Bracero* program is only the best known of the many ways U.S. and state governments have collaborated with business interests to ensure that a "reserve army of labor," as Karl Marx called it, is always readily available on both sides of the border with Mexico (see chapter 11). No, the "illegals" are not slaves in the sense of being bought and sold like cattle; but poverty has turned them into low-wage or too often no-wage slaves.[31]

Building walls and filling immigration prisons will not stop Mexicans from entering the United States by both legal and illegal means. The head of Homeland Security as of this writing, Janet Napolitano, has said, "Show me a fifty-foot wall and I'll show you a fifty-one foot ladder." Tougher restrictions only serve to keep the Mexican underclass in its place—that is, at the bottom of the labor and social-class hierarchies in both the United States and Mexico, trying ever more desperately to climb the fifty-one-foot ladder. Apart from noting that immigrants from Mexico and Central America come to the United States looking for work because they cannot find it south of the border, many self-proclaimed immigration experts do not ask why that is the case. They may, like Tancredo, inveigh against the Mexican government for not improving its economy so that jobs would be available there, and they may sometimes note that U.S. businesses and corporations are profiting by employing low-wage, "illegal" workers. But they do not inquire further into the history of U.S.-Mexican relations. How did those of us lucky enough to be U.S. citizens get to be so prosperous—many of us, anyway? And how did so many Mexicans become so poor? Many anti-immigrationists are ready to blame impoverished Mexicans themselves for their poverty, just as they are ready to blame the unemployed and the homeless in the United States for their predicaments.

Intensifying border security—by walls, by militarization, by beefing up the Border Patrol, or by vigilantism like that of the Minutemen—has a number of adverse effects on impoverished Mexicans but also on border security. For the undocumented, it increases the dangers of crossing, and not just the chances of getting caught. Many more immigrants now die in the Arizona desert than used to be the case. The perils of border crossing also increase the profits of the "coyotes" or human traffickers, who often have ties to the drug cartels. Tightening border security means that many who make it into the United States do not return to Mexico, as they frequently did in the past: most of the undocumented are here to stay, unless they are caught and deported. And the effort to round them up and deport them by ICE and other agencies increases the cost for U.S. taxpayers, who are also paying for the "war on drugs."

The vigilantism of the Minutemen and other anti-immigrant groups points to an increase of racism and hate crimes. In the 1920s, Jim Crow laws were applied to Mexicans, whether they were immigrants or U.S. citizens, and "Mexican" became "a separate racial category in the census."[32] Like freed slaves but also like members of immigrant groups such as the Chinese, Mexicans in the United States, even some who became American citizens by default through the Treaty of Guadelupe Hidalgo in 1848, have been lynched or otherwise murdered with impunity. Although they deny they are racists, for the anti-immigrationists, "Mexican" remains a racial category. Their attitude toward Mexicans—the undocumented, at least—is similar to that of many of the Whigs who opposed seizing all of Mexico in 1848: white America is today threatened by the Brown Peril from south of the border.

NAFTA, ratified in 1993 by the United States, Canada, and Mexico, was supposed to improve economic conditions for all three countries. However, since it went into effect on January 1, 1994, though many corporations have profited from it, most Americans, Canadians, and Mexicans have not. "Under NAFTA and WTO policies that forced the reduction or elimination of protective tariffs," write Jane Guskin and David Wilson, "more than 1.5 million Mexican farmers have lost their sources of income and been forced to sell or abandon their farms. Consumer prices were supposed to decline under NAFTA—yet while the prices paid to farmers for their products have plummeted, consumer food prices have risen in all three NAFTA countries. As of 2005, Mexican farmers earned 70 percent less for their corn than they did before NAFTA, while Mexicans paid 50 percent more for tortillas" (*The Politics of Immigration*, 25). One result has been a doubling of immigration, both legal and undocumented, from Mexico into the United States.[33]

The argument that Mexico should get its economy in order so its population could escape the poverty that is driving migrant laborers north fails to consider that Mexico has been obeying the dictates of American neoliberal economics ever since the Reagan years. NAFTA climaxed that obedience.[34] Today, the United States also has to get its economy in order. Has NAFTA brought benefits to farmers in the United States? Though farms both large and small have been supported through government subsidies, which support violates the free-market dogma of economic neoliberalism, the small farmer has been falling through the cracks for decades. Bank foreclosures on small farms in the United States have been going on much longer than the current plague of foreclosures on the homes of urban, middle- and working-class citizens. A key difference is that the foreclosed small farms have been gobbled up and consolidated into the large-scale holdings of agricorporations like Cargill, as has also been happening in Mexico and throughout Latin America (and, indeed, throughout the world as the latest form of colonialism).[35] But urban and suburban homes cannot be consolidated and rendered profitable in the same way. They become profitable mainly through resale, and if the pool of potential individual homebuyers shrinks (because many of them have already lost their homes as well as their jobs), then the urban real estate market nosedives. In a world where only the rich can hang on to their homes and only the corporations can buy up agricultural land, poverty and the poor are bound to multiply exponentially.

Also in 1994, after the meltdown of the Mexican peso, President Bill Clinton and Alan Greenspan seemingly saved the day through a $50 billion emergency loan, although the loan was mostly a "bailout of U.S. banks, brokerage firms, pension funds and insurance companies."[36] In *Empire's Workshop*, Greg Grandin writes,

> Washington's rescue stabilized the peso and allowed the economy to re-cover, yet structural problems remained, including high rates of nonpro-ductive speculative investment, declining wages in proportion to growth, and staggering levels of poverty. Most disruptive, the importation of cheap goods decimated domestic manufacturing and small-scale farming, which could not compete with U.S. agro-industry.[37]

Grandin adds that "the NAFTA model provided no mechanisms to incorporate displaced peasants into the new global economy, except pushing them to travel north to supply cheap labor to service the American economy" (200). Meanwhile, manufacturing jobs in the United States were disappearing, as transnational corporations moved their production facilities to, among other places, the *maquiladoras* south of the U.S.-Mexican border.[38]

Besides cheap labor, another way Mexico contributes to the U.S. economy is through the so-called war on drugs and the importation of narcotics into the United States. Of course, illegal drugs are consumed in Mexico, but, by far, the greatest amount of drug consumption occurs north of the Rio Grande. According to John Gibler,

A study by the Mexican government found that the country's economy
would shrink by 63 percent if the drug business were to disappear. Mexico
is the largest foreign supplier of marijuana and methamphetamines to the
United States and is responsible for 70 to 90 percent of all the cocaine that
enters the country.[39]

The U.S. economy, the study revealed, "would shrink by 19 to 22 percent
without the drug business."[40]

Apart from the illegal but multibillion-dollar trade in drugs, many legal U.S. businesses profit from this so-called war, including the gun trade
and the prison-industrial complex. In Mexico, permits for guns are hard
to come by, but in Arizona and Texas, all sorts of guns are readily available
(see chapter four). Narco cartels are better equipped with firepower than
the Mexican army. That army is now occupying entire cities such as Ciudad Juárez and Reynosa but has done more to contribute to the violence
than shut it down. "After some ten thousand soldiers . . . arrived in Juárez,"
writes John Gibler in *To Die in Mexico*, "the execution rate nearly *doubled*"
(199). The narcos kill with impunity; only 5 percent of the murder cases in
the drug war are even investigated, and over 40,000 people, many of them
"collateral damage," have been slain (ibid., 202). Gibler notes that "U.S.
policy has not stopped the flow of drugs, but it has outsourced most of
the killing" to Mexico (203). Nevertheless, the United States now has the
highest incarceration rate of any country in the world. Illegal drugs and
the unending but utterly futile "war" against them have been a major boon
to the new private prison industry and have helped perpetuate Jim Crow
racism in a supposedly colorblind mode.[41] Neither the United States nor
the Mexican government seems willing to legalize narcotics, which would
help end the violence—that might be bad for capitalism (both legal and
illegal) on both sides of the border.

Narco violence belongs to the dark side of Mexico's long history of
injustice and oppression, lawlessness and rebellion. A far more positive
rebellion began with the emergence of the EZLN or the Zapatista National Liberation Army of Chiapas in 1994. The Zapatistas have helped
inspire the global justice movement against transnational capitalism and
the reign of economic neoliberalism. After Hernan Cortes and his followers defeated Montezuma and the Aztec empire in 1521, for the next
several centuries the indigenous societies of Mexico were devastated by
war, slavery, and disease. Yet many of them were stronger and better orga-

nized than indigenous societies north of the Rio Grande. The Mayas and other indigenous groups, today numbering some twelve million people, constitute about 11 percent of the total population of Mexico, compared to native peoples in the United States, who make up less than 1 percent of the population. This greater size of the indigenous population of Mexico helps explain why the Zapatista struggle for the recognition and rights of all of the indigenous of Mexico has also been at the forefront of the world-wide "global justice" or "alterglobalization" resistance to transnational corporate capitalism (see chapter twelve).

Why did the Zapatista rebellion begin in Chiapas? One reason is that Chiapas is one of the poorest states in Mexico. Novelist Paco Taibo, in a 1994 article in *The Nation*, writes,

> An agrarianist friend explains to me that 15,000 indigenous people have died of hunger and easily curable diseases in Chiapas in the past few years. Without crop rotation, the fields are not very productive. The price of coffee has dropped, so the landowners have seized more land for cattle. They create conflicts between the [indigenous] communities and assassinate community leaders. Although the land cannot feed any more people, the population has been growing by 6 percent annually with the arrival of indigenous refugees from Guatemala and the internal migration of Indians whose land has been taken by the owners of the large haciendas.[42]

It might have been the same old story, except that the Zapatistas managed to attract worldwide attention through radio, the Internet, and the press. And even though it is in theory a leaderless, completely democratic, and mostly nonviolent "army" (it is an "army" that aims to put an end to armies), its charismatic leader, Subcomandante Marcos, is now nearly as famous as Che Guevara.

The collective declarations and communiqués of the EZLN, most of them by Marcos, make up an extraordinary account of what has been wrong with Mexico throughout its history. The first paragraph of "The First Declaration of the Lacandón Jungle" offers an overview: "We are the product of 500 years of struggle: first against slavery, then during the War of Independence against Spain..., then to avoid being absorbed by North American imperialism, then to promulgate our constitution and expel the French empire from our soil. Later the dictatorship of Porfirio Díaz denied us the just application of the Reform laws and the people rebelled; leaders like Villa and Zapata emerged: poor men just like us."[43] The "we" in the declaration refers not just to the EZLN but to all of the Mayan communities of Chiapas and, indeed, to all of Mexico's indigenous people. The declaration presents a shorthand version of the rebellions and revolutions that constitute the history of Mexico up to the revolution of 1910–20. "Mexico's history of revolt is as deep as its history of exploitation," writes John Gibler in *Mexico Unconquered* (29). That country's "original inhabitants did not simply bow their heads to foreign authority and violence," he adds; "they rejected attempts to be dominated. The indigenous revolted all across the country, continuously and steadily throughout the entire colonial period" (29), indeed, throughout the entire history of Mexico down to the Zapatistas.

The Zapatista uprising took place on the first of January 1994, the date when NAFTA went into effect and the year the Mexican peso crashed. These events are two seemingly opposed but causally linked outcomes of economic neoliberalism. Marcos announced that NAFTA was "the death sentence for the indigenous people" of Mexico. It has been called that as well for all of Mexico's peasant farmers.[44] But it was also a point of origin of what Tom Hayden calls "the war between the forces of market modernity and the world of the wretched of the earth." That last phrase— "wretched of the earth"—echoes Frantz Fanon's title of his brilliant dissection of Western imperialism and racism. Dividing the world's wealth between rich and poor individuals, classes, nations, and regions, capitalist modernity has produced catastrophic levels of inequality by conquest, dispossession, oppression, and genocide that can only be undone by the resistance of the victims and by those brave and knowledgeable enough to join them in combating oppressive conditions everywhere. Confronting poverty, starvation, violence, and mass unemployment in Mexico, the Zapatistas have brought worldwide attention to the domination of transnational corporations and neoliberal economic dogma. Marcos has called the battle against these forces of the wealthy and powerful "the Fourth World War." The enemies of the Zapatistas "are carrying under their arms the economic and police plans that have been drawn up in the boardrooms of international greed."[45] With the commencement of the Occupy Wall Street movement in the United States on September 13, 2011, "We are all Chiapenecos"—or at least, 99 percent of us are. Viva Zapata!

SIX

Waste and Value: Thorstein Veblen and H. G. Wells

COAUTHORED WITH RICHARD HIGGINS

Trashmass, trashmosh. On a large enough scale, trashmos. And—
of course—macrotrashm! . . . Really, just think of it, macrotrashm!

—STANISLAW LEM, *THE FUTUROLOGICAL CONGRESS*

A WASTEFUL PREAMBLE

As the self-proclaimed "science of value" economics—whether neoliberal, Keynesian, Marxist, or anything else—has always had trouble defining its main subject. Early attempts to identify value with something substantial and nonrelative—the labor theory of value, the gold standard, and so forth—gave way in the latter third of the nineteenth century to price theory and the doctrine of marginal utility. As that was happening, value seemed to grow indistinct from its antitheses: depending on circumstances, anything and everything could be considered valuable. Among other observers, Thorstein Veblen and H. G. Wells are exemplary for their insistence that waste could be valuable and values wasteful. They thus point ahead to a key aspect of the postmodern condition: the indeterminacy of values, signaled by the theme of valuable waste in, for example, Don DeLillo's 1997 novel *Underworld*.

Introducing *Filth: Dirt, Disgust, and Modern Life*, William Cohen declares that "polluting or filthy objects" can "become conceivably productive, the discarded sources in which riches may lie" (x). Riches, though, have often been construed as waste. The reversibility of the poles—wealth and waste, waste and wealth—was becoming especially apparent with the

96

emergence of so-called consumer society, and several of its first analysts, including Veblen and Wells, made this reversibility central to their ideas.[1] But such reversibility has a much longer history, involving a general shift from economic and social theories that seek to make clear distinctions between wealth and waste to modern ones where the distinctions blur, as in Veblen and Wells; in some versions of postmodernism, the distinctions disappear altogether.

Cohen also writes, "As it breaches subject/object distinctions ... filth ... covers two radically different imaginary categories, which I designate polluting and reusable. The former—filth proper—is wholly unregenerate" (x). Given the reversibility of the poles (and various modes of the scrambling or hybridization of values), what is the meaning of "filth proper"? Proper filth? Filthy property? Is there any filth that is not potentially "reusable" and, hence, valuable? Shit is valuable as fertilizer, garbage as compost, and so on. Inversions and identifications of the two poles are possible if not always common in all cultures. Under capitalism, they become increasingly commonplace. Capitalist modernity, then, can be defined as the age in which even filth began to seem valuable and postmodernity as the age in which anything has whatever value a consumer places on it. In *Waste and Want*, Susan Strasser writes, "what counts as trash depends on who's counting" (3). Our era, perhaps the end point or last stage of capitalism,[2] is one in which everything can be turned to account, and yet nothing—not even the worker who turns into the valued consumer after work—seems to be worth anything. Shopping malls and Wal-Mart have institutionalized this postmodern fact of life.[3]

The equation between waste and money is perhaps as old as money itself. It emerges as a central element of socioeconomic theory, however, only with consumer society, after the initial phase of the Industrial Revolution from the 1780s to the 1850s. The shift in economics from emphasizing production to emphasizing consumption, marked by the marginalist revolution of the 1870s, was paralleled by the increasing subjectivism of aesthetic theory associated with the fin de siècle decadent movement and early literary and artistic modernism.[4] Like the atomistic conception of decadence, the equally atomistic (individualistic, egoistic) notion of limitless consumption meant, in part, that anyone's values or desires were as worthy or as wasteful as anyone else's. The marketplace, where all values are valuable and everything has its price, was the central institution of the new consumer society, and the marketplace was increasingly equated with the total fungibility of mass democracy. Important diagnoses of these trends come from Veblen and Wells, one an American maverick economist and the other a British novelist, historian, and Fabian socialist.

This transatlantic similitude suggests that the equation can be found elsewhere at about the same time, from roughly 1870 down to World War I, in, for example, John Ruskin's notion of "illth," or in Friedrich Nietzsche's theory of "the transvaluation of all values," which influenced Georges Bataille's insistence on the primacy of expenditure.[5] In *The Insatiability of Human Wants*, Regenia Gagnier supplies other examples from the same period. The equation of wealth and waste achieves a postmodern apotheosis of sorts in the lucubrations on consumer society of Jean Baudrillard (who with Veblen in mind writes, "The consumption of leisure is a species of potlatch"), and more generally in "rubbish theory" from Michael Thompson to Arthur Kroker and Michael Weinstein, an apotheosis explored in fictional form in DeLillo's *Underworld*.

After a brief survey of the paradoxical imbrication of waste and wealth in economic thinking from John Locke to Karl Marx, we turn to Veblen and Wells. Though the two seem to have been unaware of each other's work, both were early advocates of a cultural modernism that, in some of its avatars, repudiated consumerist materialism in favor of a functionalist efficiency that sought to "supplant ornament" with "utility."[6] In that formulation, "ornament" signifies wasteful expenditure. Both Veblen and Wells looked to science, technology, and efficiency as means to limit waste. They were Victorian and modernist enemies of waste in ways that at least some modernist thinkers, including Bataille and the surrealists, would reject.[7] But like Bataille and other modernists, Veblen and Wells saw waste as pervasive—so much so, that for them as for many postmodernists, it was perhaps the very basis of value.[8] Waste is fundamental if only because, as Mary Douglas among others has observed, cultural value hierarchies arise and maintain themselves by defining and rejecting it. This means in part that, for every positive value, there is a negative that is in some way equated with waste (and a negative value is, after all, still a value). It also means that value hierarchies can be contested through symbolic inversion, whereby what is normally understood as positive or as valuable comes to be viewed as the reverse—value is seen as waste, and vice versa. Both Veblen and Wells practiced what might be called a sour social science or a sarcastic objectivity, revealing the hollowness of a capitalism in which value is no longer tied to productivity or utility and whose ultimate product is a social and cultural wasteland. In DeLillo's *Underworld,* it is no longer possible to distinguish between waste and value. Postmodernity has been defined both as "incredulity toward metanarratives" and as the collapse of value hierarchies.[9] If today waste and value are interchangeable, or even indistinguishable from each other, that is because of the lax teleology—democratic and economic entropy—that both Veblen and Wells were among the first to analyze in economic terms. For Veblen and Wells, "value creates waste, and waste impels the search for new constructions of value,"[10] although, for DeLillo, it does not appear that the search leads anywhere beyond individuals and their rational—that is, irrational—choices.[11]

WASTE IN ECONOMIC THEORY
BEFORE VEBLEN AND WELLS

Economics understands economies in terms of production and consumption, regulated by supply and demand. Mediating between these poles in all modern and now postmodern societies is money that, as one standard metaphor has it, lubricates exchange at all levels and points of industrial and commercial contact. And as all lubricants can do, money often spills out of the channels intended for it: economies, whether capitalist, socialist, or other (even primitive), are subject to leakage, and such leakage (over expenditure, speculation, embezzlement, bribery, excess taxation, and the like) is one meaning of waste. But money in general, whenever it remains tied to a metallic or other substantial base, is metaphorically tied to waste: a material dross that resists its "transformation . . . into a purely symbolic representative of its essential function," which is to serve as the dematerialized general equivalent for all values.[12] As Georg Simmel puts it in *The Philosophy of Money,* "The development of money is a striving towards the ideal of a pure symbol of economic value which is never attained" (191). One upshot of "never attained" is that money inevitably remains tied to materiality and, hence, to waste.

Paradoxically, the squandering of money by spendthrifts and gamblers may seem to promote its quasi-religious "striving towards the ideal" by shedding the dross, or at least by treating it lightly. After all, the Bible advises the rich to divest themselves of their riches if they are to enter heaven. Although the economic and utilitarian rationality attendant upon capitalism dictates against such advice, forms of wasteful expenditure have their religious significance in primitive gift economies, spectacularly exemplified by the practice of potlatch. In *Visions of Excess*, Bataille counters "the insufficiency of the principle of classical utility" in bourgeois economics with the "principle of loss" or wasteful expenditure, which he identifies with both religion (including potlatch ceremonies) and poetry ("The Notion of Expenditure," 116–29). In any event, in some circumstances, wasting money has the appearance, at least, of a spiritual elimination of waste: ridding oneself of "filthy lucre."[13] This is perhaps also one reason that spending on luxuries, or what Veblen famously called "conspicuous consumption," at times seems virtuous, as with unworldly millionaire Adam Verver in Henry James's *The Golden Bowl*.

The wasting of money can be understood as the elimination of waste through the demand that it creates for ever-greater levels of productivity and efficiency. But whether spent wastefully or rationally, spent money is what greases the wheels of mechanical and economic progress. Simmel further notes, "Money carries within itself the structure of the need for luxuries, in that it rejects any limitation upon desire for it—which would be possible only through the relation of definite quantities to our capacity to consume. Yet money, unlike a precious metal used for jewelry, does not need to balance the unlimited desire for it by a growing distance from direct needs, because it has become the correlate of the most basic needs of life as well" (*Philosophy of Money*, 251). In Britain during the eighteenth century, the discourse on luxury was concerned with "conspicuous consumption" as a type of waste that threatened national security.[14] In his essay "Of Public Credit," David Hume contended that the creation of the national debt and the stock market had fostered "a stupid and pampered luxury" (172). Throughout history, moreover, luxury had been one of the causes of the decline and fall of empires. But hadn't it also and equally been, and obviously so, a sign of the triumph of empires? Once any economy overcomes scarcity and is able to provide its participants with more than bare subsistence, the question of what to do with the excess—the "surplus value," to use Marx's phrase—arises. Luxury names one solution to that problem, and it is almost always, according to Enlightenment theorists such as Hume, the wrong, wasteful solution. But the other, supposedly rational solution—to plow the excess back into more production—only exacerbates the problem by leading to more commodities, more wealth and prosperity, and in short to more money, more luxury, and more wasteful spending.[15] Capitalism, it seems, is an economic system geared to the transformation of waste into ever-more waste; according to its spendthrift logic, instead of two separate islands, utopia and wasteland turn out to be the same place.

Although the problem of conspicuous consumption can be seen in embryo in the eighteenth-century discourse on luxury, it was not a main issue for the early capitalist economists (Adam Smith through John Stuart Mill). Of course, they had to account for various types of waste that are the inevitable by-products of the production of wealth. What value to attach to the tailings produced by an iron mine, for example? They worried much about the wasting of capital through inefficiency, depreciation, nonuse, and unwise investment; they worried less about wasteful individual consumption, and little or not at all about the paradox, implicit in the concept of luxury, of wealth as waste.

According to the early economists, waste was a regrettable but minor, perhaps even irrelevant, phenomenon. In a sense, waste was a noneconomical phenomenon—a sort of waste category or "externality" in relation to rational production and consumption. Certainly, they attached some (monetary) value to some forms of waste, most notably "waste lands" or territories, which from the perspective of European imperialism meant much of the rest of the world. They agreed with John Locke, who in his *Two Treatises of Government* had linked property to the cultivation of land and its noncultivation to waste. In Locke's influential formulation, "waste land" is identified both with "Nature" and with the potential for great wealth, readily available throughout the world for those who will settle on it, cultivate it, and convert it into productive property. And Locke also identifies property with the use of money. Throughout the world, he writes, "there are still great tracts of ground to be found, which the inhabitants thereof, not having joined with the rest of mankind in the consent of the use of their common money, lie waste, and are more than the people who dwell on it, do, or can make use of, and so still lie in common; though this can scarce happen amongst that part of mankind that have consented to the use of money" (139). Here, as in the economists from Smith to Mill, money rationally aligns itself with both property and productivity; in *Two Treatises,* at least, the question of wasting money does not arise, and the paradoxical identification of money and waste not at all.[16]

Locke's portrayal of "the Indians" as nonindustrious and ignorant both of cultivation and of money suggests that they themselves are waste or human refuse. This suggestion foreshadows numerous European portrayals of supposedly noncivilized peoples around the world as surplus or waste populations: if incapable of becoming "civilized," then they deserve what many came to see as their inevitable extinction.[17] And if there were surplus populations in "waste lands" abroad, so also were there waste peoples at home—most famously, the overpopulating poor in Thomas Malthus's *Essay on Population* (see chapter eleven). From the Malthusian perspective, the poor are always overpopulation, an excrescence or cancerous growth on the body politic. While some savages might improve and even advance to civilization, almost by definition the European poor were unimprovable. "To remove the wants of the lower classes" is impossible, Malthus declares; "the pressure of distress on this part of a community is an evil so deeply seated that no human ingenuity can reach it" (38). Money only adds to the dilemma, because the more money the poor possess, the greater their inducement to overpopulate. In other words, their expenditures beyond bare subsistence can only produce more waste (or wasted lives). For some observers, such as Victorian sage Thomas Carlyle, it was just a short step from recognizing "waste" populations at home to seeing home—Britain, in Carlyle's case—as an industrial wasteland.

Adam Smith had at least been optimistic that the poor, through thrift and hard work, could gain a modicum of "luxury." Indeed, Smith redefined that term in part by extending it as a possibility to all levels of society, and not just the "opulent." One question Smith addresses in *The Wealth of Nations* is what to do with wealth, once a nation or an individual possesses it. He uses "opulence" interchangeably with both "luxury" and "wealth," and from "luxury," he removes some of the moral and political stigma that earlier thinkers had attached to it. Nevertheless, starting with Malthus, the capitalist economists often equated the poor themselves with waste: wasted lives equal waste matter. In the Reverend Sidney Godolphin Osborne's pungent phrase, they are "immortal sewerage." Osborne's 1853 essay of that title, written in the wake of the Irish Famine of 1845–50, advocates "the draining of civilization" through emigration to waste lands abroad. So, too, in 1826, economist J. R. McCulloch, in his essay "Emigration," urging Parliament to transport at least one-seventh of the population of Ireland to the colonies, warned that a "tide" of Irish paupers was "inundating" England: "Half-famished hordes ... are daily pouring in from the great officina pauperum" or sewer of Ireland. Pauperism "will find its level. It cannot be heaped up in Leinster and Ulster without overflowing upon England and Scotland."

From the Malthusian perspective of early economics, prosperity is the goal, but prosperity produces overpopulation and, for the vast majority, poverty: wealth inevitably results in human waste. Smith did not reach that dismal conclusion, but Malthus made it a key issue for subsequent economists. Smith, however, considered another, more traditional version of the wealth as waste equation by arguing that "the prodigal" or spendthrift "encroaches upon his capital. . . . By diminishing the funds destined for the employment of productive labour, he necessarily diminishes ... the quantity of that labour[,] which adds a value to the subject upon which it is bestowed, and, consequently, the value of the annual produce of the land and labour of the whole country, the real wealth and revenue of its inhabitants" (438–39). Smith fails to recognize that what "the prodigal" spends, wasting his private "capital," may well pay for "productive" labor of various sorts. He divides labor into "productive" and "unproductive" categories and then links "prodigality" only to the latter. For Smith, "prodigality" or "profusion" means wasting money on "the passion for present enjoyment," which implies (among other types of wasteful activities) frivolous entertainment:

> Of two or three hundredweight of provisions, which may sometimes be served up at a great festival, one-half, perhaps, is thrown to the dunghill, and there is always a great deal wasted and abused. But if the expense of this entertainment had been employed in setting to work masons, carpenters, upholsterers, mechanics, etc., a quantity of provisions, of equal value, would have been distributed among a still greater number of people who would ... not have lost or thrown away a single ounce of them.[18]

In this passage, Smith does not consider the possibilities that "masons, carpenters," and so on might be employed to help produce the "great" and wasteful "festival" in the first place, much less that they might very well partake of that festival. There is no reason that a "productive" worker cannot be employed for the "profusion" of others, nor that, at least when not working, he cannot himself be a "prodigal."

Perhaps through a similar line of reasoning, Marx in *Capital* offers only the briefest consideration of workers in relation to "luxury." During his comments on "luxury production," directly in response to Smith, Marx notes that there are circumstances when "wages generally rise, and the working class actually does receive a greater share in the part of the annual product destined for consumption" (3:486–87). However, because his main theme is the immiseration of the working class under capitalism, he cannot go farther than this, to imagine a situation in which workers themselves begin to imitate the upper classes through wasteful spending on frivolous entertainment or ostentatious display. Workers may be ignorant (blinded by ideology), but they are not wasteful because they possess nothing to waste: surplus value belongs to the capitalists. Yet because they are productive, but treated as waste, workers—Marx hoped—would become revolutionaries. Human nature, however, was perhaps both more productive and more prodigal than Marx assumed.[19]

Marx was certainly right in contending that capitalism in general is wasteful, and especially so in regard to the lives of the working class. "From the standpoint of the capitalist," Marx declares, any expenditure on the health, safety, and education of the workers "would be a senseless and purposeless waste. Yet for all its stinginess, capitalist production is thoroughly wasteful with human material, just as its way of distributing its products through trade, and its manner of competition, make it very wasteful of material resources, so that it loses for society what it gains of the individual capitalist" (3:180). In short, the ultimate "prodigal" is not the private spendthrift or gambler but capitalism. Marx was right in many ways, not least in claiming that capitalism wastes lives and resources. It remained for Veblen to recognize that, through all aspects of its economy and culture, modern (and now postmodern) capitalism—or so-called consumer society—is characterized by its prodigal, wasteful ways.

VEBLEN'S GILDED AGE

If, for Malthus, the ultimate forms of both economic and human waste were represented both by savagery and overpopulation (or by primitive humankind and modern paupers), Veblen thought differently: "peaceable" savages were exemplars of "the instinct of workmanship," and the wastefulness of modern capitalism lay only partly in poverty, or the immiseration of workers; it lay also in war and in its ability to generate and squander surplus value or wealth, which, in turn, promoted the survival of "barbarian"—not "savage"—"predatory" customs into the present. Though benefiting from "machine discipline," modern civilization is threatened by the wasteful ways of the new "barbarians." The struggle for the future lay between the "vested interests," who wasted, and "the technicians. There is no third party."[20] On one side are the "parasites" who squander; on the other, those who promote technoscientific efficiency. Veblen's most familiar concept, "conspicuous consumption," means also "conspicuous waste," which functions "to absorb any increase in . . . industrial efficiency or output of goods, after the most elementary physical wants have been provided for."[21]

In Veblen's *Theory of the Leisure Class,* as Theodor Adorno puts it, "Leisure and waste are granted their rights, but only 'aesthetically'; as economist Veblen will have nothing to do with them" ("Veblen's Attack on Culture," 84). In other words, while Veblen insists on the centrality of leisure, luxury, and waste to modern capitalism, he does so through the lens of techno-rationality, including the values of efficiency, "industry," and "the instinct for workmanship." The result is a necessary disjuncture between rational method and irrational subject that helps produce his "corrosive sarcasm."[22] Repeatedly, Veblen tries to give his key terms, including "waste," "conspicuous consumption," and "pecuniary emulation," a technical significance to pry them loose from their moralizing connotations, but his very choice of these terms makes him, as Adorno recognizes, as much satirist as scientist.[23]

Veblen voiced many of the concerns that other "progressives" and socialists of his era expressed. He did not agree with William Graham Sumner, under whom he studied economics at Yale, that success in business indicated Darwinian "fitness" in the struggle for life, but perhaps he did agree with Sumner's 1885 pamphlet *Protectionism: The Ism That Teaches That Waste Makes Wealth.* He certainly agreed with Henry Demarest Lloyd, who, in his 1894 exposé of the Standard Oil Company, *Wealth against Commonwealth,* wrote, "The man who should apply in his family or in his citizenship this 'survival of the fittest' theory as it is practically professed and operated in business would be a monster, and would be speedily made extinct."[24] According to Louis Filler, *Wealth against Commonwealth* "can be regarded as the first muckraking book" (26), and *Theory of the Leisure Class* belongs in the same genre—a text exposing the fallaciousness of modern social arrangements, including the production and squandering of wealth during America's "Gilded Age." *Theory of the Leisure Class* and Veblen's other books and essays were written with the same moral vision and intensity as many contemporary realistic novels, which portrayed the lifestyles of the rich as vacuous ostentation and "pecuniary emulation"—William Dean Howells's *The Rise of Silas Lapham* (1885), for example, or Edith Wharton's *House of Mirth* (1905).[25]

Like Veblen, earlier economists tried to restrict or eliminate this moralizing strain from their supposedly scientific discourse. Unlike Veblen, however, they often wound up with a "hedonistic calculus" that reduced all values to prices, and economic motivations to a utilitarian psychology that was both one-dimensional and unfathomable (whatever gives anyone pleasure is valuable, for whatever reason). In the 1870s, William Stanley Jevons, theorizer of marginal utility and, hence, of consumer society, struck the first word from the traditional phrase "political economy" while helping mathematize economics.[26] But economics obviously kept its critical—political and moralizing—edge in socialist thinkers, including Veblen, although his socialism, like that of H. G. Wells, was highly idiosyncratic. And even orthodox economics moralized in its popular versions, as in Samuel Smiles's 1875 *Thrift:* "Extravagance is the pervading sin of modern society. It is not confined to the rich and moneyed classes, but extends also to the middle and working classes" (252). Veblen might have added to this proposition that, when the lower classes practice "extravagance," they do so because of "emulation," which—like Antonio Gramsci's concept of hegemony—helps explain why those classes do not rebel against "the leisure class."

Veblen recognizes that economic processes are not the rational, efficient, progress machine that the early economists and Smiles posited. Even Marx, Veblen notes, through his materialist version of Hegelianism, treats economic history as a progressive teleology. Both capitalist economics and Hegelian/Marxist dialectics install a thin rationality at the heart of history—a rationality that, according to Veblen, Darwinism eliminates: "The evolutionary point of view . . . leaves no place for a formulation of natural laws in terms of definitive normality."[27] The end—

goal, but also meaning or value—of any evolutionary sequence is never predetermined by any version of progressive teleology.

Adam Smith's belief in the "invisible hand" that regulates markets is typical of early economists' tendency to treat economies as rational progress machines. This was, according to Veblen, a secular version of "natural theology."[28] In contrast, Veblen recognizes that economies cannot be isolated from their societies and cultures—that they are inextricably bound with values, processes, and institutions that, from the viewpoint of both the classical economists and Marx, are neither rational nor predictable. For Veblen, moreover, the main psychological force underlying capitalism is not the profit motive, the utilitarians' pleasure principle, or rational self-interest, but "emulation," "the strongest and most alert and persistent of the economic motives proper": "In an industrial community this propensity for emulation expresses itself in pecuniary emulation; and this, so far as regards the Western civilised communities of the present, is virtually equivalent to saying that it expresses itself in some form of conspicuous waste."[29] According to Veblen, there is something "invidious" to begin with about "ownership" and "property." Property did not derive in the first instance from the need to settle and cultivate land, as Locke believed, but from "predation" and war. Including women and slaves, "property set out with being booty held as trophies of the successful raid," Veblen writes; it follows that "the motive that lies at the root of ownership is emulation" (*Theory of the Leisure Class*, 27, 25). He continues: "Ownership began and grew into a human institution on grounds unrelated to the subsistence minimum. The dominant incentive was from the outset the invidious distinction attaching to wealth, and . . . no other motive has usurped the primacy at any later stage of development" (ibid., 26). In short, although civilization has entered a "quasi-peaceable" stage of cultural evolution, "barbarism" has continued into the modern, industrial, capitalist era in the semi-tame but nevertheless "predatory" form of the "leisure class" itself.

The barbarian leisure class acts as a drag on progress: "The office of the leisure class in social evolution is to retard the movement [forward] and to conserve what is obsolescent"[30] and, of course, both obsolescence and the retardation of progress name two more types of waste. Veblen includes both hereditary aristocracies and bourgeois nouveaux riches in the modern leisure class, both acting as brakes on democracy as well as on industrial efficiency and progress. The businessman, too, belongs to this wasteful category; contrary to some social Darwinists, such as Sumner and Herbert Spencer, the businessman's financial success does not mean he is "fittest" to survive in "the struggle for existence." Veblen had no doubt that "The life of man in society is a struggle for existence."[31] But the members of the leisure class, whose barbarian ancestors were fit enough, have come to be "sheltered" from economic necessity. Businessmen still live by "predation," however, practicing "chicane" rather than conquest to profit from the labor and intelligence of others. In so doing, they contribute to the unfitness of capitalist society to survive.

If businessmen indulge in "conspicuous consumption" and "pecuniary emulation" in their private lives, they also engage in wasteful behaviors on the production side of the ledger. According to Veblen, "sabotage" is practiced by management as well as workers; the term refers to any activity that impedes productivity. To maintain profitability by limiting supply, businessmen regularly throw economic monkey wrenches into the machinery.[32] Obviously, too, any enterprise that produces and sells goods for "conspicuous consumption" is "parasitic" on the community at large. Advertising is an example, as are "competitive selling" and war. Such activities undermine the society that engages in them: "A disproportionate growth of parasitic industries, such as most advertising and much of the other efforts that go into competitive selling, as well as warlike expenditure and other industries directed to turning out goods for conspicuously wasteful consumption, would lower the effective vitality of the community to such a degree as to jeopardize its chances of advance or even its life."[33]

Once production exceeds necessity, fashion in food, clothing, and shelter comes to the fore as an essential element of capitalism. According to sociologist Jukka Gronow, fashion is "a typical form of waste." Citing Veblen, Gronow adds that fashion "leads to a faster exhaustion of products: when the style is out of fashion, the product is useless even if it is still in perfect condition" (*The Sociology of Taste,* 40). And with fashion in commodities, the importance of consumer "taste" emerges. Veblen maintains that there is an innate faculty of judgment or taste for the beautiful but that, in modern "pecuniary culture," genuine taste is almost never separable from a vulgar, wasteful preference for "expensiveness," whether beautiful or not: "The marks of expensiveness come to be accepted as beautiful features of the expensive articles" (*Theory of the Leisure Class*,130). In everyday practice, in short, taste is no different from "invidious distinction," which amounts to saying that taste makes waste.

For Veblen, "emulation" and "the law of conspicuous waste" (*Theory of the Leisure Class*,116) apply to most areas of modern culture and society. Besides the consuming parasitism of "the leisure class," there is the annoying wastefulness involved in snobbism, whereby the middle and even lower classes struggle not just to make ends meet but also to emulate the "leisure class," typically by spending beyond their means. In the area of "devout observances," moreover, Veblen sees nothing but "conspicuous consumption" and waste at work (ibid., 293–331). He says he is not talking about religion as such but only about clerical and liturgical fashions; yet he points to modern "animism" as an "archaic" remnant of barbarian belief, and he cannot resist including a paragraph on saints and angels as members of "a superhuman vicarious leisure class" (ibid., 317). Nor do secular culture and "the higher learning" come off any better—that is to say, any less wastefully. As he would later do in *The Higher Learning in America* (1918), Veblen treats colleges and universities as having fallen under the "pecuniary" spell of "the leisure class." This has led to much wasteful expenditure of time and energy on such useless topics as dead languages and "the classics," while the useful sciences have languished. And rivaling the classics as "honorific," sports—"not only a waste of time, but also a waste of money"—have begun to take "primacy in leisure-class education" (ibid., 397). Veblen considers, however, that sports and other competitive leisure activities are less wasteful of life and property than the barbarian practice of war. Thus, in modern "peaceable" conditions, "chicane" replaces "devastation," though "only in an uncertain degree" (ibid., 240).

For Veblen, Darwinian fitness accords with the values he most clearly approves: scientific rationality, efficiency, and industry, which he equates with (potential) social progress. However, the evolutionary model conceals a contradiction. Certainly, evolution is productive, but is it thrifty and efficient like the steam engine or the dynamo? On the contrary, evolution in nature is enormously prodigal—Darwin's famous "tangled bank"—and so it is also in capitalist society. "Veblen demonstrates that society functions uneconomically in terms of its own criteria," Adorno writes ("Veblen's Attack on Culture," 84); in doing so, he demonstrates also the failure of earlier economic discourse to comprehend the central-ity of the forms of wasteful prodigality it had underestimated or con-demned. Thus, Veblen agrees with Marx's analysis of capitalism as prog-ress and catastrophe together, or as "creative destruction."

H. G. WELLS AND DON DELILLO

From the 1850s on, numerous novelists in Britain as well as America ex-pressed versions of Veblen's theme of conspicuous consumption while suggesting that wealth and waste were in some sense identical, or at least opposite sides of the same coin. Thus, in *Our Mutual Friend*, Charles Dickens makes the equation between wealth and waste explicit in Boffin's valuable mountain of "dust" or garbage. And the shady financier Merdle in *Little Dorrit* and Anthony Trollope's equally shady Augustus Melmotte in *The Way We Live Now* reveal how fraudulent forms of money and credit can be simultaneously wealth-begetting and wasteful. Both Merdle and Melmotte are forerunners of Veblen's businessmen and financiers, who rake in money from industry without doing anything genuinely produc-tive themselves. They are also forerunners of H. G. Wells's Teddy Pon-derevo, inventor and huckster of the quack medicine "Tono-Bungay."

Like Veblen, Wells sought to synthesize Darwinism and socialism through what he called "evolutionary speculation."[34] Veblen hoped "the instinct of workmanship," embodied in engineers and technicians, might one day free society from the barbaric customs, including war, of the leisure class; Wells hoped science and industrial efficiency would release humankind "more and more from the stranglehold of past things," leading to a future utopia under a pacific world government (*Experiment*, 2:648). Standing in the way of genuine progress was a capitalism that, through its false forms of productivity (making money from nothing, from "parasit-ism," or from shoddy goods), threatened to squander any chance for a ra-tional outcome of history. In Wells's most ambitious novel, *Tono-Bungay*, a sweeping portrait of society in the panoramic style of Dickens and Trol-lope, waste is the central theme—indeed, Wells thought of that term as an alternative title for his "condition-of-England novel." Wells shares with Veblen a desire to see something redeeming and rational emerge from the wasteland of consumer society, like the order and efficiency he advocated in his nonfiction books.[35] But just as for Veblen, biological imperatives and the indeterminacy of evolution threaten to undermine his hopes for the future (see Morton, *The Vital Science*). And to evolution, Wells added the also threatening idea of entropy.

By the end of the century, novelists and intellectuals had begun to associate entropy—the inevitable wasting away of energy, as indicated by the Second Law of Thermodynamics—with both the squandering of wealth and the "degeneration" of traditional conceptions of cultural and moral value under the impact of capitalism and the arrival on the political and economic scene of "the masses." For many turn-of-the-century intellectuals, the masses were Malthus's specter of illiterate, overpopulating paupers now equipped with the vote, with half-educations, and with money to throw away on vulgar entertainments and tawdry goods.[36] Among fin de siècle British writers who take up these issues, none is closer to Veblen in his alertness to the complicities and contradictions between wealth and waste than Wells, who is also one of the first novelists to make entropy a major theme.[37]

In *Tono-Bungay*, Wells captures many of the features of a wasteful, leisure-class culture. The novel depicts an ostensibly progressive story of capitalist entrepreneurship and "self help." The narrator and protagonist, George Ponderevo, recounts his rise from a lower-middle-class, provincial background. After squandering his early promise as a scientist, George is hired by his Uncle Teddy to help produce and market Tono-Bungay, a patent medicine that, for a while, is hugely successful. As an entrepreneur, Uncle Teddy embodies the characteristics that Veblen ascribed to businessmen in general. Veblen's entrepreneurs are "simply supersalesmen," as Daniel Aaron puts it; "adepts at getting something for nothing . . . 'sabotagers' of industrial productiveness," parasites who succeed by "exploiting mass credulity" (*Men of Good Hope*, 223).

Uncle Teddy associates what he is doing with America. "'I wish to heaven,'" he tells his nephew, "'I'd been born in America—where things hum'" (72). This is the America—and Britain—of entrepreneurial hype and financial bluff. Uncle Teddy's "passage from trade to finance" (225) reveals his increasing distance from any genuine productivity. He admits, "'I'd like to know what sort of trading isn't a swindle in its way. Everybody who does a large advertised trade is selling something common on the strength of saying it's uncommon'" (144). Reflecting on the fraudulent business practices he and his uncle engage in, George frequently sounds like Veblen; toward the end of the novel, he acknowledges, "I and my uncle were no more than specimens of a modern species of brigand, wasting the savings of the public out of the sheer wantonness of enterprise" (399). Mainly through advertising, George and his uncle quickly become rich, but just as rapidly the bubble bursts and their financial empire collapses— a rise and fall that follows an entropic pattern infusing the narrative and, Wells believed, history itself.[38] Embedded within this entropic pattern are various forms of waste, which are all symptomatic of a rotten society and the wasting away at the heart of the British Empire. The chief emblem of this waste is the patent medicine Tono-Bungay, a commodity—which George derisively calls "mitigated water"—whose value is created by hype and marketing rather than any actual utility. While there is little or no "conspicuous consumption" in buying it, the patent medicine is a symbol for the generative power of capitalism, which can produce wealth from wishful thinking. Soon, Uncle Teddy diversifies by producing and marketing Tono-Bungay Hair Stimulant, Tono-Bungay Mouthwash, Tono-Bungay Lozenges, and Tono-Bungay Chocolates. George concludes, however, that "he created nothing, he invented nothing, he economised nothing," while adding no "real value to human life at all" (237). Through advertising, Uncle Teddy is able to transform Marx's general formula for capital, M-C-M, into a formula for capitalizing on waste, M-W-M, "in which waste provides the middle term for capital's reproduction."[39]

For George, the chief ethical dilemma is that he knows from the outset that Tono-Bungay is worthless. For Uncle Teddy, however, that is exactly the point: "the quickest way to get wealth," he claims, "is to sell the cheapest thing possible in the dearest bottle" (149). The patent medicine's value derives from illusion. Its promotion is financed by the penniless uncle by playing investors "off one against the other" (141); in their scramble for wealth, they are eager to invest in the next new thing even if it is worthless. For the consumers of Tono-Bungay, Uncle Teddy claims that faith is all that his customer's desire, a faith that "makes trade! . . . A romantic exchange of commodities and property. Romance. 'Magination" (145). Even George's bohemian friend, Ewart, sees the patent medicine as "poetry" created by advertising, a fantasy pursued by its purchasers who wish to be "perpetually young and beautiful." "You are artists," he says of George and his uncle: "The old merchant used to tote about commodities; the new one creates values. He takes something that isn't worth anything

... and he makes it worth something" (168–69). Or as Veblen puts it, once "business" has divorced itself from "industry," its "realities" become mere "money-values, that is to say matters of make-believe. . . . The business man's care is to create needs to be satisfied at a price paid to himself."[40]

Indeed, Tono-Bungay does produce wealth, leisure, and opportunity. Even its purchasers who are apparently throwing their money away gain, as Ewart claims, a faith or illusion that may have a value of its own. But for George, the fortune and power gained not just through Tono-Bungay, but through capitalism more generally "is all one spectacle of forces running to waste, of people who use and do not replace, the story of a country hectic with a wasting aimless fever of trade and money-making and pleasure-seeking" (412). Uncle Teddy, for example, converts much of his wealth into a wildly wasteful instance of conspicuous consumption. In an ironically titled chapter, "Our Progress," George gives the reader a tour through a series of houses purchased and built by Uncle Teddy, each one bigger and more spectacular than the last. One implication is that everything is up for sale, including England's tradition-bound country estates. His uncle becomes, George claims, part of "that multitude of economically ascendant people who are learning to spend money." He continues, "They plunge, as one plunges into a career; as a class, they talk, think, and dream possessions" (264–65). Like garbage, they "stink" of money (266).

Houses, however, have a relative permanence that runs counter to the riot of wasteful expenditure and consumption that Wells depicts. Architecture slows the circulation of money and commodities and, in that sense, undermines the dematerialized workings of capitalist productivity and prodigality. Accordingly, the beginning of the end of the Tono-Bungay financial empire lies in Uncle Teddy's final, unfinished architectural project, Crest Hill, a "twentieth-century house" that "grew, and bubbled like a salted snail, and burgeoned and bulged and evermore grew" (292). Like the Back Bay mansion that Silas Lapham builds in Howells's novel, Crest Hill is a marvel of ostentation, only far more so. "Sooner or later," George declares, "modern financiers of chance and bluff . . . all seem to bring their luck to the test of realisation, try to make their fluid opulence coagulate out as bricks and mortar, bring moonshine into relations with a weekly wages-sheet. Then the whole fabric of confidence and imagination totters—and down they come" (294). According to this logic, the value of conspicuous consumption, including its use of signs that stand in for wealth, is diminished if overly materialized or preserved. At the same time, Wells suggests that the genuine wealth and cultural value identified with that which has a certain material solidity and permanence, such as Bladesover, the traditional country house that George contrasts to Crest Hill, have been changed beyond recognition.

The deceptive nature of material possessions is further illustrated by a subplot late in the novel. To recoup their financial losses, George and his uncle engage in another ill-conceived venture: to convert "quap," a rare radioactive mineral found on a West African island, into much-needed cash. George travels to the island where he quite gratuitously shoots and kills a "native"—wasting a life. When George tries to sail back to England with a load of quap—after a trip that replicates the imperial violence of resource extraction in, for example, King Leopold's Congo—the radio-active cargo eats through the hull, sinking the ship. The quap episode signals a dark turn in the narrative, an apparent speeding-up of entropic processes, and provides a stunning figure for George's loss of faith in human progress; in the final analysis, George thinks, human endeavors will all lead to "no splendid climax and finale, no towering accumulation of achievements but just—atomic decay!" (355). Like Tono-Bungay, quap may be potentially of immense value, yet it also epitomizes the waste and decay that Wells sees at work in capitalist modernity.

Nevertheless, however much Wells attempts to make waste carry the weight of his critique, it constantly threatens to transform itself into something valuable. This is evident in the novel's representation of the consumers of Tono-Bungay—the masses. From time to time Wells, like Malthus, intimated that certain populations were superfluous, and, in *Anticipations,* he even advocated the extermination of "countless, need-less, and unhappy lives" through "the euthanasia of the weak" (303–8; and see chapter 11). George describes London as "the unorganised, abundant substance of some tumorous growth-process, a process which indeed bursts all the outlines of the affected carcass and protrudes such masses as ignoble comfortable Croydon, as tragic impoverished West Ham." The masses and the suburbs are a cancer on the body politic.[41] "Will those masses ever become structural," George asks, "will they indeed shape into anything new whatever, or is that cancerous image their true and ultimate diagnosis?" (109). But waste, like the wealth and abundance generated from Tono-Bungay, can simultaneously be valuable. However diseased and useless, the masses and the city they inhabit are also described by George in stimulating, desirable terms. Shortly after the passage about the cancerous masses, George asserts that London was "so enlarging and broadening. . . . The whole illimitable place teemed with suggestions of indefinite and sometimes outrageous possibility, of hidden but magnificent meanings" (113).

So, too, at the end of his story, after describing the novel's manuscript as an incoherent "heap" and after deciding that he is himself an embodiment of "decay," George nevertheless claims that "something comes out of" the "crumbling and confusion, of change and seemingly aimless swelling, of [the] bubbling up and medley of futile loves and sorrows" (419). Even when describing a romantic affair following his failed marriage, George vacillates between seeing love as wasteful and as somehow precious: "Love . . . is a thing adrift, a fruitless thing broken away from its connections . . . [but] it glows in my memory like some bright casual flower starting up amidst the debris of a catastrophe" (403). George would have us believe that everything fits into his entropic vision of eventual, total destruction, and yet each of these examples points to something of value in the midst of "catastrophe." "Something comes out of" the waste and wreckage of modern capitalism, including George's own growing self-knowledge and maturation.

The novel expresses Wells's reflections on waste and value, but it is also itself, as cultural commodity, a form of both waste and value. Its value resides in part in its critique of the other forms of waste and entropy it depicts, but, in the last chapter, George asserts that he should have called his manuscript *Waste* (412). Moreover, the novel regularly exhibits its failure and anti-progressiveness in diegetic terms. For a narrator who identifies himself as a technically inclined positivist similar to Veblen, George exhibits a surprising enthusiasm for describing the illusions of advertising, mass cultural forms, and "pecuniary emulation." He frequently also falls into various attitudes of aimlessness and indecision; even his futuristic experiments with airplanes are mostly dilettantish. George's life gains an ironic value, however, when his technical interests lead him finally to invent new munitions and war machines, expressing something like Veblen's high valuations of efficiency, engineering, and "industrial workmanship." Both Wells and Veblen, however, placed the machines of war in the immense and growing category of waste. At the very end of his story,

George sails into the future having achieved the critical and ideological distance necessary to write his novel (and then to reject it as "waste"). But the cost of gaining both self-knowledge and critical objectivity about the general wastefulness of capitalism and human history is his militarized self at the helm of his experimental "X2 Destroyer," itself a product of modern industrial know-how and super-utility that can and presumably will inflict the ultimate "wasting" on whatever it targets.

A century after Veblen and Wells, the value of many commodities and patterns of economic and social behavior continues to be bound inextricably with their wasteful and often fantastic features.[42] E-money has accelerated the apparently entropic process by which waste and value have become increasingly interchangeable. Derivatives, junk bonds, toxic assets, bankruptcies, and foreclosed homes, leading to the 2007 economic crash, exacerbate the postmodern profusion and confusion of waste and value. Arthur Kroker and Michael Weinstein have identified postmodern "excremental culture" as "a waste-management system . . . a vast plumbing machine for managing the discharge of image effluents." Some postmodern industries, moreover, now treat waste products as so many "resources out of place."[43] In an age that Zygmunt Bauman describes as "liquid modernity," though nothing seems valuable, nothing is allowed to be valueless.[44] Today, there is money, and a lot of it, to be extracted from waste, whether through its reclamation (recycling) or through trying to deep-six it like Wells's sunken quap. Simultaneously, in postmodern culture, the value of waste proliferates as a metaphor for that which eludes a rationalized, instrumentalized utility. In DeLillo's *Underworld*, for example, the central character, Nick Shay, is a waste-management expert. On assignment early in the narrative, he visits the recently closed Fresh Kills landfill on Staten Island:

> He looked at all that soaring garbage and knew for the first time what his job was all about. Not engineering or transportation or source reduction. He dealt in human behavior, people's habits and impulses, their uncontrollable needs and innocent wishes, maybe their passions, certainly their excesses and indulgences but their kindnesses too, their generosity, and the question was how to keep this mass metabolism from overwhelming us. (185)

At one level, like Wells's novel, *Underworld* is a tale of hypercapitalism, of consumption and superabundance as an engine of desire and excess that ultimately produces mountains of trash. As Ruth Helyer puts it, the novel "demonstrates the problems, not only of disposing of waste, but of identifying waste in the first place" ("'Refuse heaped many stories high,'" 987). But as with Wells's treatment of entropy, it also expresses a theory of history that allows DeLillo to embrace rather than completely reject the logic of waste. Radioactive waste, like Wells's quap, is one of the categories that most concerns DeLillo. Although the threat of ultimate annihilation hovers in the wings, DeLillo's waste-management expert nevertheless reads garbage's irreducible materiality as the price of the ineffability and ordinariness of human activity, as though waste signifies unquantifiable and obscure features of existence, such as passions, habits, impulses, and excesses—perhaps even priceless experiences that no amount of money can buy.[45] "Maybe we feel a reverence for waste," Nick says, "for the redemptive qualities of the things we use and discard" (809). Quoting this remark, Todd McGowan comments: "In *Underworld,* waste is everywhere, and it has become holy" (124).

From the standpoint of capitalist economics and of the writers cited here, there is nothing, not even waste, that is not potentially valuable or value-producing. The production of value is also wasteful, and there is nothing valuable that is not potentially wasteful or waste-producing. Nor are the paradoxical linkages between waste and value merely the result of natural cycles of growth and decay. They arise in large measure because, like an empty bottle of Tono-Bungay, the concept of value at the heart of capitalist economics is hollow, a container waiting to be filled by whatever individual agents—producers or consumers—wish to put in it, whether gold dust or quack medicine. In this regard, Veblen's critique of economic orthodoxy as merely a "hedonistic calculus" is correct. Like money and debt, value and waste are two ends of a spectrum that—today more than ever, when waste management has become big business and shopping or consumption-as-usual is touted as how the average American can best wage the war on terror—forms a closed circle.

PART TWO

POSTMODERN CONDITIONS

SEVEN

Shopping on Red Alert: The Rhetorical Normalization of Terror

Terror has long been terrible: but to the actors themselves it has
now become manifest that their appointed course is one of Terror;
and they say, Be it so. "Que la Terreur soit à l'ordre du jour."

—THOMAS CARLYLE, *THE FRENCH REVOLUTION* (1837)

Waiting for my flight, I hear the announcement: "The Department of
Homeland Security has just raised the terror threat level to orange. Be on
the lookout for any suspicious activity." The girl drinking pop has purple
streaks in her hair. A suit-and-tie man reads *The Wall Street Journal.* A
woman in fringed leather jacket yaks at her cell phone. The only suspicious character may be the pale young man with the backpack pacing
nervously near the counter. Why so nervous? Suddenly he returns my
stare. Am I suspicious? Going through security, they seized my toothpaste. My miniscule tube weighed 2.5 ounces (or less). "This needs to be
in a plastic bag," said the guard; "If you want it back. . . ." "Never mind;
I'll buy some when I get there." I did not ask why my toothpaste would
be safer in a plastic bag.

In the hotel gift shop, I paid six dollars for a giant tube of Crest—the
only size they had. Because I could not take it on the flight home, I left
it for the maid. Are toothpaste sales skyrocketing? I tried to think about
the relationship between toothpaste and terrorism; I could not think of
any. However, during a press conference on October 11, 2001, President
Bush (W) advised,

> The American people have got to go about their business. We cannot let the terrorists achieve the objective of frightening our nation to the point where we don't—where we don't conduct business, where people don't shop.[1]

This was hardly Franklin Delano Roosevelt's "the only thing we have to fear is fear itself." It was instead one of many occasions when W's rhetoric, wittingly or otherwise, worked to normalize terror. For W and the Bush-ites, the standard message was this: despite the U.S. military's "shock and awe" response to 9/11, we may never be able to let down our guard against our shadowy new enemies—"the terrorists," whoever they are. But we can still shop (unless we drop).[2]

FIRE SALES

No one doubts that, since 9/11, "terror" has become "the order of the day." Massive, terrifying military power has been deployed—far beyond anything "the terrorists" can muster—to ensure that it has. "Orwellian 'Bushspeak,'" of course, attributes terrorism entirely to the other side.[3] Meanwhile, not just W-speak but the rhetoric of the mass media and of many other politicians and governments, including un-American ones (Russia's, for example), renders terror routine, the "new normalcy." Government is no different from shopping, equally terrorized. About his "Master Terror Watch List," Attorney General John Ashcroft said in 2003 that it would "provide one-stop shopping" for the feds.[4] According to terrorism expert Charles Kegley, "Crisis, the Chinese proverb maintains, comprises both danger and opportunity. The opportunity before us is to understand the character of the new threats and to deal with them in ways that allow the world to adjust to the 'new normalcy' of life in the midst of fear" (*The New Global Terrorism*, 2). Perhaps Kegley does not really mean that the purpose of understanding "the new threats" is not to eliminate terrorism, but merely to help people adjust to "fear" as part of the "'new normalcy'" (a phrase he puts in scare quotes, without citing a source). Nevertheless, he adds, "This fear now *is* normal. Terror and the chronic threat it arouses have become constants" (3). Here, too, Kegley's word-ing is oddly topsy-turvy: isn't it the "chronic threat" of terrorist attacks that arouses "terror," rather than the other way around? But in current parlance, "chronic threat" and "terror" are apparently synonymous, as are "terrorism" and "terror." Kegley's language is characteristic of the tautological discourse of terror that has become normal since 9/11. We are repeatedly said to be terrified by "terror" itself, with or without help from "the terrorists."

The elision of "terrorism" and "terror" is symptomatic of how the Bushites seized on 9/11 as, in W's words, an "opportunity to strengthen America."[5] "Terrorism" is not routine, but "terror" can be. If the aim of the Bush regime was to frighten us so that we would change our political if not our business or shopping habits, how is that different from the aim of the terrorists? To instill fear in the minds of the populations they target is one terrorist objective, and they have succeeded—so the rhetoric of terror implies. Some business habits, moreover, have changed. Toothpaste sales may have gone up, like duct tape sales during the anthrax scare; but in the wake of 9/11, air travel plummeted (so to speak), and a number of airlines declared bankruptcy. A whole new "fear industry" emerged, including such outfits as ChoicePoint, which became "the largest personal database company in America," ready to snoop where the FBI, CIA, and NSA legally cannot.[6] And there are the private security firms like Blackwater (now Xe); in Iraq, mercenaries employed by such firms made up the second largest force after the U.S. military.[7]

Apart from the rise of Islamic "jihadism," 9/11, and the invasions of Afghanistan and Iraq, is anything new about the supposedly new normalization of terror? Perhaps its mass-mediation since the introduction of television in the 1950s is its most novel feature.Certainly terrorism is not new. Nor are "weapons of mass destruction" and their use, even by non-state terrorists. During the Nazi nightmare, Walter Benjamin declared that, for "the oppressed," history is always "a state of emergency." That is the case today for Afghans, Iraqis, Somalis, Tibetans, and millions of others in the impoverished and embattled "failed states" of the world.[8] But in the United States' shining "city on the hill"? Citing Benjamin, Michael Taussig writes, "In talking terror's talk are we ourselves not tempted to absorb and conceal the violence in our own immediate life-worlds, in our universities, workplaces, streets, shopping malls, and even families, where, like business, it's terror as usual?" ("Terror as Usual," 4). Taussig stresses the violence and terror that permeate everyday life, though these are not unique to our era. What is unique is "terror's talk," the rhetorical overkill that, in the guise of warning the public about the supposedly new "chronic threat," treats terror as foreign, assailing us from abroad, and therefore ironically as extraordinary, something entirely novel in our lives. As ideological mystification, nothing works better to conceal the ordinary terror of everyday life than the notion of the supposedly alien terror that attacks us out of the blue—while we are shopping or just going about our business.

Besides telling us to keep on shopping, W also advised Americans to be suspicious of our neighbors—everywhere around us, terrorists may be "lurking." If we are suspicious of our neighbors, moreover, they will be suspicious of us.[9] And why not? After all, it is now normal to have your toothpaste seized at airports, your shoes x-rayed, and your travels through the aisles of your local Wal-Mart videotaped, because, no matter how unafraid you are, you may be somebody other people should fear. Though you know you are just a shopper and not a terrorist, how can we tell you are not? Prove it. What books have *you* checked out from your library lately? We are all plenty scared (or told we are)—look out especially for people with dark complexions and foreign accents, even in your local Wal-Mart (they may be temps, however, rather than terrorists).

Instead of treating terrorism as exceptional and, even after 9/11, not nearly so lethal to ordinary Americans as traffic accidents, smoking, or bee stings, the rhetoric of the Bush regime and the press rendered "terror" pervasive and downright homey, though coming from abroad (we are peaceful; they are not—and they are right on our doorsteps). The title of the new "Department of Homeland Security" sounds like a unit in Sears or Macys, while also suggesting that what it aims to defend us against— terrorism? terror? or just insecurity?—has come home to roost. Further, one obvious indication that terror is now like shopping or the weather is Homeland Security's color-coded terror alerts. They are, of course, terrorism alerts; but they are usually called terror alerts. The terrorists do not have to strike again to keep the country in a state of red or orange alert: Homeland Security will do that for us, thank you. Like hailstorms or hurricanes, moreover, supposedly the terrorists may go on attacking forever, but with ups and downs, just like barometer readings. Whether the terror alerts are as accurate as weather forecasts is beside the point; they do not need to be accurate to demonstrate that terror (we are told) now permeates every facet of daily life. And that is just the point: a ter- rorized public is a docile one, willing to accept whatever the government says will protect us from even bigger doses of terror—so let's take our umbrellas and go shopping before the mall explodes.[10]

W's "war on terror" also helped normalize terror as the new national emotion (if there was a national emotion before 9/11, perhaps it was happiness, as in "life, liberty, and the pursuit of happiness"). Both the Bushites and the media seized on the notion that 9/11 was a "new Pearl Harbor" and that it might be the start of World War III. In contrast to the American and "coalition-of-the-willing" forces that invaded Afghanistan and Iraq, however, the enemy military was difficult to identify and, as in the case of 9/11, self-destroying. W himself acknowledged, "These people don't have tanks. They don't have ships. They hide in caves. They send suiciders out."[11] Except for the U.S. invasions, "war" seems hyperbolic, as does "jihad."

Moreover, as with "terror alert," what should be called the "war on terrorism" is typically shortened to the "war on terror." Thus, prematurely announcing "mission accomplished" on the deck of the USS *Abraham Lincoln* (May 1, 2003), W declared, "The battle of Iraq is one victory in a war on terror that began on September the 11th, 2001 and still goes on."[12] Folks, it is not just terrorism we are fighting: it is terror itself, the greatest bogeyman of all. Besides, since all wars are terrifying, any "war on terror" is over before it begins—this second tautology suggests that such a conflict produces the very thing it seeks to combat. How do you allay or defeat terror, an emotion all normal humans are equipped to feel on terrifying occasions, while the mass media are constantly blaring, like air-raid sirens, that your country is waging war against that phantasmatic but universal (normal) emotion? It is possible to catch or kill a terrorist, but not terror.

The semantic difference between "terrorism" and "terror" may seem insignificant, but, in statement after statement by the Bushites and the media, "terror" is treated as routine. For many reasons, terror*ism* cannot be routine. One is that it aims to disrupt routines, and another is that the Bushites need to claim they are effectively waging war against it. Yet terror (we are told) pervades the very air we breathe. The rhetoric of terror shoves aside all other issues—the economy, the environment, education, health care, corporate and political scandals. Yet both the international and the domestic measures to combat terrorism have been more about public relations than about actually protecting the public. Thus, in *The Terrorism Trap*, Michael Parenti writes,

Many of the measures taken to "fight terrorism" have little to do with actual security and are public relations ploys designed to (a) heighten the nation's siege psychology and (b) demonstrate that the government has things under control. Hours after the September 11 attacks, the US Navy deployed aircraft carriers off the coast of New York to "guard the city," as if a mass invasion were in the offing. National guardsmen . . . armed with automatic weapons patrolled the airports. Flights were canceled until further notice. Sidewalk baggage check-ins and electronic tickets were prohibited for a time, all supposedly to create greater security.[13]

One can add to Parenti's list numerous items such as warrantless wiretapping and seizing unbagged toothpaste. The Bushites were upset when the wiretapping was leaked to the media, but the leak did not hurt the general cause of persuading the public that a massive, shadowy struggle is going on, right here in the "homeland," between the terror cops and terror. Yet adequate measures to improve port security, to protect nuclear power plants, and to stop the Chinese from importing toxic toys and pet food have not been taken. Meanwhile, Hurricane Katrina demonstrated how unprepared government at any level is to handle a new emergency—to those who were injured, killed, or rendered homeless by that perfect storm, a disaster every bit as terrifying as 9/11.

CAN'T SHOP? TRY LOOTING

In Katrina's wake, there was not much shopping going on in New Orleans. But according to the media, looting was, and it seemed to be just as big a deal as the flooding. For awhile, looting out-headlined the bungling of relief by W, FEMA, and on down the governmental ladder to the cops, including several cops who shot unarmed black people. After 9/11, we—or rather, Afghanistan and Iraq—got "shock and awe," which we got to watch on TV. After Katrina, the mostly black victims got nothing (if they did not get shot); we also got to watch them on TV struggling with the flood and the nonrelief. "Brownie, you're doing a heck of a job," W told the bungler in charge of FEMA.[14] Why were the responses by W and his minions to 9/11 (shock-and-awe) and Katrina (bungling) so dramatically different? The hurricane killed 1,800 people, more than half the number of people who died in the World Trade Center. But Katrina destroyed most of New Orleans and disrupted tens of thousands of lives. By the beginning of 2007, when this essay was written, over half of the former residents remained "in exile," and many of these had been "evicted from emergency housing" in Baton Rouge, Houston, and elsewhere.[15] New York City survived 9/11—shopping went on there as usual; it was not clear, three years after the hurricane, that New Orleans had survived.[16]

There are two main reasons that the Bush regime reacted swiftly and with full military force to 9/11 and then reacted so ineptly to the devastation of New Orleans. One is "the military-industrial complex," our own enormous terror machinery. America is the country with by far the most weapons of mass destruction, and besides using them in Afghanistan, Iraq, and elsewhere, it does a regular business peddling them to the "failed states" who shop for them.[17] If you want to buy missiles, bombers, or tanks, the United States has the edge on the market. In his 1961 farewell address, President Dwight Eisenhower warned America about the growing menace of the U.S. military and the defense industries. Ike knew that "the military-industrial complex," as he dubbed it, was already influencing far too many aspects of American politics and economics. Rather than heeding Ike's warning, W and his neoconservative henchmen viewed 9/11 as their chance to call the American military and gut-level patriotism into action. Perhaps as part of his lame-duck effort to bring peace and democracy to the Middle East, W signed a deal in January 2008 to sell "state-of-the-art" weapons to Saudi Arabia for $20 billion.

The second reason for the different responses to 9/11 and Katrina is racism. Even before the Iranian hostage crisis of 1979, the American media regularly stereotyped Islam and people of Middle Eastern descent in negative terms. The Oklahoma City bombing in 1995 was immediately blamed on Islamic terrorists, even though the bomber was a disgruntled American veteran, Timothy McVeigh. A 1995 review by Fairness and Accuracy in Reporting noted that the mass media frequently speak of "Islamic violence," but never of "Christian violence" as in attacks on abortion clinics.[18] Films and TV programs often feature sinister Arabs or Muslims cooking up criminal plots; mainstream movies that offer sympathetic portrayals of Islamic characters are almost nonexistent. Needless to say, 9/11 has only increased the stereotypical association of Middle Easterners (minus Israelis) with terrorism.

One upshot of all the stereotyping has been an explosion of that old version of domestic terrorism—hate crimes. According to the FBI's annual reports, hate crimes aimed at mosques, Muslims, and people perceived as Middle-Eastern "spiked" after 9/11 and continue at much higher levels than before that tragic date. On July 9, 2005, a Molotov cocktail was thrown into the mosque in my usually peaceful hometown (Bloomington, Indiana), and six months later two bombs damaged a Cincinnati mosque, to cite just two of many incidents. The Council on American-Islamic Relations points out that hate crimes often go unreported because "victims do not dare go to the authorities." The crimes are compounded by official harassment: hostile cops and immigration agents, snoops in search of terrorists. Thousands have left the United States, seeking refuge in Canada or returning to Pakistan, Egypt, and elsewhere.[19]

Furthermore, most of the victims of Hurricane Katrina were African Americans. Many did not own cars and could not leave before the storm hit. Many also lived in the neighborhoods where the worst flooding occurred. As already noted, immediately after the storm, newscasts headlined rumors about black gangs looting and shooting other people. There was some looting and shooting, but much of it was done by the cops.[20] And Blackwater arrived before most federal agencies and charities, supposedly to help with relief efforts but actually to beef up security and prevent more looting. Its mercenaries were already patrolling the streets of "Baghdad on the Bayou" when Homeland Security hired them.[21] TV images of "looting, lawlessness, and chaos" were "racist and inflammatory," writes Jeremy Scahill in his study of Blackwater. "What was desperately needed was food, water, and housing. Instead what poured in fastest were guns. Lots of guns" (323).

Entire sections of New Orleans—poor, mainly black neighborhoods—may never recover, and public housing is being demolished. Though ACORN, Habitat for Humanity, and other nongovernmental organizations are helping low-income residents rebuild, government has been less than helpful. Many of the mainly white powers-that-be have seen the aftermath of Katrina as an opportunity to restore New Orleans without an African American underclass. As rapper Kanye West said, "George Bush does not care about black people." At least, W does not care about poor black people unless he and his cronies can find ways to keep them from voting. As the storm approached New Orleans, in New York City Condoleezza Rice went shoe shopping.[22]

While the mainstream media attended to looting in flooded New Orleans, the looting of Iraq has received very little attention. Oh, yes, there was something about the looting—presumably by Iraqis—of that country's "national treasures" from museums and libraries in Baghdad. Perhaps (it was suggested) U.S. troops could have done more to prevent that from happening, but, after all, they had their hands full guarding Iraq's other national treasures—its oil wells. Archaeologist Paul Zimansky called the looting of the museums and libraries "the greatest cultural disaster of the last 500 years."[23] The Bushites did not think it was all that serious, however. According to Chalmers Johnson, Rumsfeld "compared the looting to the aftermath of a soccer game" and declared: "Freedom's untidy. . . . Free people are free to make mistakes and commit crimes" (Nemesis, 47).

As to other aspects of "rebuilding" Saddam Hussein's "failed state," L. Paul Bremer made sure its government-run agencies and industries were privatized, with major U.S. corporations making off with the loot—or with a lot of it, anyway.[24] There has been some grumbling in the press about the billions of dollars that have gone unaccounted for—somebody's loot, of course, but when it is in such enormous quantities, it seems qualitatively different from a few poor black folks taking food from 7–11's just to survive in their flooded city. In the American mass media, the looting of Iraq's—and world history's—cultural treasures has been almost invisible, in contrast to the so-called looting in New Orleans. When referred to at all, the missing billions looted from Iraq is discussed under the rubric of "corruption," which media stereotyping long ago identified as something Iraqis and other Middle Easterners engage in—unlike Americans or American corporations such as Halliburton or Enron. If the Bushites have their way, the long-anticipated looting—you cannot call it shopping—of Iraqi oil by U.S. corporations will soon begin.

TELEVANGELICAL TERRORS

What happened on 9/11 was a spectacular video event—Al-Qaeda could not have wished for a better, more terrifying result in terms of media coverage. Neither could the Bushites.

Rumsfeld's "shock-and-awe" and Bush's "mission-accomplished" posturings are just two of now countless instances of American politicians' reacting to television as much as to terrorism—or exploiting them simultaneously. Al-Qaeda's videotapes are also smash hits. Years before 9/11, ABC's Ted Koppel opined,

> Without television, terrorism becomes rather like the philosopher's hy-
> pothetical tree falling in the forest: no one hears it fall and therefore it has
> no reason for being. And television, without terrorism, while not deprived
> of all interesting things in the world, is nonetheless deprived of one of the
> most interesting.

Quoting this remark, Zulaika and Douglass note that Koppel "himself [is]
a product of terrorism news" (*Terror and Taboo,* 7). The same is true for
other television newscasters who operate as terror mongers rather than as
critical analysts of such mongering. If you are shopping around for terror,
TV news is a better place to start than zombie movies.[25]

For the policymakers and the Pentagon, "the order of the day" since
9/11 has been fighting "terror" by "counterterror"—that is, by using the
methods of the terrorists themselves. The "shock-and-awe" bombard-
ments, the arrest and often torture of thousands without due process, the
deliberate rejections and violations of international treaties and laws, the
flouting of the U.N. (John Bolton: knock off the top ten floors of the U.N.
building, and they won't be missed), the wiretapping and other forms of
surveillance under the Patriot Act, are sold with apocalyptic (supposedly
Christian) invocations of good versus evil and of God and Armageddon.
The religious rhetoric also serves both to sanctify "counterterror" as official policy and to normalize terror. These are all now aspects of business
as usual. Meanwhile, Al-Qaeda turns the religious equation around with
its invocations of good versus evil, Allah and Armageddon, and W or Dick
Cheney as Beelzebub.[26]

No doubt Al-Qaeda wishes that it could bring American business
crashing down like the Twin Towers, symbols of that business. No doubt,
too, members of both the Clinton and Bush regimes wish they had captured or killed bin Laden, although they had plenty of opportunities to do
so that they failed to pursue.[27] But just as Al-Qaeda cannot stop Americans from shopping, neither can the Bushites win the war on terror that it
is so furiously and futilely waging in Iraq and elsewhere. Indeed, winning
that unwinnable war would put the Bushites out of business. Of what value
is peace to a self-proclaimed "war president"? The events of 9/11 gave the
Bushites their *raison d'être* as well as their cover for going after the oil. The
war on terror is now unfolding in its myriad bloody ways—in Afghanistan, in Iraq, in the Philippines, in Colombia—but also in the Gaps and
Guccis, the Targets and Wal-Marts of the world. Wherever there are ter-

rorists who hate America and want to destroy us, supposedly the antiter-
rorists forces of the U.S. government will be ready for them, W in the lead:

> We're tracking down terrorists who hate America one by one. We're on
> the hunt. We got 'em on the run, and it's a matter of time before they learn
> the meaning of American justice.[28]

That sort of cowboy talk hardly squares, however, with the very different
claim that, in the words of Dick Cheney, the war on terror may go on for
a "long, long time, perhaps indefinitely,"[29] much to the benefit of oil and
defense industries like Halliburton.

The war on terror may go on forever or until the end of the world,
because (we are told) it is the ultimate war of good against evil. Although
Bush now tries to avoid the word "crusade" in talking about his war on
terror, paradoxically the apocalyptic language that he and the Christian
right apply to the fray once again helps normalize terror. Shopping may
be normal, but the Bible is the revealed truth—hence, ultranormal from
a fundamentalist perspective. Shopping and Armageddon are not poles
apart; they go hand in hand—they happen every day. Now is the hour of
Wal-Mart and also of the Beast.[30] To defeat the terrorists, we need to shun
the devil and to keep a grip on our purses and purchases. None of this is
abnormal because, throughout history (that is, after the Fall), Satan has
been trying to slay business-as-usual—the American, Christian way of
life, a.k.a. shopping. W & Co. understand that there are other religions
than born-again Christianity even in the United States. Yet according
to rightwing evangelists like Jerry Falwell and Pat Robertson, America
is a "Christian country." As Stephen Colbert put it in his remarks to the
White House correspondents on May 3, 2006: "And though I am a committed Christian, I believe that everyone has the right to their own religion.... I believe there are infinite paths to accepting Jesus Christ as your
personal savior."

Colbert did not go on to say that God speaks directly to W, but he did
not need to. The White House correspondents understand that the great
"Decider" is in close personal touch with Our Heavenly Father. Or so W
claims: "I trust God speaks through me. Without that, I couldn't do my
job."[31] Again: "God told me to strike at Al-Qaeda and I struck them, and
then He instructed me to strike at Saddam, which I did, and now I am
determined to solve the problem of the Middle East."[32] When Pat Robert-

son resigned as head of the Christian Coalition late in 2001, evangelicals came to view W as "the de facto leader of the Christian Right."[33] On the Christian Broadcasting Network, Robertson assured his viewers that, if W should ever make a mistake, "God picks him up because he's a man of prayer and God's blessing him."[34] For evangelicals, apart from having a born-again Republican as president and commander-in-chief, one nice feature of the war on terror is that the terrorists will fry eternally in the fiery pit, where torture is the norm. I wonder, however, if W ever wonders if shopping goes on as usual in heaven?

Speaking to Congress on September 20, 2001, W declared, "The course of this conflict is not known, yet its outcome is certain. Freedom and fear, justice and cruelty, have always been at war. And we know that God is not neutral between them." If these two sides "have always been at war," when will it ever end? And if God really is on the side of freedom and goodness, why doesn't it end? There can be no timetable for withdrawal from Armageddon. Even if he has had to stop calling his war on terror a "crusade," W knows what it is: both normal and ultimate. And he knows as well that "Every nation in every region now has a decision to make. Either you are with us or you are with the terrorists." So, too, that redoubtable Christian Tom DeLay, echoing W,

> The war on terror is not a misunderstanding. It is not an opportunity for negotiation or dialogue. It's a battle between good and evil, between the Truth of liberty and the Lie of terror. Freedom and terrorism will struggle—good and evil—until the battle is resolved. These are the terms Providence has put before the United States, Israel, and the rest of the civilized world. They are stark, and they are final.[35]

In this formulation, "terror" stands for three different "final" notions, all muddled together: it is at once the fear the terrorists are seeking to instill in us; it is terrorism as such; and it is the ideology of the terrorists—"the Lie of terror." And besides just plain evil, we know—or Tom DeLay knows—what that ideology is: it is radical Islam, subbing for communism.

So long as the war on terror is cast as a "crusade" or a "clash" between incompatible "fundamentalisms" or even "civilizations," rhetorically there is no room for compromise: such a war can only end in the total destruction or ultimate damnation of one side or the other. But what or who exactly is this enemy, this other side? Surely not an entire civilization or religion? Even though it sounds brave and decisive to declare that the world is split down the middle—the good and free Christians (most Americans) on one side and the bad and unfree Muslims on the other—thoughtful Christians and Muslims understand that evil inhabits every human breast and that Satan is a character in both the Bible and the Koran. So is Jesus.

Nevertheless, Democrats and Republicans alike have bought into the Bushites' war on terror and the apocalyptic, gunslinger rhetoric that has been selling it like snake oil since 9/11. During his 2003 campaign for the presidency, John Kerry tried to out-terrorize the Republican terror mongers with the refrain "I will capture or kill all the terrorists." Okay, big guy—go round 'em up. We should all be thankful that Kerry did not give a religious spin to his rhetoric, though that may be one reason that he lost the election. And yet both parties and the mainstream media routinely reproduce "the apocalyptic worldview that now dominates our government—and that is also thriving elsewhere in the world, frequently *against* this government," as Mark Crispin Miller notes: "It is a Manichaean worldview, purist, fierce, explosive, and uncompromising, yet terrorstricken too and livid with self-hatred" (*Cruel and Unusual*, 106).

"From his bunker," writes Greg Palast, "Mr. Cheney has created a government that is little more than a Wal-Mart of fear" (*Armed Madhouse*, 37). Just how terror-stricken most Americans are is hard to tell, however. According to a Gallup poll taken in January 2005, 38 percent of Americans claimed they were "very concerned" or "concerned" that they themselves might be victims of a terrorist attack. But that means 62 percent were not all that concerned. Most people I know are more afraid of global warming or of what W will do next than of new terrorist attacks.

THE AGE OF TERROR? HAVE A NICE DAY

Since 9/11, at least eighty books have appeared using "the age of terror" or of "terrorism" as title or subtitle.[36] "Age" is a historical designation, of course, so is this claim good history or only hysteria? Statistics seem to bear it out, yet much depends on definitions and also on how reliable the numbers are now and have been in the past. One familiar statistic is that, in 2006, terrorist acts topped ten thousand for the first time in history. But when did such acts begin to be counted, and what exactly counts as a terrorist act? If the experts cannot agree on a definition (and they cannot), then it is difficult to see what such a number means. Suicide bombings in Iraq may be terrorist acts, but they could just as well be counted as acts of war. Killing civilians instead of combatants is one measure of terrorism, but then United States, Israeli, British, and NATO forces do that routinely. Innumerable acts of war have killed millions of noncombatants throughout history. If acts of war are counted as versions of terrorism, the number goes through the roof. By such a reckoning, during World War II or the Vietnam War, there were far more terrorist acts destroying millions more lives than 9/11 or even its aftermaths in Afghanistan and Iraq.

Though the phrase "Age of Terror(ism)" cropped up occasionally before 9/11, the destruction of the World Trade Center catapulted it into a cliché. Clichés are often true, but there are several problems with this one. For one thing, besides the issues of definition and statistics, those who assert that ours is the Age of Terror are operating as prophets rather than historians. Their alleged Age of Terror begins with 9/11 or very recently so that this "age" lies mainly ahead of us. Many of the prophets seem to believe that terrorism, supposedly more or less confined to the Middle East until now, has been globalized by 9/11; perhaps this justifies interpreting that date as the start of a new era. But terrorism is not the recent invention of Islamic madmen; it is perhaps as old as humankind. That is a terrifying idea, though peace and law and order have equally long histories—and history continues.

Unlike many of the politicians and pundits, the academic experts at least recognize that terrorism has a past as well as a future. Albert Parry, Walter Laqueur, and other historians point out that the terms "terrorist" and "terrorism" were coined in the 1790s, during the French revolutionary "Reign of Terror." Unlike today's terrorists, however, the Jacobin terrorists were in power; they were, moreover, like their American revolutionary counterparts, democratic advocates of "the rights of man." In 1793, faced with the threats of invasion from abroad and subversion at home, the Committee of Public Safety, headed by Robespierre, made "terror the order of the day." That is a quotation from Robespierre himself, who believed "the republic of virtue" could only be secured by making it "the terror" of "the oppressors." "Bliss was it in that dawn to be alive," wrote William Wordsworth; however, the dawn of modern democracy also opened the era of industrial execution via the guillotine. Its use during the Reign of Terror is a clear example of state terrorism, but so were the repressive measures of the monarchy that the French Revolution overthrew.

That terror could be deliberately adopted as state policy was evident to Machiavelli, who advised his prince "it is better to be feared than loved." Many "princes" have understood this: history is rife with examples of state terrorism. Today's Age-of-Terror proclaimers, however, often ignore state terrorism. Thus, in *No End to War: Terrorism in the Twenty-First Century*, Laqueur includes only a couple of pages on "state-sponsored terrorism" (223–25), and his examples are the usual suspects: Libya, Iran, Syria, and so forth—but not Israel and not the United States. This is a standard ploy on the part of those terrorologists who practice what Edward Herman calls the "pseudo-science" of terrorology (*The Real Terror Network*, 53). Many of the experts who proclaim that 9/11 is the dawn of the Age of Terror are quite selective about what they identify as terrorism.

In contrast, Herman distinguishes between what he calls "retail" or nonstate and "wholesale" or state terrorism (12). Can the retail terrorism of Al-Qaeda or even the Aryan Nation be understood minus the context of wholesale state terrorism? Though a distinguished historian, Laqueur dismisses those like Herman who stress that context. He thinks Noam Chomsky's "neoanarchist" insistence that it is "wrong to study substate political violence (i.e., terrorism) in isolation" renders "the study of terrorism impossible"; Chomsky's is "a manifestly absurd approach" (*No End to War*, 140). So, Laqueur chimes in with the pundits and politicians who, as Philip Herbst notes in *Talking Terrorism*, prefer "a definition of terrorism that excludes violent acts of the powerful and their clients." Terrorism is, thus, "the violence perpetrated by groups" or individuals "against a government or its citizens," but not the other way around."[37]

If waging a "preemptive war" of "shock and awe" with thousands of civilian casualties counts as terrorism, then Laqueur's is the incoherent, "absurd approach." When has the torture of prisoners held by a state not constituted terrorism? If planting roadside bombs is terrorism, what about dropping cluster bombs and using depleted uranium shells? Laqueur claims that it is a waste of time to try to define terrorism. Even limiting it as he first did in *Terrorism* (1977) to "an insurrectional strategy that can be used by people of very different political convictions" does not help: "No definition of terrorism can possibly cover all the varieties . . . that have appeared throughout history."

For the first edition of *Political Terrorism: A Research Guide* (1977), Alex Schmid listed over one hundred definitions. The experts agree, of course, that terrorism exists, and many of them also insist that states practice it, even when the official label is "counterterrorism." Modern examples of state terrorism include those analyzed by Patricia Marchak in *Reigns of Terror:* the Ottoman Empire during the Armenian genocide, the USSR during the "Great Terror" under Stalin, the Nazi Holocaust, and so on, through Cambodia's "killing fields" and Yugoslavia's "ethnic cleansings." Herman's *The Real Terror Network* adds numerous examples from U.S. "counterterrorist" activities in Central and South America.[38] As both Marchak and Herman note, "counterterrorism" is typically just as terroristic (if not more so) as what it claims to be combating. Now and in the past, Marchak comments, "the vast majority of crimes against humanity, and by far the largest number of deaths and disappearances have been caused not by small groups of revolutionaries, but by organized states against their own citizens and the citizens of other countries."[39] Genocides are frequently, although not always, versions of state terrorism. Perhaps because of this, Laqueur does not deal with them. But downplaying both genocides and state terrorism while stressing only the violent deeds of nonstate actors produces myopic results.

Before dubbing our era "the Age of Terror," the politicians, pundits, and terrorologists should also ask if it makes sense to name any complex historical period for a single emotion. After all, when was the age of regret or of joy? "The Age of Anxiety" became something of a cliché for the 1930s, but it is difficult to think of other examples. Rather than identifying terror as the main characteristic of our era, it may be more reasonable to think of it as a universal political emotion. In *Fear: The History of a Political Idea*, Corey Robin notes that terror may even be the most basic political emotion, the one that binds humans together in search of security. In the 1600s, Thomas Hobbes made "terror the order of the day" in political theory. Because the "state of nature" is one of "continual fear, and danger of violent death," humans formed communities to escape it.[40] But Hobbes also argued that people would not obey such moral "laws" as "justice, equity, modesty, mercy . . . without the terror of some power, to cause them to be observed" (*Leviathan*, 129). The terror of nature is what forces people to band together; the terror of the king or the law is what keeps them together.

Hobbes was an authoritarian upholder of monarchy. Opposed to his dismal view of both nature and society were such early liberal theorists as John Locke; Enlightenment philosophers from Montesquieu to Immanuel Kant opined that the fundamental emotional tie binding societies together was not fear but sympathy. People joined together in society because of "the law" and economic "self-interest," yes, but also because of "fellow-feeling," a mingling of emotional identification and mutual respect for each other. This was the optimistic view of both the French and the American revolutionaries—terrorists to their opponents—who gave us our Bills of Rights and our present-day conceptions of human worth, freedom, and possibility.

SHOPPING AROUND FOR A BETTER WORLD

Suppose Al-Qaeda were crushed, the U.S. occupation of Iraq and Afghanistan ended, differences with Iran overcome, and the conflict between Israel and Palestine settled. Terrorism might not vanish, but it would greatly diminish. An unterrified world, at peace and on its way to solving such seemingly ageless problems as global poverty, would put a self-proclaimed "war president" out of business.[41] The Department of Homeland Security could be disbanded and FEMA strengthened. The military could be radically downsized, and billions reinvested in social programs that benefit ordinary Americans. The prophetic pundits who come up with such headlines as "The Age of Terror" would have to come up with very different ones: "The Age of Peace" or of "International Harmony," perhaps. Such a prospect will not sound entirely far-fetched after recalling Bush Sr.'s 1991 declaration of "a new world order" (although he criticized himself for not being good at "the vision thing," what was on his shopping list?). Following the collapse of the Soviet Union but before 9/11, many neoconservatives shared with liberals a highly optimistic "vision thing."

Insofar as Age-of-Terror claims are predictions rather than historical accounts, they ignore the hazards of political forecasting, close relative of the "vision thing." After all, who foresaw the downfall of communism in Eastern Europe and the Soviet Union? But back then, just a bit more than two decades ago, some of the politicians and pundits who now trumpet the Age of Terror were playing a very different tune. With capitalism and liberal democracy seemingly victorious, 1989–91 was the dawn of an age of universal peace and prosperity. What has become of all those rosy "new-world-order" and "end-of-history" prophecies?

Paradoxically, the history of terrorism may offer some support for those older, hopeful forecasts. Terrorism is certainly as old as states and empires, but a case can be that the modern "Age of Terror(ism)" is winding down rather than just beginning. The two world wars, the Korean and Vietnam Wars, the Gulf War, and now the invasions and occupations of Afghanistan and Iraq offer little or no cause for hope. The ratcheting up of violence since World War II, including major genocides in Cambodia, Rwanda, Bosnia, the Congo, and the Sudan, signals the opposite of a winding down of terrorism. Like the war on terror, the Israeli-Palestinian conflict appears interminable and sure to fuel more terrorism, not less.

The good news, however, is that in some situations both repression and terror are in retreat and, just as the Bushites claimed they hoped, democracy rising. Since World War II, the United Nations and other international institutions and laws have been major gains for global peace and order (despite John Bolton). So has the emergence of the European Union. Also after the 1940s, most former colonies have gained their official, political independence from the Western empires (though, in many cases, economic dependency continues). Just as astonishing as the downfall of the Soviet empire, the Apartheid regime in South Africa has been swept away. And the recent elections in Latin America that have empowered democratic socialist leaders who are putting the welfare of the masses back on the agendas of their countries are also hopeful. Though Hugo Chávez of Venezuela is both hated and feared by the Bush regime, his advocacy of a "Bolivarian" federation may lead to a unity in South America that could help overcome centuries of imperial exploitation and repression. Moreover, human rights organizations such as Amnesty International are making headway; their reports are part of the reason that the Bush regime is hated by millions around the world—and not just by "the terrorists." Perhaps nothing caused support for the invasion and occupation of Iraq to wane so quickly as the revelations of abuses and torture at Abu-Ghraib, Guantanamo, and elsewhere.

The end of the cold war, writes Richard Falk, opened "incredible historical opportunities to create a safer and fairer world order." All the tools are at hand. The one thing needful is leadership, from the United States among other countries, with enough of "the vision thing" for pursuing disarmament, strengthening the U.N., and insisting on a "fair . . . solution of the Israel/Palestine encounter." Further, science and technology are developing new ways to manage environmental problems, to cure or eliminate many diseases, and to overcome global poverty. Besides the deaths and destruction wrought by 9/11, its main cost may well prove to be delaying the realization of these hopeful possibilities for decades—or however long the "Age of Terror" takes to get over itself. Let us hope "age" turns into something much shorter. Perhaps what is new about terrorism today, apart from the rhetorical hype that sustains it, is its exhaustion—its angry impotence in light of the desire of the vast majority for peace, stability, prosperity, and freedom. After all, as the motto of the World Social Forum has it, "Another world is possible."

EIGHT

The State of Iraq

It is easier to stay out than to get out.

—MARK TWAIN, *FOLLOWING THE EQUATOR*

Having invaded Iraq, occupied it, surged it, and turned it into a democracy with an economy blessed by free trade, it would be crazy for the United States to withdraw from it now. Yet that is exactly what President Obama is doing—ordering our boys (and gals) out of a place they have been occupying for nearly a decade. Given the great expense of American treasure and Americans in the Iraq War, John McCain's hundred-year Reich makes good sense versus Obama's surrender. Far more sensible, however, would be the one solution that no American politician including Joe Lieberman has yet proposed: *Turn Iraq into the fifty-first state of the Union.*[1]

Think how fitting it would have been, as one of his first acts in office, for Obama, who promised change we can believe in, to have transformed that fine piece of oil-rich real estate into a new, vibrant state of the United States! What is the purpose of state building, after all? And what better reward could there be for the Iraqis (the non-Al Qaeda types, that is, even if they are all Muslims) after years of dictatorship, sanctions, shock and awe, waterboarding, regime change, and Abu Ghraib? Grant all Iraqis except the jihaders American citizenship. After all, wasn't the Bush regime trying to remake Iraq in the image of America? They will love us for our freedoms.

Opponents of the fifty-first-state solution will say that Iraq is an independent country with its own elected government. Why, then, are our oilers, plumbers, and contractors still occupying it? Why, after Obama has withdrawn the troops, have the troops not withdrawn?[2] The opponents will also say that Iraq is a foreign country and that America does not turn foreign, faraway places into new states. Former Secretary of Defense Donald Rumsfeld said it well: "We've never been a colonial power. We don't take our force[s] and . . . try to take other people's real estate or . . . resources, their oil. That's just not what the United States does. . . . That's not how democracies behave." And ex-President George W. Bush, who majored in history at Yale and ought to know, has noted with his customary flare for accuracy, "America has never been an empire."

On the contrary, America has always done the opposite of empire building. It takes failed states and turns them into thriving democracies and lovers of free markets. It is in the business of state building. Despite threats to secede, the United States today is an "uninalienable" union of very successful states.[3] Regarding the argument that Iraq is far away, what about Alaska, the forty-ninth state, or Hawaii, number fifty? Both are far away. As to foreign, Hawaii once belonged to the Hawaiians, and Alaska to Russia! Today, Alaska, despite its long winters and dark nights, is home to Sarah Palin and the polar bear. Of course, at the outset in both Hawaii and Alaska, a few Americans had arrived to show the natives how to manage their affairs. Hawaii will come up later, along with the Philippines, Japan, Korea, Taiwan, China, and Vietnam. Many more Americans flocked to Alaska after Secretary of State William Seward purchased it from Russia for $7,200,000 in 1867. That was less than 2 cents an acre. Some people called it "Seward's Folly," but it should have been called "Russia's Folly." The Russians went home. The oil, timber, salmon, gold, seals, moose, and deer flies remained. So did the polar bear.

Though still a long way off, Alaska would be connected to the United States by land if, during the War of 1812 or on any later occasion, American statesmen had been wise enough to embrace the Canadian provinces and send the British packing. As many of our best statesmen like President James Madison recognized, statehood for Canada was perfectly doable. After all, except for the Indians, Eskimos, and French, most Canadians spoke English. Many Canadians were originally Americans who unwisely moved north during the American Revolution. Probably for most of them,

Americanization would be a sweet homecoming. Independence at last! Disputes over fishing rights in the 1880s caused some U.S. patriots once again to call for turning Canada into new American states. As a rhymester poetized in a Detroit newspaper,

> We do not want to fight,
> But, by jingo, if we do,
> We'll scoop in all the fishing grounds
> And the whole dominion too!

Perhaps some Canadians, especially the French, might object to being Americanized. Many of them to this day claim that they are already Americans, merely because Canada is located in North America! In any case, bringing Canada into the Union would help promote the borderless world or flat earth we've been looking forward to ever since NAFTA or even Chief Pontiac. To this day, Canadians flock to Detroit or Seattle when they want to go shopping or can't afford vacations in the tropics.

It is true that sometimes Americans flock to Canada to go fishing or to get health care on the cheap. Something similar is now happening in Iraq, which is already teeming with American operators, diplomats, spies, bureaucrats, truckers, salesmen, geeks, demo men, loan sharks, plumbers, and policy wonks. The tourists are on their way. Unlike Alaska, no purchase is necessary, because American corporations have already bought up most of Iraq. Are all those Americans just going to pull up their stakes and leave? Not likely! Soon they may even outnumber the Iraqis, as today in Russia's Folly (aka Alaska) Americans outnumber the Eskimos. Of course, not all Iraqis will be ready to become American citizens. For individual Iraqis, there should be an application process, as there is for immigrants to the United States. If an Iraqi seems unhappy about it or behaves suspiciously, he could be interrogated. And if, during interrogation, he reveals terrorist sympathies, he could be waterboarded or renditioned.

But, the antistatists will argue, Iraqis are not just foreigners who live in a faraway place: they belong to a different race, they believe in another religion, and they have been brought up in a backward civilization. The antistatists will be wrong, however, because America is a melting pot of many different races, religions, and even civilizations. Talk about a clash of civilizations! That's the United States for you. Many Iraqis already live in America, and most of them are law-abiding citizens—or not, as the case may be. Think how eagerly Iraqi Americans will welcome all the new Iraqi Americans living in Iraq! What a voting bloc they will form! At first, non-Iraqi Americans might not be too keen about it. They may not want a mosque in their neighborhood. But they should remember that Iraq was once the cradle of civilization, the original Babylon. And conversion, like citizenship, is always possible.

Keep in mind, too, that America is still very young. It has plenty of time and room for growth. All thirteen original colonies at first belonged to the Indians, who were just as foreign as the Iraqis are today. They were uncivilized savages, speaking foreign languages and worshipping totem poles. Thomas Jefferson purchased the Louisiana Purchase from the French, not the Indians. Furthermore, Jefferson declared that "our confederacy must be viewed as the nest from which all America, North and South, is to be peopled." In other words, after the British and the French, Jefferson was ready to tackle the Spanish and Portuguese all the way down to the South Pole. If Jefferson thought it made sense to turn Brazil into a new state of the United States, then it is surely thinkable to do that favor for Iraq.

Of course, it was not for the benefit of the natives (Indians) that the Pilgrims created the colonies that they later converted to states of the young American republic. The situation in Iraq is different because there the main benefiters of statehood will be the natives. Attempts were made to pacify and civilize the Indians, but when these failed, Congress voted to remove the Indians still surviving east of the Mississippi River west of it to places like Oklahoma, which was not yet a state. In Iraq, many wild, disorderly natives have already been removed. Statehood caught up with the Indians, however. Oklahoma, which turned out like Iraq to have a lot of oil, entered the Union in 1907, becoming the forty-sixth state. How many Okies complain about statehood now?

Florida is also a good example of American state building. Before overseeing Indian removal in the 1830s, Andrew Jackson marched into that godforsaken, malarial swamp, which at the time belonged to Spain. Jackson said he was there to pacify the Seminoles, who along with some escaped slaves and pirates were on the warpath. While polishing off the Seminoles, Jackson got the brainstorm of capturing a couple of Spanish outposts. In 1819, Spain and the United States signed a treaty that gave Florida to America in exchange for our giving up any thought of welcoming Texas into our growing family of states. At the time, Texas was part of Mexico, which also belonged to Spain. In 1821, Mexico declared its independence from Spain, TKO-ing the Texas part of the 1819 treaty. Although Florida's original inhabitants were foreigners, in 1845 it was declared the twenty-seventh state of the Union, with much fanfare and rejoicing by the owners of its beaches, hotels, saloons, and future retirement communities. Not to mention Disneyworld, a state in itself. So it matters not if a future state contains foreigners or even belongs to another country.

Statehood for Florida was easy compared to Texas. Despite belonging to Mexico and being populated by Mexicans and Indians, in the 1820s east Texas was settled by the Austin family after relatively minimal gunplay (but they all carried, as per the Second Amendment). Then came the Alamo. Remember the Alamo? At that historic site, the Mexicans slaughtered almost two hundred non-Mexican Texican heroes (as Texans were first called) including Davy Crockett and Jim Bowie (remember the Bowie knife?). There was an even bigger massacre at a godforsaken place called Goliad, which, unlike the Alamo, nobody remembers today. The surviving Texicans fought back, defeating the Mexicans at the Battle of San Jacinto. Then came statehood—Texas was admitted to the Union as state number twenty-eight, also in 1845, right after Florida.

In considering Iraq for statehood, remember that both Florida and Texas had recently belonged to Spain and Mexico and that the original inhabitants of both new states were foreigners who spoke little or no English. They were either heathens or Roman Catholics, which made no difference whatsoever to Manifest Destiny. Like Oklahoma and Texas, moreover, Iraq has plenty of oil. It also has plenty of mosques and Muslims, but that's okay. And it has both ancient and modern ruins, plus looted museums, not to mention Halliburton, Xe (aka Blackwater), and a Green Zone. The place could be tidied up by adding a few more corporate franchises and a baseball team or two. It does not need more ruins. Flat Earther Thomas Friedman claims that, if a country has a McDonalds's franchise, then, just like America, it is at peace with the world. It will quit hankering after weapons of mass destruction. Or as President Bush so eloquently put it, "See, free nations do not develop weapons of mass destruction." So bring on McDonalds and any other corporations still lacking in Baghdad and Basra. Let the good times roll!

Besides Florida and Texas, there are many other examples of American state building—in fact, every state in the Union. And there are many other places like Canada that have been considered for statehood but unwisely rejected. Mexico itself, for instance. After the Texicans sent the Mexicans packing, there dawned on President James Polk the statesmanlike idea of invading the rest of Mexico. When American troops under General Zachary Taylor moved the border of Texas south to the Rio Grande, the Mexicans objected and shot a couple of American heroes. So Taylor invaded all the way down to the Halls of Montezuma. That the Mexicans surrendered so easily shows how keen they were to become Americans, just like today. No matter how high or far the United States builds its Great Wall, you can be sure there will be plenty of Mexicans scrambling over or digging under it, determined to become Americans. Why isn't Mexico building a wall? Why just the United States?

In any case, by defeating Mexico in 1848, America acquired a whole slew of new states, even though all those faraway states were then populated by foreigners—Mexicans and Indians. In the order of their happy admission to the United States, the new states included California (1850), Nevada (1864), Colorado (1876), Wyoming (1890), Utah (1896), New Mexico (1912), and Arizona (1912). If this sounds like empire building, it was not; it was just more happy state building. The happy idea of turning all of Mexico into states occurred to some U.S. patriots, but was tossed out because of anti-Mexicanism. Mexicans were said to be a mongrel race made up of a bunch of Indians, some Spanish, and a few blacks. Nobody wanted them except for picking fruit and landscaping. Sam Houston, whose last name adorns one of Texas's great cities, said, "The vigor of the descendants of the sturdy north will never mix with the phlegm of the indolent Mexicans." Houston should see Houston today.

Because so many Americans believed that Mexicans were beneath them, all of Mexico never became new states. A tragic mistake. If it had, there would be no need for a Great Wall of America, the Border Patrol, or Drug Cartels. People could freely come and go in all directions. Drugs would also be practically free—you could get them from vending machines on either side of the nonexistent border. American corporations would be unable to outsource American jobs south of that border. Illegals would automatically be legalized with no loose talk about amnesty. But there would still be plenty of cheap labor, because San Diego and Los Angeles would become even more chicanofied, while Cancun and Acapulco would become even more gringofied. Tacos and margaritas all around!

But why stop with Mexico? How many times in the last two centuries has the United States sent gunboats, the marines, and the CIA into places like Panama, Haiti, and Grenada? Does the United States ever need to send gunboats into Kentucky? Why does our government maintain an expensive naval base and jail in a tiny corner of Cuba when, at the end of the war with Spain, we could have turned that entire beautiful and bountiful island into a new state? Instead, in 1901 Congress passed a law guaranteeing its independence, which nipped Cuban statehood in the bud. "Independent" from what? Cubans? If we had turned Cuba into a state, look at how many problems we might have solved. Fidel Castro might still be wandering around in the jungle.. The CIA would not have tried to blow him up with exploding cigars. There would have been no Bay of Pigs. JFK might still be president. The Cubans living in Miami could go home again, where they belong.. And in all likelihood, there would now be a major-league baseball team playing for Havana—the Havana Habaneros, perhaps. Not to mention a McDonalds franchise.[4]

There have been many opportunities for statehood elsewhere in the Caribbean and Central America. The Contras and Ollie North secretly clobbered the Sandanistas during Irangate, but apparently President Reagan did not even consider statehood for Nicaragua. Very unstatesmanlike! Grenada is an even bigger historical embarrassment. Why was Reagan in 1983 so keen on invading Grenada? Because of some minor unrest in that wee but sunny tropical island, Reagan ordered in the troops. However, instead of turning Grenada into a new state, our happy-go-lucky president released it back into the political wilderness. What was he thinking? It seems in hindsight that the invasion of Grenada was just a ploy in the cold war, Reagan's attempt to show the Evil Empire that we would stop at nothing, not even the tiniest speck in the ocean.

And then there is Panama. For years far-sighted Americans wanted to dig a canal there. But in 1900, Panama belonged to Colombia. And the Colombian legislature turned thumbs down. So Teddy Roosevelt ordered American gunboats to prevent Colombian forces from landing while American troops seized Panama City and Colon. That is how Panama became an independent country—not a new state, however, which was again a tragic mistake. The canal was dug, but Panama remains a banana republic to this day, ruled by gangsters like Manuel Noriega. This mistake led to Operation Just Cause, when the first President Bush bombed Panama City and sent in the troops. They caught Noriega, but nearly two dozen U.S. soldiers died along with several hundred Panamanians. This was excessive. The Panamanians resented being bombed. And in 1999, the United States turned the canal over to Panama! All this could have been avoided if Roosevelt had taken up the White Man's Burden and turned Panama into a new state.Besides Cuba, at the end of the War with Spain, the United States liberated a few other places, including the Philippines and Guam. Hawaii had already been turned into a U.S. territory when American patriot Sam Dole, not content with growing sugar cane, toppled Queen Liliuokalani from her throne and installed himself as the new president. A patriot in Honolulu cabled Washington: "The Hawaiian pear is now fully ripe, and this is the golden hour for the United States to pluck it." President Ben Harrison heartily approved. He had also helped America to a share of Samoa, divvying it up with Great Britain and Germany.[5] Besides approving the liberation of Hawaii, Harrison by 1890 had added six more states to the Union, even though practically nobody lived in them except Indians: North Dakota, South Dakota, Montana, Washington, Idaho, and Wyoming.

President Grover Cleveland who came after Harrison for some reason thought that Dole's actions were not supported by the Hawaiians. He even tried to restore Queen Likeaukulele to her throne. But Dole stood his ground. Like the Texican heroes, he proclaimed an independent Republic of Hawaii in 1894. Cleveland caved in, recognizing the new future state. The weak-kneed Cleveland was succeeded by President William McKinley, who was not as farsighted as Harrison but more so than Cleveland. McKinley saw to it that Hawaii became a territory of the United States in 1898, with Dole as its head. From sugar cane, Dole and his fellow patriots expanded to pineapples and tourism. Queen L. passed away. As already noted, Hawaii became the fiftieth state of the Union in 1959.

Guam is another story.[6] So is the Philippines. It is much larger than Guam and, like Hawaii, consists of many mountainous, unsinkable islands. At the outset of the War against Spain, McKinley did not know where the Philippines were. But after Admiral Dewey sank the Spanish fleet in Manila Bay in 1898, McKinley decided it would be a good idea for Americans to replace the Spaniards, if for no other reason than that God told him to. McKinley said that his policy toward the Philippines would involve "benevolent assimilation" rather than empire building, but he probably did not mean any sort of mixing of our all-American Anglo-Saxon bloodlines with "our little brown brothers."[7] He wanted to civilize and Christianize the Filipinos, even though most of them were already civilized Roman Catholics.

Neither McKinley nor the man who replaced him, Teddy Roosevelt, ever seriously considered statehood for the Philippines. As far as the antistatists were concerned, treating those far-away and foreign islands like a colony was bad enough—statehood was out of the question. One opponent of statehood said that the Filipinos were "utterly alien to us" and "incapable of being assimilated to the Anglo-Saxon." Another claimed that assimilating the islands would only worsen "the Negro Problem" at home. And still another said that the United States would be swamped by "the hordes of Chinese" and the "semi-savage races" of the Philippines, "engulfing our people and our civilization." So the Yellow Peril mingled with the Brown Peril and the Negro Peril, completely nixing the possibility of statehood for the Philippines.

It is a mystery, however, why that did not happen in the case of Hawaii. Today two-thirds of the population of our fiftieth state is not close to being Anglo-Saxons, but that did not stand in the way of Sam Dole's statesmanship. Part of the answer also has to do with Pearl Harbor. That dastardly attack made Americans feel that Hawaii was an uninalienable part of the United States, bonded by bombing forever, with or without statehood and no matter how brown or yellow its complexion. Bombing or getting bombed does not exactly square with benevolent assimilation or statehood. And yet war has a way of flattening the world that is often quite amazing. Perhaps if the Japanese had bombed Subic Bay instead of Pearl Harbor, the Philippines would have become the fiftieth state of the Union, while Hawaii would today be just a backwater—the Dole Private Pineapple Kingdom and Resort Hotels. And after America flattened Hiroshima and Nagasaki with A-bombs, consider what happened next. Japan surrendered; American troops moved in; and with lots of American help, the Japanese economy was restored to such a tune that, within three decades, it was giving the United States fits with cars and electronics. This, too, could easily have been prevented if, after the A-bombing, Japan had been benevolently assimilated as a new American state.

As Manifest Destiny surged like a tidal wave to the Pacific coast and then beyond it to places like Guam and Hawaii, some other territories were in its path. After the Chinese drove them out, Chiang Kai-Shek and his troops went to Taiwan, which has remained a political yo-yo ever since between the Chinese communists and the American capitalists. As to China proper, if American statesmen in 1900 or thereabouts had had the wisdom to establish U.S. corporations and shopping malls in Shanghai and Beijing, many later problems could have been avoided—the tragic case of Vietnam, for one, which also tragically was never turned into a state.

There are very few places in the world that should not be considered for statehood in the United States, and Iraq is not one of them. With Iraq as a new state, equal to Alabama or Rhode Island, the headaches of the Middle East could be cured overnight. The Palestinians would jump at the chance for statehood. Israel might be a holdout, until it saw the other dominoes falling around it: Tunisia, Egypt, Libya, Syria. . . . Every one of these supposedly independent countries is, like Iraq, populated by foreigners, speaking foreign languages, and practicing a non-Christian religion. But with statehood, they would cease to be foreigners. Their clashing civilizations would join the melting pot.

With Americans streaming into these new states, benevolent assimilation would go far more quickly than we can now imagine. Consider the speed with which Mormons and Pentecostals, not to mention Wal-Mart and McDonalds, have made converts all over the world. There might be unrest and even outbreaks of terrorism in some of the infantile states, but with the American military everywhere embedded, these could be easily squelched. And while Americans would have to tolerate a babble of foreign tongues for awhile, English would soon be spoken everywhere. Pakistan, Venezuela, North Korea, France—granted statehood, trouble spots like these would clear up overnight.

But, a skeptic might say, this is sheer Americanism run amuck. Therefore, rather than stressing the Manifest Destiny of America to benevolently assimilate the rest of the world, we will conclude this frankly patriotic foray into the global prospects for statehood by refocusing on the state of Iraq. Just imagine its almost limitless possibilities! The new U.S. embassy in Baghdad, largest and most expensive in the world, could be turned into the largest and most expensive U.S. state capital in the world.

The Green Zone could become the Green Zone National Park: all it needs is a few trees and Blackwater—that is, Xe—park rangers. America's military bases could be turned into well-armed and secure state police posts also run by Xe. Fast food and laundry could be supplied on the cheap by Halliburton. Abu Ghraib could still be Abu Ghraib (talk about turning it into a major tourist attraction complete with dogs, sadistic guards, sexual humiliations, and waterboarding seems premature). The oil wells are already in place, only not as productive as they should be—unlike those in Oklahoma, for example.

As far as Americans are concerned, Iraq has already become a state of mind—though so far not a very attractive one. But if statehood is granted to that currently unhappy land, suiciders would throw away their explosives and dance in the streets of Baghdad. Leftover land mines and cluster bombs could be safely detonated with little or no collateral damage. All over the world, the price of gasoline would drop. With a new American state on its border, Iran would surrender its nukes and itself apply for statehood. And next? Afghanistan, of course! The Taliban could join the Tea Party. The world would then indeed be flatter, yet ever advancing and rejoicing under the Stars and Stripes!

NINE

On the Postmodernity of Being
Aboriginal—and Australian

I am still
The black swan of trespass on alien waters.

—"ERN MALLEY"

What does it mean to be Aboriginal in today's Australia? Most people of Aboriginal descent live in cities, often in conditions of unemployment and dire poverty, often dependent on meager government support. Those lucky enough to receive an adequate education and to move into the middle class still suffer from the effects of racial discrimination. As the 1997 report on "The Stolen Generations" revealed, moreover, perhaps as many as one-third of the Australians who are of Aboriginal descent can no longer trace their family origins.[1] These are likely to be mixed-race people; either they or their parents had been "stolen"—removed from their Aboriginal families—presumably in order to be assimilated into white Australia. Yet even if they wanted to, they have never been allowed to assimilate fully. Nor can they return to what might be called a "traditional" lifestyle.

According to the 2012 *Yearbook of the Australian Bureau of Statistics,* in 2008 about half of the population of Aboriginals and Torres Straits Islanders, or approximately a quarter million people, "identified with a cultural group (meaning a tribal or language group, a clan, a mission or a regional group)," but this does not indicate the degree to which any of them practiced a traditional way of life. Only about one-tenth, or fifty thousand, spoke an indigenous language as their main one. The Bureau adds,

In 2008, an estimated 65,000 Aboriginal and Torres Strait Islander children aged 3–14 years (42%) were spending some time with an Aboriginal or Torres Strait Islander leader or elder—31% at least one day a week and a further 12% less frequently. Children living in remote areas were much more likely than those in non-remote areas to have been spending time with an elder at least one day a week (49% compared with 25%).

But a declining percentage of children were "living in remote areas," and, in any event, remoteness is no guarantee that a culture can be certified as traditional or authentic. Yet like indigenous peoples everywhere in the world, Australian Aboriginals are under constant pressure to prove their authenticity, even though their attempts to do so lead to their treatment as second-class citizens by white Australia.

LOCATING SALLY MORGAN'S *MY PLACE*

In the fall of 1992, at a hotel near Alice Springs, Australia, my wife and I found ourselves sitting across a swimming pool from Judith Drake-Brockman. She figures in a book we had just read, Sally Morgan's best-selling autobiography *My Place* (1987). She was the daughter of wealthy Western Australian pastoralist Howden Drake-Brockman, who may also have fathered Morgan's grandmother and mother. We recognized her because her photo had just appeared in the October 1992 issue of *The Daily Legend*, "the official journal of the Honda Masters Games." The seventy-two-year-old Drake-Brockman was in Alice Springs to compete in the Masters Games's swimming competition. My wife said that she felt like going over to her and telling her that her father's treatment of Morgan's mother and grandmother was shameful.

Drake-Brockman would later tell her own story, largely as a response to *My Place*, in her 2001 autobiography, *Wongi-Wongi*. There she repeats what she told Sally Morgan, that Morgan's grandmother's father was Maltese Sam and her mother's father was an Englishman named Jack Grime.[2] Morgan's granduncle, however, Arthur Corunna, was certain this is not the case and that Howden Drake-Brockman fathered Daisy (the grandmother), as well as himself and his half-brother Albert: "Are you gunna take the word of white people against your own flesh and blood?" He admits that "I got no papers to prove what I'm sayin'," and adds, "Nobody cared how many blackfellas were born in those days, nor how many died" (Morgan, *My Place*, 155).

Morgan's *My Place* was one of many books we acquired on that trip to Australia. I was especially in search of books by Aboriginal authors, and Morgan was then viewed, apparently without much controversy, as an Aboriginal author. I also purchased texts by Mudrooroo (Narogin), including his historical novel about the extinction of the Tasmanian race, *Doctor Wooreddy's Prescription for Enduring the Ending of the World* (1983), and the 1990 anthology he coedited with three other authors, *Paperbark: A Collection of Black Australian Writings*. Its publisher, University of Queensland Press, declares in a blurb on its cover that it is "the first collection to span the diverse range of Black Australian writings."[3]

I was researching and observing both past and present white-Aboriginal relations. Those relations were glaringly obvious at Alice Springs and Uluru (Ayres Rock), but their present-day manifestations were not evident in Tasmania, except as displays in the Hobart Museum. According to the standard narrative, the Tasmanian Aboriginals, different in several respects from the mainland Aboriginals, had been completely exterminated by the time the (supposedly) last full-blooded native died in 1876. But supposed certainties in Australian history like the fate of the Tasmanians were, I would soon learn, just as uncertain as the identity of the father or fathers of Sally Morgan's mother and grandmother, and, consequently, just as uncertain as her Aboriginality. Besides, like many other authors who deem themselves to be Aboriginal, Morgan is a "half-caste." She had grown up in Perth and, as a child, believed her family was of East Indian origin, far removed from traditional Aboriginal culture. Her sister Jill enlightens her:

> "You know what we are, don't you?"
>
> "No, what?"
>
> "Boongs, we're Boongs!" I could see Jill was unhappy with the idea.
>
> ... "What's a Boong?"
>
> "A Boong. You know, Aboriginal. God, of all things, we're Aboriginal!"

But what did it mean to be Aboriginal? At that moment of revelation, all Sally Morgan could think of is that Aboriginals are "like animals" and that "they feel close to the earth and all that stuff." Jill sees the issue differently: "It's a terrible thing to be Aboriginal. . . . You can be Indian, Dutch, Italian, anything, but not Aboriginal!" (*My Place*, 98)

But Sally and Jill are also half-castes or rather octoroons. Is that better or worse than being a full-blooded "Boong"? Even if their maternal grandfather was not Howden Drake-Brockman, he was in all likelihood white. With each revelation about her and her family's origins, *My Place* raises more questions. The ultimate revelation is that Howden Drake-Brockman begot Daisy, or Sally Morgan's grandmother, and then committed incest with Daisy, who gave birth to her mother. But even without "Aunt Judy" Drake-Brockman's denials about her own father as also Sally Morgan's, the issue of paternity for Morgan remains unsettled, as does also the issue of what it means, in 1980s Australia, to be a "half-caste" or "mixed blood" Aboriginal. With every new revelation in Morgan's autobiography, "my place" threatens to turn into many places or perhaps no place at all, while nothing seems definitively Aboriginal. And, thus, the question has arisen, "Is Sally Morgan really an Aboriginal author?"[4] The authenticity, in the sense of truthfulness, of her story may be beyond question (except by Judith Drake-Brockman), but the authenticity of Morgan's identity as an Aboriginal has been widely questioned.

Matters did not become more certain on my later visits to Australia, but just the opposite. On my second visit, to Western Australian University in Perth, I observed, as I had earlier in Alice Springs, city-dwelling Aboriginals living in abject poverty: they appeared to have lost anything that could conceivably be called authentic Aboriginality. And on my third trip, this time to a postcolonial conference at the University of Queensland in Brisbane, I learned about the recent publication of the first volume of Keith Windschuttle's *The Fabrication of Aboriginal History*. In it, he argues that the many authors who have claimed the Tasmanian Aboriginals were totally exterminated mainly through violence and disease were misinformed. Yes, the first Tasmanians died out, but, according to Windschuttle, only because of the dysfunctionality of their own primitive culture. For instance, he claims that they were not attacked by Tasmania's white settlers; they were instead the attackers, while the humane colonizers tried to preserve their race.

Windschuttle's second volume, published in 2009, denies the massive evidence, painstakingly assembled by Peter Read and many other scholars, about the "Stolen Generations," or the removal from the late

1800s into the 1970s especially of half-caste Aboriginal children from their families. It appears that Windschuttle, editor of the conservative journal *Quadrant*, is prepared to deny all the major aspects of white-Aboriginal history that other scholars have accepted as fact. If taken literally and seriously, his attempts to puncture holes in the standard treatments of frontier conflict in Australia seem to puncture holes in the very idea of historical evidence. For Windschuttle, Australian history—perhaps history itself in the sense of historiography—appears to be a vast conspiracy to conjure genocide out of thin air. *Fabrication* led me to respond to it in *Victorian Studies*, a journal I edited from 1980 to 1990, in an essay titled "'Black Armband' versus 'White Blindfold' History in Australia."[5] I sided with the chorus of Black Armbanders like historians Henry Reynolds, Brian Attwood, and Stuart Macintyre, who had begun accusing Windschuttle of genocide denial.[6]

I do not wish to revisit the influential silliness of Windschuttle's revisionist history, but merely to stress that he is an author prepared to question what in the past has been accepted as the standard history of an entire continent. Perhaps for Windschuttle, as for Henry Ford, history itself is "bunk." Paradoxically, Windschuttle's project shares a number of features with many other postmodern narratives or deconstructions of narratives, both in Australia and elsewhere, including Morgan's *My Place.* That is the case also, I believe, with Aboriginal literature in general, which in a forerunner to this chapter I referred to as "fake(?) Aboriginal literature."[7]

THE MYSTERIOUS VANISHING OF
MUDROOROO NAROGIN

Accounts of Aboriginal literature usually view the mid-1960s as its beginning point. In 1964, Kate Walker (Oodgeroo Noonuccal) published her first volume of poetry, *We Are Going,* and the next year Colin Johnson (Mudrooroo or Mudrooroo Narogin) published the first novel by an Aboriginal author, *Wild Cat Falling.* The name changes of these two authors are symptomatic of the difficulties Aboriginal writers have in establishing their identities and cultural credentials. Unlike Oodgeroo, Mudrooroo did not grow up on an Aboriginal reserve or have an Aboriginal tongue as his first language. In large measure because of her family ties and her political activism, Oodgeroo never lost touch with her Aboriginality. Mudrooroo, on the contrary, lost his Aboriginality altogether: he vanished, it seems, into the time warp between modernity and postmodernity, during which both he and his globalizing readership found it impossible to distinguish between racial and cultural authenticity—or inauthenticity. Yet paradoxically, in some of her poems Oodgeroo expresses the elegiac theme of the vanishing of all Aboriginal culture, as in the title poem to her first volume:

> The scrubs are gone, the hunting and the laughter.
> The eagle is gone, the emu and the kangaroo are gone from this place.
> The bora ring is gone.
> The corroboree is gone.
> And we are going.

However one understands the Aboriginality of either Oodgeroo or Mudrooroo, sometimes David Unaipon's *Native Legends* (1929) is viewed as "the 'first work' of Aboriginal literature."[8] But his text was republished in London in 1930 by white anthropologist William Ramsay-Smith, who failed to credit Unaipon with its authorship. Aboriginal storytelling was typically viewed by Westerners as an anonymous, collective enterprise and free grist for the mill of (white) anthropology. So perhaps there was nothing unusual about Ramsay-Smith's literary piracy. The continent itself, after all, had been stolen from its Aboriginal inhabitants by its British invaders. Starting with the First Fleet and the establishment of a penal colony at Botany Bay in 1788, the invaders promptly lied about what they were doing. According to them, the continent's Aboriginal inhabitants had no conception of property or of owning the land they inhabited. The invaders soon promulgated the legal doctrine of *terra nullius,* or nobody's land, as if the Aboriginals did not even exist. *Terra nullius* was finally overturned by the High Court in 1992 in the Eddie Mabo land rights case, the year of my initial trip to Australia.[9]

Literature by white Australian authors is only about a century older than literature by Aboriginal authors. Assigning the former to modernity and the latter to postmodernity suggests the recentness, in terms of historical periods, of Australian culture and nationhood after 1788, although Aboriginal culture, the so-called Dreamtime, has often been treated as both ancient and ageless, as in Bruce Chatwin's *The Songlines.* The question of the postmodernity of both white and Aboriginal Australian literatures, however, is not merely one of period. That question depends on how one understands cultural or literary authenticity, which can get confused with the authenticity of authors' racial identities. With its origins not just in settler colonialism but in convict history, Australian culture, including both white and Aboriginal culture, has found it especially difficult to know how to deal with the issue of authenticity. At times, Australian writers and artists have turned their sense of inauthenticity to their advantage, as, for example, in Peter Carey's novel *My Life as a Fake* and Simon Caterson's monograph *Hoax Nation*. Further, while questions of authenticity often posed major problems for authors and artists identified with modernity, including Australian colonial authors, postmodern culture in general is characterized by a wide range of types of inauthenticity, which includes both white and Aboriginal literatures today.

No more than Oodgeroo, however, did Mudrooroo think he was being inauthentic when he asserted his Aboriginal identity and wrote about Aboriginal characters and their experiences. After all, for three decades, Mudrooroo was considered Australia's most important Aboriginal novelist and literary critic. Yet his first novel, *Wild Cat Falling*, and all the rest of his writing, seems to have entered a postmodern purgatory because, starting in 1996, his racial authenticity, like Sally Morgan's, has been called into question. Apparently, his forebears were not Aboriginal but part white and part African or African American (Oboe). "To complicate matters," Maureen Clark points out, "the hardships Mudrooroo suffered in his youth—separation from his family, followed by years spent in Australia's welfare and penal institutions—represent for many the 'authentic' Aboriginal experience of dislocation and pain."[10] Obviously, this is not the "'authentic' Aboriginal experience" demanded by officialdom adjudicating land rights, by New Age spiritual tourists, or even by many Aboriginals.

In *Uncanny Australia*, Ken Gelder and Jane Jacobs argue that, whether coming from whites or from Aboriginals, the pressure for the latter be "primitive" and "traditional," by locking "Aboriginal people into a form of otherness that modernity needs," is a product of "neocolonial racism."[11] By insisting that Aboriginal authors should narrate only a limited range of stories or experiences, the demand for authenticity takes the form of discursive oppression. So, too, in examining the authenticity of Morgan's *My Place*, Gareth Griffiths contrasts "the closed and limited construction of a pure authentic sign" to the "endless and excessive transformation of the subject positions possible within the hybridized."[12] Because all identities are plural, divided, and in various ways hybrid, to insist on a nonhybridized authenticity is to render all authors' claims to Aboriginal or even to Australian identity suspect. After all, no one expects all white male Australians to behave like Crocodile Dundee.

If modernity has involved the extinction of "natives" everywhere mainly through settler colonialism, disease, violence, and racial hybridization or miscegenation, postmodernity in some of its forms involves the recognition of that extinction.[13] Yet, paradoxically, in Australia as in all other societies formed through settler colonization, writers wishing to establish their and their texts' ethnic, national, or racial authenticity confront what Terry Goldie calls "the impossible necessity of becoming indigenous."[14] In the context of postmodern, capitalist globalization, both white and Aboriginal Australians struggle to maintain their identities as Australians and also as either white or Aboriginal, against the corroding forces especially of mass-mediated commodification and superficial multiculturalism—the forces pressuring them to vanish into mere simulacra of what they had hoped to become.

But assuming that Mudrooroo is racially non-Aboriginal although he is culturally Aboriginal, how does that affect the authenticity of his writings? "The curse of authenticity," as Adam Shoemaker puts it in considering Mudrooroo's (and Australia's) dilemma, involves several types of that key but elusive epistemological value. Obviously, any author can write an inauthentic story (fake, fictional, fantastic, untrue in detail but true as representation, etc.). But can a biologically inauthentic author write a culturally authentic story, which is what Mudrooroo seems to have done in *Wildcat Falling, Dr. Wooreddy's Prescription for Enduring the End of the World* (1983), *Master of the Ghost Dreaming* (1991), and his other novels? Before 1996, Mudrooroo did not know that he was not of Aboriginal descent. "I'm not a Caucasian masquerading as a blackfella," he told Shoemaker in 2001; "I'm some sort of a blackfella masquerading as a blackfella."[15] With the revelation that he is not the "blackfella" he thought he was, Mudrooroo seems to have given up writing and left Australia for India, where he has taken up Buddhism.

With Sally Morgan in mind, Sonja Kurtzer notes that "Indigenous authors are having difficulties within their own communities in having their life experiences recognized as authentic and this in part is due to the demand for particular kinds of stories from 'white' audiences."[16] But why should an author's descent or racial makeup or even his or her original culture be a factor in judging the aesthetic quality and even the veridicality of that person's writing? In assessing the literary qualities of *Wild Cat Falling* or his other writings, Mudrooroo's genetic makeup should be irrelevant.

Perhaps harder to assess are the writings of Sretan Bozic, the author of *The Track of Bralgu* (1973) and other works under the presumably Aboriginal pseudonym "B. Wongar." It turns out that Bozic is a Serbian immigrant who married an Aboriginal woman and lived for several years among Aboriginals in the Northern Territory. In his autobiography *Dingo Den* (1999), Bozic acknowledges his Serbian origins. There is no doubt, however, that the success of his earlier publications benefited from his assumed Aboriginal identity.[17] Bozic's story raises this question: can a white person "go native" thoroughly enough to become Aboriginal? Becoming a "white blackfella" is the obverse of the assimilationist policy followed for many years by the Australian government, which aimed at turning Aboriginals into—from a white perspective—civilized Australians. In any event, unlike Leon Carmen, the Sydney cab driver who wrote as "Wanda Coolmatrie" (thus assuming both a fake Aboriginal and a fake gender identity), Bozic-Wongar had in some measure become culturally Aboriginal.[18]

The critics have not questioned the accuracy of "B. Wongar's" portrayals of Aboriginal characters and culture. But the fact that he at first disguised his Serbian descent has landed his fiction in the category of literary hoaxes, and there have been many of those in Australian literary history. In contrast, Donald Stuart, another writer who married an Aboriginal woman and has lived among Aboriginals, has written novels such as *Ilbarana* (1971) and *Malloonkai* (1976) about the early history of Aboriginal-white relations that have not been categorized as hoaxes. As historical fiction about first contact, Stuart's stories bear comparison to Mudrooroo's *Dr. Wooreddy*. Yet, of course, historical fiction, no matter how factually accurate, is always inauthentic, in the sense that its authors are writing about times and situations they have not experienced.

As Mudrooroo grew up, he too acquired an Aboriginal cultural identity that has been the main basis of his writing. While *Wild Cat Falling* and the other Wild Cat novels are more or less autobiographical, that is not true of the rest of Mudrooroo's fiction. *Dr. Wooreddy,* for example, deals with the extinction of the Tasmanian Aboriginals, a "race" that supposedly died out in 1876, with the death of "Queen" Trugernini. Mudrooroo's racial origins have as much or as little to do with the authenticity of *Dr. Wooreddy* as do Stuart's with *Ilbarana* or white author Robert Drewe's with the authenticity of *The Savage Crows* (1976), another historical novel based on the Tasmanian tragedy. *Dr. Wooreddy, Ilbarana,* and *The Savage Crows* deserve to be judged as are all historical novels—or, for that matter, as are all literary works that are not based on the immediate personal experiences of their authors.

Meanwhile, Mudrooroo seems to have been lost in the vast shuffle of capitalist globalization, which may well be the fate of Aboriginal culture in general. "The aerial reef ballet staged in imaginary water was a miracle. My favourite bit was the fluttering swarm of jellyfish. The whole lyrical synthesis of the Aboriginal Dreamtime and the modern age was an unrelenting wow." So wrote Clive James about Ric Birch's spectacle for the opening of the 2000 Olympics in Sydney. Birch, James asserted, was "the Diaghilev of the Southern Hemisphere."[19] The oxymoronic fusion of "the Aboriginal Dreamtime" and "the modern age" in both the spectacle and James's essay is typical of much "modern" Australian culture. However, the contradiction at the center of this fusion, or confusion, seems more postmodern than modern, in a way that characterizes the cultures of other postcolonial settler societies: Canada, New Zealand, South Africa, and the United States.[20] All these societies are undergoing capitalist globalization: the 2000 Olympics, including Birch's internationally televised commodification of the Aboriginal Dreamtime, is an obvious example.[21] And in all these societies, writers wishing to establish their or their texts' national, racial, or ethnic credentials confront "the impossible necessity of becoming indigenous"(Goldie 13). In the context of postmodern, capitalist globalization, which bleaches and blends (supposedly harmoniously) all identities in a mass-mediated wash of commodification, multiculturalism, and superficial cosmopolitanism, this necessity is just as impossible to fulfill for indigenous as for nonindigenous writers.

In all postmodern cultures, commodification reigns supreme, and how can any commodity, even if it is original and one of a kind, be Aboriginal? "When Australia hosts an international event or seeks to entice overseas visitors, consumers or corporations," declares Aboriginal writer

Larissa Behrendt, "it is not shy about using images of Aboriginal people or symbols. . . . One need look no further than the incorporation of a boomerang as part of the official Olympic motif."[22] The boomerang has gone global and can never be repossessed by Aboriginals as their exclusive invention or property: no patent pending. What about the Dreamtime? Who owns the 2000 version of the Dreamtime, and how much did it cost? Whether Birch asked these questions is beside the point; but he obviously appropriated some version of the Dreamtime—not his own—for the spectacle that wowed James.

The primitivism expressed in many claims to or nostalgic aspirations for Aboriginality by both nonindigenous and indigenous Australians alike is obviously affected by commodification. Tourism to Uluru, Kakadu, and other Aboriginal sites is an example, and so are New Age bestsellers like Lynn Andrews's *Crystal Woman: Sisters of the Dreamtime* (1987) and Marlo Morgan's *Mutant Message from Down Under* (1990). These examples of "indigenous popontology"[23] portray their white heroines discovering spiritual wisdom among primitive nomads. Besides the desire for a spirituality lacking in modern and postmodern civilization, primitivism typically involves a back-to-nature fantasy, so that Aboriginality is identified with the Australian landscape—the desert, the "bush" or "outback." In white discourse from the colonial period to Marlo Morgan, the Aboriginals are typically merged with the landscape, part of Australia's exotic fauna. But with postmodernity comes the rapid commodification and even disappearance of nature. To the extent that the entire continent has been invaded and possessed by non-Aboriginal Australians, it, too, is now commodified; it has, in a sense, been removed from nature and pressed into the service of so-called civilization, or globalizing capitalism. After the Mabo and Wik land rights court decisions of the 1990s, Aboriginal possession of tribal land and sacred sites is being reasserted through elaborate legal proceedings. However, very little land owned by white Australians or by corporations has reverted or will revert to Aboriginal ownership. In short, all the land that comprises Australia has been colonized, and most of it has been commodified and will remain so for the foreseeable future.

The commodification of Aboriginal motifs during the 2000 Olympics is only one of the issues evoked by Birch's work and James's praise of it. As the terms "modern" and "postmodern" suggest, the temporal divide between the Aboriginal Dreamtime and James's "wow" is now key. Through no fault of their own, Birch and James are as far removed from the original Aboriginal Dreamtime as I am. And through no fault of her own, today's Aboriginal writer—Behrendt, for instance—is inevitably anachronistic, coming after or perhaps even before her time (that is, her time according to Western clocks). Postmodernity is also anachronistic, a dreamtime perhaps (capitalist, globalized, surrealistic) but also a time out of time, a futuristic falling away from the Western forward march of progress, an acknowledgment that the clocks are running in reverse or at any rate are unreliable. If the original Aboriginal Dreamtime was authentic, the postmodern condition is the dreamtime of the inauthentic.

Aboriginal writers like Sally Morgan and Mudrooroo are caught in the same chronotope or time warp that causes non-Aboriginal writers also to be, inevitably, postmodern. The point is not simply the periodizing one that, because they live in the postmodern era, all authors are now postmodern. Rather, the postmodern condition entails veridical confusions, falsifications, or reversals, so that what might be called "fake" Aboriginal writing might also be viewed as authentically postmodern, although not authentically Aboriginal.

"NIX MY DOLLY, PALS, FAKE AWAY!"[24]

There have, of course, been many modern attempts by non-Aboriginal authors to portray or mimic Aboriginal values and experience. What have the critics said about the authenticity—or lack thereof—of their portrayals and versions of mimicry? Poetry by the Jindyworobaks and novels such as Katherine Prichard's *Coonardoo* (1929) and Xavier Herbert's *Capricornia* (1938) are examples. The earliest major attempt "to develop a truly indigenous white Australian culture, using Aboriginal culture—or rather, their superficial understanding of it"—was the Jindyworobak movement, which commenced in 1938. Adam Shoemaker writes that "most of the original Jindyworobaks told their readers next to nothing about Aboriginal people. Rather, their usage of the ostensible trappings of black Australian languages was indicative of a kind of souvenir mentality."[25] Prichard and Herbert show sympathy for their Aboriginal characters, if not greater understanding of Aboriginal culture than did the Jindyworobaks.

It is not surprising, moreover, that "fake" Aboriginal writing includes a number of prominent hoaxes that have plagued, puzzled, and entertained Australian and, indeed, transnational readers. Besides the stories by "B. Wongar" (Bozic) and *My Own Sweet Time* (1994) by "Wanda Coolmatrie," there are the highly popular New Age "walkabout" tales by two American writers. Andrews's *Crystal Woman* and Marlo Morgan's *Mutant Message Down Under* do not purport to be authored by Aboriginals; they do, however, purport to be the true stories of their authors' spiritual walkabouts with Aboriginals. Morgan's *Mutant Message Down Under* has been condemned as a hoax by Aboriginal groups, whose leaders have traveled to the United States seeking an apology from her.[26] As a purveyor of Aboriginal spirituality, Lynn Andrews, "the Beverly Hills shaman," is just as phony as Morgan, but seems to have received less publicity in Australia (Aldred, "Plastic Shamans").

As in the cases of Morgan, Mudrooroo, and Bozic, moreover, both Aboriginal and non-Aboriginal writers have, at least since the 1960s, been puzzled and plagued by issues of identity. Thus, self-proclaimed Aboriginal writer Archie Weller, author of *The Day of the Dog* (1988) and other literary works, "has white skin and he cannot prove his belief that his great-grandmother was part-Aboriginal."[27] But neither can Weller's belief be disproven. So, too, the authenticity of Roberta Sykes's autobiographical works, starting with *Snake Cradle* (1997), has been challenged by other Aboriginal writers.[28] Since authenticity and its opposites are relative terms, even these works, like the narratives by Morgan, Mudrooroo, and Bozic, have some degree of authenticity. But with the postmodern condition comes the difficulty or perhaps impossibility of attaining any degree of authenticity whatsoever, so that hoaxes acquire a kind of perverse veridicality—not truth, of course, but the honesty of being thoroughly dishonest or inauthentic.

Fake Aboriginal writing and puzzling Aboriginal or part-Aboriginal identities by no means exhaust the history of hoaxes and authorial identity problems in current Australian culture. Of course, there have been many similar hoaxes in the United States, for example, including texts about Native American cultures, such as Carlos Casteneda's *The Teachings of Don Juan: A Yaqui Way of Knowledge* (1968), that are now known to be hoaxes, and texts by supposedly Native American authors who have turned out not to be Native American—Forrest Carter's *The Education of*

Little Tree (1976), for example. Nor is it exclusively fake Aboriginal texts that have caused Simon Caterson to dub Australia the "hoax nation" par excellence. For a new, relatively small nation-state, whose origin goes back to the First Fleet in 1788 and the establishment of a penal colony at Botany Bay, literary hoaxes exacerbate Australia's "cultural cringe"[29] and its "obsession with the issue of legitimacy."[30]

There have been many types and degrees of hoaxes in Australian as in North American literary history, but by the 1990s Australia was experiencing "a flood of disclosures about hoaxes and impostures."[31] Such hoaxes expose "the crisis of authority for white settler Australians in their claims to legitimate possession of nationhood in post-Mabo Australia" (Nolan and Dawson, *Who's Who?* ix). Assuming that the entire continent before 1788 belonged to the Aboriginals, the legal fiction on which white possession was based, *terra nullius,* which, as previously mentioned, the High Court overturned in 1992 in the Eddie Mabo case, was itself a hoax—and a rationalization for invasion and genocide. The Australian situation may be dramatic, of course, but is not unique because modern nation-states and national identities—and not just those in former settler colonies—have been forged out of war, violence, and the expropriation of land and other resources, a process that is still going on in the Middle East and many other parts of the world.

Perhaps because of its convict past, hoaxes and other versions of fakery have seemed to constitute one of the basic ingredients of Australian culture from the beginning. Hoaxes in Australian literature start with the texts attributed to transported pickpocket George Barrington, the first person to receive a pardon in New South Wales. According to Simon Caterson,

> The 'Prince of Pickpockets,' as he was portrayed in the popular press . . . seems to have been the first Australian literary celebrity of any kind— though there's no evidence that he actually wrote any portion of the numerous bestselling books published in several languages under his name that describe his imagined life in Australia (24).

Barrington's case was soon followed by the captivity stories of Eliza Fraser, who found herself "in the company of Aborigines" after the *Stirling Castle* was shipwrecked off the northeast coast of Australia in 1836. In the first account she gave of her "captivity," she said very little about her treatment by the Aboriginals. But after her return to England, she embellished her story considerably, as did others who capitalized on the sensational possibilities—cannibalism, for example—that they inserted into it. As "the first white woman to encounter Aborigines in the wild," Mrs. Fraser has today acquired "mythical status" via such retellings as Patrick White's 1976 novel *A Fringe of Leaves* and the film in the same year by David Williamson and Tim Burstall, *Eliza Fraser*.[32] Did the Aboriginals capture or rescue her? Was she ever threatened with being killed and eaten? Her own additions to her story after she returned to England led to her being widely viewed as a fraud.

In the twentieth century, the most notorious Australian literary hoax is the poetry of "Ern Malley" starting in 1944, the topic of Peter Carey's postmodern novel *My Life as a Fake* (2003). According to Bill Ashcroft, "No event has captured the attention, and the imagination, of Australian critics as completely as the Ern Malley hoax."[33] Carey is well aware that the most authentic—*and* least original—aspect of his tall tale are the quotations from Ern Malley, attributed in the novel to the Australian monster/poetic genius Bob McCorkle, who, in turn, is the Frankensteinian invention (or hoax) of failed poet Christopher Chubb. Carey recognizes that a "genealogy of fraudulence," as Graham Huggan puts it, "coexists with the historical development of Australian literature itself."[34]

How could it be otherwise? Modern Australia's brief history is rooted in a recent colonial, convict, and genocidal past that, in regard to the last two issues, many of its writers and officials have wanted to "whitewash."[35] As noted earlier, the literary theft of David Unaipon's *Native Legends* (1929) is only a microcosm of the colonizers' theft of the entire continent. And besides the entire continent, there is the issue of the "stolen generations," a genocidal theft perhaps best known outside Australia through the movie *Rabbit-Proof Fence,* based on the 1996 book by Aboriginal author Doris Pilkington-Nugi Garimara. Hers is one of many accounts of people having lost or having come close to losing touch with their Aboriginal roots (ancestral families, communities, languages, beliefs, and customs)—accounts that include Sally Morgan's *My Place*. It is also not surprising that the motif of stolen or lost children is a major one in Australian literature and film, as in the movies *Walkabout* and *Picnic at Hanging Rock,* although most stories that feature this motif are about lost white children.[36]

In terms of notoriety, Ern Malley is followed closely in the Australian pantheon of literary hoaxes by *The Hand That Signed the Paper* (1994), whose author, Helen "Demidenko" Darville, claimed to be a Ukrainian emigrant recollecting the Holocaust. In 1993, Darville's novel won the prestigious Vogel Literary Prize for an unpublished work by an author less than thirty-five years old. As Susanna Egan notes, "The Demidenko scandal that erupted in 1995 challenged the literary and academic establishments in Australia for their ineptitude in monitoring the cultural identities that constitute Australia" ("The Company She Keeps," 15). Probably next in notoriety to the Ern Malley and Demidenko frauds is *Forbidden Love* (2004) by Norma Khouri, supposedly a true story of an honor killing in Jordan, which Caterson says is "the most commercially successful literary hoax ever exposed in Australia" (*Hoax Nation*, 12).

Lurking behind Khouri, Demidenko, Ern Malley, and other hoaxes is the suspicion that Australian identities of all sorts are unstable, perhaps more fictional or even fraudulent than other nationally based identities. If authenticity is supposedly at least partly based on descent or race, the "White Australia" policy that was hegemonic during much of the twentieth century has been belied on several counts. A key source of genealogical information for white Australians can be found in the computerized databases available in prison museums. Many of the first immigrants, including convicts, were Irish rather than Anglo-Saxon in origin. Other early immigrants were Asian or African in descent.[37] In the early 1900s, an argument for the assimilation of Aboriginals was based on the theory that they were actually a primitive branch of the Caucasian or white race.[38] There is never any secure basis of authenticity in notions of racial purity.

Ironically, far from leaving race behind, postmodern commodification and globalization have put a premium on racialized authenticity, however preposterous and no matter how it is measured. Aesthetic measures of authenticity—usually based on judgments about originality and/or verisimilitude—are slippery and subjective. Hence, for the purposes of advertising and marketing, authenticity tends to be measured by an untenable standard of racial purity. In regard to "primitive art," Shelly Errington comments,

> "Authenticity" more and more designates . . . that the artist is an authentic Australian Aboriginal, Native American, or whatever. In the United

States, legislation has been passed to guarantee this; airport gift shops, for example, are legally obliged to label things as (for instance) "Southwest Style Jewelry" or words to that effect, rather than as "Authentic Navajo Jewelry," unless they are made by authentic Navajos. Authenticity has been transferred from the object to the author.[39]

Culture offers more logical grounds for assessing authenticity than biology, yet obviously individuals can adopt aspects of new cultures or can experience other cultures in ways that give them some measure of expertise beyond their culture of origin. Hence, a writer like Sretan Bozic may be more knowledgeable about "traditional" Aboriginal culture than an Aboriginal author who has grown up in Melbourne or Sydney.

For many Aboriginal authors like Sally Morgan, it is the experience of being of mixed-race descent and of the forms of racist oppression visited upon "half-breeds" that is authentic, in the sense of personal, lived experience. If neither to be fully Aboriginal nor fully white is to be caught between two impossibilities—pure black or pure white—then the demand to produce something that can be called authentically Aboriginal writing is itself one that can only produce various degrees of inauthenticity or, indeed, of hoaxes. This is simply the mirror opposite of the contradictory situation in which the descendants of colonial settlers in Australia, New Zealand, Canada, and elsewhere find themselves. Writing about literature in colonies of white settlement, Anna Johnston and Alan Lawson remark,

> The typical settler narrative . . . has a doubled goal. It is concerned to act out the suppression or effacement of the indigene; it is also concerned to perform the concomitant indigenization of the settler. In becoming more like the indigene whom he mimics, the settler becomes less like the atavistic inhabitant of the cultural homeland whom he is also reduced to mimicking. The text is thus marked by counterfeiting of both emergence and origination.[40]

In short, the literature of the colonizer "is also reduced" to inauthenticity, a "counterfeiting" that invariably leads to a general cultural condition of hoaxing, as diagnosed in the U.S. context by Herman Melville in *The Confidence Man*. Melville, Edgar Allan Poe, and Mark Twain all understood that in America, with its history of slavery, the extinction of Native Americans, and racial hybridization, hoaxing was a paradoxically honest way to tell the truth.

The search for cultural authenticity also places a premium on speech rather than writing. According to Terry Goldie, "Speech is deemed to be more natural than writing and therefore the oral culture is much closer to nature than one that writes."[41] White settler literature was, of course, from the outset a version of print culture. And supposedly authentic Aboriginal literature has often been restricted to mythology, folklore, and oral storytelling. Yet oral cultures need to be rendered in print in order to move beyond immediate speech acts. In *The Songlines,* an Aboriginal man performs for Bruce Chatwin and his friend Arkady a song representing "the travels of the lizard Ancestor" (105). The performance is in English and lasts about three minutes. At the end of it, Arkady tells Chatwin that it "was not of course the *real* Lizard song, but a 'false front,' or sketch performed for strangers. The real song would have named each waterhole the Lizard Man drank from, each tree he cut a spear from, each cave he slept in, covering the whole long distance of the way" (106). Nevertheless, Chatwin inserts a short, three-paragraph rendition of the unreal lizard song that he heard into his text—that is, a lizard song at several removes from the real one. The final rendition is an abbreviation of the already abbreviated lizard song. Through a text like Chatwin's—or, for that matter, through Theodore Strehlow's *Aranda Traditions,* which Chatwin admires—the "real" Aboriginal songlines are an ever-receding mirage. This is not to say that *The Songlines* is a hoax—far from it: Chatwin acknowledges the impossibility of his being able to offer more than a third- or fourth-hand version of "the *real* Lizard song." Chatwin's travelogue is epistemologically the antithesis of a New Age fake like *Mutant Message Down Under.* It is instead similar to Carey's *My Life as a Fake:* both achieve a certain ironic authenticity by acknowledging the impossibility of ever achieving the nonironic authenticity claimed by hoaxes.

CONCLUSION

Terry Goldie writes that the first of the "phantoms" evoked by Mudrooroo and Demidenko is the "illusory figure of absolute authenticity" ("On Not Being Australian," 97). One implication of Mudrooroo's personal story is that, if there is such a thing as an authentic Australian, then that person must be a traditional Aboriginal, unspoiled by white civilization. In those terms, there are no longer any traditional Aboriginals. In *The Cun-*

ning of Recognition, anthropologist Elizabeth Povinelli writes that "no indigenous subject can inhabit the temporal or spatial location to which indigenous identity refers—the geographical and social space and time of authentic Ab-originality" (49). This is the corollary of Goldie's insistence on the "impossible necessity" for the white citizens of former settler colonies to become "indigenous." Povinelli has in mind the impossibility of today's Aboriginals to maintain and practice "traditional" customs and laws—that is, the customs and laws exactly as their ancestors maintained and practiced them. Like Sally Morgan, moreover, many Australian writers who identify as Aboriginal are of mixed-race descent. And many twentieth-century texts, whether by white, Aboriginal, or mixed-race authors also feature "half-caste" or mixed-race characters like Harley, the narrator and protagonist of Kim Scott's *Benang.* Harley is an "octoroon" who his grandfather, a Scotsman, hoped would be "the first white man born" through interbreeding the races. The "recessive" genes of the Aboriginals, whose race some scientists and officials considered a forerunner of the Caucasian race, would supposedly give way to superior, dominant white traits. The only outward sign that Harley is part Aboriginal is his freckles. Breeding out the "race" was the eugenics theory (mis)informing the assimilationist policy of the 1920s and 1930s, advocated in the novel by A. O. Neville, an actual "Protector" of Aboriginals in Western Australia. Quotations from Neville's racist writings pepper *Benang.*

In both racial and literary terms, the stress on authenticity is misleading, especially when it is considered that any translation of an oral source into a printed text is, in some sense, already inauthentic. In her study of early Aboriginal writing, Penny van Toorn notes that "there is no denying that in many parts of Australia important traditional Indigenous life-ways have not survived the introduction of literacy," and she asks, "Does such erosion attest to the destructive powers of literacy itself?" (*Writing Never Arrives Naked,* 11). Perhaps so. At least, it is certain that European civilization has involved the destruction of Aboriginality and, perhaps with that destruction, any chance that modern and postmodern Australian culture, whether produced by whites or by Aboriginals, can achieve authenticity, except by acknowledging its inevitable inauthenticity. Today, the commodified Dreamtime, rendered for capitalist, globalized consumption, can only speak the truth of the hoax.

McLuhan, Crash Theory, and
the Invasion of the Nanobots

The truth of contemporary science is not so much the extent of
progress achieved as the scale of technical catastrophes occasioned.

—PAUL VIRILIO, *THE INFORMATION BOMB*

A maverick professor of English, Marshall McLuhan became a public
intellectual by dint of his commentaries on communications technologies and how they had shaped history and were shaping the present and
future. Though initially highly critical of them, McLuhan also appeared
perfectly happy to serve as a pundit or guru for the mass media and for
commercial advertising firms. Perhaps he was not critical enough. In any
case, recent work on new technologies and the emergence of "the information society" suggests that McLuhan has entered a sort of academic
purgatory, even though many of his ideas—or the ideas that he expressed,
at any rate—are everywhere. Many scholars do not bother to cite him. In
Theories of the Information Society, for example, Frank Webster does not
mention McLuhan, while Darin Barney cites only his "famous aphorism
. . . 'the medium is the message'" in *Prometheus Wired* (56). So, too, in *The
Informational City,* probably the most important sociological analysis to
date of the paradigm shift to the information age, Manuel Castells ignores
McLuhan. This is not to say that he, Webster, Barney, or other recent
scholars should necessarily do otherwise; after all, McLuhan published
The Gutenberg Galaxy and *Understanding Media* over four decades ago.
Nevertheless, as Christopher May notes, McLuhan's "discussion of
the transformative potential of new communications technologies and

practices remains influential, inasmuch as many of his ideas find their way into current discussions, albeit unacknowledged."[1] Certainly, McLuhan was asking important questions, even if his answers were often inadequate or weakly supported. If that judgment is true from the vantage point of the information age, it is also true concerning his ideas about earlier historical moments.[2] Perhaps, then, Donald Theall's claim that we should view McLuhan as a "modernist artist" rather than as a historian, philosopher, or social scientist is the fairest way to judge him.[3] Theall writes that "McLuhan has frequently been misunderstood by heavy, sombre academics, since he played games, he used wit and satire, and he employed a strategy of decentering and fragmentation" (*The Virtual Marshall McLuhan*,17). All this is true, though it also helps explain why "heavy, sombre academics" will continue to ignore him.

Theall makes some intriguing points, however, about similarities between McLuhan's ideas and the emergence of French poststructuralist theory also starting in the 1960s.[4] Theall cites John Fekete writing in 1982: "Derrida takes up again and again, without reference to McLuhan, the same themes . . . : logocentrism, phonocentrism, the eye, the ear . . . the impact of the phonetic alphabet, abstraction, writing, linearity as the repression of pluri-dimensional thought, simultaneity, synaesthesia, etc."[5] For other French theorists, including Roland Barthes and Jean Baudrillard, there was an acknowledged interest in "McLuhanism" in the 1960s and 70s. In *A Thousand Plateaus,* Gilles Deleuze and Félix Guattari drew on McLuhan for the idea that the modern world is moving in "two directions: worldwide ecumenical machines, but also a neoprimitivism, a new tribal society" (360). In their earlier *Anti-Oedipus,* with the "Gutenberg galaxy" in mind, they claimed that "the significance of McLuhan's analyses [is] to have shown what a language of decoded flows is, as opposed to a signifier that strangles and overcodes the flows" (240). This "language of decoded flows" supported their concepts of the "mechanosphere," "nomadism," "deterritorialization," "machinic assemblages," "bodies without organs," and humans as "desiring machines." Versions of all these ideas can be found in McLuhan.

McLuhan continues to be important to a radical branch of postmodernist, posthumanist cultural theory in France and elsewhere. This branch merits the title "crash theory," a phrase that I take from Arthur Kroker and Michael Weinstein's *Data Trash.* An apocalyptic version of postmodernism, crash theory treats technology as inexorably pushing humanity toward annihilation, or at least toward the "implosion" of reality into something like its opposite. Besides Kroker and Weinstein, the main crash theorists I will consider are Paul Virilio and Jean Baudrillard, both of whom acknowledge at least some influence from McLuhan. I will also consider several recent computer and robotics scientists who pay little if any attention either to McLuhan or to the postmodern crash theorists, but whose ideas about the consequences of technological innovation are clearly versions of crash theory.

The crash theorists represent one highly apocalyptic line of speculation about "the postmodern condition," a line indebted both to McLuhan and to poststructuralism. The scientists engaged in current debates about GRAIN, or the "megamerger of [the] super sciences" of genetics, robotics, artificial intelligence, and nanotechnology,[6] though expressing a McLuhan-like ambivalence toward the technological innovations they are simultaneously promoting and deploring, go beyond even the crash theorists with some of their doomsday scenarios. McLuhan may have been prescient in regard to some of the social and psychological effects of new communications media, but he did not fully foresee the impact of cybernetics and the computer revolution and did not at all foresee the apocalyptic prospects that have dawned through GRAIN, even though the first annunciations of these new sciences and technologies occurred during his lifetime. McLuhan emphasized communications media, but GRAIN technologies are not easily distinguishable from such media. On the contrary, artificial intelligence, codes such as DNA, and communication between the parts of systems, whether organic or inorganic (or hybrid) are fundamental to the emergent GRAIN technologies that promise and threaten to change the world forever.

MCLUHAN AS TECHNOPROPHET

Foreshadowed by McLuhan, crash theory is in part the logical outcome of the technological determinism that McLuhan occasionally disowned but that is central to his thinking. All versions of technological determinism are inherently dystopian because they always transfer agency from humans to machines—they are always expressions of alienation. Paul Grosswiler has argued that "McLuhan's method, like the early Marx's radical dialectical method, was not a mechanistic, technological determinism."[7] That view depends, however, on just how much weight one gives to McLuhan's disclaimers about technodeterminism and, conversely, how much stress one puts on some of his best-known formulations, such as "the medium is the message."[8] The consensus among scholars who write about McLuhan is, indeed, that he often expresses versions of technodeterminism. A brief version of history from McLuhan's perspective might be this: in the beginning, men created machines; later on, machines took over, dominated, and even began to create men—in the sense, at least, that the machinery of mass communications now creates and directs human consciousness.

William James distinguished between "hard" and "soft" versions of determinism.[9] Taken in isolation (or perhaps, out of context), many of McLuhan's assertions about the historical impacts of new technologies are clearly "hard"; but he backtracks often enough to make a reasonable case that he is only a "soft" determinist. And as Bruce Bimber argues, "a so-called soft determinism cannot be called determinism at all"[10]—thus, it is possible to maintain that McLuhan was not a technodeterminist. However, my reading of McLuhan's most important texts—*The Gutenberg Galaxy* and *Understanding Media*—suggests otherwise. McLuhan's typical formulations about modern history (Renaissance or even the Middle Ages forward) put the cart before the horse, the machine before the human. He regularly makes the key move that defines technodeterminism: he personifies and gives historical agency to new machines and media; in doing so, he also reifies or erases human agency from the historical narratives that he constructs. Although they do not point to McLuhan as an example, the editors of *Does Technology Drive History?* note that "popular narratives" convey a vivid sense of the efficacy of technology as a driving force of history: a technical innovation suddenly appears and causes important things to happen. It is noteworthy that these minifables direct attention to the consequences rather than the genesis of inventions.[11] McLuhan's most familiar claims about history take this form: the printing press causes the Reformation and the rise of modern nationalisms; now the electronic media are reversing the linear, centralizing tendency of modernity and producing the detribalizing "global village."

Judith Stamps, Neil Postman, and others (myself included) have discussed similarities between McLuhan's theories and Karl Marx's, as well as those that have emerged from various Marxisms, including the Frankfurt School and the cultural studies movement.[12] One of those similarities has to do with determinism—or the degree of it, rather—in both McLuhan's and Marx's versions of history. Marx was certainly capable of aphoristic statements that can be interpreted as technodeterminist: "The hand-mill gives you society with the feudal lord, the steam-mill, society with the industrial capitalist."[13] Marx's more general economic determinism—especially the thesis that the "economic mode of production" or "real foundation" gives rise in every society to the ideological superstructure—is, however, a version of "soft" determinism—or, in other words, is not strictly deterministic. This is partly because of his other most prominent thesis, that the driving force of historical change is class conflict. And class conflict, Marx believed, produced revolution, including the final revolution that would usher in the classless society of the future. Marx clearly thought that the domination of any given mode of production was subject to revolutionary *Aufhebung* or dialectical upheaval through human agency: "Workers of the world unite! You have nothing to lose but your chains."

In contrast to Marx, McLuhan's typical formulations are about the historical and psychological changes to the human "sensorium" caused by the abrupt (and mysterious or unexplained, at least by McLuhan) appearance of some new machine or medium of communication. He rarely considers how new machines come to be invented, distributed, and used, except in the most abstract sense, though invention, distribution, and uses—plural—would put human agency back into the picture. His stress on the general, totalizing (that is, undifferentiated) effect of a new machine or medium willy-nilly (whether intentionally or otherwise) gives massive historical agency to machines and subtracts it from humans, whether inventors or owners and users.

For McLuhan, new media are both major historical events and mundane miracles (it is no accident that he was a faithful Catholic), though they can be demonic as well as angelic. And indeed, because he saw new media as potent forces, intervening in human history in unpredictable ways, McLuhan remains influential, at least among the crash theorists. Nevertheless, claims that he was a prophet or even just prescient about the era of computers and the Internet strike me as special pleading. Thus, according to Paul Levinson, "The handwriting for coming to terms with our digital age was on the wall of McLuhan's books."[14] Perhaps so, although given television and, for that matter, early computers, "our digital age" was easy enough to predict in the 1960s. Norbert Wiener was attempting to introduce (and simultaneously apologize for) a cybernetic, technologized concept of (post)human identity as early as 1950.[15] McLuhan writes, "by means of electric media, we set up a dynamic by which all previous technologies that are mere extensions of hands and feet and teeth and bodily heat-controls—all such extensions of our bodies, including cities—will be translated into information systems."[16] In the 1960s, however, that statement would have been more accurate—and sounded less prophetic—if McLuhan had used the present instead of the future tense. Further, McLuhan derived his main ideas about the electronic media from television, not from computers. And there were other technologies that were on the horizon during his lifetime that he paid little or no attention to: besides computers, which he did pay some attention to, these include robotics, genetic engineering, nanotechnology—that is, GRAIN.

What was most original about *The Gutenberg Galaxy* and *Understanding Media* was perhaps not McLuhan's ideas but the way he presented those ideas as paradoxes, startling claims, headlines, seemingly new insights such as "the medium is the message." Besides that striking paradox—which at least in its wording was original—the other most frequently cited McLuhanism is the idea of an emergent "global village," caused mainly by the rapidly "globalizing" effects of the electronic mass media. Notions of a shrinking, wired world, however, go back to responses to telegraphy and the first transatlantic cable hookup in the nineteenth century.[17] McLuhan's additional claims that the electronic global village is both "imploding" and undergoing "retribalization" are more original, especially in light of the recent balkanization, warfare, and genocides in Eastern Europe, Russia, the Middle East, and much of Africa. In *Globalization: The Human Consequences,* sociologist Zygmunt Bauman sums up a great deal of recent commentary on this topic, cites McLuhan not once, and yet writes, "Neo-tribal and fundamentalist tendencies, which reflect and articulate the experience of people on the receiving end of globalization, are as much legitimate offspring of globalization as the widely acclaimed 'hybridization' of top [elite] culture."[18] McLuhan could not have said it better himself.

In any case, Levinson's claim that McLuhan's stance toward new media is that of a prophet is at least accurate in regard to his rhetoric. McLuhan may have been a Joycean trickster-artist and witty poseur, as Theall makes him out to be, but he also wrapped himself in the mantle of the seer of new media. He was never sure enough of any of his ideas to issue straightforward jeremiads against technological innovations and new media; but neither was he sure enough to welcome them as ushering in the New Jerusalem. Crash theory is more consistently dystopian than was McLuhan, although there is often an undercurrent of celebration in its assertions of technological doom and anticipations of fulfilled prophecy.

Part of the similarity between crash theory and McLuhan lies in his penchant for making sweeping claims about history, such as these from *The Gutenberg Galaxy:* "A nomadic society cannot experience enclosed space" (64); "The medieval world ended in a frenzy of applied knowledge" (117); and "Heidegger surf-boards along on the electronic wave as triumphantly as Descartes rode the mechanical wave" (248). Imagining Heidegger surfboarding on anything at all is certainly amusing; but one feature that all these statements share with many of the other headlines (or section headings) in *Galaxy* is their oracular quality. These are more than just aphorisms and more than just headlines; they are pronouncements on vast, complicated historical transformations or social conditions that imply that their author is almost omniscient or has some kind of inner (supernatural?) scoop on past, present, and future that ordinary mortals—even Heidegger and Descartes, unwitting surfers—do not have. Along with technological determinism, it is McLuhan's oracular rhetoric that makes him a forerunner of crash theory. The prophetic, apocalyptic aspects of McLuhan's ideas show up again in Kroker, Weinstein, Virilio, and Baudrillard, though with less ambivalence about possible historical outcomes.

CRASH THEORY

The crash theorists tend to be dismissive of McLuhan as a techno-optimist, utopian, or even cryptotheologian, but they also recognize that McLuhan was not always merely a naïve cheerleader for technological innovation. In *Data Trash,* Kroker and Weinstein write, "McLuhan's 'global village' with its promise of technology as a religious 'epiphany' has passed" (52). This judgment may be partly correct, but their own brand of apocalyptic postmodernism begs to be read as a continuation of McLuhanism by other means. After all, later in their manifesto about the "virtual" trashing of the human, they write, "Cross McLuhan's nervous system outerized by the media, with Nietzsche's 'last man' . . . and you get crash theory" (143), which is their theory. Kroker and Weinstein try to distance themselves from McLuhan, but Kroker's first book, *Technology and the Canadian Mind: Innis /McLuhan /Grant,* traced the tradition of theorizing about the links between technology and history to which he and Weinstein belong.

Baudrillard, whose theory of "simulation," "hyperreality," and the "implosion" of the mass media into "posthistory" echoes some of the language of *The Gutenberg Galaxy* and *Understanding Media,* is explicit about his indebtedness to McLuhan: "even if I did not share the technological optimism of McLuhan, I always recognized and considered as a gain the true revolution which he brought about in media analysis."[19] Adopting McLuhan's "cybernetic concept of implosion," Baudrillard claims that what "implodes" in the postmodern condition is the distinction between simulation and reality. In *In the Shadow of the Silent Majorities,* Baudrillard acknowledges his debt to McLuhan and goes beyond his predecessor by contending that "the medium is the message signifies not only the end of the message, but also the end of the medium" (102). Both meaning and the media disappear into the simulacral maelstrom of "hyperreality."[20]

In *The Illusion of the End* (1992), Baudrillard both predicts and contradicts the ultimate Big Bang of all history. Capitalism is cannibalizing everything and virtualizing it into simulation, spectacle, image, copy without original. And/or there is the—more real? or more hyperreal?— threat of nuclear or some other even more advanced form of world-military annihilation. There are, at any rate, no alternatives either to the end of history or to its simulated illusion, whichever is happening: "For hyperreality rules out the very occurrence of the Last Judgement or the Apocalypse or the Revolution. All the ends we have envisaged elude our grasp and history has no chance of bringing them about, since it will, in the interim, have come to an end."[21] History as farce? For Baudrillard, as for McLuhan, the chief weapons of destruction seem to be television and cinema, though, in *The Spirit of Terrorism,* Baudrillard, like Virilio in *Ground Zero,* interprets 9/11 as an all-too-real, apocalyptic globalization of terror through television and the Internet. More than the other crash theorists, Baudrillard shares with McLuhan a quasi-theological investment in end-of-reality, end-of-history rhetoric and in simulations or electronic representations of those ends. Flaming icons?

Starting in the late 1960s, Paul Virilio has stressed the importance of wartime and war-related research for technological innovation. As James Der Derian, editor of *The Virilio Reader,* says, "There is certainly more than a hint of millenarian doom to Virilio's work" ("Introduction," 11). Der Derian also points out how, in *The Insecurity of Territory* (1976), Virilio introduced "the concepts of *deterritorialization, nomadism,* and the *suicidal state,* which Deleuze and Guattari pick up and brilliantly elaborate in their most significant work, *A Thousand Plateaus*" (10). In any event, Virilio also cites McLuhan, but only to dismiss him as a quasi-religious optimist about the effects of technology.[22] Yet in his section on weapons in *Understanding Media,* McLuhan recognizes the impetus that war has given to technological innovation, though he is less insistent than Virilio that technology in general can be understood as weaponry, or at any rate as in some sense always destructive. According to Virilio, even information becomes, in the age of the Internet, an "information bomb."[23]

Virilio's themes of speed and "speed pollution" are directly linked to war because "speed is the essence of war."[24] The goal of "the suicidal state," implicit in its drive to perfect its weaponry, is "pure war" and the annihilation not just of its enemies but of itself.[25] The computer and the postmodern "cult of information," moreover, are outgrowths of the global war machine or what Norbert Wiener, shortly after World War II, called "the military-communications complex."[26] In *The Art of the Motor,* Virilio writes, "Originating in civil and international war as well as in army logistics, the modern information complex cunningly preserves the deadly features of these" (54). He adds that "the media evolve in tandem with the army" (56) and that, even when no actual combat is happening between nation-states (though it is always happening somewhere), the media still seek to annihilate distance, real space and real time: "Territorial distance and media proximity make an explosive cocktail" (57).

Virilio's account of the developing "postindustrial 'technosphere'"[27] involves what he calls "dromology"—that is, the critical analysis of the effects of speed (and especially, the "light speed" involved in electronic devices including computers)—although this, again, is a theme in McLuhan: "The stepping-up of speed from the mechanical to the instant electric form reverses explosion into implosion."[28] The language of "explosion" and "implosion" that McLuhan uses in relation to media effects is echoed by all the crash theorists. The metaphor of the bomb, as in Virilio's *Information Bomb,* represents the extreme version of technology run amok. According to crash theory, even the seemingly most benign machines—computers, for instance—are hurtling forward toward "escape velocity" and the ultimate smash up, the Big Bang that will end reality and history altogether. For Virilio, moreover, the bomb is not just a metaphor:

> The metaphor of nuclear catastrophe . . . is no longer a stylistic trope, but . . . an accurate enough image of the damage to human *activity* caused by this sudden implosion-explosion of computerized *interactivity* which Albert Einstein predicted in the 1950s would probably constitute a second bomb, after the purpose-built atomic one.[29]

For McLuhan, too, "explosion" and "implosion" are real enough: they describe catastrophic historical transformations caused by new technologies. Unlike the postmodern crash theorists, however, he does not use these terms to predict the end of the world. Nevertheless, in *Understanding Media,* McLuhan writes,

> We know . . . the kind of energy that is released, as by fission, when literacy explodes the tribal or family unit. What do we know about the social and psychic energies that develop by electric fusion or implosion when literate individuals are suddenly gripped by an electromagnetic field . . . ? . . . The fusion of people who have known individualism and nationalism is not the same process as the fission of . . . oral cultures that are just coming to individualism and nationalism. It is the difference between the "A" bomb and the "H" bomb. The latter is more violent, by far.[30]

Even though Virilio does not cite him often, and then only critically, it is difficult not to detect the angelic-demonic, utopian-dystopian figure of McLuhan in the wings, so to speak, of Virilio's catastrophic accounts of "the nihilism of Western technology."[31] In a passage like this one, Virilio might as well be quoting McLuhan: "Like some gigantic implosion, the circulation of the general accident of communication technologies is building up and spreading, forcing all substances to keep moving in order to interact globally, at the risk of being wiped out, being swallowed up completely."[32] For Virilio, moreover, "speed" accelerates everything into a fast-forward leading to the ultimate technological, industrial "accident": "the coming crash of postindustrial production" (*Open Sky*, 73), the "*general global accident* which could well have radio-activity as its emblem" (ibid., 83), the pending "unprecedented accident, representing the end of the road for history" (ibid., 125–26), the "*general* accident which globally undermines all 'presence' and promotes a 'telepresence' without consistency" (ibid., 131)—this is the "temporal catastrophe" (ibid., 134) that is about to sweep away, or perhaps has already swept away, history, human freedom, and individual mobility, identity, and sanity. So, whether the world ends in nuclear holocaust or not, it is still speeding headlong, accelerator to floorboard, to the terminal Big Bang.

Adopting McLuhan's "cybernetic concept of implosion," Baudrillard claims that what "implodes" in the postmodern era is the distinction between simulation and reality. So, too, Kroker et al. write that "the USA implodes into the dark and dense nebula of its final existence as an aesthetic hologram of science as the American way."[33] This is "crash history" as media event, or rather as "virtualized" computer event, the final end of "the ecstasy of exterminism."[34] Kroker and Weinstein echo McLuhan's electronic "outerings" by calling the Internet an "externalization" of the human psyche, but instead of the consummation of consciousness as in some passages in McLuhan, in their *Data Trash*, the Internet signifies the arrival of a "posthuman" monstrosity. "Data trash" is specifically the detritus of the human body as it is cannibalistically devoured by the "virtuality" of the "information leviathan" (150). In the "electronic abattoir" of postmodernism, we are all doomed to be flayed alive and rewired as mere simulations of ourselves.[35] Here, on the terminal "digital beach," the "data-net" hatches as a monstrous new species through "the externalization of the human nervous system (McLuhan)."[36]

GRAIN

Perhaps McLuhan intended to be a "soft" determinist—that is, according to Bruce Bimber, not really a determinist at all—but again, many of his boldest assertions express versions of technodeterminism, and there is also McLuhan's stress on the modern (and now postmodern) acceleration of technological innovation. This theme foreshadows Virilio's "dromology" with its twinned emphases on speed and the ultimate accident, and it relates to the idea of "technological momentum" elaborated by, among others, Thomas Hughes in *Does Technology Drive History?* In contrast both to technological determinism and to notions of "social construction," through which technology tends to be viewed optimistically as directly responsive to human designs and wishes, technological momentum "avoids . . . extremism" and still allows for human agency, though it also suggests that time is running out.[37]

Somewhere between Bimber's notion that "soft" determinism is not strictly deterministic at all and the idea of "hard" determinism, technological momentum suggests that the rate of innovation, which is also the rate at which we are surrounding ourselves with new machines on which we become increasingly dependent, may lead to a version of strict determinism—a historical catastrophe whereby the machines really do take over and start running human affairs. In an attention-grabbing article for *Wired* (April 2000), whose first issue proclaimed on its masthead that McLuhan was its "patron saint," computer engineer and CEO Bill Joy writes, "The 21st-century technologies—genetics, nanotechnology, and robotics . . . are so powerful that they can spawn whole new classes of accidents and abuses" ("Why the Future Doesn't Need Us," 242).[38] Joy claims that "we are on the cusp of the further perfection of extreme evil, an evil whose possibility spreads well beyond that which weapons of mass destruction bequeathed to the nation-states" (ibid.). This "evil" stems partly from the prospect that the new technologies, or some of them at any rate, will be within the reach of individuals as well as governments, but partly also from the possibility that they will spin out of the control of everyone: "robots, engineered organisms, and nanobots share a dangerous amplifying factor: They can self-replicate. A bomb is blown up only once—but one bot can become many, and quickly get out of control" (ibid., 240).

The inspiration for Joy's dystopian vision about self-amplifying technologies running amok came partly from Ray Kurzweil, also a computer scientist and inventor, who, in his 1999 bestseller, *The Age of Spiritual Machines: When Computers Exceed Human Intelligence,* predicted that, in just a few decades, computers would be capable of replicating all aspects of human intelligence and, following Moore's Law, would leave us in the dust. (An important indicator of technological momentum, Moore's law states that computer power has been doubling and will continue to do so every eighteen months.) Although Kurzweil is more optimistic than Joy, "destruction of the entire evolutionary process" is a distinct possibility (*ibid.*, 256).[39]

The key apocalyptic event predicted by Kurzweil, the moment when computers surpass human intelligence, has been dubbed "The Singularity" by another scientist, Vernor Vinge. Vinge is also a science fiction writer, and several of his stories—*A Fire upon the Deep* (1992), "True Names," *Marooned in Real Time*—deal with the consequences of the Singularity. Other sci-fi writers who do so include Karl Schroeder (*Ventis,* 2001) and Charles Stross (*Singularity Sky,* 2003). Citing Vinge and the Singularity in *Enough: Staying Human in an Engineered Age* (2003), Bill McKibben contends that the convergence of the GRAIN technologies could lead to the extinction of humanity.[40] McKibben also cites Thomas Pynchon, who in 1984 wrote: "if our world survives, the next great challenge to watch out for will come—you heard it here first—when the curves of research and development in artificial intelligence, molecular biology, and robotics all converge. Oboy."[41]

In a 1993 article titled "The Coming Technological Singularity: How to Survive in the Post-Human Era," Vinge claimed that "within thirty years, we will have the technological means to create superhuman intelligence. Shortly after, the human era will be ended" (1). Vinge cites I. J. Good, who, in the 1960s, declared that "the first ultraintelligent machine is the last invention that man need ever make, provided that the machine is docile enough to tell us how to keep it under control" (2). But the proviso in Good's statement is like the wishful thinking expressed in Isaac Asimov's famous "laws" for robots, whereby they will not harm humans.[42] Good, Vinge, Joy, Kurzweil, and McKibben are in varying degrees skeptical about humans' ability to render the superintelligent computers and robots we are developing "docile" or "harmless."

So, too, in *Mind Children: The Future of Robot and Human Intelligence* (1988), Hans Moravec, whose main area of expertise is robotics, claims that we are on the verge of the displacement and perhaps even elimination of the entire human species by "intelligent robots." The very machines that Moravec is helping invent, he declares, will soon be able to "carry on our cultural evolution, including their own construction and increasingly rapid self-improvement, without us, and without the genes that built us. When that happens, our DNA will find itself out of a job, having lost the evolutionary race to a new kind of competition" (2). In this doomsday scenario, machines prove superior to humans both because they become far more intelligent and because they are made of far more durable materials. Worn parts can always be replaced, so, if the robots that replace us choose, they can be close to immortal (but never completely so, given entropy and the eventual heat-death of the universe).

Even if one rejects the experts' forecasts about computers and robots, there remain the specters of genetic engineering and nanotechnology. Debates over cloning and other aspects of genetic engineering have become as routine in the press as in science fiction. Further, if molecules in DNA chains can be manipulated to cure diseases or to create diseases, then all molecules can be manipulated to create anything and everything imaginable. As long ago as 1959, nanotechnology appeared on the horizon in Richard Feynman's talk, "There's Plenty of Room at the Bottom."[43] The key idea that Feynman broached was the possibility of building anything at all, including both new machines and organisms, from the level of atoms and molecules upward. Of all the GRAIN technologies, nanotech seems both most promising and most threatening—and, indeed, as some commentators have stressed, closer to magic than to science—because of its aim of creating virtually everything from atoms and molecules. The idea is to produce "assemblers" at the molecular level that can be programmed to arrange other molecules however one wishes. The assemblers or nanobots may be miniature robots (hence, humanoid machines), but, if they can self-replicate, have intelligence, and are capable of building or destroying just about everything under the sun, then they combine all the GRAIN ingredients.

As Colin Milburn notes, though Feynman's lecture is often cited as the point of origin of nanotechnology, his ideas and those of its other originators were anticipated by science fiction writers such as Theodore Sturgeon ("Microcosmic God," 1941) and Robert Heinlein ("Waldo," 1942, which deals with a scientist who creates smaller and smaller "hands," down to the molecular level, to do his bidding).[44] Milburn points out that, even though nanotechnologists often try to distance their discourse from science fiction, the line between a futuristic science like nanotechnology and science fiction is fuzzy or nonexistent. A major booster of nanotech-nology, K. Eric Drexler tries both to distance his futuristic science from science fiction and yet contributes to it, admitting that his enthusiasm leads him to indulge in "science fiction dreams."[45]

In 1974, Japanese scientist Norio Taniguchi coined *nanotechnology* to refer to manipulating molecules into potentially any arrangements that they are capable of forming, or, in other words, to "machining with toler-ances of less than a micron."[46] In *Engines of Creation* (1986), Drexler ex-plored these possibilities, including the development of "nanomachines" capable of "assembling" anything at all, but also of "dissembling" or de-stroying anything and, perhaps, everything. These nanomachines, like Moravec's "intelligent robots" and Kurzweil's "spiritual" computers, will have the power to reproduce themselves. They also, as Katherine Hayles, Brooks Landon, Colin Milburn, Kate Marshall, and the other contribu-tors to the anthology *Nanoculture* observe, erase the distinctions between machine and organism, human and robot. To do so invites both utopian and dystopian speculation, often simultaneously. Brooks Landon notes the frequency with which science fiction stories dealing with nanotech-nology in particular *simultaneously* invoke both the world-ending "gray goo" problem and the utopian wish for the "transcendence" of mundane reality and humankind's limitations. While Drexler's vision in 1986 was more optimistic than otherwise, he also warned of dire prospects if this quite miraculous "molecular" technology gets out of control or gets into the wrong hands.

According to Drexler, "engines of creation" can just as well be "en-gines of destruction" (*Engines of Creation*, 171–90). For instance, "Ad-vanced technology will make workers unnecessary and genocide easy" (176). Self-reproducing nanomachines or "replicators can be more potent than nuclear weapons . . . to destroy all life with replicators would require only a single speck made of ordinary elements" (174). Further, "they could spread like blowing pollen, replicate swiftly, and reduce the biosphere to dust in a matter of days" (172). Already by 1986, "this threat" had been named the "gray goo problem" by "the cognoscenti of nanotechnology" (172). And that problem is the theme of Michael Crichton's recent horror science fiction novel, *Prey*, as well as of earlier science fiction fantasies such as Greg Bear's *Blood Music* (1985), in which all humanity has been transformed "into billowing sheets of sentient brown sludge,"[47] and Wil

McCarthy's *Bloom*, "which features a runaway nanoentity called the My-cora, so insatiable that it has displaced humans from all the inner planets of the solar system."[48] So, too, in Kathleen Ann Goonan's "Nanotech Quartet" of novels, nanotechnology has escaped human control and operates as a plague, threatening the extinction of humanity. Yet, as Brooks Landon comments, in Goonan's, Bear's, McCarthy's, and other writers' futuristic scenarios, "nanotech" still offers "utopian" prospects ("Less is More," 145).

From the accounts by Drexler and its other promoters such as David Pearce, and also by science fiction writers like Greg Bear, nanotechnology, together with the other converging technologies that form GRAIN, inspire something like secular versions of "The Rapture," science and technology bringing on the apocalypse. Bill McKibben writes that these technofuturists live intellectually "at the opposite pole from the fundamentalists with their 'In Case of Rapture This Car Will Be Empty' bumper stickers. But not emotionally" (*Enough,* 102). Most science fiction about nanotechnology, such as Neal Stephenson's *The Diamond Age* and Michel Houellebecq *The Elementary Particles,* is dystopian. But Landon says that Greg Bear's *Blood Music* "makes the noosphere or thought universe that follows hard on the heels of a gray-goo-like transformation of Earth sound very much like the most wishful Christian stereotypes of heaven" ("Less is More," 145).

Whether the emphasis is dystopian ("gray goo") or utopian (enhanced intelligence, immortality, etc.), nanotechnology, as Kate Marshall puts it, "is clearly perceived as a risky business" ("Future Present," 153). Needless to say, even though he is perhaps nanotechnology's biggest cheerleader, Drexler argues that extreme caution will be necessary to keep the new nanoengines on the side of "creation" rather than "destruction."[49] And Crichton's introduction to *Prey* cites Drexler's "queasiness" about nanotechnology and the need for rules and regulations to keep it under safe human control (ix–xiii). McKibben warns, however, that the policing of new technologies, let alone giving them up altogether, is already difficult if not impossible. If an "international mafiosi" does not establish outlawed "biotech labs," then "big corporations" will find ways, whether legal or illegal, to do so (*Enough,* 165). The corporations are already doing so.

What distinguishes Joy, Vinge, Kurzweil, Moravec, and Drexler from the crash theorists (and also from McLuhan) is that they are themselves scientists, working to create the very technologies they warn against. Like Virilio in particular, they are all keenly aware of technological momentum. Moore's Law predicts that the power of computer technology multiplies almost exponentially. Other technologies such as robotics proceed more slowly but are, nevertheless, all speeding up. Kurzweil and Drexler believe that technological momentum has not yet foreclosed the possibility of humans retaining control over the new technologies that are both improving and reproducing themselves at an accelerating rate. Joy, Vinge, and Moravec might as well be called crash theorists because they suggest that machines may already have gotten beyond the control of their inventors—or, if not already, then very soon. Vinge's followers take 2014 as the date of the Singularity.[50] There is little difference between the scientists' dire warnings and Arthur Kroker's digital "exterminism," Jean Baudrillard's end of history, or Paul Virilio's ultimate Big Bang.

Perhaps because of his Catholicism, McLuhan wavered between utopianism and dystopianism. That wavering may prove to be one aspect of his thinking that will keep his ideas in circulation. While he certainly tended toward technodeterminism in many of his annunciations about new media and technologies, he apparently did not understand such determinism itself to be a version of dystopianism. However, his more utopian moments are, as Kroker suggests, also deterministic, in the sense that they approximate "religious epiphanies." But at least McLuhan did not abandon the thought that humans *should* control the technologies we create. Just what forms such control might take he did not venture to speculate—no more than do the crash theorists. Indeed, for Kroker, Weinstein, Virilio, and Baudrillard, no control seems possible: as technology accelerates, the ultimate Big Bang becomes inevitable. The GRAIN scientists also have difficulty imagining how the new technologies they are helping create can be rendered "docile" or mainly beneficial instead of destructive to *homo sapiens*.[51]

In GRAIN discourse, the tendency is to imagine technological solutions to the problems posed by technology. There is, for instance, the now common idea that "cyborgization," or the combining of machines and humans as in scenarios of downloading human psyches into computers (and thereby achieving a sort of immortality), will allow the era of the "posthuman" to continue to be at least partly human. A highly optimistic discourse about "human enhancement" and the "transhuman" or "post-human," as in the online magazine *Humanityplus,* offers "breathtaking visions of immortality, spatial transcendence, and social transformation." Utopian prospects for "redesigning the human condition" are fueled by the idea that we may become "the first species to take control of its own evolution."[52] Such thinking is often indistinguishable from apocalyptic religious discourse, as in Thomas Horn's *Forbidden Gates* (2010).[53]

The idea of humans seizing control of our own evolution is neither new, however, nor reassuring, in part because it does not constitute a political vision. Current discourse about human enhancement and creating a super species eerily echoes eugenics discourse. Moreover, new tools— DNA engineering, robots, nanobots—will not get *homo sapiens* out of the very dangerous toolbox the species is, it seems, busily locking itself inside (in two or three decades, will we still have a key?). This is evident from the dilemmas already posed by nuclear energy. The absence of a political theory of new technologies, one that would put human consciousness and agency clearly in charge of the toolbox, is partly the result of the current hegemony of globalized capitalism or "free market" ideology and its corollary, the current weakness of international institutions and laws.[54] As with nuclear weapons, leaving nation-states in charge of the latest technologies will likely prove as unsafe as letting markets and corporations rule the posthuman roost. What is superabundant in McLuhan, in crash theory, and among the GRAIN scientists (whether pessimistic or optimistic) is technological imagination. What is wanting among them is the sociological and political imagination (and, indeed, the will) to avert the disasters many of them predict by ensuring that new technologies contribute to social progress—to peace and plenty for all humanity and nature—rather than to "exterminism" and the end of the road for human history.

Like the date of Y2K or that of the Rapture, if the date of the Singularity (2014?) passes and still the world turns, that will not mean that the crash theorists and the doomsters among the GRAIN scientists have been mistaken. When prophets get their dates wrong, they often just move them forward. Y2K and the Rapture will not happen, but the Singularity will and perhaps has already occurred. Certainly Virilio is correct to stress that most new technological innovations produce unforeseen side effects and "accidents." Surely, too, the GRAIN scientists are right to warn about the increasing domination machines exercise over humans and about the possibly catastrophic consequences of genetic engineering and nanotechnology. What they are unable to predict or even imagine is how humans can shut the technological Pandora's box they have opened or, in other words, how they can control the inventions and discoveries they have loosed upon the world.

ELEVEN

Army Surplus: Notes
on "Exterminism"

The camp is the space that opens up when the state
of exception starts to become the rule.

—GIORGIO AGAMBEN, *MEANS WITHOUT END*

Currently thousands of American veterans are homeless. Over a million
are "at risk of homelessness due to poverty, lack of support networks,
and dismal living conditions in overcrowded or substandard housing."[1]
The website for the National Coalition of Homeless Veterans reports
that roughly "67,000 veterans are homeless on any given night. Over the
course of a year, approximately twice that many experience homelessness.
Only eight percent of the general population can claim veteran status,
but nearly one-fifth of the homeless population are veterans." Although
the current unemployment rate among all veterans, 6.7 percent, is lower
than the overall rate of 7.9 percent of the labor force, it is still too high.
Moreover, 56 percent of the unemployed veterans are African American
or Latino, even though they constituted only 12.8 percent and 15.4 percent, respectively, of the population of the United States. The Obama
administration has helped reduce unemployment among veterans, which
for several years was significantly higher than the national rate.[2] But how
can "our country's heroes" be homeless and unemployed in a nation that
prides itself on being a model of democracy and prosperity for the rest of
the world? How can homelessness for anyone occur in the United States?
In any prosperous, democratic society, no one should be tossed into the

gutter. Yet that is precisely what has been happening in the United States as jobs have disappeared, as banks and mortgage companies have cashed in on the foreclosure crisis, and as thousands of Americans have seen their pensions and retirement savings wiped out. The United States is devolving into a third-world country: at least forty-seven million Americans now live in poverty, a rapidly increasing number.[3]

No one, of course, talks about curing homelessness or poverty by eliminating the homeless and poor. Yet many seem to believe that the poor, like "welfare mothers" and "welfare deadbeats" a couple of decades ago, are to blame for their poverty.[4] The victims' supposedly bad behavior, however, is not what drives the socioeconomic machinery, in present-day America and in many other nations, that causes large numbers of people to fall through the cracks so that, ultimately, many of them seem no longer to belong to any society. Is this machinery responsible, at least in part, for the skyrocketing suicide rate among vets?[5] Further, can the machinery of socioeconomic exclusion, at least in some countries and in some circumstances, lead to genocide? What can cause a portion of a nation's population to be treated as worthless and, perhaps in some cases, fit only for extermination?

MARX, MALTHUS, AND MARCUS

Unemployment and homelessness are only among the more obvious forms of social and economic exclusion, or partial exclusion, that afflict millions of Americans. Government intervention could protect all veterans and, indeed, all the homeless and unemployed. More robust programs of unemployment insurance and job creation, similar to the Works Progress Administration (WPA) during the Great Depression, would help. But the Republicans in Congress will continue to block any such effort, and many Democrats are too timid or too well lobbied to press the issue. Both parties are hooked on money from corporations and wealthy donors, who often believe that all government spending is nefarious or at any rate less effective than private enterprise. But capitalism always seeks to maximize profits, while reducing its labor costs to a minimum. A corporation can do this through downsizing, automation, and shipping jobs overseas, processes that have been in full swing in the United States since the 1980s. Ineffective government may be one aspect of the machinery of exclusion; another, more important one is unregulated, globalizing, and downsizing capitalism.[6]

"The constant production of a relative surplus population of workers," Marx declared in *Capital*, "is a necessity of capitalist accumulation" (1:787). This "reserve army of labor" drove wages down and supplied new workers when new industries emerged. Earlier in the *Grundrisse*, he had written,

> It is a law of capital [and not of nature] to create surplus labour. . . . It is its tendency, therefore, to create as much labour as possible; just as it is equally its tendency to reduce necessary labour to a minimum. It is therefore . . . a tendency of capital to increase the labouring population, as well as constantly to posit a part of it as surplus population—population which is useless until such time as capital can utilize it. (399)

Marx implies the obvious: if "necessary labour" is constantly being ground down "to a minimum," then "surplus population," along with unemployment and poverty, must increase. Of course, capitalism also seeks to increase the consumption of its products, so it cannot simply turn "necessary labour" into "surplus population" with no spare change. Nevertheless, "It is . . . a tendency of capital to make human labour (relatively) superfluous, so as to drive it . . . towards infinity" (ibid.).

But, again, "infinity" cannot mean over the cliff. Besides the issue of consumption, because capitalism needs a "reserve army of labor," the idea that this "army" is "superfluous" is contradictory. The logic of capitalist accumulation does not point to the liquidation of surplus workers. Some indeterminate portion of the surplus could starve or vanish without harm to capitalism, but not all of it. Moreover, is it only capitalism that produces a surplus population? In his *Essay on Population*, first published in 1798, the Reverend Thomas Malthus famously argued that "overpopulation" was the result of "the poor" reproducing themselves at a "geometric" rate, while the food supply could only increase at an "arithmetic" rate. As Marx and Engels recognized, Malthus's argument was another way of saying "the poor ye shall always have with you," no matter what the economic mode of production.[7] According to Malthus, the tendency to overpopulate was the outcome of natural laws which had always been operative. That is why, starting with the second edition of his *Essay* in 1803, Malthus ransacked travelers' and missionaries' reports to provide examples of population pressures in non-Western societies. He also noted the various "checks," including infanticide, widow-murder, and cannibalism, that he thought offset surplus reproduction in some of those societies. Malthus argued that a "redundant population" in any society would inevitably be whittled down to the level of subsistence by the major, "positive" checks of famine, disease, and war. So, although his *Essay* turned "the population bomb" into a global threat, "overpopulation" was paradoxically an impossibility.[8] Because of the inevitability of the checks to population, Malthus also contended that social progress in any major sense was out of the question: "To remove the wants of the lower classes of society is indeed an arduous task. The truth is that the pressure of distress on this part of a community is an evil so deeply seated that no human ingenuity can reach it" (*On Population*, 37). Individual paupers could help themselves by not having more children than they could support, but otherwise measures to alleviate their poverty—whether through private charity or the poor laws—backfired by encouraging them to have more children than they could support.

Marx and Engels viewed Malthus as a hypocritical champion of the status quo. But Malthus was at least correct in arguing that the phenomenon of societies having "superfluous" numbers—meaning people who belong to those societies and yet who seem so marginal or excluded that they belong only in some negative sense—predates capitalism and has, perhaps, been universal. The phenomenon of *mass* exclusion may not have been characteristic of "primitive" or "simple" societies, though all of them were to some degree hierarchical and though many produced small numbers of outcasts and scapegoats. But mass exclusion has occurred in all of the empires and nation-states of Eastern and Western "civilizations."[9]

Since the rise of industrial capitalism, the poor have commonly been reckoned in degrees of worthlessness. In today's overheated credit economy, one does not need to be homeless or unemployed to have, in monetary terms, only negative value. That may now be true of most Americans. In any case, Adam Smith thought that, if government did not interfere with it, "the Invisible Hand" of the marketplace could render everyone, including the poor, relatively prosperous. Malthus cast a "dismal" eye on that idea.[10] "Overpopulation" rendered poverty inevitable and progress impossible, at least for the poor. But the prefix *over* meant only that some portion of a society could not be supported by its economy. Two phrases that Malthus uses repeatedly are "redundant population" and "superfluous numbers." Both imply that those who belong in this surplus category, because they cannot be rendered socially and economically useful, should be swept away. Those who rely on "poor relief" and charity, Malthus thought, were nothing more than parasites, a version of human waste.

From Malthus on, capitalist economics has treated "the lower classes" as worthless or almost so, versions of what, at the time of the Irish Famine, another clergyman called "immortal sewerage."[11] The poor might have souls like everyone else, but, on earth, they were refuse. Unlike "sewerage," however, there was no easy way to get rid of them. Even the most obvious nineteenth-century remedy for "overpopulation" and poverty—emigration—Malthus regards as merely "a slight palliative" (On Population, 346). The only other "palliative" that Malthus can think of is no palliative at all: "the total abolition of all the present parish laws" for poor relief (ibid., 37). Let them eat grass.

Malthus does not advocate exterminating the poor, but his argument involves an exterminationist logic not far removed from the many versions of rationalizing genocides. These always include the idea that the people being liquidated are worthless, no better than vermin. In Britain in the late 1830s, two pamphlets about poverty and population were republished together as The Book of Murder! by "Marcus," who claims to be contributing to "the Science of Population" (31). This small book or double pamphlet purported to be the "vade-mecum for the Commissioners and Guardians of the New Poor Law" of 1834. Along with Charles Dickens's Oliver Twist and Thomas Carlyle's Chartism, it was one of many publications attacking Malthus and the New Poor Law.[12] According to the editor of the second edition of this "diabolical" volume, its "Demon Author" advocates limiting "population by murdering all the infants born over three in each family of the poor." Lots should then be drawn to choose one-quarter of all of the third children to destroy. Regarding the Irish poor, Marcus proposes that they "shall be allowed to rear only one child to each family until their present numbers shall have been brought down." He recommends giving the doomed infants, while they are sleeping, a "deadly gas" to render their extinctions "painless."

Marcus asserts that pauper infants do not have the right to exist (The Book of Murder! 39). But he is not altogether unsympathetic to the poor.

The editor notes that the Demon Author urges reconciling "Mothers to the MURDER OF THEIR INFANTS, by presenting them with gay and lively images." The mothers

> are to be impressed with the idea that it is for the benefit of the world that they are to submit to the sacrifice, and above all, the murdered infants are to be interred in beautiful colonnades decorated with plants and flowers, which are to be called the Infants' Paradise, and which are to be the scenes of the chastened recreations of all classes!

The passage by Marcus on "the Infants' Paradise" comes toward the end of *The Book of Murder!*; it is followed by five pages on "The Theory of Painless Extinction," which might have been written by Victor Frankenstein. By this time, it is apparent that *The Book of Murder!* is a satire on Malthus and the New Poor Law.[13]

Early in his essay, Marcus proposes the formation of an "Association" aiming at "the extinction of superfluous life" (*The Book of Murder!* 31). Society has only a limited number of "places" for people to fill; the goal of the association will be "the preventing of the existing of persons for whom there [are] no places" (ibid., 13). This passage echoes Malthus's claim about the poor man who is born without a place at the table of "nature's mighty feast," which Gertrude Himmelfarb calls "the most notorious passage" in his *Essay*—a passage Malthus removed after the second edition of 1803.[14] The members of the association will agree to limit the numbers of their offspring, exterminating the excess unless the parents have already lost one or more children (ibid., 20). The implication is that, once the association grows to include most or all members of society, poverty will vanish. Marcus says that his readers may suspect him of proposing a "Utopian" goal, but he claims he is being quite realistic and practical. Yet he also says that he aims at "lifting up mankind from abasement, and . . . putting an end to the empire of pain," and also that "our design" is one of "universalizing enjoyment" (ibid., 26–27)—Benthamism run amuck. Infanticide will be the means whereby "the great ulcer of modern nations, a proletarian populousness," can be overcome (ibid., 12).

Marcus was perhaps writing with Jonathan Swift's *A Modest Proposal* (1729) in mind.[15] As a cure for poverty in Ireland, Swift's satire recommends butchering pauper children and selling them for meat. Swift and Marcus mock several aspects of upper-class attitudes to the poor, including ones expressed by Malthus. Both the *Essay on Population* and *The Book of Murder!* bring the prospect of domestic genocide or "democide" into view. By "democide," I am referring to the extermination of a category of people within a society, indistinguishable from the majority by race or nationality.[16] Irish peasants, of course, were viewed as a different race and nationality by their English and Anglo-Irish overlords. But the Act of Union of 1801 had united Ireland with England and Scotland in one nation, and any sharp dichotomy between the Celtic and Anglo-Saxon races was often rejected by nineteenth-century commentators. That racist binarism, however, helped justify the British government's inadequate response to Irish poverty and starvation.

His many critics often accused Malthus of approving of the "positive checks"—disease, famine, war—that he thought were certain to eliminate "superfluous" people, and particularly the poor.[17] Recommending mass destruction was not his intention, but he, nevertheless, envisions with apparent equanimity the extermination, through supposedly natural and inevitable causes, of vast numbers of people. *The Book of Murder!* does the same, though infanticide is highly unnatural: in the numerous missionary journals that, by the 1830s, were often bestsellers, infanticide, like cannibalism, was condemned as a diabolical custom among savages. Nevertheless, Thomas Carlyle apparently interpreted Marcus's volume as nonsatirical, probably because its exterminationist logic was so close to the Malthusian opinions expressed in Parliament and the middle-class press. "To believe practically that the poor and luckless are here only as a nuisance to be abraded and abated," Carlyle wrote in *Chartism* (1839), "and in some permissible manner made away with, and swept out of sight, is not an amiable faith" (176). But he recognized that it was a widespread "faith." Rather than being a "Demon Author," Carlyle opines, Marcus "has looked intensely on the world's woes, from a Benthamee-Malthusian watchtower, under a Heaven dead as iron" (237). Carlyle places Marcus among the "benefactors of the species, who counsel that in each parish ... instead of the Parish Clergyman, there might be established some Parish Exterminator; or say a Reservoir of Arsenic, kept at the public expense, free to all parishioners" (236). The best way to deal with paupers is just how rat-catchers deal with rats (175). Carlyle sounds less ironic, however, when he remarks, "The time has come when the Irish population must either be improved a little, or else exterminated" (183). Writing seven years before the onset of the Great Irish Famine, Carlyle no doubt supported improvement rather than extermination, but there is also no doubt that he considered extermination a possibility. Marcus, too, regarded Irish overpopulation as a problem:

> What is to be done with the lazars of Naples; or with the half-savages of Ireland, or the Ireland of France—La Vendée? Are those populations doomed to be as they are for everlasting? Any attempt to amend their condition must set out by a reduction of their numbers. This can be done only by putting them, district by district, into a state of coercion. (33)[18]

Marcus does not recommend "Exterminate all the brutes!" as does Mr. Kurtz in Joseph Conrad's *Heart of Darkness*. But the Irish must be "coerced" to have half of their babies exterminated.

Carlyle, Marcus, and Malthus were participating, during an early stage of industrial capitalism, in a much wider discourse about eliminating poverty that often implied and sometimes explicitly advocated exterminating the poor altogether. Malthus was an especially influential figure in shaping that discourse, in part because he was recognized as an authority on political economy (as economics was called from Adam Smith through John Stuart Mill). Though in his *Essay on Population,* he does not advocate arsenic or poison gas, he does insist that the poor should quit having so many children (even though he regards this as impossible for the vast majority). Further, though he is not thinking about racial improvement, Malthus anticipates eugenics. The 1948 U.N. Convention on Genocide includes forced reduction or elimination of childbearing, something eugenicists advocated, as a form of genocide.

According to Malthus, moreover, the poor alone are to blame for their poverty, a view clearly expressed in the notorious passage about "nature's mighty feast":

> A man who is born into a world already possessed, if he cannot get subsistence from his parents on whom he has a just demand, and if the society do not want his labor, has no claim of *right* to the smallest portion of food, and, in fact, has no business to be where he is. At nature's mighty feast there is no vacant cover for him. She tells him to be gone, and will quickly execute her own orders [by exterminating him]. (*On Population,* 2d ed., 531)

The absurdity of this version of victim blaming is obvious. The "man," in common with everyone else, cannot help being born into the world, and, if he is born to poor parents, he will in all likelihood remain poor. Further, "society" does not consist of a fixed number of places at "nature's mighty table." Nor does "nature" limit the number of places in any inevitable or stingy fashion ("mighty" suggests otherwise).

The capitalist process of determining what Marcus calls "places," or the types and quantities of labor it needs, is indifferent to the needs of workers. Except for the production of "the reserve army of labor," overpopulation has no bearing on this process. Nor does overpopulation ordinarily have any bearing on genocide. In *The Age of Triage*, however, Richard Rubenstein adopts a Malthusian perspective, according to which overpopulation is the principal cause of mass exterminations: "It is my conviction that both the 'overproduction' of people and programs for their elimination are an intrinsic rather than an accidental feature of modern civilization in both capitalist and communist societies" (9). From this perspective, genocide is an additional check to overpopulation. Rubinstein is persuasive about the "instrumental rationality" that has often helped rationalize genocides, but not about overpopulation as their cause. Colonial genocides were certainly not caused by overpopulation.[19] Poverty, unemployment, and starvation, which Malthus equates with overpopulation, drove many colonizers to emigrate. But the indigenous peoples they slaughtered were typically far from populous.[20] So, too, the Jews and Gypsies exterminated by the Nazis exerted no extraordinary pressure on the population of Germany and Central Europe.

Many densely populated parts of the world have never experienced genocides. While poverty may cause social conflict, moreover, no more than overpopulation can it be considered a primary cause of genocide. According to Adam Jones, conflicts aroused by poverty can assume "genocidal or political proportions . . . in tandem with features of the political system," including the operation of "an exclusionary ideology" (*Genocide*, 310). The issue of causation always involves the machinery plus ideology of exclusion, rather than poverty, race, or other qualities of the victims. (To treat those qualities as causes of genocide is again a form of blaming the victim: it makes no sense to say that the cause of the Holocaust was the Jewishness of the Jews.) Nevertheless, Rubinstein correctly argues that, when planned and executed by modern nation-states, "genocide represents the ultimate expression of the revolution of rationality with which the problem of population redundancy began in the first place"

(*The Age of Triage,* 32). In other words, the same instrumental reason that can rationalize the total destruction of unwanted populations (not necessarily *over*populations) underlies Malthus's argument and the economic and legislative consequences of that argument such as the New Poor Law of 1834. That law distinguished between the deserving and undeserving poor. The former could receive poor relief, the latter, not. If any of them starved, so be it. Malthus's claim that poor relief only caused more poverty was directly responsible for the stinginess of the 1834 legislation, with its principle of "least eligibility" and its near-starvation diet in the workhouses it established.[21]

THE POOR, THE COMMON PEOPLE, AND THE STATE OF EXCEPTION

If Malthus's claim that the pressure of population on subsistence is universal, then the question of what part of a population will be first to go to the wall is also universal. Malthus's answer, "the poor," seems obvious, especially because he treats that category as present in every age and every society. But this answer will not fit many relatively egalitarian societies where there is little or no poverty, or else where everyone is poor. In extreme circumstances such as famine, if it comes down to a decision as to who dies first, who makes that decision and on what basis? Even in highly unequal societies such as contemporary America, there is no obvious reason that "the poor" should be singled out for starvation or other forms of elimination apart from the fact that they are relatively powerless. In all societies, however, there is some sort of sovereignty, and the sovereign is whoever or whatever is empowered to make the decision about life or death. In today's society, another name for the sovereign is the state, which has the capacity to certify "particular individuals in ways that qualify them for discrimination or social exclusion."[22] The sovereign is also whoever or whatever makes the decision about "the state of exception," or the "emergency" in which the laws or the normal operating procedures can be set aside, at least in regard to "bare life."

In his analysis of sovereignty, "naked" or "bare life," and "the state of exception," Giorgio Agamben helps illuminate the machinery of social exclusion and, therefore, also of genocide. "Political power," he writes in *Means without End*, "always founds itself . . . on the separation of a sphere of naked life from the context of the forms of life" (4). In complex societies at least from the time of ancient Greece and Rome, sovereignty establishes itself by making the fundamental distinction between humans who count as citizens, or who at any rate have various readily identifiable social qualities and abilities ("the forms of life"), and those who are excluded—"bare life," the merely human without any other qualities or qualifications. The excluded ones fall outside the patterns of social stratification (classes, castes, and so on) and value, or rather they are categorized as the excluded. Yet they are not excluded from society in the manner of aliens, the external "barbarians," or foreigners, who, of course, have their own versions of sovereignty and social hierarchy. The excluded are within society and yet not of it. Summarizing Agamben, Slavoj Žižek writes that the Jews who were annihilated during the Holocaust belonged "to the species of what the Ancient Romans called *Homo sacer*—those who, although they were human, were excluded from the human community, which is why one can kill them with impunity—*and, for that very reason, one cannot sacrifice them (because they are not a worthy sacrificial offering)*" (*Welcome to the Desert of the Real*, 141).

Sovereignty has evolved from older, personified versions—the emperor or king—to the modern, "biopolitical" version. Agamben draws on Michel Foucault's ideas about "bio-power" and "biopolitics," according to which sovereignty is invested in "disciplines," notably science and technology. "Bio-power" now has authority over life and death. As both Agamben and Foucault suggest, modern biopolitics is perhaps best exemplified by eugenics. Writing about Nazism, Agamben declares, "The principles of this new biopolitics are dictated by eugenics, which is understood as the science of a people's genetic heredity."[23] Also discussing Nazism, Foucault writes, "A eugenic ordering of society, with all that implied in the way of extension and intensification of micro-powers, in the guise of an unrestricted state control ... was accompanied by the oneiric exaltation of a superior blood; the latter implied both the systematic genocide of others and the risk of exposing oneself to a total sacrifice."[24] Eugenics was not restricted to Nazi Germany, however. It had its start in Victorian Britain and was widely promoted there, in the United States, and many other places between the 1880s and World War II.[25]

Once entire categories or classes of human beings are perceived as rubbish or as mere parasites—or else, in Darwinian terms, as "unfit" to survive—the question of how to get rid of them arises. One answer came through Social Darwinism and its offshoot, eugenics. Francis Galton's project for racial improvement or "purification" was based on the fear that civilization was self-subverting because it allowed the "weak" or "unfit," like Malthus's paupers, to survive and breed. The poor who crammed into the slums of European and North American cities in the late 1800s and early 1900s gave rise to widespread anxiety about racial degeneration. Among ways to prevent that from happening were, first, as in Malthus, to keep the poor—that is, the unfit in Social Darwinian terms—from breeding, and, second, to promote breeding among the fit—that is, the upper classes. In civilized conditions, the fittest did not reproduce at a fast enough rate to outbreed the unfit. Galton thought that the key to the progress of any race was to preserve "the desirables" and eliminate "the undesirables." Elimination might be through nonviolent persuasion, but it might also take more or less coercive and even violent forms, ranging from forced sterilization to extermination.

Galton, Darwin's cousin, "first published his eugenic ideas in 1865—well before he coined the word [eugenics] itself—in a two-part article for *Macmillan's Magazine* which he subsequently expanded into a book, *Hereditary Genius,* published in 1869."[26] According to Daniel Pick, Galton's "long inquiry into heredity was perhaps the most striking example of the re-direction of questions of economic and social progress to the evolutionary problem of the body's reproduction"—in short, to biopolitics (*Faces of Degeneration,* 197). Inspired by Galton, numerous eugenics journals, organizations, and projects sprang up between the 1890s and World War II.

For H. G. Wells and many other intellectuals in the late 1880s and early 1900s, eugenics promised social, economic, and racial progress. In *Anticipations* (1901), a book of secular prophecies, Wells's most hopeful prediction concerns the emergence of what he calls "the New Republic," consisting of engineers, scientists, and other technocrats—the new rulers. In contrast, among his pessimistic forecasts is "the rapid multiplication of the unfit" (61–62)—that is, of all those millions of individuals at the bottom of "the social pyramid" whose potentially life-sustaining labor has been superseded by machinery (63). How will the society of the future rid itself of "these gall stones of vicious, helpless, and pauper masses"? (61–62). Wells's answer is that they must be prevented from multiplying or, if that fails, they must be exterminated. He looks forward to a time when eugenics, involving the "merciful obliteration of weak and silly and pointless things," would be widely accepted.

The "biopolitics" of eugenics overlooks the economic factors that produce poverty: the poor are not much different from supposedly inferior races. Agamben's biopolitical analysis of sovereignty and "bare life" also needs some version of Marxist analysis of capitalism to explain why many people are reduced to poverty in the first place. The sovereign is not the sole determinant of who winds up at the bottom or the top of the ever-shifting economic pyramid. Governmental policies of taxation, regulation, education, and distribution of revenues play a major role in shaping economies and sorting populations into social classes. Economies are relatively independent of sovereignty. But once pauperized masses appear on the scene, only sovereignty—in modern times, state power—has the authority to categorize some or all of those masses as "bare life" and, therefore, as targets of various processes of extermination.[27]

For Wells, the future problem will involve much more than just how an industrialized society should deal with its "pauper masses." It will involve how to deal with the outsized and presumably dangerous multiplication of all the world's races. Wells contends that, while the New Republic is evolving, "that other great element, which I have called the People of the Abyss, will also have followed out its destiny":

> For many decades that development will be largely or entirely out of all human control. To the multiplying rejected of the white and yellow civilisations, there will have been added a vast proportion of the black and brown races, and collectively those masses will propound the general question, "What will you do with us, we hundreds of millions, who cannot keep pace with you?" If the New Republic emerges at all it will emerge by grappling with this riddle; it must come into existence by the passes this Sphinx will guard.[28]

This Malthusian and racist "anticipation" might be described as the black and brown plus the "rejected" white and yellow racial peril. According to Agamben, "the capitalistic-democratic plan to eliminate the poor [through either economic development or extermination] not only reproduces inside itself the people of the excluded but also turns all of the populations of the Third World into naked life."[29] With the ecological catastrophe brought on by global warming, it is now conceivable that the entire continent of Africa may become a famine-stricken desert while the first world watches it expire.

Besides Galton and Wells, many writers, educators, and politicians between the 1880s and World War II supported eugenics. D. H. Lawrence, for one, might almost be echoing Marcus on the "Infants' Paradise" when, in 1908, he declared,

> I would build a lethal chamber as big as the Crystal Palace, with a military band playing softly, and a Cinematograph working brightly; then I'd go out in the back streets and main streets and bring them in, all the sick, the halt, and the maimed; I would lead them gently, and they would smile me a weary thanks; and the band would softly bubble out the "Hallelujah Chorus."[30]

And three decades later, George Bernard Shaw opined, "Extermination must be put on a scientific basis if it is ever to be carried out humanely . . . as well as thoroughly. . . . [If] we desire a certain type of civilization and culture, we must exterminate the sort of people who do not fit in."[31]

Malthus and his first critics, including Marcus and Marx, were responding, in part, to the new, biopolitical version of sovereignty evident in his argument about "redundant population" and also in the New Poor Law of 1834. This distinctly modern version of sovereignty entails the exercise of state power over the lives and bodies of entire populations, both within the boundaries of the state and in its colonial possessions. While from the Renaissance forward most colonial genocides were motivated by the colonizers' desire for the land and resources possessed by the colonized, it is more difficult to explain the mechanisms by which certain groups within metropolitan societies—"the poor," most obviously, who were not racially distinct from others—fall within the scope of exterminationist logic. Biopolitical sovereignty, however, entails the exercise of power over the lives and deaths of all its subjects, including entire categories of people deemed worthless or unfit to live. As *The Book of Murder!* indicates, according to Malthusian logic, the poor become "bare life," which also means, as Agamben says, "life that is not fit to live." And as Foucault noted in *The History of Sexuality*, the negative side of the modern, biopolitical version of sovereignty pointed the way to genocide:

> If genocide is indeed the dream of modern powers, this is not because of a recent return of the ancient right to kill; it is because power is situated

and exercised at the level of life, the species, the race, and the large-scale phenomena of population.[32]

Foucault also contends that the origin of modern "class conflict" was "race war," from which some "races" or nations emerged as dominant and others as subordinate.

In both France and England, as Marx also noted, class war was originally understood in racial terms, which continued to be applied to England's difficulties with Ireland. As European nations moved outward and colonized much of the rest of the world, the modern, biological conception of distinct races emerged. At the same time, "race war" turned inward and manifested itself as "social war" and "class struggle." "The social body is basically articulated around two races," Foucault writes, which are not "races" in the biological sense: "what we see as a polarity, as a binary rift within society, is not a clash between two distinct races. It is the splitting of a single race into a superrace and a subrace."[33] The emergence of "a State racism" is central also to the emergence of modern forms of biopolitical power and, therefore, to the emergence of the general threat of genocide (including democide). In the colonies, genocide is one of the frequent and obvious outcomes of racism, a virulent version of biopolitical discourse. At home, genocide (or democide) may be less frequent but is, nevertheless, always a possibility, as Malthus and Marcus both suggest and as the Nazi resort to eugenics and exterminism clearly illustrates. The prospect of democide arises from "a State racism ... that society will direct against itself, against its own elements and its own products. This is the internal racism of permanent purification, and it [has] become one of the basic dimensions of social normalization."[34]

Biopolitics is not limited to "the poor" or to other races. Today, it exercises sovereign authority over life and death in most "developed" societies. Agamben notes that the ambiguity of the word *people*, in its political uses involves the attribution of sovereignty to everyone ("We the people"), but also can mean nearly the opposite—the idea of "the common people" as those who are powerless and unimportant. Both meanings are central to modern democratic theory and practice. "Any interpretation of the political meaning of the term *people* ought to start from the peculiar fact that in modern European languages this term always indicates also the poor, the underprivileged, and the excluded."[35]

"The common people," thus, move toward "bare life." But "We the people" also move in a negative direction. By the end of the 1800s, discourse about "the crowd" and "the masses" threatened the transformation of everyone into "bare life."

As I noted in *Bread and Circuses,* Ortega y Gassett's *"Revolt of the Masses* is a sort of *Communist Manifesto* in reverse" (187). Ortega's "masses" do not rise up in conscious revolution against the bourgeoisie and capitalism; instead, they are unthinking "barbarians," who undermine civilization or cultural and religious authority. They have no definite class consciousness, no awareness of their interests or the interests of society in general. Ortega echoes Gustave Le Bon's *The Crowd* (1895) and the "crowd psychologists," including Freud, who followed his lead. "The crowd" is the outcome of social, cultural, and political regression. In "mass society" or the "one-dimensional" realm of "the crowd," presumably everyone falls into the category of the unfit. In T. S. Eliot's "The Wasteland," Karel Čapek's *R.U.R.,* and George Orwell's *1984,* the crowd or the masses may be alive but might as well be zombies. The discourse about mass society thus foreshadows Agamben's conclusion about the universalization of "bare life," or the condition, brought about through biopolitics, in which all citizens are also potentially *homines sacri,* available for extermination but not worth sacrificing. "We the people" are sovereign; but as the masses, "the people"—and not just "the poor"—all become fodder for the camps and for extermination.

With mass society, "the state of exception" is no longer exceptional but is instead the rule or the new norm. This is obviously true in totalitarian societies such as Nazi Germany and the Soviet Union. But it has proven easy for any democracy, including the United States, to move in the direction of the "one-dimensional society" Herbert Marcuse deplored. If nothing else, "the war on terror" has pushed the United States into what may well be a permanent "state of exception," as exemplified by, among many other symptoms, the Patriot Act.[36] Agamben cites Walter Benjamin's eighth thesis on the philosophy of history to illustrate the trend toward the normalization of "the state of exception" in all biopolitical regimes (*Means Without End,* 6): "The tradition of the oppressed teaches us that the 'state of emergency' in which we live is not the exception but the rule" (Benjamin, *Illuminations,* 257). Writing in *The Guardian* for September 7, 2011, Hina Shamsi notes,

> In the last ten years, America has become an international legal outlier in
> invoking the right to use lethal force and indefinite detention against sus-
> pected terrorists outside battle zones. If we further entrench the militari-
> sation of our counter-terrorism efforts, our nation risks becoming a legal
> pariah, to the detriment of those efforts.

"Outside battle zones" means potentially everywhere, including within
the United States. And "suspected terrorists" could be anybody, including American citizens. As many have proclaimed, moreover, "the war on
terror"—or the state of emergency since 9/11—threatens to be unending.

Concerning genocide, sociologist Helen Fein notes that victim
groups are "perceived as alien" and, hence, do not belong to "the universe of obligation of the dominant group"; that they are seen as "unas-
similable"; and that "their elimination either removes a threat (real or
symbolic) or opens up opportunities (or both)" (*Genocide,* 34). Within
these terms, it is easy to understand colonial genocides. The indigenous
peoples European colonizers encountered were always seen as "alien,"
outside the colonizers' "universe of obligation," and typically both threatening and presenting opportunities. Fein's terms, however, do not clearly
fit those cases in which a group that belongs to a society is subjected
to exterminationist measures by other groups within that society. The
"kulaks" targeted for liquidation by Stalin were, after all, Russian peasants, supposedly the ancient heart and soul of Russia. But they were also
resistant to modernization through the collectivization of agriculture.
The Jews and Gypsies during the Holocaust were viewed by the Nazis as
aliens, outside the German "universe of obligation," and both threatening
and offering opportunities at least for racial "purification." But the Nazis
also exterminated many Germans because they were deemed criminals,
insane, or mentally defective. "Alien" takes on a very different meaning
when applied to offspring of the German "race" and society.[37]

Coupled with the modern, biopolitical sovereignty of nation-states,
exterminism has frequently emerged as an official method of procedure.
State-sponsored genocides, rationalized as necessary for economic or
cultural progress, have often accompanied processes of modernization.[38] Genocides, moreover, can be aimed at populations both outside
and within the boundaries of nation-states. Whether under the aegis of
capitalism, National Socialism, or communism, the way forward for many
societies has often appeared to entail the liquidation of entire populations

who seem to stand in the way. The record of genocidal actions and policies in the history of the Soviet Union is horrific. But the history of capitalist development is hardly better. In fact, as we have seen, unregulated capitalism inevitably produces its own category of rubbish people or surplus population—Marx's "reserve army of labor."

Agamben argues that the concentration camp has become "the biopolitical paradigm of the modern": "Inasmuch as its inhabitants have been stripped of every political status and reduced to naked life, the camp is . . . the most absolute biopolitical space that has ever been realized."[39] In saying so, Agamben takes Foucault's disciplinary penitentiary one step farther, to its experiential extreme. Everyone knows about the Nazis's concentration camps and also the Soviet gulags. Is "the camp," as Agamben says, paradigmatic also in democracies—in the United States, for example? Among the earliest concentration camps in the twentieth century were those the United States established during the Philippine-American War, the much bloodier affair that followed the Spanish-American War. Even earlier, there were P.O.W. camps on both sides during the Civil War. And the reservation system into which Native Americans were herded had many of the characteristics of later camps. Then there were the internment camps for Japanese and Japanese Americans during World War II. Today's "prison-industrial complex" has also taken on many of the characteristics of concentration camps, and certainly Guantanamo and the other prisons for "detainees" (suspected terrorists) are such camps.[40] The question of "illegal aliens," furthermore, has led to the establishment of an entire system of immigration prisons. The "illegals"—mostly Mexicans—provide a sort of reserve-reserve army of labor, very useful to capitalism, that situates them at the border of "indistinction," as Agamben calls it, where human dignity and acknowledgment cease and "bare life" begins (see chapter 5).

Given the current economic crisis of capitalist globalization, it is at least conceivable that the ranks of the unemployed, the homeless, and the "superfluous" will continue to swell and to descend past any redeemable limit into "bare life," pushing supposedly democratic regimes into fascist versions of sovereignty willing to exterminate portions of their own populations deemed worthless or parasitic. Modernity emerges when sovereignty shifts from its feudal embodiment in the king to biopolitics, evident already in Malthus's *Essay on Population*. Marcus's *Book of Mur-*

der! foreshadows Agamben's *Homo Sacer.* The state increasingly takes charge of the health and bodies of its citizens. Race science leads through Darwinism to eugenics, with its positive mission of improving "the race" of a nation-state's citizens. But eugenics, like the theory of evolution itself, had its negative side: selecting those citizens who are most fit to reproduce necessarily involves identifying those who are least fit. By the early 1900s, experts in the United States, Britain, and France, as well as in Germany, were calling for sterilization and sometimes euthanasia for the insane, the mentally deficient, and criminals, judging them to be entire categories whose individual members' lives were "devoid of value." The discourse about "the masses" and "mass society" leads, moreover, toward the nihilistic denouement in which all lives are "devoid of value." "The masses" are no longer just Malthus's category of "the poor" or just Marx's "reserve army of labor," let alone the revolutionary proletariat. They are everybody. The sovereign "We the people" has its nightmare opposite in "bare life" and the threat of universal annihilation—a threat that has been a real possibility since World War II, the invention of nuclear weapons, and the "deterrence" policy of M.A.D., or "Mutually Assured Destruction," during the cold war. Today, with the proliferation of nuclear arms, universal annihilation may be even more likely.

In *The Dialectic of Enlightenment,* Max Horkheimer and Theodor Adorno contended that the only thing that can prevent Enlightenment from reaching this catastrophic dead end is Enlightenment reflecting upon itself and its consequences. But in *Negative Dialectics,* Adorno rejects this possibility: in modern mass society, administered through biopolitics, "Even in his formal freedom, the individual is as fungible and replaceable as he will be under the liquidators' boots" (362). How to avoid this nihilistic outcome is the central problem facing humanity. The standard answer is through strengthening democratic procedures and the regimes of international law and human rights, including the United Nations, while eliminating poverty as far as possible—without, however, eliminating the individuals who now constitute "the poor." That answer is at best shaky, both because of the many negative forces blocking its realization and because, even if it can be achieved, biopolitics will still hold sway, deciding on life and death and "the state of exception" or "emergency." Unfortunately, as Horkheimer and Adorno claimed, Enlightenment can easily turn totalitarian.

Many economists view the solution in terms of reviving capitalism, reversing growing unemployment by investing in greater productive capacity or "growth." They acknowledge that the global crisis is bad but have faith that, even if it needs some artificial respiration from governments in the form of stimulus money and bank bailouts, the capitalist system will right itself and continue its ever-forward march of progress. In the United States, unemployment will, it is hoped, soon shrink to normal (somewhere around 5 or 6 percent). But what is normal about unemployment? Why is it that capitalism cannott achieve full employment? What is normal about one hundred million or one million or even a thousand people starving in the Global South, let alone in the Global North?

A world in which the excluded vastly outnumber the included, in which everyone is potentially excluded: ever since the first states (civilizations) began to emerge, the poor have vastly outnumbered the rich. But, at least in precapitalist times, most of the poor were able to live off the land, mainly as serfs or peasant farmers. Many others were slaves, often well cared for because they were useful and valuable property. Today, with millions crammed into the slums of enormous, dysfunctional cities, what is to be done? An economic system that systematically produces huge numbers of superfluous people has no answer. Only when the dominance of private over public, corporate over communal ownership is reversed and only when the excluded become the focus and active center of economic and political arrangements (only when the excluded are fully included) can poverty both in the United States and throughout the world be overcome. At the very least, when Johnny comes marching home, he should not be tossed out with the garbage.

TWELVE

World Social Forum: Multitude versus Empire?

At the heart of building alternatives and localizing
economic and political systems are the recovery of the
commons and the reclaiming of community.

—VANDANA SHIVA, "THE LIVING DEMOCRACY MOVEMENT"

On a Global Exchange "reality tour" in 2005, we traveled to the fifth
World Social Forum (WSF) in Porto Alegre, Brazil. Our group included
pacifists, anticorporation activists, a contingent of young Bioneers from
California, and a practitioner of liberation theology—a Church of Christ
minister who is also an avowed atheist. The first half of the tour took us to
a number of the encampments staked out by MST (the Brazilian Landless Workers' Movement) and to an MST school in Veranópolis, which
trains the movement's leaders. We also visited a school, a recycling center,
and a women's cooperative funded through Porto Alegre's participatory
budgeting process.[1]

Estimated at two hundred thousand, an enormous march through
the streets of Porto Alegre opened the WSF. Besides those who had come
for the WSF, there were delegations from all seventeen of Brazil's political
parties and many Brazilian trade unions. The march took the general form
of a protest against the U.S. invasion of Iraq. Together with the standard
peace signs, many signs, including the one I carried, condemned President George W. Bush as a war criminal. Even while many protested the
Bush regime's warmongering, the march was not an angry event but a

celebratory one—an expression of hope and a welcoming for those who had come to the WSF from every corner of the world.

The WSF is a major factor in what its opponents like to call the "antiglobalization" movement. The new internationalism, however, that is expressed in the WSF and its numerous offshoots is not *anti*globalization. Susan George writes that it is, instead, "deeply engaged with the world as a whole and the fate of everyone who shares the planet." It is "easily more 'pro-globalisation' than its [neoliberal] adversaries" (*Another World*, ix). Instead of "antiglobalization," WSF activists refer to "the global justice" or the "alterglobalization" movement.

Despite the optimism of the neoliberal advocates of transnational corporate capitalism before the 2007–8 crash, globalization on their terms has not helped spread prosperity around the world, but the reverse. Instead of the boost to economic development that loans from the World Bank and the International Monetary Fund (IMF) were supposed to give countries in the Global South, most poor nations "are facing enormous hardship because more money is spent on debt service than on education, healthcare or poverty reduction," writes Belay Seyoum: "African countries [now] spend four times more on payments to international creditors than on education"[2]—and that was ten years ago. This is partly because loans from the IMF and World Bank have come with strings attached: the countries receiving those loans have had to agree to undertake Structural Adjustment Programs (SAPs), which typically involve austerity measures—cutting back both on social welfare (health, education, etc.) and on locally and regionally sustainable patterns of production and trade.[3] In *Planet of Slums*, Mike Davis calls this "SAPing the Third World" (151–73). "The coerced tribute that the Third World pays to the First World has been the literal difference between life and death for millions of poor people," Davis writes: "The 1980s—when the IMF and the World Bank used the leverage of debt to restructure the economies of most of the Third World—are the years when slums became an implacable future not just for poor rural migrants, but also for millions of traditional urbanites displaced or immiserated by the violence" of SAPs (148, 152). David Harvey notes as well that it would be politically "suicidal" to try to impose on the United States "the kind of austerity programme that the IMF typically visits on others."[4]

The WSF expresses a very different sort of optimism about the future —one based in grassroots activism working against the forces of economic immiseration and poverty and against environmental spoliation. During the fifth WSF, we found that optimism to be extraordinarily dynamic and compelling. To what degree the global justice movement will be able to change the world for the better remains to be seen, but, in many parts of it, including in Porto Alegre and more generally in Brazil and many other parts of Latin America, it has already changed it for the better.

THE WSF AND THE GLOBAL JUSTICE MOVEMENT

The MST encampments we visited before the start of the WSF were occupied by landless peasants brimming with hope and creative energy. Between1984 and 2005, the MST succeeded in legally obtaining small farms for over 350,000 previously landless families, out of a total landless population of about 4.5 million individuals.[5] With some state aid and MST leadership, peasants set up "black tent" encampments near the boundaries of large *fazendas* or ranches and plantations. Through an official review process, if the government finds that part or all of a *fazenda* is not being put to socially productive use, the peasants can move onto it and start their farms and communities. Since the 1800s, however, land reform in Brazil and elsewhere in Latin America has been far from peaceful. Landowners' hired thugs have assassinated MST leaders and massacred peasants. Approximately "1,600 people have been killed in agrarian conflicts since 1984" in Brazil, although only "about a hundred" of the slain belonged to the MST (Stedile, "Brazil's Landless Battalions," 40). But there is no more effective way for Brazil or other Latin American countries to combat endemic poverty than through land reform.[6]

The MST activists in the encampments and at the school in Veranópolis were well organized, well trained, and cheerfully looking forward to a better future for themselves and their families. Like participatory budgeting for which Porto Alegre is famous, MST is a highly democratic, grassroots organization: everyone is involved and participating. All the encampments have schools and teachers supplied by MST, so children who might otherwise have grown up illiterate are learning to read and write and also learning about MST and social and economic issues more generally. The children in the schools within the encampments were just as cheerful and friendly as their parents. They now have a future they can look forward to.

At the WSF, in the hundreds of white tents along the banks of the Guaiba River, we heard talks by pacifists and environmentalists, feminists and leaders of indigenous peoples, Marxists and liberation theologians; and one morning we joined the enormous crowd in a stadium to hear an impassioned speech by President Luis Inacio Lula da Silva ("Lula") of Brazil. We were later told that President Hugo Chávez of Venezuela drew an even bigger crowd, but we missed his speech. One of the few rules of the WSF is that politicians cannot participate in its proceedings, so Lula and Chávez, although they attracted huge audiences, were not part of the official program. Besides Lula and Chávez, many of the speakers were famous and included at least two Nobel Prize winners. Among others, we met the late Dennis Brutus, South African poet and anti-Apartheid activist, and Jan Nederveen Pieterse, distinguished anthropologist and analyst of globalization and economic neoliberalism. The WSF's printed program was as thick as the Sunday *New York Times,* listing discussions and panels whose participants came from 135 countries and from every continent except Antarctica.

As participants ourselves, we were joined by two of our friends and colleagues from Indiana University who had helped organize a two-day session of the forum with faculty and students from various countries— besides the United States, these included Canada, Argentina, Brazil, and Uruguay. Our topic was how to make our academic work politically more effective. Among other issues, we discussed holding teach-ins about the U.S. war machine and about the WSF; establishing peace studies programs; activist forms of service learning for our students; and forging alliances with labor unions on our campuses. I spoke about the importance of teaching postcolonial studies in U.S. colleges and universities, especially given the propensity of many American politicians and pundits to claim that the United States has never been an imperializing power. And Professor Michael Denning and the students who came with him from Yale spoke about student-labor solidarity on their campus.

The fifth WSF was larger than any previous WSF and, so far, any other gathering of global justice activists. There were over 150,000 registered participants, with perhaps an equal number of unregistered observers. We rightly judged that the press in Europe and Latin America would report this astonishing gathering, but not the mainstream press in the United States. And, indeed, when we returned home, we encountered very few people, even in our university community, who had read or heard about the WSF. This was hardly surprising: the Battle of Seattle in 1999, which helped inspire the WSFs, came as a complete surprise in the United States, even though many events led up to it. By now, other WSFs have been held in Asia and Africa (Mumbai in 2004; Karachi and Bamako, along with Caracas, in 2006; Nairobi in 2007; and Dakar in 2011). Our small delegation from Indiana University also participated in the Midwest Social Forum in Milwaukee in 2006. The first U.S. Social Forum was held in 2007 in Atlanta and a second one in 2010 in Detroit. And there have been regional global justice forums in Europe and other parts of the world.

In September 2011, the Occupy Wall Street movement also seemed to arise out of nowhere—at least, as viewed by the mainstream media in the United States—but it too has had many precedents, including the WSFs and the Battle of Seattle. As I write (January 26, 2012), Occupy protestors are camping in igloos outside the World Economic Forum in Davos, Switzerland, while the latest WSF is gathering once again in Porto Alegre.[7] A January 23, 2012, story from *Agence Presse-France* reports that the 2012 WSF will include participants from Occupy Wall Street, the Arab Spring, the "Indignados" movement in Spain, and student protestors from Chile, among many others. And its organizers will help plan for a people's summit to correspond to next June's Rio+20 environmental meeting, "to give a voice to those who resist the advances of . . . predatory development hiding behind a green face."

The Battle of Seattle, waged by approximately fifty thousand activists from many organizations—teamsters and church groups, AIDs activists and pacifists, farmers and environmentalists—disrupted a ministerial meeting of the World Trade Organization. It was not the first action in the campaign against neoliberalism and for global justice, but it was the first to be widely reported by the U.S. media.[8] *The Los Angeles Times* declared,

> On the tear gas shrouded streets of Seattle, the unruly forces of democracy collided with the elite world of trade policy. And when the meeting ended in failure . . . the elitists had lost and the debate had changed forever.[9]

If the Seattle demonstrators expressed their rejection of how the WTO does the world's business, two years later the WSF "sequel"[10] offered an "open space" for the advancement of positive alternatives: among them, fair trade versus so-called free trade, economic as well as political democracy, an end to militarism and war, food sovereignty, overcoming global poverty and canceling the debts of the poorest countries, the abolition of racial discrimination and of violence against women, protection of "the commons," and environmental sustainability.

The WSF has roots in numerous campaigns by peasants, factory workers, women, and indigenous peoples seeking to improve their lives. Joining these groups have been environmentalists, GLBT (gay, lesbian, bisexual, and transsexual) activists, socialists, pacifists, and anarchists, as well as representatives of numerous nongovernmental organizations such as Via Campesina, Oxfam, and Focus on the Global South. It owes much to the MST, to Lula's Brazilian Workers' Party, and to the practice of participatory budgeting in Porto Alegre. Widespread resistance to capitalist globalization, however, goes back at least to the era of decolonization. As they emerged between the end of World War II and the 1970s, many of the newly decolonized nations established socialist or partially socialist economies. The WSF also owes something to the civil rights movement in the United States, the opposition to the Vietnam War, and the 1968 "cultural" rebellions in North America and Western Europe.[11] Several months before Seattle, the World Economic Forum meeting in Davos encountered resistance by the MST from Brazil and by ATTAC (the Association for the Taxation of Financial Transactions and Aid to Citizens) from France.[12] These organizations took the lead in establishing the WSF in 2001.[13]

Another forerunner of the WSF was the Zapatista rebellion in Chiapas, Mexico, which has renewed "the legacy of Che Guevara, the struggle of Emiliano Zapata, liberation theology, Maya culture, and the democratic demands of Mexican society."[14] When the EZLN, or Zapatista Army of National Liberation, declared war against the Mexican government in 1994 and seized several towns in Chiapas, partly because of the national and, indeed, global media attention the rebellion attracted, the violence did not last long—the government backed off. In 1996, the Zapatistas organized the first Intercontinental Meeting for Humanity and against Neoliberalism.[15] Journalist Luis Hernandez Navarro notes that "Hundreds of personalities and organizations have participated in the *encuentros* against neoliberalism convened by zapatismo," Global Exchange among them.[16] With the help of the press and the Internet, Zapatismo soon acquired an international dimension, including many of the participants in the Battle of Seattle and in the WSF "process."[17]

As noted in chapter five, the history of the struggle for social justice in Mexico goes back much farther than 1994 or even the Mexican Revolution of 1910–20 to the earliest struggles against Western imperialism. In *Global Revolt*, Amory Starr writes, "For indigenous peoples anywhere, colonialism never ended. Theirs is an uninterrupted struggle against genocide, displacement and cultural invasion" (19).[18] The Mayas of Chiapas and elsewhere in Mexico and Central America are fighting above all to gain recognition and rights from the governing elites as well as from corporations. Over the short term, their movement and the more general movement leading to the WSF can be traced to the 1980s and the Reagan-Thatcher era that started the "dismantling of the Keynesian [welfare] state"[19] and that consolidated the ideological hegemony of economic neoliberalism.[20] Like the World Economic Forum, the WTO and NAFTA are outcomes of that hegemony.

Where the WSF "process" will lead is uncertain. But at least it has alerted much of civil society around the world to the inequities and damage caused by capitalist globalization. Whether it can meet all the utopian goals its participants advocate, the WSF and both its supporters and opponents must meet some of those goals—environmental sustainability above all—if the earth and all the species that inhabit it, obviously including humans, are going to continue to inhabit it.[21]

THE "MULTITUDE" VERSUS THE "EMPIRE"?

With the fall of the Soviet Empire and the Eastern European socialist regimes, the triumph of neoliberalism seemed to some observers to be final and absolute. Neoliberal gurus such as Milton Friedman and Alan Greenspan claimed victory for "free markets" and liberal democracy, which they also claimed were virtually identical (see chapter two). Francis Fukuyama famously declared that history had come to an end with the triumph of capitalism and liberal democracy—a prophecy almost as ludicrous as the one announcing that the Rapture would occur on May 11, 2011. After 9/11, after the invasions of Afghanistan and Iraq, after the economic crash of 2007–8, and after the Arab Spring of 2011, no one—not even Fukuyama—believes any longer that history has ended. History forges relentlessly on—not necessarily in a forward, progressive direction. Today, it is shaped increasingly by globalizing capitalism, but it is not close to any conclusion—except, perhaps, the apocalypse brought on by global warming or the one caused by nuclear warfare or by Slavoj Žižek's other "riders of the apocalypse."[22]

The WTO and the other major financial institutions now controlling international trade—the World Bank and the International Monetary Fund paramount among them—are not democratic, and neither are corporations. Because of the domination by corporations and their lobbyists, and especially after the Supreme Court's "Citizens United" ruling, the federal government in the United States is no longer democratic either but is today a plutocracy.[23] One of the main goals of the social movements that coalesced in Seattle and then again in the WSF is "expanding the practice of democracy to include the economic realm."[24] This is also a Zapatista goal: it opposes not just the Mexican government but neoliberalism and the domination of the world's economic affairs by transnational capitalism. Exemplified by NAFTA as supposedly an antipoverty, development-friendly trade agreement, "neoliberalism has been an utter failure" and is demonstrably moving the world in the opposite direction of the goals of ridding the world of poverty, hunger, and environmental spoliation.[25] According to Anuradha Mittal of the organization Food First, "The victims of free market dogma can be found all over the developing world."[26] Instead of bringing prosperity to Mexico, in NAFTA's first five years, Mexican per capita income declined by 25 percent (however, the Mayas of Chiapas had from the outset very little monetary income to decline).

At its first annual meeting in 2001, the WSF drew some twelve thousand activists representing dozens of organizations from Latin America and around the world. Due in part to the leadership of Brazilian activists including Oded Grajew, Francisco Whitaker, and João Pedro Stedile, Porto Alegre was a logical site for holding the WSF. A city of 1.3 million and a center of the MST that Stedile helped organize, Porto Alegre has also made its mark in grassroots organizing and democracy through participatory budgeting.[27] This entails having its citizens elect committees that make and vote on proposals for funding, using a sizable percentage of the city's budget for everything from new schools and clinics to workers' cooperatives and recycling facilities. Participatory budgeting has now spread to some other Brazilian cities and states.

Does the World Social Forum represent "the multitude" that will overthrow "the Empire"? These are the terms Michael Hardt and Antonio Negri employ in analyzing the current global political and economic crisis. Their first book, *Empire*, appeared in 2000, the year before the initial WSF meeting and also just before 9/11 and the U.S. invasions of Afghanistan and Iraq. "Empire" is the name Hardt and Negri give to the new power that, they contend, has replaced the old political and military empires and is gradually replacing the waning power of nation-states. "Empire" supposedly represents a qualitatively different form of sovereignty from national governments, because it has sprung ethereally out of transnational capitalism and the Internet.

Nation-states, however, though perhaps less powerful than they were two decades ago, have not vanished, and, as is obvious in the case of the United States after 9/11, they continue to exercise military might over weaker societies in the same old, imperialist fashion that created the major European empires starting in the Renaissance. Studies of U.S. imperialism such as Sidney Lens's *Forging of the American Empire*, William Blum's *Rogue State*, Noam Chomsky's *Year 501: The Conquest Continues*, Chalmers Johnson's *The Sorrows of Empire*, and Greg Grandin's *Empire's Workshop* stress the many ways the United States has dominated Latin America and other parts of the world, sometimes with and sometimes without gunboat diplomacy, military invasions, and CIA-sponsored coups and assassinations (though these have been very frequent since World War II), but always by exercising its economic clout.

If Negri and Hardt's "Empire" means primarily capitalist globalization, with or without the blessing of national governments it is having devastating effects. Both within most countries and among them, the inequality between the poor and the wealthy has been growing exponentially rather than decreasing. According to the 2003 Human Development Report, in fifty-four countries income declined over the previous decade. In that same period, the profits of the largest two hundred corporations increased by over 360 percent. In 2003, total sales of just three corporations—BP, Wal-Mart, and ExxonMobil—exceeded the total incomes of 118 of the poorest countries, home to more than eight hundred million people. Even the World Bank now admits that "Globalization appears to increase poverty and inequality.... The costs of adjusting to greater openness [that is, to 'free trade'] are borne exclusively by the poor, regardless of how long the adjustment takes."[28] Over the last three decades, in terms of per capita wealth, "The difference between the top and bottom 20 percent has doubled. . . . The richest 20 percent of the world's people consume 86 percent of the world's resources, while the poorest 20 percent get just one percent."[29] Seyoum notes that "the average African household [in 2001] consumes 20% less than it did 25 years ago" (*The State of the Global Economy 2001/2002*, 57). Instead of rising since the 1980s, the life expectancy of individuals in many African countries has fallen, partly because of AIDS but also because of poverty, famine, and other diseases such as the recent cholera epidemic in Zimbabwe. "The 'economic therapy' imposed under IMF–World Bank jurisdiction," writes Michel Chossudovsky, "is in large part responsible for triggering famine and social devastation in Ethiopia and the rest of Sub-Saharan Africa, wrecking the peasant economy and impoverishing millions of people."[30]

Globalizing capitalism is also creating more rather than less economic inequality within the countries of the North, including the United States. "Recent research using data from tax returns," write Boushey and Weller, "has found that the average real income of the bottom 90 percent of American tax payers declined by 7% between 1973 and 2000, while the income of the top 1 percent went up 148%."[31] Since 2000, as Occupy Wall Street insists, inequality in the United States has been accelerating. At least forty-seven million U.S. citizens now live below the official poverty line, while the United States is rapidly reaching income inequality similar to that in many Latin American countries.[32]

In *Globalization and Its Discontents,* Joseph Stiglitz, Nobel Prize-winning economist and former vice president of the World Bank, begins by saying, "While I was at the World Bank, I saw firsthand the devastating effects that [corporate] globalization can have on developing countries, and especially the poor within those countries" (ix). The World Bank, the IMF, and the WTO all operate according to what Stiglitz calls "unfair trade laws" (166). These international lending and trade organizations do the bidding of their member nations, but only if the governments of those nations do the bidding of multinational corporations. "Unfortunately," writes Stiglitz, "we have no world government, accountable to the people of every country, to oversee the globalization process in a fashion comparable to the way national governments guided the nationalization process" (21–22). Stiglitz was one of the featured speakers at the fourth WSF in Mumbai (and see his more recent books, especially *Free Fall* and *The Price of Inequality*).

Just as disturbing are the revelations in *Confessions of an Economic Hit Man* by John Perkins, who has also addressed the WSF. Perkins explains how leaders of poor countries have often been cajoled, bribed, or threatened into accepting enormous "development" loans—a job he used to do. Leaders who resist, as did Omar Torrijos of Panama in 1981, have frequently wound up on the CIA's hit list. Outside the United States, writes Perkins, "most of the world" knows "that Torrijos's death . . . was just one more in a series of CIA assassinations" (161)—Patrice Lumumba in the Congo (1961), Ngo Dinh Diem in Vietnam (1963), Che Guevara in Bolivia (1967), Jaime Roldós in Ecuador (1981).[33]

There are now numerous accounts of the supposedly new imperialism exercised by the United States around the globe. In *The Sorrows of Empire*, to cite just one example, Chalmers Johnson emphasizes the role played by U.S. military bases—there are approximately eight hundred of them around the world—in wielding American power in what amounts to an imperialist manner. Of course, as the old saying goes, trade follows the flag; American-based corporations are also exercising their economic clout on a global scale, along with other corporations based in Japan, Germany, and elsewhere. Yet in their first book, Hardt and Negri claim that the "imperial expansion" of today's shadowy financial empire "has nothing to do with imperialism, nor with those state organisms designed for conquest, pillage, genocide, colonization, and slavery" (*Empire*, 166–67). The old empires were territorial; the new Empire "extends and consolidates the model of network power" (ibid., 167). This is surely a misreading of today's global power structure, in part because even the oldest empires depended on communications and trade "networks."

In *Multitude* (2004), Hardt and Negri have much more to say about war, about the WTO, IMF, World Bank, and NAFTA, and also about the emergent opposition to empire, "the multitude," which they claim the WSF in some sense expresses or represents. They see the 1999 WTO protest in Seattle as one of the points of origin of the WSF, as do other commentators, but also as a forerunner of what they predict will become the revolutionary "multitude." But just what sort of revolution do they anticipate? If "empire" is not "imperialism," will the coming revolution be anything like those of the past—the American and French Revolutions, the Russian Revolution of 1917, the nationalist revolutions in the colonies of Europe's now-defunct empires, the frequent coups in Latin

America, the overthrows of the communist regimes in Eastern Europe and the Soviet Union, or the Arab Spring? If "the multitude" is not Marx's revolutionary proletariat and if it is not the aggrieved, rebellious citizens of nation-states, then what sort of revolutionary agent is it?

Hardt and Negri are fuzzy—they seem to think they are being philosophical—on details both about the multitude and about revolution.[34] On one hand, they say that "multitude is a class concept" (*Multitude,*103) and they add "All of the multitude is productive and all of it is poor" (134). How is this different from the idea of the proletariat? It is a more inclusive but also vaguer idea, and it probably involves some mixture of the working and middle classes. Perhaps it is also inclusive in the same manner as the "99%" who make up Occupy Wall Street and the other Occupy movements in the United States and around the world. Among many other thoughts, the expression "99%" implies, at least, that the middle classes have collapsed into the working classes and that both are increasingly impoverished, while the 1 percent keeps getting richer.

Marx, of course, identified the proletariat mainly with factory workers, in part because he thought the largely illiterate peasantry in the early 1800s could not represent itself, much less form a revolutionary vanguard. The anticolonial revolutions in Europe's former colonies in the twentieth century seem to have proved him wrong. For Frantz Fanon in *The Wretched of the Earth,* it was not the factory proletariat but the impoverished peasantry who carried the torch of revolution. The Zapatista rebellion is one of the most recent demonstrations of Fanon's thesis.

Ronaldo Munck asserts that Hardt and Negri leave the peasantry out of the picture. While they do say that "the peasantry is fundamentally conservative, isolated, and capable only of reaction, not of any autonomous political action of its own,"[35] and while this is "reminiscent of the most clichéd phrases of Marx about the French peasantry as 'sacks of potatoes'" (133), they also understand the peasantry to be dying out as a class category. It is fading "into the background of the economic landscape of agriculture, which tends to be populated now by huge corporations, agricultural workers, and an increasingly desperate rural poor" (*Globalization and Contestation,* 120).

It seems rather arbitrary, however, to define the peasantry as a lapsed or lapsing class. What about the MST as well as the Zapatistas? If small farmers and "agricultural workers" are not "peasants," then who are?

Munck contends that, in current struggles against capitalist globalization, peasants have occupied "a whole range of crucial sites of contestation such as the environment, gender and indigenous knowledge" (*Globalization and Contestation,* 133). Certainly, small farmers and agrarian workers have been in the vanguard of the WSF process, a fact Hardt and Negri do not seem to recognize. In *Multitude,* there is only a brief mention of the MST, which was key in establishing the World Social Forum. Nor do Hardt and Negri mention the leading role of French farmer José Bové in WSF and in the global issue of "food sovereignty." Via Campesina, the worldwide organization of "peasants"—that is, of small farmers and agricultural workers—has also played a vital role in WSF and the current upsurge of resistance to capitalist, corporate globalization. And Hardt and Negri have nothing to say about various other movements and organizations that, in the WSF process, advocate for indigenous rights and that also are peasant based. Nor do they consider the plight or the revolutionary potential of the peasants and small farmers who have been driven off of the land into the slums of today's mega cities, as in the *favelas* of Rio de Janeiro and Sao Paolo or the townships ringing Johannesburg and Capetown.

On the other hand, Hardt and Negri do acknowledge the Zapatista National Liberation Army as "the hinge between the old guerilla model and the new model of biopolitical network structures" (*Multitude,* 85). They continue,

> The Zapatistas ... demonstrate wonderfully how the economic transition of post-Fordism can function equally in urban and rural territories, linking local experiences with global struggles. The Zapatistas, which were born and primarily remain a peasant and indigenous movement, use the Internet [to communicate to a national and global public].[36]

Even though Hardt and Negri seem to downplay other peasant and indigenous organizations that have played major roles in the WSF, the "poors" in their "multitude" include the billions of peasants and also of the urban poor who are excluded from the wealth produced by the transnational corporations (*Multitude,* 135). Where do most "peasants" go when they are driven from the land? To the slums of the cities (Davis, *Planet of Slums*).

Poverty and exclusion from corporate productivity do not characterize the "immaterial labor" that Hardt and Negri see as also an intrinsic part of the multitude. By "immaterial labor," they mean all those employed in the information, communications, and educational sectors of the global economy. It is not exactly clear why they do not use the more familiar term "intellectuals." Perhaps this is because many of these "immaterial" workers are well paid and think of themselves as middle-class professionals, not as rebellious members of a growing, globalizing labor movement. And some percentage of them has managerial positions in corporations. Nevertheless, at least a small fraction of the "immaterial labor" category is also active in the WSF process, including the academics who participated in our session at the fifth WSF.

In *Multitude,* Hardt and Negri are also fuzzy about what it is the coming revolution will presumably overthrow: "We should emphasize, once again, that what the forces mobilized in this new global cycle [of struggles] have in common is not just a common enemy—whether it be called neoliberalism, U.S. hegemony, or global Empire—but also common practices, languages, conduct, habits, forms of life, and desires for a better future" (215). So is "Empire" both "neoliberalism" and "U.S. hegemony"? Is at least one nation-state, even after the era of the nation-state has supposedly lapsed, standing in the way of the multitude's "desires for a better future"? If so, then "Empire" does have something to do with imperialism in the old-fashioned sense, and especially with U.S. imperialism as it is being practiced in Iraq, Afghanistan, and around the world. The United States is still also one of the headquarters, if not the only one, of the global capitalist economy.

Just as Hardt and Negri argue that "Empire" is categorically different from "imperialism," so they argue that "the multitude" is categorically different from "global public opinion." They claim that the latter is a phrase "completely inadequate to understand the nature and power of such expressions of the networks of the multitude" as the massive, worldwide antiwar demonstrations in February 2003 (*Multitude,* 264). They seem to be splitting hairs: all revolutionary movements, even medieval jacquaries, have been motivated by some version of public opinion. And the WSFs, like the global antiwar demonstrations, are obviously expressions of at least a portion of "global public opinion."[37] As Thomas Olesen points out in *International Zapatismo,* it helps to distinguish between dominant "public spheres" and subaltern "counter-public spheres" (94). "Multitude" in the singular is no more analytical than "public opinion" or "public sphere" in the singular.

It is true, however, as Hardt and Negri contend, that the achieve-ment of a genuine democracy on a global scale is "a dream created in the great revolutions of modernity but never yet realized." Hardt and Negri continue:

> This striving for democracy permeates the entire cycle of protests and demonstrations around the issues of globalization, from the dramatic events at the WTO in Seattle in 1999 to the meetings of the World Social Forum in Porto Alegre, Brazil. This desire for democracy is also the core of the various movements and demonstrations against the 2003 war in Iraq and the permanent state of war more generally.[38]

It is true as well that the WSFs and related events and processes such as the U.S. Social Forum and, most recently, the Occupy Wall Street move-ment stress participatory democracy and grassroots organizing (Maeck-elbergh, *The Will of the Many*). Later in *Multitude,* Hardt and Negri are explicit about some of the main elements of "Empire" that the WSF and "the new cycle of struggles" oppose:

> The coming-out party of the new cycle of struggles were the protests at the WTO summit in Seattle in 1999. The Seattle protests not only initi-ated a series of protests at the summit meetings of the representatives of global power that would extend in the subsequent years across North America and Europe, but also revealed the real origins of the cycle in the innumerable struggles in the global south that had already taken place against the IMF, the World Bank, North American Free Trade Agreement (NAFTA), and other institutions of the new global power structure.[39]

They add, "The cycle of struggles has been consolidated in a certain sense at the annual meetings of the World Social Forum and the various re-gional social forums" (215).

In the foreword that Hardt and Negri wrote for *Another World Is Possible: Popular Alternatives to Globalization at the World Social Forum,* edited by Thomas Ponniah and William F. Fisher, they elaborate upon their identification of the WSF with what they think of as the seedbed for the revolutionary "multitude": "One should . . . read the papers and confer-ences presented at Porto Alegre [the way one should read] the *Cahiers de Doléances* (statements of grievances) presented to the Estates-General in France in 1789":

Over 40,000 Cahiers de Doléances were presented with lists of demands, denunciations, requests, and desires that were the basis for constructing the Third Estate as a revolutionary force. In pre-revolutionary France they perfected an art of demanding. At Porto Alegre, too, the statements and lists have the same intensity, full of denunciations and utopian desires. They reveal the horrible state of our present form of globalization, the scandal of neoliberal capitalist power, and the misery of the majority of the world's populations.[40]

This is an accurate description of the WSF. Hardt and Negri recognize that the WSF was not established to become a decision-making and action-taking organization but is rather meant to offer an international, democratic, "networking" way for various progressive, activist organizations, causes, and individuals to share viewpoints and aspirations and to express solidarity. Presumably, it is not yet the revolutionary "multitude" in action. But just what do Hardt and Negri think the "multitude" will turn out to be, and how will it take revolutionary action? How will it differ from the new social movements "that have extended from Seattle to Genoa and the World Social Forums in Porto Alegre and Mumbai and have animated the movements against war," which "are the clearest example to date of distributed network organizations" (*Multitude*, 86)? Will the multitude simply be an intensification of the movements now in play, including the WSF, Occupy Wall Street, and the Arab Spring, which, one hopes, are bringing them into clearer focus and nudging them toward more concerted actions? Or will it need to undergo a qualitative (dialectical) mutation to produce the new revolution on a global scale?

One of Hardt and Negri's habits, in both *Multitude* and *Empire*, is to attribute democratic, quasi-revolutionary properties to "networks" per se, conceived as "grassroots" and shaped like Gilles Deleuze and Félix Guattari's "rhizomes," expanding horizontally and, therefore, intrinsically inimical to hierarchical power structures.[41] Clearly, the Internet and its communications systems such as Facebook and Twitter allow individuals and groups to "network" for the first time almost instantaneously on a global scale. The Zapatistas, the groups that demonstrated in Seattle, the Arab Spring revolutionaries, and the Wall Street Occupiers have all made effective use of the Internet, as did President Barack Obama in his 2007 election campaign. And it also appears that these new social movements take on something of the "swarm" aspects of the Internet.[42] Hardt and Negri write that "the Zapatista rebellion had grasped the novelty of the new global situation. . . . The Zapatistas are famous for their global Internet communication."[43] But is networking intrinsically revolutionary? It does seem to be intrinsically democratic: "The democratic network is a completely horizontal and deterritorialized model. The Internet . . . is the prime example of this democratic network structure" (*Multitude,* 299). Hardt and Negri, however, reluctantly admit that networks can be "oligopolistic" and hierarchical, with authoritarian centers and effects.[44] After all, corporations, in both horizontal and vertical modes of their organization, are networks. These include the corporate-controlled communications networks such as CBS, CNN, and Fox. And, just like the Zapatistas or the WSF, corporations make use of the Internet, even controlling major aspects of it—Google, Yahoo, Amazon, Facebook, and so forth.

On their model, "Empire" itself seems to be an immense electronic spider's web being woven through and around defunct nation-states.[45] However, the spider itself consists of both nation-states and corporations. Hardt and Negri fall back on the distinction between form and content because "the fact that a movement is organized as a network . . . does not guarantee that it is peaceful or democratic" (*Empire,* 93). Revolutions, moreover, typically involve violence on both sides. Just how the "peaceful and democratic," "distributed network" of the multitude will overthrow Empire without resorting to violence is unclear. Indeed, it perhaps makes as much sense to think of Al-Qaeda as the revolutionary force that will overthrow globalized capitalism as it does to cobble together a multitudinous "multitude" made up only of the good sorts of revolutionaries—the "productive" "poors" of the world and the progressive "networkers" of "immaterial labor."

Yet the new social movements *are* networking to overthrow unfair trade rules and more generally the domination of the world's economy by transnational corporations. At the same time, the organizations and individuals that gather at the WSFs are both nonviolent and democratic.[46] Various pacifist organizations have been major participants in the WSFs. Global Exchange is a pacifist organization, and so are Code Pink, Women's International League of Peace and Freedom, and Witnesses for Peace—all represented at the fifth WSF. In Porto Alegre, we had interesting discussions with members of the pacifist Gandhi Institute from New Delhi. Most of the events and speeches we attended were quite radical but also pacifist. It is, in any case, difficult to imagine how a violent revolution could be forged from the dispersed and widely diverse ingredients that make up the WSF or the more general global justice movement. Moreover, contrary to what Hardt and Negri expect from the revolutionary multitude, the WSF and its many regional and local offshoots are serving as focal points for progressive "global public opinion." Of course, revolutions can be nonviolent: Gandhi came close to achieving one in India; the final downfall of the Apartheid regime in South Africa is another example; and so is the "Singing Revolution" in Estonia in 1991. At the fifth WSF, in the speeches we heard, Gandhi and Martin Luther King Jr., with their practice of nonviolent civil disobedience, were as often invoked as Castro and Che Guevara, although, in our travels through Brazil before, during, and after the WSF, the most popular tee shirt featured Che, and the next most popular featured Castro. Probably by now Subcomandante Marcos tee shirts are catching up. Are they free market or fair trade commodities? That depends on how they are manufactured and marketed.

WSF GOALS

I do not know if Empire—or the domination of the world by corporations, by neoliberal economic policies, and by U.S. neoimperialism—can be overthrown or even radically reformed by nonviolent means, though I hope that happens. Hardt and Negri are vague about how the revolution they foresee will occur, in part because they are vague about how Empire differs from imperialism and about how the multitude can be something more revolutionary than "global public opinion."[47] At any rate, as a network of progressive movements, the WSF is facilitating numerous local and regional protests and rebellions against capitalist globalization. Perhaps some of these can occur and succeed only through violence, like the Zapatista rebellion in its first several weeks, though Subcomandante Marcos declares he speaks as the member of an army whose goal is to eliminate armies: "the zapatistas are soldiers, so that one day there will be no soldiers."[48] The Zapatistas do not aim to overthrow the government and seize power in Mexico; they aim instead to get the government to carry through with its previous agreements about land reform, human rights, and other issues. But perhaps also, every revolution and every army has wished it could achieve victory nonviolently.

As Negri and Hardt contend, different from previous rebellions and revolutions by peasants and indigenous peoples is the way that the Zapatistas have been able to network with other movements around the world, including the WSF. In large measure because of networking, Empire—whether or not it is a completely new form of capitalist global sovereignty beyond nation-states—is proving itself vulnerable, at least to some extent, to countless local initiatives like the MST and the Zapatistas. As José Corrêa Leite writes in *The World Social Forum: Strategies of Resistance,*

> what seemed to be emerging organically out of the World Social Forum (despite the best efforts of some of the organizers) was not a movement for a single global government but a vision for an increasingly connected international network of very local initiatives, each built on direct democracy.[49]

The WSF offers an "open space" and time for further networking among many, very diverse groups and individuals in the current struggle for global justice. It is "contributing to altering the ideological climate in today's world, helping to break the hegemony of the values of marketization, neoliberalism, and growing militarism."[50] Its current function is to influence and shape "global public opinion" and governmental policy rather than to produce some new orthodoxy, revolutionary or otherwise. "The WSF is a *process* and not just an *event,*" writes Leite; "and it is *part of a bigger movement.* With the multiplication of forums, some organized at the continental level, others at the city level, the WSF has become a worldwide process. It helps to provide continuity to the new internationalism that, since Seattle, has been spreading around the world, confronting neoliberal globalization" (137).

That much of the world is getting poorer has led critics and activists of many persuasions to call for reforming or abolishing the World Bank, IMF, and WTO, and for either reforming or cancelling such "free trade" agreements as NAFTA that have promoted both capitalist globalization and increasing inequality and poverty. Aspects of capitalist globalization that fuel criticism and protest include the scrapping of welfare programs in many countries; the undermining of organized labor (partly through the globalized "outsourcing" of production, with the familiar loss of jobs at home, and partly through direct, often violent opposition to unionization); the relentless commodification of global resources, including such "commons" as water and forests; the proliferation of "weapons of mass destruction," with the United States as the world's major arms trafficker; and global warming and environmental destruction. The current version of globalization, dominated both by transnational corporations and by U.S. military power, looks to many observers to be a continuation of imperialist rule of the West over the rest, rather than its supposed opposites: Hardt and Negri's Empire on the one hand or the "free trade" utopia of prosperity for all promised by neoliberal economic orthodoxy on the other.

Major themes at every WSF have included the reduction or outright cancellation of the enormous and growing debts supposedly owed by the poor countries to the World Bank, the IMF, and other lending agencies and banks in the wealthy countries. Organizations such as ATTAC and British-based Jubilee 500, whose main goal is debt cancellation, are among the dozens of nongovernmental organizations participating in the WSFs. George Monbiot in *Manifesto for a New World Order* writes,

> That the colonized world, whose wealth has been plundered for 500 years, should be deemed to owe the rich world money, and that this presumed debt should be so onerous that every year $382 billion, which might have been used to feed the hungry, to house the poor, to provide healthcare, education, clean water, transport and pensions for people who have access to none of these amenities, is transferred from the poor world to the banks and financial institutions of the rich world in the form of debt repayments is an obscenity which degrades all those of us who benefit from it. It is an obscenity perpetuated by the very system which was, or so we are told, designed to bring it to an end.[51]

To many, including former UN Secretary Kofi Annan, who advocates debt cancellation for the African countries, getting out from under financial mountains of debt is the necessary first step for the poor countries to at long last start on the path of sustainable economic production and stability.

Related to debt cancellation are the issues of "fair trade" and of "food sovereignty." The first refers to the necessity of protecting the livelihoods of peasants and small, local producers and distributors of food and other goods and services against the so-called free market dominated by trans-national corporations. The second refers to the right of individuals and local communities to grow and market their own food in ecologically sustainable ways: "We call for democratic agrarian reform. Land, water, and seeds must be in the hands of the peasants. We promote sustainable agricultural processes. Seeds and genetic stocks are the heritage of humanity."[52] All three issues involve opposition to the so-called, but wildly misnamed, free trade demands of the WTO, the World Bank, and the IMF to grow cash crops for export while giant agribusinesses such as Monsanto and Cargill dump surplus crops (often genetically engineered) into local markets, thus undermining the livelihoods of millions of small farmers. In the United States, one upshot of this process has been the so-called immigration crisis, as millions of Mexicans and Central Americans, driven off the land in their home countries, seek work in the still relatively prosperous North (see chapter 5).

Connected to the issue of food sovereignty is the practice of corporations patenting and monopolizing seeds and other organic products such as pharmaceuticals, many of which have been developed and collectively owned—shared, that is—by peasant and indigenous communities for centuries. There is also growing opposition throughout the world to corporations developing and forcing genetically modified organisms onto the market, with or without the knowledge of consumers about their possible environmental and health consequences. These issues constitute Žižek's second and third "riders of the apocalypse" (see my "Preface"). They are related, in turn, to another major WSF theme, the protection of the global "commons."

The authors of *Alternatives to Economic Globalization* write that there are three types of "common heritage resources":

> The first category includes the water, land, air, forests, and fisheries on which everyone's life depends. The second includes the culture and knowledge that are collective creations of our species. Finally, more modern common resources are those public services that governments perform on behalf of all people to address such basic needs as public health, education, public safety, and social security, among others.[53]

The list could be extended by adding other items—oil, for example. Does the oil underlying the ground of Iraq belong to the Iraqi people? Can the rights to its extraction and sale be claimed by foreign corporations, without the consent of the Iraqis? And so forth.

In the past, despite colonization and the establishment of huge, privately owned estates, every village and locality had its "commons," its parcel of land where all people had a right to plant their gardens or graze their sheep. Today, all countries and cities still have versions of such commons: forests, parks, public gardens, beaches, plazas that belong to the public. But, as the controversy over drilling for oil in the Arctic Wildlife Refuge and in other protected areas such as national parks indicates, the pressure is on to privatize what remains of these public lands in the United States and everywhere else on the planet.

Water is one resource that corporations like Bechtel and Coca Cola are trying to privatize and bottle up, and then resell to the world. A number of sessions at the fifth WSF focused on protecting water as a common possession, not a commodity. These sessions featured talks by such activists as Canadian Maude Barlow, author of *Blue Gold: The Fight to Stop the Corporate Theft of the World's Water.* The struggle for the commons relates directly to ecological issues; a number of the groups that participate in the WSF are primarily focused on the environment, including the young, idealistic members of the Bioneers who traveled to Brazil, as we did, with Global Exchange. Besides sessions focused on debt cancellation, fair trade, food sovereignty, and protecting the commons, the fifth WSF also held sessions that dealt with disarmament and ending militarism and war, including the wars in Afghanistan and Iraq; women's rights sponsored by, among other organizations, Code Pink and WILPF; and ending racism, emphasized in sessions of the World Dignity Forum.

As U.S. citizens, we encountered no animosity at the WSF or elsewhere in Brazil. But the anger toward the Bush administration, because of its invasion of Iraq, its practice of torture, and its support of capitalist globalization at all costs, was everywhere apparent. During the closing ceremonies, as at earlier WSFs, participants posted on a huge wall hundreds of proposals for creating "a better world." And nineteen WSF organizers produced a "manifesto" of proposals that amount to a summary of all of the Forums to date. The goals of the WSF include the following:

· Global peace and security, including disarmament of all "weapons of mass destruction" everywhere.

- Economic justice, including the cancellation of the massive external debts of the poorer countries of the world and the rebuilding of their educational, health, and welfare systems.
- Adherence to fair labor practices and environmental standards by all corporations and governments.
- Protection of the "global commons," including water and other increasingly precious resources such as forests, fish, and wildlife, from privatization and exploitation by corporations.
- Progress toward ending global warming and achieving environmental stability and sustainability.
- Creation of a democratic global polity, or a system of international law and social justice including the strengthening of the U.N. and existing international treaties and institutions such as the World Court.
- National and international policies that protect the rights of indigenous peoples and their cultures, as well as of all other ethnic, cultural, and religious minorities.

Is the WSF process utopian? Of course it is. In an imperfect world, utopianism is a necessity. And if the WSF is utopian, it is no more so than the 1948 U.N. Universal Declaration of Human Rights, which reads in part,

> Everyone has the right to a standard of living adequate for the health and well-being of himself and of his family, including food, clothing, housing and medical care and necessary social services, and the right to security in the event of unemployment, sickness, disability, widowhood, old age or other lack of livelihood. . . . Motherhood and children are entitled to special care and assistance. All children, whether born in or out of wedlock, shall enjoy the same social protection.

Susan George, who quotes the declaration in her book on the WSF, *Another World Is Possible If. . . .* (140), points out that, after World War II, "For perhaps the first time in history, the world really could afford to provide access to a decent life for every person on earth" (137). As we have seen, however, so-called free trade via the corporate globalization of capitalism has not produced increased prosperity for the vast majority of people, not even in the United States. With the current collapse of the American and global economies, it is ludicrous for neoconservatives and economic neoliberals to keep on insisting that capitalist globalization, carried on by transnational corporations, offers the best of all possible worlds.

If ever people everywhere needed to think in utopian terms, it is surely now, as we confront economic breakdown; continued war and violence in the Middle East; the proliferation of nuclear and other weapons of mass destruction; genocide in the Sudan, the Congo, and elsewhere; accelerating, instead of diminishing, world poverty and hunger; global warming and environmental degradation; and the privatization of the global commons. On a planet where the sources of hope seem to be disappearing as rapidly as species, the World Social Forum, whose motto is "another world is possible," is one of the most hopeful processes now occurring. A far better world is possible than the one that has been concocted "in the boardrooms of international greed."[54] If it takes a revolution to arrive there, then let it begin, as Subcomandante Marcos says, "with the speed of dreams."

NOTES

Preface

1. Slavoj Žižek, *Living in the End Times* (London: Verso, 2010), x.
2. See Jim McGuigan, *Cultural Populism* (London and New York: Routledge, 1992).

1. Class Warfare and Cultural Studies

1. See, for example, Dick Hebdige, *Subculture: The Meaning of Style* and Ken Gelder and Sarah Thornton, eds., *The Subcultures Reader.*

2. Though the original emphasis of cultural studies in the works of Williams, Thompson, and Hoggart was clear about social class, starting in the 1970s, there was a movement away from class issues toward ones of race and gender and also toward what Jim McGuigan has called "cultural populism." Because both race and gender are linked in many ways to social class, however, emphasizing these categories did not necessarily detract from the earlier emphasis on social class. But as McGuigan argues, it is in the "populist" direction that the critical edge of cultural studies, focused on social justice, tends to get lost in celebrations of mass culture: whatever the common people enjoy must necessarily be democratic and deserving of recognition. This is a position hard to distinguish from the very economism that insists markets are infallible and the customer is always right.

3. See my *Crusoe's Footprints: Cultural Studies in Britain and America,* 112–18.

4. Jameson, *Signatures of the Visible,* 35.

5. ISA: short for "ideological state apparatus." See Louis Althusser, "Ideology and Ideological State Apparatuses" in *Lenin and Philosophy.*

6. See my *Bread and Circuses: Theories of Mass Culture as Social Decay,* especially chapters 5 and 6.

7. See Lutz Niethammer, *Posthistoire: Has History Come to an End?*

8. In a new version of this old theme, Sheldon Wolin argues that the takeover of the U.S. political system by megacorporations, lobbyists, and the very wealthy has created conditions for an "inverted totalitarianism." See *Democracy Incorporated.*

9. Starting in 2004–5, there have been many books and articles dealing with class war in contemporary America. These include Thomas Frank's books, and also Joe Bageant,

Deer Hunting with Jesus: Dispatches from America's Class War (2007); Lou Dobbs, *War on the Middle Class* (2006); Jeff Faux, *The Global Class War* (2006); Thom Hartmann, Greg Palast, and Mark Crispin Miller, *Screwed: The Undeclared War against the Middle Class . . .* (2006); and Benjamin Page and Lawrence Jacobs, *Class War? What Americans Really Think about Economic Inequality* (2009). A somewhat earlier entry into the fray is Frederick Strobel and Wallace Peterson, *The Coming Class War and How to Avoid It* (1999).

10. Baudrillard, *Selected Writings*, 122.

11. Vattimo, *The End of Modernity*, xlviii.

12. *Postmodernism*, 407.

13. Eagleton, *The Illusions of Postmodernism*, 60. See also Wood, *The Retreat from Class: A New "True" Socialism.*

14. Fraser, *Justice Interruptus*, 2.

15. Quotations from W are from Jacob Weisberg, ed. "The Complete Bushisms," http://www.slate.com/articles/news_and_politics/bushisms/2000/03/the_complete _bushisms.html, accessed on October 9, 2012.

16. For the origins of our present top-down class warfare in the 1970s, see Jacob Hacker and Paul Pierson, *Winner-Take-All Politics,* especially 116–120; Joseph Stiglitz, *The Price of Inequality;* Michael Lewis, *The Big Short;* Jeff Madrick, *Age of Greed;* and Peter Edelman, *So Rich, So Poor,* among many other accounts.

17. In *The Marx-Engels Reader,* 473.

18. Whenever the issues of inequality and poverty come up, other conservatives also like to accuse their opponents of fomenting class warfare. In 1997, Lawrence Summers, then the deputy secretary of the Treasury, called those pushing to abolish the estate tax "selfish." He was attacked by GOP apparatchik Ken Khachigian for indulging "in the rhetoric of class warfare and view[ing] with socialist passion the opportunity to confiscate another's wealth." Quoting Khachigian's remark in "The Real Class War," Michelle Cottle also cites "a seniors association . . . calling for Summers to be fired for promoting 'class warfare' and the tenets 'of the Communist Manifesto.'" As Cottle points out, "Conservatives love to fling around terms like 'socialist' and 'class warmonger' whenever someone suggests that policy makers tend to favor rich, influential special interests" (13).

19. Paul Krugman, *The Great Unraveling,* 279.

20. For these and related figures, see the website of Citizens for Tax Justice, "The Bush Tax Cuts: The Latest CTJ Data March 2007," http://www.ctj.org/pdf/gwbdata .pdf, accessed December 9, 2012.

21. How much W really understands or cares about "saving" Social Security seems evident from a number of his comments about it. On November 3, 2000, for example, he opined, "They want the federal government controlling Social Security, like it's some kind of federal program."

22. The year 1973 is also the starting date for the rise of what Naomi Klein calls "disaster capitalism." In that year, neoliberal economists from the University of Chicago helped the new Chilean dictator, Augusto Pinochet, inaugurate "free market" reforms in that country, dismantling its welfare state. Seven years later, Reagan in the U.S. and Margaret Thatcher in Britain began their assault on labor and so-called "big government" in favor of private enterprise.

23. "If the total income growth of these years [1979–2005] were a pie . . . the slice enjoyed by the roughly 300,000 people in the top tenth of 1 percent would be half again as large as the slice enjoyed by the roughly 180 *million* in the bottom 60 percent. Little

wonder that the share of Americans who see the United States as divided between 'haves' and 'have nots' has risen sharply over the past two decades." Hacker and Pierson, *Winner-Take-All Politics*, 3.

24. As Lawrence Mishel, Jared Bernstein, and Heather Boushey note in *The State of Working America*, "Supporters of the U.S. model generally acknowledge the relative inequality in the United States but argue that the model provides greater mobility, greater employment opportunities, and greater dynamism than do more interventionist economies. The evidence, however, provides little support for this view" (431). On the contrary, "poverty is deeper and harder to escape in the United States, and much less is available in the way of adequate social policy relative to other" developed countries.

25. I have, of course, already mentioned several exceptions, such as Barbara Ehren-reich and Bill Moyers. There is also the redoubtable media pundit Lou Dobbs, whose *War on the Middle Class* takes up the issue precisely because economic inequality is now eroding bourgeois—and not just working class—living standards. "Even writing the words 'class warfare' makes me uncomfortable," Dobbs says, but he insists it is, never-theless, an accurate description of what is happening in the U.S. today (23).

26. In "The Class War Has Begun," Frank Rich contends that "the right was ahead of the class-war curve." Their target, however, was not innocent billionaires (who al-ways seem to have started out as small business folks and who are, in any case, routinely praised as "job creators") but Barack Obama and the "elites" in Washington and in the universities: Sarah Palin sounded the charge when she stuck up for "the real America" against the elites during the 2008 campaign. The real America, as she defined it, was in small towns—"those who are running our factories and teaching our kids and grow-ing our food." In other words, it is the middle class (or at least its white precincts) that fell behind while the rich got richer. The *Über*-class she and her angry followers would take to the guillotine, however, is not defined by its super-wealth. It is first and foremost exemplified by potentates in the federal government, especially the Ivy League cohort of Obama—closely followed by the usual right-wing populist bogeymen, the pointy-headed experts in fancy universities and the mainstream-media royalty with their "'gotcha' questions" (2). See http://nymag.com/news/frank-rich/class-war-2011-10/, accessed December 10, 2012.

2. "It's the Economy, Stupid!"

1. Writing about the "classical economists" of the late 1700s and 1800s, maverick economist Thorstein Veblen complained that Adam Smith's doctrine of the "invisible hand" was a surrogate secular religion that imparted to later capitalist economists a "devout optimism" (245). He declared that "this perfect competitive system [of the free market], with its untainted 'economic man,' is a feat of the scientific imagination, and is not intended as a competent expression of fact. It is an expedient of abstract reasoning" (269). Michael Perelman comments that contemporary economics emphasizes "elegant mathematical solutions," which "require models that depict a world in which everything works smoothly and predictably; in other words, perfectly functioning markets have de-sirable mathematical properties" (*Confiscation*, 180). It is just that "perfectly functioning markets" do not exist in the real world. In *The Dismal Science*, Stephen Maglin also ar-gues that economics is not a science but a "normative" enterprise, cloaked in mathemat-ics, aimed at demonstrating that "markets are good for people" (5; 291–92). In *Capitalism*

Hits the Fan, Richard Wolff compares neoliberal economic orthodoxy to evangelical fundamentalism (100–102).

2. Teller-Elsberg et al., *Field Guide to the U.S. Economy,* xiii; see also Perelman, *Confiscation,* 88–93.

3. Throughout I cite the fifth edition of Mankiw's textbook, published just as the 2007–2008 recession or depression was beginning. There is now a sixth edition. I emailed Mankiw to ask what changes he had made in it, particularly in light of the 2007–08 crisis. He sent me the website for his blog, http://gregmankiw.blogspot.com/2011/03/whats-new-in-new-edition.html (last accessed October 16, 2012). Several of the revisions focus on financial crises, and chapter 33 includes a new "case study" on the current "recession." The changes listed do not suggest any major changes in Mankiw's basic neoliberal principles.

4. Mankiw is also author of *New Keynesian Economics* (Cambridge, MA: MIT Press, 1991) and *The Reincarnation of Keynesian Economics* (Cambridge, MA: National Bureau of Economic Research, 1991). According to Perelman, "less than a decade after Keynes published his major book, economists had already succeeded in recasting his work in mathematical form in an attempt to show that it was consistent with the very theories that he set out to attack. In the process, they managed to wring much of the heretical tone from Keynes's work" (*Railroading,* 38).

5. Mankiw, "The Case Against the Living Wage," 70.

6. *Principles,* 5.

7. Mankiw also reproduces a 2004 column by conservative George F. Will, "The Economics of Progress," which approvingly cites Mankiw's judgment that the outsourcing of jobs is a sign of America's economic dynamism—lost jobs will be replaced by more and better jobs. For Will and Mankiw, Mankiw is the incarnation of economic wisdom, versus the concerns about outsourcing and unemployment expressed by economic ignoramuses such as Democrats John Kerry and John Edwards and even Republican Dennis Hastert (*Principles,* 189). On Mankiw's position regarding unemployment and the outsourcing of American jobs, see Fred Goldstein, *Low-Wage Capitalism,* 39–40.

8. Quoted in Perelman, *Confiscation,* 194.

9. *Confiscation,* 184.

10. The students also complained, "As your class does not include primary sources and rarely features articles from academic journals, we have very little access to alternative approaches to economics. There is no justification for presenting Adam Smith's economic theories as more fundamental or basic than, for example, Keynesian theory" (http://hpronline.org/campus/an-open-letter-to-greg-mankiw/?mid=51, last accessed October 16, 2012).

11. Quoted in Lifschultz, "Could Karl Marx Teach Economics," 280.

12. Quoted in ibid., 284.

13. For a brief, lively account of the fate of heterodox economists in the academy, including David Ruccio, see Christopher Hayes, "Hip Heterodoxy." Along with Jack Amariglio, Ruccio is a founding editor of the journal *Rethinking Marxism.* Together they have authored *Postmodern Moments in Modern Economics,* a work that demonstrates the significance of various aspects of postmodernist theory, including Althusserian Marxism and Derridean deconstruction, for economic theory.

14. Bourdieu, *Acts of Resistance,* 226; see also Frank, *One Market under God;* Quiggin, *Zombie Economics,* 3; and Žižek, *First as Tragedy, Then as Farce,* 19.

15. Hudson, "Dress Rehearsal for Debt Peonage"; see also Lifschultz, "Could Karl Marx Teach," 284; Perelman, *Confiscation* 169–97.

16. Gilles Raveaud points out that, according to Mankiw's bestselling textbook, reality "is made up of isolated individuals. But it is a world where fairness prevails: everybody gets what they deserve. It is also a world where, thanks to the magic effect of markets, private enterprise and property rights, standards of living rise constantly. It's a beautiful world . . . if only it existed" ("Neo-Con Indoctrination").

17. "Fundamentally there are only two ways of coordinating the economic activities of millions. One is central direction involving the use of coercion—the technique of the army and the modern totalitarian state. The other is voluntary co-operation of individuals—the technique of the market place" (*Capitalism and Freedom*, 13). Friedman published *There Is No Such Thing as a Free Lunch* in 1975.

18. *The MIT Dictionary of Modern Economics* has a brief article on "the Veblen effect," which it describes as "the phenomenon whereby as the price of a good falls some consumers construe this as a reduction in the quality of the good and cease to buy it. The result is that the market demand curve will exhibit a steeper slope than would otherwise be predicted. It could even slope upwards in contradiction of the law of demand" (Pearce, 449).

19. "The psychology invoked by economists," writes George Brockway, "has . . . borne little relationship to that studied by psychologists" (*End of Economic Man*, 17). James Galbraith points out that "modern behavioral economics has begun—but only begun—to notice" the many ways humans behave inconsistently, often with little or no regard to economic self-interest. Together with the myth of the market as a perfect machine, for the orthodox economist, "economic man is a machine to whom whimsy and evolution are unknown" (*Predator State*, 22). And Stephen Marglin writes that so far behavioral economics has not done enough to challenge any of the basic assumptions of orthodox economics (*Dismal Science*, 5). Besides psychology, mainstream economists seem weak in what C. Wright Mills called "the sociological imagination," which is why I refer to Durkheim as well as Freud.

20. The transatlantic slave trade began in the 1600s as a mercantilist enterprise. By the end of the 1700s, it had become a fully capitalist enterprise.

21. This is the argument as well of heterodox economist Stephen Marglin in *The Dismal Science: How Thinking Like an Economist Undermines Community*. For Marglin, communities and markets are in many ways antithetical modes of organizing societies and economies.

22. This is not to suggest that the capitalist economists were reacting against Marx. For one thing, *Das Kapital* was not translated into English until 1883. But it is significant that capitalist or orthodox economics was reordering itself as the mathematized science of prices and marginal utility just as capitalism was coming under intense theoretical critique and opposition.

23. *Railroading*, 25.

24. It appears to be the aim of the Koch brothers and the various think tanks and politicians they fund to privatize as much of government as possible. In this regard, they are adhering to Milton Friedman's neoliberal beliefs. The Kochs' organization ALEC (the American Legislative Exchange Council), made up of hundreds of Republican state legislators and corporate executives, provides model legislation aiming at defunding public employees' unions, public education, and, indeed, as many public enterprises as

possible. See, for example, John Nichols, "ALEC Exposed"; Beau Hodai, "Publicopoly Exposed"; and Hightower and Frazer, "Billionaires' Front Groups Attack Workers, Public Schools, and Young Voters."

25. Coyle et al., *Capitalist Punishment*, 15.

26. Anderson et al., *Field Guide*, 68.

27. Hartmann, *Unequal Protection*, 218.

28. Mokhiber and Weissman, *Corporate Predators*, 9.

29. If "monopoly power" is "usually limited," in what sense is it still "monopoly power"?

30. In *Globalization and Contestation*, Ronaldo Munck sums up the neoliberal attitude toward corporations: "Corporations are seen as virtuous as well as dynamic agents of progressive change. Globalization will, according to this view, lead to a decline of inequality and poverty worldwide as the market works its magic" (2). Munck points out that exactly the opposite has happened.

31. Healthcare results in Great Britain, France, Denmark, and many other countries are also superior to those in the United States. In 2000, the World Health Organization ranked the U.S. thirty-seventh in the world in healthcare outcomes. The results have not improved since then. See the online CIA Factbook for 2009, https://www.cia.gov/library/publications/the-world-factbook/.

32. Žižek, *First as Tragedy*, 94.

33. In analyzing "the roots of poverty," Milton Fisk contends that "increasing productivity in a competitive economy makes workers superfluous and hence poor" ("Roots of Poverty," 74). He also notes that it is in the interest of capital to keep the supply of labor higher than the demand for it.

34. Quoted in Olson, "Greenspan under Fire."

35. A commonly used phrase on the Left is "capitalist crisis," but the phrase by itself is ambiguous: whether it means that capitalism produces crises or that capitalism is the crisis is unclear.

36. See Kindleberger, *Manias, Panics, and Crashes*.

37. Goldstein, *Low-Wage Capitalism*, 277.

38. Tonelson, *Race to the Bottom*, 15.

39. Prashad, *Fat Cats and Running Dogs*, 55.

40. Ibid.

41. In his study of the current "global crisis," Chris Harman points out that "recurrent economic crises" are an inevitable aspect of the "zombie capitalism" that none of the fixes of the orthodox economists can cure (58). See also David Harvey's definition of economic crises in *The Enigma of Capital* (246).

42. See, e.g., Harvey, *The New Imperialism*, 160.

43. See also Perkins; Harvey, *Enigma*, 15.

44. Klein, *Shock Doctrine*, 18.

45. In *Bad Samaritans: The Myth of Free Trade and the Secret History of Capitalism*, Ha-Joon Chang, a Cambridge University economist, writes, "During the period of controlled globalization underpinned by nationalistic policies between the 1950s and the 1970s, the world economy, especially in the developing world, was growing faster, was more stable and had more equitable income distribution than in the past two and a half decades of rapid and uncontrolled neo-liberal globalization" (31).

46. Laxer, *Undeclared War*, 249.

47. Gray, *False Dawn*, 16.

48. Pieterse, *Is There Hope for Uncle Sam?* 67.

49. In *The New Imperialism,* David Harvey writes of the relentless process of capitalist "accumulation by dispossession" through "stock promotions, ponzi schemes, structured asset destruction through inflation, asset-stripping through mergers and acquisitions, and the promotion of levels of debt incumbency that reduce whole populations even in the advanced capitalist countries to debt peonage" (147). Similarly in *Bait and Switch,* Barbara Ehrenreich points out that "On many fronts, the American middle class is under attack as never before. For example, the 2005 federal bankruptcy bill, which eliminates the possibility of a fresh start for debt-ridden individuals, will condemn more and more of the unemployed and underemployed to a life of debt peonage" (236).

50. Wolff, "Capitalism Hits the Fan," 38.

51. Harvey, *Enigma*, 1.

52. "Debt covered up the failures of the social contract and the economic model. It did not succeed in protecting workers from rising debt payments, lost healthcare benefits, withering pensions or job turnover. . . . The Bush administration made conditions significantly worse. The economy was thriving, but hourly wages fell between 2002 and 2007 for the typical worker . . . and for the first time since World War II, median family income did not rise as a result of economic recovery. . . . Access to borrowing was the salve that soothed the harsher reality of lower real wages. Now indebted Americans are paying a large price, losing homes and livelihoods" (Madrick, "Beyond Rubinomics," 15).

53. Krugman, "The Debt-Peonage Society," *The New York Times,* March 8, 2005, http://www.nytimes.com/2005/03/08/opinion/08krugman.html, accessed October 16, 2012.

54. See, for instance, Grandin, *Empire's Workshop;* and see chapter 5.

55. Mankiw's comments on "the commons" are restricted to a few remarks about air pollution and wildlife species. In a brief account of "the tragedy of the commons," he imagines a medieval town sharing common grazing land but allowing the sheep to overpopulate. This fable supposedly illustrates that property held in common is never so well cared for as private property (*Principles,* 232–34).

3. Tea Party Brewhaha

Unless otherwise noted, quotations from Sharron Angle, Michele Bachmann, Glenn Beck, Christine O'Donnell, Rush Limbaugh, Sarah Palin, Tom Tancredo, and Mark Williams come from http://politicalhumor.about.com.

1. Recently, Beck's program was removed from the Fox Channel, presumably because he had become too extreme, even for Fox. I wrote this essay prior to the recent Republican campaign to choose a presidential candidate for the 2012. The views expressed by the candidates have often echoed Tea Party sentiments—and ignorance.

2. Susanne Pharr, Eric Ward, Tarso Ramos, et al., "Fight the Right: Looking Forward, Looking Back," in Flanders, ed., *At the Tea Party,* 327.

3. FreedomWorks supports the Border Integrity and Immigration Reform Act promoted by, among others, Representative Mike Pence of Indiana, who was elected governor in 2012. According to Pence, this is "a bill that is tough on border security and tough on employers who hire illegal aliens, but recognizes the need for a guest worker program that operates without amnesty and without growing into a huge new govern-

ment bureaucracy." "Without amnesty" means it will not provide any route to American citizenship for those who have entered the country illegally.

4. Quoted in Khimm, "Tom Tancredo."

5. Quoted in Ballvé, "Tea Party Dabbles in Immigration Politics."

6. Quoted in Easley, "Limbaugh Defends AZ Immigration Law with Obama Salt Conspiracy Theory."

7. Republicans claim the 2010 election gave them a sweeping mandate. Between tearful moments, John Boehner, as he was being anointed Speaker of the House, averred, "The American people have spoken." Not exactly. Democrats retained a majority in the Senate. Many who voted for Obama in 2008 did not vote in the midterm election, especially not for the "blue-dog" Democrats who failed to take progressive stances such as supporting a public option in the health care bill. Those who voted for Republicans often did so out of frustration or anger about the economy. And now Boehner and the old guard Republicans have had to grapple with the intransigence of the Tea Partiers, who find the old guard faint of heart. In the 2012 election, the Tea Party lost some of its clout even in the House of Representatives, but it hasn't gone away.

8. *Taming Cannibals: Race and the Victorians* (Ithaca, NY: Cornell University Press, 2010).

9. Hofstadter, "Paranoid Style, 24–25.

10. Ibid., 27–28.

11. Ibid., 29.

12. As Peter Hart and Steve Rendall point out in "At Last a Citizen Movement the Corporate Media Can Love," "Antipathy toward Obama as a black Democratic president goes some way toward explaining why, if the Tea Partiers are really motivated by opposition to government spending, the movement didn't launch years earlier in response to George W. Bush's skyrocketing budget deficits" (237), two illegal wars, and tax cuts for the wealthy.

13. Like the two respondents to my letter to the editor, the majority of Tea Partiers believe the U.S. is or ought to be a Christian nation. As Palin told Bill O'Reilly on Fox television, "Go back to what our founders and our founding documents meant—they're quite clear—that we would create law based on the God of the bible and the Ten Commandments."

14. O'Donnell, who believes there is more evidence for God's having created the world in six days than for any other theory of creation, has also claimed that "American scientific companies are cross-breeding humans and animals and coming up with mice with fully functioning human brains," which in a roundabout way contradicts her view that monkeys are not still evolving into humans.

4. Shooters

1. The American mass media at first used "Cho Seung-Hui" and then changed to "Seung-Hui Cho." Because he signed his play scripts "Seung Cho," I refer to him in this essay as "Seung." Since I wrote this essay for their inaugural issue at the invitation of the editors of *Situations,* a number of other shooting rampages have occurred in the U.S., including the massacres in Tucson, Arizona and in Aurora, Colorado. Between 2007 and 2012, nothing has been done to tighten gun control in Virginia, Arizona, or elsewhere. On the contrary, there has been an uptick in calls for allowing even more

Americans to carry concealed weapons, including carrying them on college campuses. Virginia Tech, meanwhile, was fined $55,000 by the Department of Education for waiting too long to alert students that Seung was on the loose. It also, in March 2012, lost a suit brought by two families for the same reason; they were awarded $4 million. The verdict is being appealed. And the campus has had a number of other scares, the most serious being the decapitation of a woman in a campus coffee shop in 2009; and on Dec. 8, 2011, the shooting of a police officer by twenty-two-year-old Ross Ashley, who then took his own life.

2. Interview shown on ABC6 News, http://www.kaaltv.com/nw/article/view/113059. See also CBS News, "Cho Family Statement," February 12, 2009, http://www.cbsnews.com/8301-501803_162-2712709.html?tag=contentMain;contentBody, accessed December 9, 2012.

3. More relevant is how Virginia Tech's professors, administrators, counselors, and others dealt with a young man who displayed symptoms of mental illness. Katherine Newman writes, "We might expect adults who routinely deal with adolescents, such as school personnel, to be able to spot mental illness. It turns out to be exceptionally difficult, largely because problems like clinical depression or schizophrenia may be in their early stages, lacking some of the symptoms that manifest themselves later in life" (*Rampage*, 60). Seung was, however, twenty-three, and, on a number of occasions, his parents had sought help for him through church, before he left for the university.

4. The term is Robert Jay Lifton's. See Lifton, "An Ideology of 'Gunism,'" B11.

5. Seung was a legal resident alien rather than citizen of the U.S., so the Korean American label is, on one level, questionable.

6. Quoted in Begley, "The Anatomy of Violence," 43.

7. Žižek, *For They Know Not What They Do*, 110.

8. Thomas, "Making of a Massacre," 26.

9. Ryan and Fricker, "'This Is Someone That I Grew Up with and Loved....'"

10. *Rampage*, 63.

11. Park, "I Hope He's Not Korean," B5.

12. Quoted in ibid.

13. There has been a greater response by Koreans and Korean Americans to the fact that Seung was a resident alien from South Korea than any "backlash" by non-Korean Americans. See the op-ed pieces by Katharine H. S. Moon and Adrian Hong, which were also posted on the website of the National Association of Korean Americans.

14. The Conspiracy Theory Research List (hereafter CTRL), 1.

15. CTRL, 2.

16. Thomas, "Making of a Massacre," 25.

17. CTRL, 2.

18. Ibid., 4.

19. Ibid., 3.

20. Because of privacy restrictions, Virginia Tech will not reveal Seung's academic record. But it will perhaps sometime be pieced together in various ways. There is some indication that, prior to the shootings, he had stopped going to class, though I have no solid evidence for that possibility. Those among Seung's victims who were about to graduate received posthumous degrees; Virginia Tech obviously declined giving Seung a posthumous degree.

21. Gardner and Cho, "Isolation Defined Seung's Senior Year."

22. CTRL, 3.

23. Quoted in ibid.

24. Thomas, "Making of a Massacre," 24.

25. For a pdf of the entire play, see http://investigation.blog.lemonde.fr/files/2007/04/cho-seung-hui-richard-mc-beef.1176883245.pdf.

26. Brantlinger, "(Re)Turning to Marx," 242; see also Newman, "Before the Rampage"; and Brown and Merritt, *No Easy Answers*. Stressing the rationality rather than insanity of mass killers in school settings, Katherine Newman writes, "School shooters are problem solvers. They are trying to turn the reputations they live with as losers into something more glamorous, more notorious. . . . How do they go about it? Sadly, becoming violent, going out in a blaze of glory, and ending it all by taking other people with them is one script that plays out in popular culture and provides a road map for notoriety" ("Before the Rampage," B20).

27. Thomas, "Making of a Massacre," 29.

28. Ibid., 27.

29. Ibid., 27.

30. Ibid., 28.

31. Goldstein, "Seung Seung-Hui's Commitment Papers."

32. *Rampage*, 247.

33. There have been massacres of students at universities in many countries for political reasons, like the shootings at Kent State and Jackson State in 1968. Outside the U.S., however, so-called random massacres by crazed individuals on campuses have been rare.

34. Gopnik, "Shootings," 28.

35. I am using "fetish" in both of its major definitions: commodity fetishism and sexual fetishism. The gun is obviously a commodity with metaphorical sexual attributes, as in Jerry Adler's "Story of a Gun" for *Newsweek*.

36. Brown and Merritt, *No Easy Answers*, 16.

37. For the story of guns and gunfighting in American history back to "frontier times," see Slotkin, *Gunfighter Nation*.

38. Quoted in Begley, "The Anatomy of Violence," 44.

39. Quoted in Bok, *Mayhem*, 57.

40. For the relationship between celebrity and mass murder, especially serial killing, see David Schmid, *Natural-Born Celebrities*.

41. Seltzer, *Serial Killers*, 6.

42. Seltzer distinguishes between serial killers and mass murderers such as Seung, but that distinction is not important in assessing the cultural "pathology" he explores in *Serial Killers*. See also Schmid, *Natural-Born Celebrities*, 68–72.

43. Denby, "Men Gone Wild," 88.

44. Quoted in Begley, "The Anatomy of Violence," 44.

45. Thomas, "Making of a Massacre," 29.

46. Bok, *Mayhem*, 3.

47. Begley, "The Anatomy of Violence," 45. "Since 1970, the number of guns in the United States has doubled, to about 200 million," writes Newman: "One might conclude that access to guns is spreading rapidly, but the increase has actually been fueled by people who are already gun owners acquiring additional firearms. The proportion of adults who own guns has stayed relatively constant since 1980 at about 30 percent. This is not

a low number; it is the highest proportion of any industrialized country, but it hasn't changed much over the years" (*Rampage,* 69).

48. Quoted in Begley, "The Anatomy of Violence," 44.

49. Ibid., 46.

5. What Is the Matter with Mexico?

1. John Kenneth Turner, *Barbarous Mexico,* 10.

2. Ibid., 55.

3. Ibid., 67.

4. Jon Ross, *The Annexation of Mexico from the Aztecs to the I.M.F.,* 20.

5. Ibid.

6. Rodriguez, *Mongrels, Bastards, Orphans, and Vagabonds,* 47.

7. Marx noted that "slavery is hidden under the form of peonage" for the vast majority of Mexican peasants, who owned no land and were, hence, reduced to the status of agricultural laborers. This was true throughout Latin America, where vast tracts of land had been appropriated by the Spanish conquistadors, the Catholic Church, and the first well-to-do colonists.

8. Gibler, *Mexico Unconquered,* 95.

9. Turner, *Barbarous Mexico,* 111.

10. Hamnett, *A Concise History of Mexico,* 159.

11. Harvey, *The New Imperialism,*137–82.

12. See, for instance, Galeano, *Open Veins of Latin America,* 72–73.

13. Gonzalez, *Harvest of Empire,* 52.

14. Gibler, *Mexico Unconquered,* 94. In the early 1800s, Alexander von Humboldt, writing about the silver mining center, Guanajuato, declared, "Perhaps nowhere is inequality more shocking. . . . The architecture of public and private buildings, the women's elegant wardrobes, the high-society atmosphere: all testify to an extreme social polish which is in extraordinary contrast to the nakedness, ignorance, and coarseness of the populace" (ibid., 48). He might have been writing about Mexico in general.

15. See Huffington, *Third-World America,* for instance.

16. Quoted in Lens, *The Forging of the American Empire,* 132.

17. Quoted in Ross, *The Annexation of Mexico,* 39.

18. Ngai, *Impossible Subjects,* 50.

19. Gonzalez, *Harvest of Empire,* 44.

20. Boyer, *The Enduring Vision,* 480.

21. Quoted in Zinn, *A People's History of the United States,* 155.

22. Schroeder, *Mr. Polk's War,* 123.

23. Zinn and Arnove, *Voices of a People's History,* 156.

24. Heidler and Heidler, *The Mexican War,* 145.

25. Gibler, *Mexico Unconquered;* Hamnett, *A Concise History of Mexico,* 154–55.

26. Heidler and Heidler, *The Mexican War,* 145.

27. See Ramos, *La Ola Latina.*

28. See Wessler, "Thousands of Kids Lost from Parents in U.S. Deportation System," *Colorlines,* November 2, 2011.

29. Besides Tancredo, anti-immigration ideologues like Lou Dobbs see "illegals" as a threat to American workers, a category that presumably includes legal Mexican resi-

dents and Mexican American citizens (Aviva Chomsky, *"They Take Our Jobs!"* 11–29). Dobbs was recently exposed as a hypocrite when it was revealed that he has employed undocumented Mexicans, but he is not the only hypocrite (Macdonald, "Lou Dobbs, American Hypocrite"). At any rate, by inundating the low-wage end of the labor market, the undocumented help to keep wages low for everyone. They also make unionization that much more difficult and wage theft that much easier.

30. Cohen, *Braceros;* Mize and Swords, *Consuming Mexican Labor.*

31. On wage theft, see Bobo, *Wage Theft in America.* On Marx's "reserve army of labor," see *Capital* 1:784. Looking back to the 1950s, Aviva Chomsky writes that "Operation Wetback," launched in 1954, led to the deportation of more than a million Mexicans. That effort "provides another example of the dueling logic of U.S. attitudes towards Mexicans." She adds that "Operation Wetback" occurred during the *Bracero* program, "which was bringing about 200,000 Mexicans a year into the country as guest workers":

> The deportations meant that there were fewer workers available for agriculture, and that more were recruited as braceros—about 300,000 in 1954, and 400,000 to 450,000 a year in subsequent years. Deportations and recruitment served the same purpose: they provided workers, but ensured that the workers remained "aliens" without rights. And they reinforced the notion that citizens and people with rights were white people. (100)

Much the same is happening today. Round ups and deportations by Immigration and Customs Enforcement (ICE) increase; border crossings by desperately poor Mexicans increase. Many companies and employers who hire Mexican workers would rather not check them for documentation; they might have to start paying them more if they did.

32. Ngai, *Impossible Subjects,* 7.

33. In *Consuming Mexican Labor: From the Bracero Program to NAFTA,* Ronald Mize and Alicia Swords write, "NAFTA's promise to improve conditions for Mexicans has proven untenable. Rather, neoliberal [economic] policies concentrate wealth *and* poverty in cities, while impoverishing the countryside" (204). For a close-up look at how NAFTA has affected Mexican farmers, see David Bacon, "Mexico's Great Migration."

34. It also has not helped that Ronald Reagan and American presidents after him have rarely hesitated to intervene in Central American countries. The CIA-assisted toppling of democratically elected Jacobo Árbenz in Guatemala began a cascade of U.S. meddling, in the name of anticommunism, in Nicaragua, El Salvador, Panama, and elsewhere. "All told, U.S. allies in Central America during Reagan's two terms killed over 300,000 people, tortured hundreds of thousands, and drove millions into exile" (Grandin, *Empire's Workshop,* 71). Many of those who fled their homes and countries added to the upsurge of migration from Mexico into the United States.

35. See Allen, "Global Land Grab."

36. Quoted in Grandin, *Empire's Workshop,* 200.

37. Ibid.

38. Chacón and Davis comment that, since the U.S. war against Mexico of 1846–48, the latter country has "continuously subsidized the growth of the U.S. economy by exporting whole generations of workers to the north, providing much of the labor that built the industrial and agricultural infrastructure of the nation, as well as much of its cultural foundation. Nevertheless, the legacy of the Mexican contribution is both ig-

nored and distorted in order to deny Mexican immigrants' historic connection to the land and their right to legitimately participate in the U.S. political system as citizens" (*No One Is Illegal*, 191).

39. Gibler, *Mexico Unconquered*, 55.

40. Ibid., 310, n16.

41. See Alexander, *The New Jim Crow.*

42. Taibo, "Zapatistas! The Phoenix Rises," 24.

43. Hayden, *The Zapatista Reader*, 218.

44. Mize and Swords, *Consuming Mexican Labor*, 195.

45. Marcos, *Speed of Dreams*, 254.

6. Waste and Value

1. According to Cohen, "Particularly in the nineteenth century, human excrescences get tangled up in fantasies of emergent value, and polluting substances spill into their apparent opposite, the recyclable source of hidden riches" (xiv). As both Regenia Gagnier (*The Insatiability of Human Wants*) and Catherine Gallagher (*The Body Economic*) have demonstrated, such "fantasies of emergent value" became especially apparent in the second half of that century, in tandem with the marginalist revolution in economics and the first signs—department stores, mass advertising campaigns, and the like—of consumer society. At the same time, however, "the history of shit" is coextensive with history itself (Laporte).

2. See, for instance, Žižek, *Living in the End Times.*

3. Shopping malls are no longer primarily sites of consumption, but "lonely places" in which "what is truly fascinating is expenditure, loss, and exhaustion" (Kroker and Kroker, *Panic Encyclopedia*, 208).

4. See Gagnier, *The Insatiability of Human Wants.*

5. For "illth" in both Ruskin and Charles Dickens's *Our Mutual Friend*, see Gallagher, *The Body Economic*, 86–117.

6. Wollen, *Raiding the Icebox*, 18.

7. Connor, *Theory and Culture Value*, 71–80.

8. Assuming that postmodernity is, in Fredric Jameson's phrase, "the cultural logic of late capitalism," according to that logic, money, via computerization, appears to float free of all material encumbrances, taking on the quasi-theological non-properties of credit (or fiduciary "faith"). In much postmodernist fiction and film, including DeLillo's *Underworld*, reality has an unreal or "irreal" (close to insubstantial, but not surreal) quality even as the world seems to be inundated with the excrement—"data trash" (Kroker and Weinstein), garbage, ruins, literal shit—of a consumer culture that seems to have no external limits but only the internal possibility of becoming clogged by its own manic excess or overproduction.

9. See Lyotard, *The Post-Modern Condition*; Huyssen, *The Great Divide.*

10. Richards, *The Imperial Archive*, 95.

11. The reduction of "taste" to the "rational choices" of individual consumers by recent economics can equally well be understood, as both Veblen and Wells understood it, as a *reductio ad absurdum*; that is, to the irrational choices of individuals that add up only to, for Veblen, "conspicuous consumption" and "pecuniary emulation," and for Wells, to "mitigated water" or "Tono-Bungay."

12. We take "waste" as a larger, perhaps more vacuous, category than "filth," in part because of its economic meanings as inefficiency and squandering of money or resources. These, too, can be treated as "filth," of course, at least metaphorically. To "lubrication," compare the metaphoric monetary term "liquidity." Like "value," "waste" has countless specific meanings. It is a capacious garbage bin for whatever one cares to throw into it. Its most general meaning, allowing it to cover all the specific meanings, is that which is deemed to have either no value or only negative value.

13. Sigmund Freud famously writes that "wherever archaic modes of thought . . . persist . . . money is brought into the most intimate relationship with dirt. . . . We . . . know the superstition which connects the finding of treasure with defecation" ("Character and Anal Eroticism," 296). See also Laporte, *History of Shit,* viii; and Cohen and Johnson, *Filth,* xiii.

14. See Sekora, *Luxury.*

15. This is, of course, the solution according to orthodox, capitalist economics. For Marx, the solution entailed the revolutionary abolition of "surplus value" and with it private property and the exploitation of labor.

16. "And thus came in the use of money," Locke declares, "some lasting thing that men might keep without spoiling, and that, by mutual consent, men would take in exchange for the truly useful but perishable supports of life" (*Two Treatises,* 139–40). Locke does not consider the possibility that "men" might exchange money for what is not useful—in other words, that they might waste it—much less that the "lasting thing" could itself be identified with waste (could be, for instance, considered "spoils," or the result of exploitation: one society's prosperity based on laying waste to another society). In his essays on money and the recoinage controversy of the 1690s, however, Locke does ruminate about the wasting away of money through, for instance, the clipping of coins. See Constantine Caffentzis, *Clipped Coins.*

17. See Brantlinger, *Dark Vanishings.*

18. Smith, *Wealth of Nations,* 449.

19. Cf. Thorstein Veblen, "Socialist Economics in Karl Marx," in *The Portable Veblen,* 275–96.

20. Veblen, *Engineers and the Price System,* 134.

21. Veblen, *Theory of the Leisure Class,* 110.

22. Michaels, *The Gold Standard and the Logic of Naturalism,* 51.

23. Daniel Aaron calls Veblen "a moralist" whose America "was a land full of Yahoos" (*Men of Good Hope,* 213). Susan Strasser writes that Veblen both "analyzed and satirized the rise of consumerism and the expansion of 'pecuniary emulation'" (*Waste and Want,* 198). Though disapproving of "prodigality," Adam Smith had certainly approved of progress, wealth, and prosperity in national terms. From Malthus through Marx and Mill, however, economics had great difficulty in maintaining a scientific as opposed to moralistic stance toward its main subject, the production and consumption of wealth. In several essays, Veblen criticizes his predecessors for basing their arguments on concepts of "natural law" and societal norms that hypostatized capitalism and the "beneficent" workings of free markets. Of the achievements of the classical economists," he writes, "the science may be justly proud; but they fall short of the evolutionist's standard of adequacy" (*The Place of Science in Modern Civilisation,* 59). He means in part that they treat economics without regard to institutional, cultural, and historical factors; they also treat present arrangements as morally superior to all others, yet Veblen's own terminology is insistently moralizing.

24. Lloyd quoted in Hofstadter, *Social Darwinism in American Thought,* 120.

25. American realists from Howells through John Dos Passos were influenced by Veblen. See Alfred Kazin, *On Native Grounds,* 130–35; Clare Eby, *Dreiser and Veblen;* and Michael Spindler, *Veblen and Modern America,* 126–41. Howells's two articles on *The Theory of the Leisure Class* "helped to launch Veblen's book" (Aaron, *Men of Good Hope,* 209). Unlike American realists before World War II, H. G. Wells seems not to have been aware of Veblen, which makes his thematization of "waste" in *Tono-Bungay* all the more suggestive of a cultural conjuncture that included both the United States and Britain during which that concept surfaced in a variety of contexts.

26. For the marginalists, writes Regenia Gagnier, "Value no longer inhered in goods themselves . . . but in others' demand for the goods. Political economy's theory of the productive relationship between land, labor, and capital thus gave way to the statistical analysis of price lists or consumption patterns" (*The Insatiability of Human Wants,* 4). From the 1870s on, the orthodox economists dealt "with wealth rather than welfare" (ibid., 44). Because of his emphasis on consumption, it is tempting to see Veblen as contributing to the marginalist revolution. But the evolutionary and ethnological factors in his work make him more akin to Nietzsche than to, say, William Jevons. And he was always some version of a socialist. See "Limitations of Marginal Utility," in Veblen, *Place of Science,* 231–51.

27. *Engineers,* 76.

28. Ibid., 144.

29. *Theory of the Leisure Class,* 110.

30. Ibid., 198.

31. Ibid., 188.

32. *Theory of Business Enterprise,* 1–64.

33. Ibid., 44.

34. *Experiment,* 2:644.

35. Haynes, *H. G. Wells,* 118.

36. See John Carey, *The Intellectuals and the Masses.*

37. Richards, *The Imperial Archive,* 88. In "The Dustbins of History," Natalka Freeland asks, "Why does waste removal figure so prominently in late-Victorian utopias?" She notes that this was a major theme in earlier "social-problem" novelists writing in a realistic mode. But entropy was a theme for both writers of utopias and of realistic novels (Freeland in Cohen and Ryan, 225–49). Freeland focuses on Wells's *The Time Machine,* though *Tono-Bungay* is just as obviously about entropy and "waste removal." For the entropic trajectory of history, see Wells's *Anticipations* (1901) and also his *Outline of History* (1920).

38. See, for instance, Wells's 1895 science fiction classic, *The Time Machine.*

39. Kupinse, "Wasted Value," 57. Kupinse adds that the major preoccupation of *Tono-Bungay* is the "abandonment by 'modern commerce' of established determinants of value and waste" (51).

40. "Captain of Industry," 384.

41. Kuchta, *Semi-Detached Empire,* 36–56.

42. In *The Barbarian Temperament,* sociologist Stjepan Meštrović takes up many of these themes, with Veblen as his main precursor of postmodernism.

43. Taiganides, "Wastes Are Resources out of Place."

44. See Evans, "Taking Out the Trash," 106–9.

45. Ibid., 131–32.

7. Shopping on Red Alert

1. Quoted in Miller, *Cruel and Unusual,* 297.

2. I wrote this essay before the end of President Bush's second term. Have the election of Barack Obama, the killing of Osama bin Laden, and the withdrawal of American forces from Iraq ended "the war on terror"? No, they have not; they have only served further to normalize that "war." See, for example, Glenn Greenwald, "Obama's Illegal Assaults," which is subtitled "How Once-controversial 'War on Terror' Tactics Became the New Normal."

3. Kellner, *From 9/11 to Terror War,* 19.

4. Quoted in Goodman and Goodman, *The Exception to the Rulers,* 116.

5. Quoted in Parenti, *The Terrorism Trap,* 2.

6. Palast, *Armed Madhouse,* 38–45.

7. Scahill, *Blackwater,* xxvi.

8. "Failed state" discourse is partly a recent attempt by neoconservatives in the U.S. to justify "preemptive war" against states deemed "failed," largely because they have opposed U.S. policies and because they are alleged to be harboring terrorists. Compare Fukuyama, *State-Building* and Chomsky, *Failed States.*

9. See, e.g., Kellner, *From 9/11 to Terror War,* 19.

10. In calling on Congress to help create the Department of Homeland Security, W averred, "I want all agencies involved with protecting America under one umbrella" (quoted in Domke, *God Willing?* 129).

11. Weisberg, "The Complete Bushisms." W has also referred to "the terrorists" as "these hateful few . . . who kill at the whim of a hat" (September 17, 2004). In that formulation, the "hateful few" do not sound much like an army necessitating either a defensive or a "preemptive" war.

12. Quoted in Everest, *Oil, Power, and Empire,* 3.

13. Parenti, *The Terrorism Trap,* 5; see also Falk, *The Great Terror War,* 119.

14. "Truth," 1.

15. Davis, *In Praise of Barbarians,* 254.

16. Three years later, in April 2010, the BP oil rig *Deepwater Horizon* suffered a catastrophic explosion that killed eleven. The subsequent oil "spill," unchecked for eighty-five days, spewed more than two hundred million gallons of oil into the Gulf, wrecking havoc on wildlife in the sea and on the shoreline from Louisiana to Florida, dealing another blow to the city.

17. Apparently in denial about what the U.S. has been using in Afghanistan and Iraq, W said on October 3, 2003, "Free nations do not develop weapons of mass destruction" ("Truth," 9).

18. Hagopian, *Civil Rights in Peril,* 103.

19. Ibid., 45.

20. On September 4, 2005, seven officers, responding to rumors of sniping from Danziger Bridge, shot six people, killing two and wounding four others. These people do not seem to have been armed. As people tried to cross another bridge into Jefferson Parish, police from there fired over their heads to force them to turn back. Five New Orleans officers were also fired for looting (Bates and Swan, *Through the Eye of Katrina,* 402).

21. Scahill, *Blackwater,* 327.

22. Congressman Barney Frank calls what is happening to black New Orleans "a policy of ethnic cleansing by inaction" (quoted in Davis, *In Praise of Barbarians*, 228).

23. Quoted in Johnson, *Nemesis*, 47.

24. Juhasz, *The Bush Agenda*, 185–260; Klein, *The Shock Doctrine*, 325–40.

25. Kellner, *From 9/11 to Terror War*, 49–70.

26. Phillips, *American Theocracy*, 206.

27. St. Clair, *Grand-Theft Pentagon*, 22–26.

28. Quoted in Miller, *Cruel and Unusual*, 291.

29. Quoted in Kellner, *From 9/11 to Terror War*, 20.

30. Domke, *God Willing?* 26.

31. Quoted in Phillips, *American Theocracy*, 208.

32. Quoted in Burbach and Tarbell, *Imperial Overstretch* 16.

33. Domke, *God Willing?* 162.

34. Quoted in ibid., 16.

35. Quoted in Miller, *Cruel and Unusual*, 270.

36. Based on the World Libraries Catalogue website as of 2010. About half the titles or subtitles use "age of terrorism"; the other half use "age of terror." Before 9/11, according to WorldCat, only nine titles or subtitles included these phrases, and a couple of these do not refer to the present "age."

37. Herbst, *Talking Terrorism*, 167.

38. See also Gareau, *State Terrorism and the United States*.

39. Marchak, *Reigns of Terror*, vii; Herman, *The Real Terror Network*, 83; Falk, *The Great Terror War*, 76.

40. *Leviathan*, 100.

41. A more immediate and terrifying problem is global warming, which, among other destructive impacts, threatens to exacerbate global poverty enormously through droughts, famines, and violence over land and water rights.

8. The State of Iraq

1. I apologize if this essay reminds anyone of Mark Twain's "To the Person Sitting in Darkness." Twain was mad about the American takeover of the Philippines. If I am angry about anything, it is all those missed opportunities for statehood including the Philippines. Twain was laughable. What is laughable about statehood?

2. Obama has now announced to much hoopla that the troops really have left Iraq. What about the thousands of hired guns that are still there? And the thousands of troops who have been moved next door to Kuwait, waiting eagerly for their chance to return? Anyway, the case for statehood I offer here can be applied to Kuwait, of course, and when we invade Iran to that fortunate country as well.

3. According to President Bush, "We hold dear what our Declaration of Independence says, that all have got uninalienable rights, endowed by a Creator."

4. And then there is Puerto Rico, along with Cuba one of the islands we took over from Spain in 1898. To this day, it is not yet a state. What are we waiting for? There are just as many Puerto Ricans in New York City as in Puerto Rico.

5. Apparently because of this triple play, statehood was never seen as a possibility for Samoa—not even American Samoa.

6. Even though it is "where America's day begins," Guam has always seemed too tiny to be considered for statehood. That is why I am putting it in a footnote. But the U.S. military occupies almost all of it, which makes it just as secure as Fort Knox. If America decided on statehood for Guam, even if the Guamites objected, what could they do about it? But global warming may soon settle the matter. What is the value of a submerged state?

7. Bill Taft, who became the first American governor of the Philippines before he became president, dubbed the Filipinos "our little brown brothers." He must have assimilated a few of them.

9. On the Postmodernity of Being Aboriginal—and Australian

1. Read, *A Rape of the Soul So Profound*, 26.

2. Morgan, *My Place*, 152–53.

3. I began to explore race relations in Britain's settler colonies and in India in the early 1980s, when I started teaching graduate seminars on literature and the British Empire in the 1800s. When I spent a month in Australia in 1992, I visited a number of cities, museums, and settlements where I observed interactions between whites and Aboriginals at first hand, and I began to study Aboriginal literature. It is standard to date its origins in the 1960s, when Kate Walker (Oodgeroo Noonuccal) published her first volume of poetry and when Colin Johnson (Mudrooroo) published his first novel, *Wild Cat Falling*.

4. See Attwood, "Portrait of an Aboriginal as an Artist."

5. *Victorian Studies* 46, no. 4 (Summer 2004): 655–74.

6. See Robert Manne, ed., *Whitewash*.

7. Brantlinger, "Notes on the Postmodernity of 'Fake' (?) Aboriginal Literature."

8. Huggan, *Australian Literature*, 47.

9. Reynolds, *The Law of the Land*.

10. Clark, "Mundrooroo," 104.

11. Gelder and Jacobs, 60.

12. Griffiths, "The Myth of Authenticity," 76.

13. Besides Oodgeroo's "We Are Walking," see, for example, Rey Chow's "Where Have All the Natives Gone?"

14. Goldie, *Fear and Temptation*, 13.

15. Quoted in Shoemaker, "White on Black/Black on Black," 19.

16. Kurtzer, "Wandering Girl," 187.

17. Caterson, *Hoax Nation*, 146.

18. Adam Shoemaker mentions the "overwhelmingly positive assessment" of Bozic's writing by Livio Dobrez (also not an Aboriginal, however), who stresses "Wongar's sense of ethnic and migrant isolation, his endurance of racism, his understanding of Aboriginal religion and—above all—his postmodern glimpse of the apocalypse in books such as *Karan* (1985) and *Gabo Djara* (1987)" ("Tracking," 339). It hardly matters that Bozic believes he is a Yugoslavian reincarnation of an Aboriginal (ibid.). Shoemaker comments that "the late 1990s debate over authenticity not only disempowers Aboriginal writers; in the most extreme cases it threatens to disempower them from citizenship in the Black Australian literary nation. Here the cases of Mudrooroo and Archie Weller are particularly prominent ones, although the intemperate eye of racial censure has also extended, at times, to Eric Wilmot, Sally Morgan and others" (ibid., 341).

19. James, "Party Town," 25.

20. By using "postmodern" and "postcolonial" in the same sentence, I do not mean to suggest that the two terms are synonymous. "Postcolonial" is an unsatisfactory term for a variety of reasons, most importantly because it suggests what is patently false— that the relationship of the dominant, white societies in today's "postcolonies" is no longer a dominating one. But "postcolonial" seems preferable to its alternatives. I am grateful for help with this essay to various Australian friends and colleagues, including Simon Caterson, Helen Gilbert, Anna Johnston, and Chris Tiffin.

21. For a more detailed and more critical account of the opening ceremony at the 2000 Olympics, see Catrina Elder, *Being Australian*, 31–39. Concerning how Aboriginality was represented in Ric Birch's display for the 2000 Olympics, Gary Kamiya, a founding editor of Salon.com, wrote in that journal on September 15, 2000: "As for the lengthy scenes paying homage to Australia's Aboriginal people, they could be viewed, if one were cynical, as ass-covering kitsch." The Olympics was preceded by the Festival of the Dreaming in Sydney, starting in 1997. In a brief article for *Wired* (September 19, 1997), Stewart Taggart wrote that the "hazy pre-history known only as 'Dreamtime'" has gone global. He cites Rhoda Roberts, director of the festival, that even the remotest Aboriginal communities "are so well-connected by the Internet and satellite communications that native artists can collaborate on artistic projects in progress." Certainly, Aboriginal painting has gone global, along with many fraudulent versions of such indigenous artwork; see the web site for Aboriginal Art Online, but also Simon Caterson, *Hoax Nation*, 153–55.

22. Behrendt, "What Lies Beneath," 5.

23. Povinelli, "Consuming *Geist*," 514.

24. Popular song from William Harrison Ainsworth's bestselling 1840 novel about highwayman Jack Sheppard.

25. Shoemaker, *Black Words*, 57.

26. See, for example, Sitka, "Cultural Mutilation Uptop."

27. *Sydney Morning Herald*, quoted in Caterson, *Hoax Nation*, 144.

28. Nolan and Dawson, xii.

29. See Phillips, *The Australian Tradition*.

30. Hodge and Mishra, *Dark Side of the Dream* x.

31. Nolan and Dawson, *Who's Who?* viii.

32. Schaffer, *In the Wake of First Contact*, 1.

33. Ashcroft, "Reading Carey Reading Malley," 29.

34. Huggan, *Australian Literature*, 110.

35. See Manne, ed., *Whitewash*.

36. See Pierce, *The Country of Lost Children*.

37. See, for example, Pybus, *Black Founders*.

38. Anderson, *The Cultivation of Whiteness*, 230.

39. Errington, *The Death of Authentic Primitive Art and Other Tales of Progress*, 141.

40. Johnston and Lawson, "Settler Colonies," 369.

41. Goldie, *Fear and Temptation*, 113. In *Orality and Literacy*, Walter J. Ong declared, "By contrast with natural, oral speech, writing is completely artificial. There is no way to write 'naturally'" (82). If authenticity is equated with closeness to nature and, hence, to orality, the difficulty is obvious: writing is inevitably inauthentic and may be most hoax-like when it purports to be a direct conduit to speech. Of course, this is an untenable

way to gauge the authenticity of an individual piece of literature, yet the premium placed upon orality in relation to Aboriginality involves a contradiction that pervades all written renderings of preliterate cultures. As Jacques Derrida puts it in his deconstruction of Rousseau's and Lévi-Strauss's valorization of the supposed innocence and immediacy of speech, "The ideal profoundly underlying this philosophy of writing is . . . the image of a community immediately present to itself, without difference, a community of speech where all the members are within earshot. . . . Writing is here defined as the condition of *social inauthenticity*" (*Of Grammatology*, 136). One upshot is that all written, literary renderings of Aboriginality, even the most strictly autobiographical accounts, fail to be authentic in these terms. However, another is that the concept of authenticity has here exceeded any useful, meaningful limits.

10. McLuhan, Crash Theory, and the Invasion of the Nanobots

1. May, *The Information Society*, 8.

2. Thus, in *The Printing Revolution in Early Modern Europe*, Elizabeth Eisenstein notes, "By making us more alert to the possibility that the advent of printing had social and psychological consequences, McLuhan performed . . . a valuable service. But he also glossed over multiple interactions that occurred under widely varying circumstances" (92).

3. Theall, *The Virtual Marshal McLuhan*, 15.

4. Ibid., 125–37. For McLuhan and poststructuralism, see the essays by Richard Cavell and Douglas Kellner in *Transforming McLuhan*. For McLuhan and Paul Virilio, see the essay in the same volume by Bob Hanke.

5. Quoted in Theall, *The Virtual Marshal McLuhan*, 131.

6. Mulhall, *Our Molecular Future*, 30.

7. Grosswiler, *Method Is the Message* 5.

8. McLuhan did on occasion protest that he was not a technodeterminist. Thus, in a 1967 interview he declared, "My entire concern is to overcome the determinism that results from the determination of people to ignore what is going on. Far from regarding technological change as inevitable, I insist that if we understand its components we can turn it off any time we choose. Short of turning it off, there are lots of moderate controls conceivable" (quoted in Rosenthal, *McLuhan*, 19). But McLuhan was never really interested in figuring out how "we can turn it off," much less conceiving of "moderate controls" to temper the social or psychological effects of new media. The cavalier language here (or is it merely naive?)—"we can turn it off any time we choose"—contradicts his typical mode of argumentation, which entails giving agency to technology and reifying humans.

9. Smith and Marx, "Introduction," xii.

10. Bimber, "Three Faces of Technological Determinism," 81.

11. Smith and Marx, "Introduction," x.

12. Paul Grosswiler acknowledges that "McLuhan consistently attacked or dismissed Marx" (*Method Is the Message*, 3), but he, nonetheless, offers a thorough "rethinking" of McLuhan through Marxist "critical theory." In *Unthinking Modernity*, Stamps, likewise, offers a useful comparison of the ideas of Harold Innis and McLuhan with those of Theodor Adorno and Walter Benjamin. I compare McLuhan to Marx and the Frankfurt School more briefly in *Bread and Circuses*, 263–73. In *Technopoly*, Postman

notes some of the basic similarities between Marx and McLuhan, though he adds, "By connecting technological conditions to symbolic life and psychic habits, Marx was doing nothing unusual. Before him, scholars found it useful to invent taxonomies of culture based on the technological character of an age" (22).

13. Quoted in Bimber, "Three Faces of Technological Determinism," 90n17.

14. Levinson, *Digital McLuhan*, 2.

15. See, for instance, Wiener's *The Human Use of Human Beings: Cybernetics and Society.*

16. *Understanding Media*, 57.

17. See Standage, *The Victorian Internet*, 74–104.

18. Bauman, *Globalization*, 3.

19. "The Masses," 208; see also Kellner, *Jean Baudrillard*, 66–76.

20. Baudrillard, *Simulations*, 54.

21. Baudrillard, *Illusion*, 8.

22. Virilio, *Art of the Motor*, 9–10.

23. Virilio, *Ground Zero*, 2; *Information Bomb*. In contrast, McLuhan suggests that technological innovation and its unequal distribution cause war, rather than the other way around: "Previous wars can now be regarded as the processing of difficult and resistant materials by the latest technology, the speedy dumping of industrial products on an enemy market to the point of social saturation. War, in fact, can be seen as a process of achieving equilibrium among unequal technologies, a fact that explains [Arnold] Toynbee's puzzled observation that each invention of a new weapon is a disaster for society, and that militarism itself is the most common cause of the breaking of civilization" (*Media*, 344).

24. Virilio, *Reader*, 46.

25. Virilio, *Ground Zero*, 37.

26. Virilio, *Reader*, 153. For "the cult of information," see Theodore Roszak, *The Cult of Information.*

27. Virilio, *Open Sky* 51.

28. McLuhan, *Understanding Media*, 35.

29. Virilio, *Open Sky*, 86.

30. McLuhan, *Understanding Media*, 50.

31. Virilio, *Open Sky*,97.

32. Ibid., 81.

33. Kroker, Kroker, and Cook, *Panic Encyclopedia*, 228.

34. Kroker and Weinstein, *Data Trash*, 2, 105.

35. In contrast to the crash theorists, McLuhan in seemingly optimistic mode can write, "The computer . . . promises . . . a Pentecostal condition of understanding and unity" perhaps leading to "a perpetuity of collective harmony and peace" (*Understanding Media*, 80). This sounds rosy enough, even "paradisal"—an overcoming of the old divisiveness of "the Tower of Babel"—though the "general cosmic consciousness which might be very like the collective unconscious dreamt of by Bergson" will, it seems, come at the expense of language. The future, global era of "harmony and peace" will also be an era of "speechlessness," whatever that means (ibid., 80). And just how "cosmic consciousness" meshes with Bergson's "collective *unconscious*" is a puzzle. As is well known, McLuhan borrowed the idea of the "noosphere" or world-brain from Teilhard de Chardin as well as from Bergson.

36. Kroker and Weinstein, *Data Trash*, 104.

37. Hughes, *Does Technology Drive History?* 104.

38. I am grateful to Ivan Amato for informing me about the article by Bill Joy and about K. Eric Drexler's *Engines of Creation*.

39. And see Kurzweil's *The Singularity Is Near: When Humans Transcend Biology*, (2005).

40. McKibben, *Enough*, 101–02.

41. Quoted in ibid., 92.

42. Kaku, *Visions*, 133–34. On Vinge and the concept of the Singularity, see Mulhall, *Our Molecular Future*, 27–29, and also Edwards, "Surviving the Singularity."

43. Mulhall, *Our Molecular Future*, 31; Kaku, *Visions*, 268.

44. Milburn, "Nanotechnology in the Age of Posthuman Engineering," 122.

45. Quoted in ibid., 119.

46. Mulhall, *Our Molecular Future*, 32.

47. Milburn, "Nanotechnology in the Age of Posthuman Engineering," 124.

48. Landon, "Less Is More, Much Less Is Much More," 144.

49. In their anthology, *Digital Delirium*, Arthur and Marilouise Kroker interview nanotechnologist B. C. Crandall, who says, "the potential for losing our evolutionary purchase on the planet is very real, as is the possibility of boldly carrying DNA to where no man—and no woman—has gone before" (169). Crandall's main idea about how to survive the consequences of nanotechnology seems to be the colonization of other worlds after ours becomes uninhabitable.

50. McKibben, *Enough*, 102.

51. Drexler includes a thoughtful chapter, "Strategies and Survival," dealing with possible institutional and political ways of controlling the new technologies (*Engines of Creation*, 191–202), but this is not typical of the other GRAIN scientists.

52. Allenby and Sarewitz, *The Techno-Human Condition*.

53. Among the proliferation of accounts, *The Techno-Human Condition* (2011) by Braden Allenby and Daniel Sarewitz is well researched and balanced. See also Allen Buchanan, *Better Than Human: The Promise and Perils of Enhancing Ourselves* (2011); Andrew Clark, *Natural-Born Cyborgs: Minds, Technologies, and the Future of Human Intelligence* (2003); and Joel Garrau, *Radical Evolution: The Promise and Peril of Enhancing Our Minds, Our Bodies—and What It Means to be Human* (2005).

54. In *Toward a Rational Society*, first published in German in 1968, Jürgen Habermas wrote, "Our problem can then be stated as one of the relation of technology and democracy: how can the power of technical control be brought within the range of the consensus of acting and transacting citizens?" (57). So far as I am aware, neither Habermas nor anyone else has provided any very satisfactory answers to that question. And such answers are certainly not going to come from crash theory and probably not from the GRAIN scientists.

11. Army Surplus

1. National Coalition for Homeless Veterans: http://www.nchv.org/index.php /connect/story/faq_knowledge, accessed Nov. 2, 2012.

2. Maze, "Obama Unveils Major Jobs Initiative for Vets." In *Nemesis,* Chalmers Johnson notes the importance of "military Keynesianism" in keeping unemployment low—until recently, that is (273).

3. See, for example, Huffington, *Third-World America*.

4. Republican vice-presidential candidate for 2012, Paul Ryan, is a fan of Ayn Rand and, hence, of the social Darwinist belief that the poor deserve what they get or rather don't get. And presidential candidate Mitt Romney's comment that 47 percent of Americans want handouts from the government and don't take responsibility for their lives registers the same belief.

5. In 2009 and 2010, there were many reports about the "epidemic" of suicides among veterans. According to VA Secretary Eric Shinseki, "Of the more than 30,000 suicides in this country each year, fully 20 percent of them are acts by veterans. That means on average 18 veterans commit suicide each day" (Clifton, "Suicide Rate Surged among Veterans"). A more recent estimate cited by *Time* magazine (July 23, 2012) places the suicide rate at "one a day."

6. In *Zombie Capitalism*, Chris Harman writes, "Thousands of factories, stores and offices are closing across Europe and North America. Unemployment is shooting upwards. Twenty million Chinese workers have been told they have to return to the villages because there are no jobs for them in the cities. An Indian employers' think tank warns that ten million of their employees face the sack. A hundred million of the world's people in the Global South are still threatened with hunger because of last year's doubling of grain prices, while in the richest country in the world, the United States, three million families have been dispossessed from their homes in 18 months" (7).

7. See Meek, ed. *Marx and Engels on the Population Bomb*.

8. See Ehrlich, *The Population Bomb*.

9. "Simple" societies often produce individual outcasts, however. The term *civilization* is now applied, at least by anthropologists, to all societies. By Eastern and Western civilizations, I am referring to those relatively large polities that have writing, centralized governments, agricultural economies, and cities.

10. Malthus was the main reason that Thomas Carlyle called economics "the dismal science."

11. Osborne, "Immortal Sewerage," in *Meliora; or, Better Times to Come*.

12. *The Book of Murder!* was republished in the Chartist newspaper *The Northern Star*. It was familiar to Marx and Engels; the latter cites it in his 1844 *Outlines of a Critique of Political Economy* (Meek, *Marx and Engels on the Population Bomb*, 59).

13. Among modern readers, Gertrude Himmelfarb in *The Idea of Poverty* takes Marcus at face value (125). See Harold Boner, *Hungry Generations*, 138–41 and 213n28 for more on Marcus's reception. The rambling weirdness of Marcus's argument may not be a sign of his satiric intent, but there are some other, clearer signs. Apart from Marcus's proposal for "the infants' paradise" (42) and his lunatic "theory of painless extinction" (43–48), both of which come at the end of *The Book of Murder!* his single mention of Malthus also betrays his satiric intent. Marcus expects even "complainants" to further the work of his association, which will receive them like "a work-factory . . . ready to employ them. And since the complaint and the remedy will march hand in hand, there will be no tone of disconsolate misery nor of angry importunity; such as that of the pauper-crowd, object of querimonious dread to MALTHUS" (29). Except from a literary or rhetorical standpoint, however, it hardly matters whether *The Book of Murder!* is satirical or not. The fact that some of its readers, both in the 1800s and more recently, have taken it at face value suggests the similarity between Malthusianism and the logic of exterminationism.

14. Himmelfarb notes that the passage about "nature's feast" appeared only in the second edition of Malthus's *Essay*, presumably because so many of his critics cited it (*The Idea of Poverty*, 122). This is what Marcus appears to be doing.

15. See Rawson, *God, Gulliver, and Genocide*.

16. For "democide," see Rummel, *Death by Government*. See also Jones, *Genocide*, 308–9.

17. Himmelfarb, *The Idea of Poverty*, 129.

18. La Vendée was a province of France consisting of numerous impoverished, reactionary peasants.

19. See Moses, *Empire, Colony, Genocide*.

20. In her study of totalitarianism, Hannah Arendt contends that, besides "superfluous wealth," "another by-product of capitalist production" was "the human debris that every crisis, following invariably upon each period of industrial growth, eliminated permanently from producing society.... That they were an actual menace to society had been recognized throughout the nineteenth century and their export had helped to populate the dominions of Canada and Australia as well as the United States. The new fact in the imperialist era is that these two superfluous forces, superfluous capital and superfluous working power, joined hands and left the country together" (*Imperialism*, 30).

21. The principle of least eligibility meant that the situation of any "pauper" applying for relief had to seem less "eligible" to receive it than even the poorest of workers who were able to maintain themselves and their families without relief.

22. Devah Pager, *Marked: Race, Crime, and Finding Work in an Era of Mass Incarceration*, quoted in Alexander, *The New Jim Crow*, 148.

23. Agamben, *Homo Sacer*, 84.

24. *History of Sexuality*, 150.

25. For eugenics in the U.S., see Paul Lombardo, *A Century of Eugenics in America*, and Edwin Black, *War against the Weak*.

26. Kevles, *In the Name of Eugenics*, 3.

27. Besides direct forms of genocide such as military annihilation, processes of extermination can be and often are indirect, such as simply neglecting to come to the aid of portions of a population affected by epidemics or famine. This is why, for example, Irish nationalists accused British authorities of genocide during the Irish Famine of 1845–50.

28. Wells, *Anticipations*, 199.

29. Agamben, *Means without End*, 35.

30. Quoted in Bradshaw, "Eugenics," 43.

31. Quoted in ibid., 42.

32. Foucault, *The History of Sexuality*, 137.

33. Ibid., 61.

34. Ibid., 62.

35. Agamben, *Means without End*, 29.

36. In "After September 11: Our State of Exception," Mark Danner notes the "normalization" now taking place in the U.S. due to "the war on terror." Danner's version of "*homines sacri*" is, however, detainees in that war, rather than the excluded within U.S. society. President Obama's "failure to close Guantanamo, after vowing on his second day in office to do so within the year, shows how deeply the state of exception has embedded itself in our politics."

37. The Khmer Rouge regime under Pol Pot aimed to liquidate Vietnamese but also targeted thousands of Cambodian intellectuals and city people in its attempt to establish a rural, communist utopia. The same pattern was evident during the Chinese "cultural revolution." The murders of street children by Brazilian police and undercover killers may not qualify as genocide but is another instance of a society identifying an internal population as worthless or threatening and, therefore, deserving only of extermination.

38. See Bauman, *Modernity and the Holocaust.*

39. Agamben, *Means without End,* 41.

40. The Reagan "revolution" and the installment of economic neoliberalism as orthodoxy led to the cancerous growth of "the prison-industrial complex." As David Harvey notes, the triumph of neoliberalism "was accompanied in the US by a politics of criminalization and incarceration of the poor that had put more than 2 million behind bars by 2000" (*The Enigma of Capital and the Crises of Capitalism,* 15). See also Alexander, *The New Jim Crow* and Pager, *Marked.*

12. World Social Forum

1. By "we," I am referring also to my wife, Ellen Brantlinger, to whom this book is dedicated. MST stands for Movimento dos Trabahadores sem Terra. For background on Porto Alegre and the MST, see Iain Bruce, ed., *The Porto Alegre Alternative;* Gret and Sintomer, *The Porto Alegre Experiment;* Stedile, "Brazil's Landless Battalions"; and Wright and Wolford, *To Inherit the Earth.* For Global Exchange, see its website, http://www.globalexchange.org/, accessed December 10, 2012.

2. Seyoum, *The State of the Global Economy 2001/2002,* 225.

3. See Anderson, *Field Guide to the Global Economy;* IFG, *Does Globalization Help the Poor;* Stiglitz, *Globalization and Its Discontents.*

4. Harvey, *The New Imperialism,* 76.

5. Stedile, "Brazil's Landless Battalions," 34; Wright and Wolford, *To Inherit the Earth.*

6. Part of the reason for the Zapatista rebellion is that Mexican President Carlos Salinas, who signed up for NAFTA, also reprivatized the *ejidos* or agricultural communes on which the livelihoods of indigenous peoples depended.

7. The WSF is held at a time that corresponds to the annual meeting of the World Economic Forum, so the Occupiers in Davos are helping the WSF cause.

8. For a sense of the many groups and movements involved in the 1999 anti-WTO protest, see Janet Thomas, *The Battle in Seattle:* "It's estimated that at least 700 groups were represented at the WTO demonstrations in Seattle. Most of the groups represented civil society; they were not affiliated with governments, although some were agencies that were affiliated with the United Nations" (86). See the lists of organizations she provides on pp. 86–87 and 218–28. For timetables indicating the evolution of the global justice movement, see "Two Decades of Resistance" in IFG, *Does Globalization Help the Poor?* 14–20, and "Chronology" in Leite, *The World Social Forum,* 230–40.

9. Quoted in Danaher and Mark, *Insurrection,* 7.

10. Klein, *Fences and Windows,* 199.

11. In *The Will of the Many,* Marianne Maeckelbergh writes, "The journey that led to Seattle is a political trajectory that 'begins' in the 1960s. In the decades since the 1960s,

many commentators have declared the 1960s movements a failure and others have credited them only with lasting cultural changes . . . but perhaps the most important effect of the 1960s movements will turn out to be their role in shaping the alterglobalization movement" (8).

12. Cassen, "On the Attack."

13. Joining with the Brazilians in founding the WSF were Bernard Cassen and the other leaders of ATTAC, established in France in 1998 to advocate the "implementation of taxes on all [international] financial transactions," an end to tax havens for corporations, and other measures to combat the "antisocial policies of organizations such as the IMF, World Bank, WTO, and OECD" (Leite, *The World Social Forum*, 212; Cassen, "On the Attack").

14. Leite, *The World Social Forum*, 44; see also chapter five. As noted in chapter five, the Zapatistas came to international attention on January 1, 1994, the date that NAFTA went into effect. Their spokesman, Subcomandante Marcos, declared that NAFTA is "a death sentence for indigenous peoples" (quoted in Anderson, *The Global Resistance Reader*, 92). "The disaster of NAFTA" has caused increasing unemployment in the U.S., but it has done far worse to the Mexican economy: "just from 1994 to 2002, Mexico lost over one million agricultural jobs," swelling the ranks of the destitute and of migrants streaming north in search of any kind of work in the U.S. (Gibler, *Mexico Unconquered*, 121, 127). That "free trade" should cause such tragic results means it deserves to be called "unfair trade" or worse. It is trade dominated by the world's largest corporations, with no concern for peasants and the poor in any nation, including the U.S. For accounts of the resistance of indigenous peoples around the world to capitalist globalization, see Mander and Tauli-Corpuz, eds., *Paradigm Wars*, and Meyer and Alvarado, eds., *New World of Indigenous Resistance*.

15. Collier, *Basta! Land and the Zapatista Rebellion in Chiapas*, 190.

16. Navarro, "The Revolt of the Globalized," 43; see also Klein, *Fences and Windows*, 208–23.

17. See Olesen, *International Zapatismo*.

18. In its first "Declaration from the Lacandón Jungle" (1994), the EZLN asserted that its struggle was five hundred years old.

19. Bello, *Deglobalization*, 28.

20. See Anderson, *Field Guide to the Global Economy*; IFG, *Does Globalization Help the Poor?*; Pieterse, *Globalization or Empire?*

21. The World Bank has just issued a report predicting global disaster if "radical measures" are not taken right away to stop global warming: "Humans must immediately implement a series of radical measures to halt carbon emissions or prepare for the collapse of entire ecosystems and the displacement, suffering and death of hundreds of millions of the globe's inhabitants, according to a report commissioned by the World Bank." Hedges, "Stand Still for the Apocalypse."

22. See "Preface," 1; his "riders," by the way, do not include nuclear warfare.

23. See, among many similar commentaries, Hacker and Pierson, *Winner-Take-All Politics*; Lessig, *Republic, Lost*; Madrick, *Age of Greed*; and Wolin, *Democracy Incorporated*.

24. Danaher and Burback, *Globalize This!* 10.

25. Pieterse, *Globalization or Empire?* 14.

26. IFG, *Does Globalization Help the Poor?* 35.

27. See Bruce, ed., *The Porto Alegre Alternative*.

28. IFG, *Does Globalization Help the Poor?* 1. Besides the World Bank, both the U.N. Development Program and the CIA have acknowledged the failure of capitalist globalization to cure worldwide poverty (Cavanagh, Mander, et al., *Alternatives to Economic Globalization*, 30).

29. Hawken, "Skeleton Woman Visits Seattle," 15.

30. IFG, *Does Globalization Help the Poor?* 37.

31. Boushey and Weller, "What the Numbers Tell Us," 31.

32. See, for example, Huffington, *Third-World America*. Today, there is "an extraordinary concentration of wealth among a small group of the super rich in many countries. The world's 225 richest people [had] a combined wealth of over 1 trillion US [dollars] in 1997, an amount equal to the annual income of the poorest 47% of the world's people" (Seyoum, *The State of the Global Economy 2001/2002*, 58). This is an amount also approximately equal to the indebtedness of the third world to the WB, the IMF, and other sources of international credit. It may only be one-third of the amount, however, that it will eventually cost the U.S. for its invasion and occupation of Iraq (Stiglitz and Bilmes, *The Three-Trillion Dollar War*).

33. See the list in William Blum, *Rogue State*, 38–40.

34. See Balakrishnan, ed., *Debating Empire*, and also Pieterse, *Globalization or Empire?* 36.

35. Munck, *Globalization and Contestation*, 122.

36. Hardt and Negri, *Multitude*, 85.

37. For an analysis of the WSF in relation to Jürgen Habermas's concept of the "public sphere," see Smith et al., *Global Democracy*, 33–42. The global justice movement is sometimes also referred to as "civil society," which again means something like "global public opinion."

38. Hardt and Negri, *Multitude*, 67.

39. Ibid., 215.

40. Hardt and Negri, "Foreword," xviii.

41. Hardt and Negri are as much influenced by the vitalist, poststructuralist theories of Deleuze and Guattari about nomadism, deterritorialization, desiring machines, and so forth as by Marx, Frantz Fanon, and other theorists of political and economic revolution.

42. Klein, *Fences and Windows*, 22.

43. Hardt and Negri, *Multitude*, 266. The Zapatistas do not just rely on the Internet, however. In 2002, for example, they started a radio broadcast—"Radio Insurgente," the "voice of the voiceless." Its programs can be accessed globally over the Internet at www .radioinsurgente.org (accessed Nov. 5, 2012).

44. As the coauthors of *Global Democracy and the World Social Forums* point out, the WSF is ideally a horizontal, democratic network but has had to struggle against vertical, hierarchical tendencies (Smith et al., 28–48).

45. Cf. Klein, *Fences and Windows*, 22.

46. On violence versus nonviolence, see Benjamin, "The Debate over Tactics." On violence by the police during the Battle of Seattle, see the essay by Paul Hawken in the same volume, "Skeleton Woman Visits Seattle."

47. Stripped of its many allusions to other recent theories and theorists, Hardt and Negri's argument does not sound much different from Karl Polyani's thesis in *The Great*

Transformation that capitalism was attempting to establish "one big self-regulating market" (70), but that this attempt was being met by a powerful counter-movement "from within society to protect itself from the anarchy of the market" (Munck, *Globalization and Contestation*, ix). According to Foucault, power always breeds resistance; in fact, in many instances, power seems to produce its own resistance, as when the prison system produces delinquency (*Discipline*, 277). So history becomes, Foucault claims, an "endlessly repeated play of dominations" (*Language*, 150). Prospects of liberation, thus, seem doomed always to be overtaken by new forms of domination. Is there any reason to adopt a more hopeful attitude? Even if I choose "no" as the answer, I still want to be on the side of liberation, democracy, and social justice. To take such a position, moreover, inevitably expresses the hope that it will come about. And supporting that hope is the unpredictability of history. Who could have predicted the fall of the Soviet Union or of the Apartheid regime in South Africa or of the Zapatista rebellion or of the Battle of Seattle or of the Arab Spring or of Occupy Wall Street? And it is conceivable that, as Slavoj Žižek argues, the convergence of numerous "end-time" crises—of capitalism, of global warming, of the various liberating movements mentioned in this essay—history must alter its course in the direction of liberation in general. Or so I hope, though it is impossible to know for sure.

48. Marcos, *The Speed of Dreams*, 266.

49. Leite, *The World Social Forum*, 174.

50. Ibid., 138.

51. Monbiot, *Manifesto for a New World Order*, 158.

52. Leite, *The World Social Forum*, 185.

53. Cavanagh, Mander et al., *Alternatives to Economic Globalization*, 64.

54. Marcos, *The Speed of Dreams*, 254.

WORKS CITED

1. Class Warfare and Cultural Studies

Althusser, Louis. "Ideology and Ideological State Apparatuses." *Lenin and Philosophy.* New York: Monthly Review Press, 1971.

Anderson, Perry. *The Origins of Postmodernity.* London: Verso, 1998.

Aronowitz, Stanley, and William DiFazio. *The Jobless Future: Sci-Tech and the Dogma of Work.* Minneapolis: University of Minnesota Press, 1994.

Bageant, Joe. *Deer Hunting with Jesus: Dispatches from America's Class War.* New York: Random House, 2007.

Baudrillard, Jean. *Selected Writings.* Edited by Mark Poster. Stanford, CA: Stanford University Press, 1988.

———. *Simulations.* Translated by Paul Foss, Paul Patton, and Philip Beitchman. New York: Semiotext(e), 1983.

Brantlinger, Patrick. *Bread and Circuses: Theories of Mass Culture as Social Decay.* Ithaca, NY: Cornell University Press, 1983.

———. *Crusoe's Footprints: Cultural Studies in Britain and America.* New York: Routledge, 1990.

Cottle, Michelle. "The Real Class War." *Washington Monthly,* July/August 1997, 12–17.

Derrida, Jacques. *The Politics of Friendship.* Translated by George Collins. London: Verso, 1997.

———. *Specters of Marx: The State of the Debt, the Work of Mourning, and the New International.* Translated by Peggy Kamuf. New York: Routledge, 1994.

Dobbs, Lou. *War on the Middle Class: How the Government, Big Business, and Special Interest Groups Are Waging War on the American Dream and How to Fight Back.* New York: Viking Penguin, 2006.

Eagleton, Terry. *The Illusions of Postmodernism.* Oxford: Blackwell, 1996.

Ehrenreich, Barbara. "Earth to Wal-Mars." In *Inequality Matters,* edited by James Lardner and David A. Smith, 41–53.

Edelman, Peter. *So Rich, So Poor: Why It's So Hard to End Poverty in America.* New York: The New Press, 2012.

Faux, Jeff. *The Global Class War: How America's Bipartisan Elite Lost Our Future—and What It Will Take to Win It Back.* Hoboken, NJ: John Wiley and Sons, 2006.

Frank, Thomas. *Pity the Billionaire: The Hard-Times Swindle and the Unlikely Comeback of the Right.* New York: Henry Holt, 2011.

———. *What's the Matter with Kansas?* New York: Metropolitan Books, 2004.

Fraser, Nancy. *Justice Interruptus: Critical Reflections on the "Postsocialist" Condition.* New York: Routledge, 1997.

Friedman, Milton. *Capitalism and Freedom.* Chicago: University of Chicago Press, 1962.

Gelder, Ken, and Sarah Thornton, eds. *The Subcultures Reader.* London: Routledge, 1997.

Goodman, Leonard C. "Wall Street Pulls Obama's Strings." *In These Times,* September 2011, 12.

Hacker, Jacob, and Paul Pierson. *Winner-Take-All Politics: How Washington Made the Rich Richer and Turned Its Back on the Middle Class.* New York: Simon and Schuster, 2011.

Hartmann, Thom, Greg Palast, and Mark Crispin Miller. *Screwed: The Undeclared War against the Middle Class—and What We Can Do About It.* San Francisco: Berrett-Koehler, 2006.

Harvey, David. *The Condition of Postmodernity.* Oxford: Basil Blackwell, 1989.

Hebdige, Dick. *Subculture: The Meaning of Style.* London: Methuen, 1979.

Hoggart, Richard. *The Uses of Literacy: Changing Patterns in English Mass Culture.* Boston: Beacon Press, 1961.

Ivins, Molly, and Lou Dubose. *Shrub: The Short but Happy Political Life of George W. Bush.* New York: Vintage, 2002.

Jameson, Fredric. *Postmodernism: or, The Cultural Logic of Late Capitalism.* Durham, NC: Duke University Press, 1991.

———. *Signatures of the Visible.* New York: Routledge, 1992.

Klein, Naomi. *Shock Doctrine: The Rise of Disaster Capitalism.* New York: Metropolitan Books/Henry Holt, 2007.

Krugman, Paul. *The Great Unraveling: Losing Our Way in the New Century.* New York: Norton, 2004.

Laclau, Ernesto, and Chantal Mouffe. *Hegemony and Socialist Strategy: Towards a Radical Democratic Politics.* London: Verso, 1985.

Ladd, Everett, and Karlyn Bowman. "The Nation Says No to Class Warfare." *USA Today Magazine,* May 1, 1999, 24–27.

Lardner, James, and David A. Smith, eds. *Inequality Matters: The Growing Economic Divide in America and Its Poisonous Consequences.* New York: The New Press, 2005.

Lessig, Lawrence. *Republic, Lost: How Money Corrupts Congress—and A Plan to Stop It.* New York: Hachette, 2011.

Lewis, Michael. *The Big Short: Inside the Doomsday Machine.* New York: W. W. Norton, 2011.

Lydersen, Kari. "North American Solidarity Agreement." *In These Times,* July 2011, 18–21.

Lyotard, Jean-François. *The Postmodern Condition: A Report on Knowledge.* Translated by Geoff Bennington and Brian Massumi. Minneapolis: University of Minnesota Press, 1984.

Madrick, Jeff. *Age of Greed: The Triumph of Finance and the Decline of America.* New York: Knopf, 2011.

Marcuse, Herbert. *One-Dimensional Man: Studies in the Ideology of Advanced Industrial Society.* Boston: Beacon Press, 1964.

Marx, Karl, and Friedrich Engels. *The Marx-Engels Reader.* Edited by Robert C. Tucker. 2d ed. New York: Norton, 1978.

McGuigan, Jim. *Cultural Populism.* New York: Routledge, 1992.

Mishel, Lawrence, Jared Bernstein, and Heather Boushey. *The State of Working America: 2002/2003.* Ithaca, NY: Cornell University Press, 2003.

Moyers, Bill. "Which America Will We Be Now?" *The Nation,* November 19, 2001, 11–14.

Niethammer, Lutz. *Posthistoire: Has History Come to an End?* Translated by Patrick Camiller. London: Verso, 1992.

Page, Benjamin, and Lawrence Jacobs. *Class War? What Americans Really Think about Economic Inequality.* Chicago: University of Chicago Press, 2009.

Perucci, Robert, and Earl Wysong. *The New Class Society: Goodbye American Dream?* 2d ed. Lanham, MD: Rowman and Littlefield, 2003.

Powers, Kirsten. "To Romney, Detractors Suffer from Envy." *The Daily Beast,* January 13, 2012. http://www.thedailybeast.com/articles/2012/01/13/to-romney-detractors-suffer-from-envy.html. Accessed October 9, 2012.

Prashad, Vijay. *Fat Cats and Running Dogs: The Enron Stage of Capitalism.* Monroe, ME: Common Courage Press, 2003.

Press, Eyal. "Ruling Class Warriors." *The Nation,* January 23, 2006, 4–5.

Rich, Frank. "The Class War Has Begun." *New York,* October 23, 2011, 20–30.

Stiglitz, Joseph. *The Price of Inequality: How Today's Divided Society Endangers Our Future.* New York: W.W. Norton, 2012.

Strobel, Frederick, and Wallace Peterson. *The Coming Class War and How to Avoid It.* Armonk, NY: M. E. Sharpe, 1999.

Thompson, E. P. *The Making of the English Working Class.* New York: Vintage, 1963.

Vattimo, Gianni. *The End of Modernity.* Translated by John R. Snyder. Baltimore: The Johns Hopkins University Press, 1991.

Weisberg, Jacob. "The Complete Bushisms: Updated Frequently." *Slate.* http://politics.slate.msn.com. Accessed October 9, 2012.

Williams, Raymond. *Culture and Society.* New York: Columbia University Press, 1983.

Wolin, Sheldon S. *Democracy Incorporated: Managed Democracy and the Specter of Inverted Totalitarianism.* Princeton, NJ: Princeton University Press, 2008.

Wood, Ellen Meiskins. *The Retreat from Class: A New "True" Socialism.* London: Verso, 1986.

2. "It's the Economy, Stupid!"

Anderson, Sarah, John Cavanagh, and Thea Lee. *Field Guide to the Global Economy.* New York: The New Press, 2000.

Bakan, Joel. *The Corporation: The Pathological Pursuit of Profit and Power.* New York: Free Press, 2004.

Bourdieu, Pierre. *Acts of Resistance: Against the Tyranny of the Market.* New York: The New Press, 1998.

Brockway, George. *The End of Economic Man: Principles of Any Future Economics.* New York: Norton, 1995.

Center for Popular Economics, CPE Globalization Briefs. "Has Neoliberalism Delivered?" Amherst, MA, 2010. http://www.populareconomics.org/wp-content/uploads/2011/05/HasNeo.pdf. Accessed October 19, 2012.

Chang, Ha-Joon. *Bad Samaritans: The Myth of Free Trade and the Secret History of Capitalism.* New York: Bloomsbury Press, 2008.

Coyle, Andrew, Allison Campbell, and Rodney Neufeld, eds. *Capitalist Punishment: Prison Privatization and Human Rights.* Atlanta: Clarity Press, 2003.

DiMaggio, Dan. "Harvard Students Demand Alternative Economics Course." *Dollars & Sense* 248 (July–August 2003): 31.

Ehrenreich, Barbara. *Bait and Switch: The (Futile) Pursuit of the American Dream.* New York: Henry Holt, 2005.

Fisk, Milton. "The Roots of Poverty." *New Politics* 10, no. 2 (Winter 2005): 71–81.

Frank, Thomas. *One Market under God: Extreme Capitalism, Market Populism, and the End of Economic Democracy.* New York: Anchor Books, 2001.

Friedman, Gerald, Fred Moseley, and Chris Sturr, eds. *The Economic Crisis Reader: Readings in Economics, Politics, and Social Policy from "Dollars & Sense."* Boston: Economic Affairs Bureau, Inc.: 2009.

Friedman, Milton. *Capitalism and Freedom.* Chicago: University of Chicago Press, 1962.

Galbraith, James K. *The Predator State: How Conservatives Abandoned the Free Market and Why Liberals Should Too.* New York: Free Press, 2008.

Goldstein, Fred. *Low-Wage Capitalism: What the New Globalized, High-Tech Imperialism Means for the Class Struggle in the U.S.* New York: World View Forum, 2008.

Grandin, Greg. *Empire's Workshop: Latin America, the United States, and the Rise of the New Imperialism.* New York: Metropolitan Books, 2006.

Gray, John. *False Dawn: The Delusions of Global Capitalism.* New York: The New Press, 1998.

Harman, Chris. *Zombie Capitalism: Global Crisis and the Relevance of Marx.* Chicago: Haymarket Books, 2010.

Hartmann, Thom. *Unequal Protection: How Corporations Became "People"—and How You Can Fight Back.* San Francisco: Berrett-Koehler, 2010.

Harvey, David. *The Enigma of Capital and the Crises of Capitalism.* Oxford: Oxford University Press, 2010.

———. *The New Imperialism.* Oxford: Oxford University Press, 2003.

Hayes, Christopher. "Hip Heterodoxy." *The Nation,* June 11, 2007, 18–24.

Hightower, Jim. *Thieves in High Places: They've Stolen Our Country—and It's Time to Take It Back.* New York: Viking, 2003.

Hightower, Jim, and Phillip Frazer. "Billionaires' Front Groups Attack Workers, Public Schools, and Young Voters." *The Hightower Lowdown,* June 7, 2011, 1–4. http://www.hightowerlowdown.org/node/2680. Accessed October 16, 2012.

Hodai, Beau. "Publicopoly Exposed: How ALEC, the Koch Brothers, and Their Corporate Allies Plan to Privatize Government." *In These Times,* July 11, 2011), 14–19. http://www.inthesetimes.com/article/11603/. Accessed October 16, 2012.

Hudson, Michael. "Dress Rehearsal for Debt Peonage." Interview on Dandelionsalad.com. August 28, 2009. http://dandelionsalad.wordpress.com/2009/08/28/michael-hudson-dress-rehearsal-for-debt-peonage/. Accessed October 16, 2012.

Kindleberger, Charles P. *Manias, Panics, and Crashes: A History of Financial Crises.* 4th ed. New York: John Wiley and Sons, 2000.

Klein, Naomi. *The Shock Doctrine: The Rise of Disaster Capitalism.* New York: Henry Holt, 2007.

Krugman, Paul. "The Debt-Peonage Society." *The New York Times,* March 8, 2005.

Laxer, James. *The Undeclared War: Class Conflict in the Age of Cyber Capitalism.* Toronto: Penguin, 1998.

Lifschultz, Lawrence S. "Could Karl Marx Teach Economics in the United States?" In *How Harvard Rules: Reason in the Service of Empire,* edited by John Trumpbour, 279–86. Boston: South End Press, 1989.

Madrick, Jeff. "Beyond Rubinomics." *The Nation,* January 12, 2009, 14–8.

Maier, Mark. "From the Classroom to the White House: Economics according to N. Gregory Mankiw." *Dollars & Sense: Real World Economics,* July/August 2003. http://www.dollarsandsense.org/archives/2003/0703maier.html. Accessed October 16, 2012.

Mankiw, N. Gregory. "The Case against the Living Wage." *Harvard Magazine,* November–December 2001. http://harvardmagazine.com/2001/11/ways-and-means-harvards.html. Accessed October 16, 2012.

———. *Principles of Economics.* 5th ed. Mason, OH: South-Western Cengage Learning, 2008.

Marglin, Stephen. *The Dismal Science: How Thinking like an Economist Undermines Community.* Cambridge, MA: Harvard University Press, 2008.

Marshall, Gordon, ed. *The Concise Oxford Dictionary of Sociology.* Oxford: Oxford University Press, 1994.

Mokhiber, Russell, and Robert Weissman. *Corporate Predators: The Hunt for Mega-Profits and the Attack on Democracy.* Monroe, ME: Common Courage Press, 1999.

Munck, Ronaldo. *Globalization and Contestation.* New York: Routledge, 2007.

Nichols, John. "ALEC Exposed." *The Nation,* August 1–8, 2011, 16–17. http://www.thenation.com/article/161978/alec-exposed. Accessed October 16, 2012.

Olson, Elizabeth. "Greenspan under Fire." http://upstart.bizjournals.com/news-markets/top-5/2008/10/23/Greenspan-at-House-Hearing.html. Accessed December 10, 2012.

"An Open Letter to Greg Mankiw." *Harvard Political Review,* Nov. 2, 2011. http://hpronline.org/campus/an-open-letter-to-greg-mankiw/?mid=51. Accessed October 16, 2012.

Pearce, David W., ed. *The MIT Dictionary of Modern Economics.* 4th ed. Cambridge, MA: MIT Press, 1995.

Perelman, Michael. *The Confiscation of American Prosperity: From Right-Wing Extremism and Economic Ideology to the Next Great Depression.* New York: Palgrave Macmillan, 2007.

———. *Railroading Economics: The Creation of the Free Market Mythology.* New York: Monthly Review Press, 2006.

Perkins, John. *Confessions of an Economic Hit Man.* San Francisco: Berrett-Koehler Publishers, 2004.

Pieterse, Jan Nederveen. *Is There Hope for Uncle Sam? Beyond the American Bubble.* London: Zed Books, 2008.

Posner, Richard. *A Failure of Capitalism: The Crisis of '08 and the Descent into Depression.* Cambridge, MA: Harvard University Press, 2009.

Prashad, Vijay. *Fat Cats and Running Dogs: The Enron Stage of Capitalism.* Monroe, ME: Common Courage Press, 2003.

Quiggin, John. *Zombie Economics: How Dead Ideas Still Walk among Us.* Princeton, NJ: Princeton University Press, 2010.

Raveaud, Gilles. "Neo-Con Indoctrination—The Mankiw Way." *Adbusters.com* July 16, 2009. https://www.adbusters.org/magazine/85/neocon-indoctrination-mankiw-way .html. Accessed October 16, 2012.

Ruccio, David, and Jack Amariglio. *Postmodern Moments in Modern Economics.* Princeton, NJ: Princeton University Press, 2003.

Schneider, Alison. "A Harvard Economist Hits the Jackpot." *The Chronicle of Higher Education,* October 10, 1997, A12.

Schwenninger, Sherle R. "Redoing Globalization." *The Nation,* January 12, 2009, 30–32. http://www.thenation.com/article/redoing-globalization. Accessed October 16, 2012.

Stiglitz, Joseph. *Freefall: America, Free Markets, and the Sinking of the World Economy.* New York: W.W. Norton, 2010.

Strassmann, Diana. "Not a Free Market: The Rhetoric of Disciplinary Authority in Economics." In *Beyond Economic Man: Feminist Theory and Economics.* edited by Marianne Ferber and Julie Nelson, 54–68. Chicago: The University of Chicago Press, 1993.

Tabb, William K. *The Amoral Elephant: Globalization and the Struggle for Social Justice in the Twenty-First Century.* New York: Monthly Review Press, 2001.

Teller-Elsberg, Jonathan, Nancy Folbre, and James Heintz. *Field Guide to the U.S. Economy.* Rev. ed. New York: The New Press, 2006.

Tonelson, Alan. *The Race to the Bottom: Why a Worldwide Worker Surplus and Uncontrolled Free Trade Are Sinking American Living Standards.* Boulder, CO: Westview Press, 2002.

Veblen, Thorstein. "The Preconceptions of the Classical Economists." In *The Portable Veblen,* edited by Max Lerner, 241–74. New York: Viking, 1971.

Wolff, Richard D. "Capitalism Hits the Fan." In *The Economic Crisis Reader,* edited by Gerald Friedman et al., 37–40.

———. *Capitalism Hits the Fan: The Global Economic Meltdown and What to Do about It.* Northampton, MA: Olive Branch Press, 2010.

Žižek, Slavoj. *First as Tragedy, Then as Farce.* London: Verso, 2009.

3. Tea Party Brewhaha

Ballvé, Marcelo. "Tea Party Dabbles in Immigration Politics," *News America Media,* February 5, 2010. http://news.newamericamedia.org/news/view_article.html?article_id =b4cc03dbd6820b4b82cb77f47573dce2. Accessed October 21, 2012.

Easley, Jason. "Limbaugh Defends AZ Immigration Law with Obama Salt Conspiracy Theory," *PoliticusUSA,* April 27, 2010. http://www.politicususa.com/limbaugh-salt -obama.html.Accessed October 21, 2012.

Egan, Timothy. "Building a Nation of Know-Nothings." *New York Times,* August 25, 2010. http://opinionator.blogs.nytimes.com/2010/08/25/building-a-nation-of-know -nothings/. Accessed October 20, 2012.

Flanders, Laura, ed. *At the Tea Party.* New York: OR Books, 2010.

Hart, Peter, and Steve Rendall. "At Last a Citizen Movement the Corporate Media Can Love." In *At the Tea Party,* edited by Laura Flanders, 23–39.

Hofstadter, Richard. *The Paranoid Style in American Politics and Other Essays.* New York: Alfred A. Knopf, 1965.

Khimm, Suzy. "Tom Tancredo: Muslim Immigrants Spread Sharia Law," *Mother Jones*, February 11, 2011. http://www.motherjones.com/mojo/2011/02/tom-tancredo-cpac-muslim-immigrants-sharia. Accessed October 20, 2012.

Kim, Richard. "The Mad Tea Party." In *At the Tea Party*, edited by Laura Flanders, 130–38.

"Know Nothing." *Wikipedia*. http://en.wikipedia.org/wiki/Know_Nothing. Accessed October 20, 2012.

Pharr, Susanne, Eric Ward, Tarso Ramos, et al. "Fight the Right: Looking Forward, Looking Back." In *At the Tea Party*, edited by Laura Flanders, 322–32.

4. Shooters: Cultural Contexts of the Virginia Tech Tragedy

ABC6 News. "Statement from Sun-Kyung Seung, Sister of Seung-Hui Seung." April 20, 2007. http://www.kaaltv.com/nw/article/view/113059.

Adler, Jerry. "Story of a Gun." *Newsweek*, April 30, 2007, 37–39.

AOL News. Texts of the plays were originally provided by a classmate of Seung-hui Cho's, Ian MacFarlane, at http://newsbloggers.aol.com/2007/04/17/cho-seung-huis-plays. They are now separately available at various websites.

Baxter, Sarah. "American Psycho." *Timesonline,.* The London *Sunday Times*, April 22, 2007. http://www.freerepublic.com/focus/f-news/1821481/posts. Accessed October 23, 2012.

Begley, Sharon. "The Anatomy of Violence." *Newsweek*, April 30, 2007, 40–44.

Bok, Sisela. *Mayhem: Violence as Public Entertainment*. Reading, MA: Addison-Wesley, 1998.

Bourdieu, Pierre. *The Field of Cultural Production: Essays on Art and Literature*. New York: Columbia University Press, 1993.

Brantlinger, Ellen. "(Re)Turning to Marx to Understand the Unexpected Anger among 'Winners' in Schooling: A Critical Social Psychology Perspective." In *Late to Class: Social Class and Schooling in the New Economy*, edited by Jane Van Galen and George Noblit, 235–68. Albany: State University of New York Press, 2007.

Brown, Brooks, and Rob Merritt. *No Easy Answers: The Truth behind Death at Columbine*. New York: Lantern, 2002.

CBS News. "Cho Family Statement," February 12, 2009. http://www.cbsnews.com/8301-501803_162-2712709.html?tag=contentMain;contentBody. Accessed December 9, 2012.

CNN. *"The Situation Room,"* April 17, 2007. http://web.lexis-nexis.com.

CTRL [Conspiracy Theory Research List]. "Seung's Family Background—Oddities Abounding." www.mail-archive.com/ctrl@listserv.aol.com/msg121329.html. Accessed October 23, 2012.

Denby, David. "Men Gone Wild: 'Shooter' and '300.'" *The New Yorker*, April 2, 2007, 88–89.

Gardner, Amy, and David Seung. "Isolation Defined Seung's Senior Year." *The Washington Post*. May 6, 2007.

Goldstein, Bonnie. "Seung Seung-Hui's Commitment Papers." *Slate Magazine*, April 24, 2007. http://www.slate.com/articles/news_and_politics/hot_document/features/2007/cho_seunghuis_commitment_papers/_7.html. Accessed October 23, 2012.

Gopnik, Adam. "Shootings." *The New Yorker*, April 30, 2007, 27–28.

Goss, Kristin A. "Good Policy, Not Stories, Can Reduce Violence." *The Chronicle Review: The Chronicle of Higher Education,* Section B. 4, May 2007, B10.

Hong, Adrian. "Koreans Aren't to Blame." *The Washington Post,*April 20, 2007, A31.

Kim, Richard. "One of My Own." *The Nation,* May 14, 2007, 5–6.

Lifton, Robert Jay. "An Ideology of 'Gunism.'" *The Chronicle Review: The Chronicle of Higher Education,* Section B. 4, May 2007, B11.

Moon, Katharine H. S. "Don't Politicize Massacre." *The Chicago Tribune,* April 20, 2007.

Newman, Katherine S. *Rampage: The Social Roots of School Shootings.* New York: Basic Books, 2004.

———. "Before the Rampage: What Can Be Done?" *The Chronicle Review: The Chronicle of Higher Education,* Section B. 4, May 2007, B20.

Park, Edward J. W. "I Hope He's Not Korean." *The Chronicle Review: The Chronicle of Higher Education,* Section B. 4, May 2007, B5.

Parry, Ryan, and Martin Fricker. "'This Is Someone That I Grew Up with and Loved . . .': Seung's Sister Apologises for Murders." *The Mirror,* [London], April 21, 2007.

Schmid, David. *Natural-Born Celebrities: Serial Killers in American Culture.* Chicago: University of Chicago Press, 2005.

Seltzer, Mark. *Serial Killers: Death and Life in America's Wound Culture.* New York: Routledge, 1998.

Slotkin, Richard. *Gunfighter Nation: The Myth of the Frontier in Twentieth-Century America.* New York: Atheneum, 1992.

Thomas, Evan. "Making of a Massacre." *Newsweek,* 149: 18 (April 30, 2007), 22–31.

Žižek, Slavoj. *For They Know Not What They Do: Enjoyment as a Political Factor.* London: Verso, 1991.

5. What Is the Matter with Mexico?

Alexander, Michelle. *The New Jim Crow: Mass Incarceration in the Age of Colorblindness.* New York: The New Press, 2010.

Allen, Terry J. "Global Land Grab." *In These Times,* September 2011, 14–19.

Anzaldúa, Gloria. *Borderlands/La Frontera: The New Mestiza.* San Francisco: Aunt Lute Book Company, 1987.

Bacon, David. "Mexico's Great Migration." *The Nation,* January 23, 2012, 11–18.

Bañuelos, Juan. "No One Is Living Now in My Country." In *First World, Ha Ha Ha! The Zapatista Challenge,* edited by Elaine Katzenberger, 199–200. San Francisco: City Lights Books, 1995.

Bobo, Kimberley A. *Wage Theft in America: Why Millions of Working Americans Are not Getting Paid—and What We Can Do about It.* New York: New Press, 2009.

Boyer, Paul S., et al. *The Enduring Vision: A History of the American People, vol. 1: to 1877.* Boston: Houghton Mifflin, 2005.

Chacón, Justin Akers, and Mike Davis. *No One Is Illegal: Fighting Racism and State Violence on the U.S.–Mexico Border.* Chicago: Haymarket Books, 2006.

Chomsky, Aviva. *"They Take Our Jobs!" and 20 Other Myths about Immigration.* Boston: Beacon Press, 2007.

Cohen, Deborah. *Braceros: Migrant Citizens and Transnational Subjects in the Postwar United States and Mexico.* Chapel Hill: University of North Carolina Press, 2010.

Galeano, Eduardo. *Open Veins of Latin America: Five Centuries of the Pillage of a Continent.* New York: Monthly Review Press, 1973.

Gibler, John. *Mexico Unconquered: Chronicles of Power and Revolt.* San Francisco: City Lights Books, 2009.

———. *To Die in Mexico: Dispatches from inside the Drug War.* San Francisco: City Lights Books, 2011.

Gilly, Adolfo. *The Mexican Revolution.* New York: The New Press, 2005.

Gonzalez, Juan. *Harvest of Empire: A History of Latinos in America.* New York: Penguin Books, 2000.

Grandin, Greg. *Empire's Workshop: Latin America, the United States, and the Rise of the New Imperialism.* New York: Owl Books, 2006.

Guskin, Jane, and David L. Wilson. *The Politics of Immigration: Questions and Answers.* New York: Monthly Review Press, 2007.

Hamnett, Brian R. *A Concise History of Mexico.* 2d ed. Cambridge: Cambridge University Press, 2006.

Harvey, David. *The New Imperialism.* Oxford: Oxford University Press, 2003.

Hayden, Tom, ed. *The Zapatista Reader.* New York: Thunder's Mouth Press/Nation Books, 2002.

Heidler, David, and Jeanne Heidler. *The Mexican War.* Westport, CT: Greenwood, 2006.

Huffington, Arianna. *Third-World America: How Our Politicians Are Abandoning the Middle Class and Betraying the American Dream.* New York: Crown Publishers, 2010.

Lens, Sidney. *The Forging of the American Empire: From the Revolution to Vietnam: A History of U.S. Imperialism.* 1971. Chicago: Haymarket Books, 2003.

Macdonald, Isabel. "Lou Dobbs, American Hypocrite." *The Nation,* October 25, 2010, 11–15.

Marcos [Subcomandante]. *The Speed of Dreams: Selected Writings, 2001–2007,* edited by Cenak Pena-Vargas and Greg Ruggiero. San Francisco: City Lights, 2007.

Mize, Ronald L., and Alicia C. S. Swords. *Consuming Mexican Labor: From the Bracero Program to NAFTA.* Toronto: University of Toronto Press, 2011.

Ngai, Mae. *Impossible Subjects: Illegal Aliens and the Making of Modern America.* Princeton, NJ: Princeton University Press, 2004.

Ramos, Jorge. *La Ola Latina: Cómo los Hispanos Están Transformando la Política en los Estados Unidos.* New York: HarperCollins, 2005.

Rodriguez, Gregory. *Mongrels, Bastards, Orphans, and Vagabonds: Mexican Immigration and the Future of Race in America.* New York: Pantheon Books, 2007.

Ross, Jon. *The Annexation of Mexico from the Aztecs to the I.M.F.* Monroe, ME: Common Courage Press, 1998.

Schrag, Peter. *Not Fit for Our Society: Nativism and Immigration.* Berkeley: University of California Press, 2010.

Schroeder, John H. *Mr. Polk's War: American Opposition and Dissent, 1846–1848.* Madison: The University of Wisconsin Press, 1973.

Taibo, Paco Ignacio, II. "Zapatistas! The Phoenix Rises." In *The Zapatista Reader,* edited by Tom Hayden, 21–30.

Tancredo, Tom. *In Mortal Danger: The Battle for America's Border and Security.* Nashville, TN: WND Books, 2006.

Turner, John Kenneth. *Barbarous Mexico.* Chicago: Charles H. Kerr, 1910.

Wessler, Seth Free. "Thousands of Kids Lost from Parents in U.S. Deportation System." *Colorlines: News for Action.* Nov. 2, 2011. http://colorlines.com/archives/2011/11 /thousands_of_kids_lost_in_foster_homes_after_parents_deportation.html. Accessed October 26, 2012.

Zinn, Howard. *A People's History of the United States.* New York: Harper Perennial, 1995.

Zinn, Howard, and Anthony Arnove. *Voices of a People's History of the United States.* New York: Seven Stories, 2004.

6. Waste and Value: Thorstein Veblen and H. G. Wells

Aaron, Daniel. *Men of Good Hope: A Story of American Progressives.* New York: Oxford University Press, 1961.

Adorno, Theodor. "Veblen's Attack on Culture." In *Prisms,* translated by Samuel and Shierry Weber, 73–94. Cambridge, MA: MIT Press, 1983.

Bataille, Georges. *Visions of Excess: Selected Writings, 1927–1939.* Edited and translated by Allan Stoekl. Minneapolis: University of Minnesota Press, 1985.

Baudrillard, Jean. *La société de consommation.* Paris: Denoël, 1970.

Bauman, Zygmunt. *Liquid Modernity.* Cambridge: Cambridge University Press, 2000.

Brantlinger, Patrick. *Dark Vanishings: Discourse on the Extinction of Primitive Races, 1800–1930.* Ithaca, NY: Cornell University Press, 2003.

Caffentzis, Constantine George. *Clipped Coins, Abused Words, and Civil Government: John Locke's Philosophy of Money.* Brooklyn, NY: Autonomedia, 1989.

Carey, John. *The Intellectuals and the Masses: Pride and Prejudice among the Literary Intelligentsia, 1880–1939.* New York: St. Martins, 1992.

Cohen, William A. "Introduction: Locating Filth." In *Filth,* edited by Cohen and Johnson, vii–xxxvii.

Cohen, William A., and Ryan Johnson, eds. *Filth: Dirt, Disgust and Modern Life.* Minneapolis: University of Minnesota Press, 2005.

Connor, Steven. *Theory and Cultural Value.* Oxford: Blackwell, 1992.

DeLillo, Don. *Underworld.* New York: Simon and Schuster, 1997.

Douglas, Mary. *Purity and Danger: An Analysis of Concepts of Pollution and Taboo.* London: Routledge and Kegan Paul, 1966.

Eby, Clare Virginia. *Dreiser and Veblen: Saboteurs of the Status Quo.* Columbia: University of Missouri Press, 1998.

Evans, David H. "Taking Out the Trash: Don DeLillo's *Underworld,* Liquid Modernity, and the End of Garbage." *Cambridge Quarterly* 32, no. 2 (2006): 103–32.

Filler, Louis. *Crusaders for American Liberalism.* Yellow Springs, OH: The Antioch Press, 1961.

Freeland, Natalka. "The Dustbins of History: Waste Management in Late-Victorian Utopias." In *Filth,* edited by Cohen and Ryan, 225–49.

Freud, Sigmund. "Character and Anal Eroticism." In *The Freud Reader,* edited by Peter Gay, 293–97. New York: Norton, 1989.

Gagnier, Reginia. *The Insatiability of Human Wants: Economics and Aesthetics in Market Society.* Chicago: University of Chicago Press, 2000.

Gallagher, Catherine. *The Body Economic: Life, Death, and Sensation in Political Economy and the Victorian Novel.* Princeton, NJ: Princeton University Press, 2006.

Gronow, Jukka. *The Sociology of Taste.* New York: Routledge, 1997.

Harvey, David. *The Condition of Postmodernity*. Oxford: Basil Blackwell, 1989.

Haynes, Rosalynn. *H. G. Wells: Discoverer of the Future: The Influence of Science on His Thought*. New York: New York University Press, 1980.

Helyer, Ruth. "'Refuse heaped many stories high': DeLillo, Dirt, and Disorder." *Modern Fiction Studies* 45, no. 4 (1999): 987–1006.

Hobson, J. A. *Veblen*. London: Chapman and Hall, 1936.

Hofstadter, Richard. *Social Darwinism in American Thought*. Rev. ed. Boston: Beacon Press, 1955.

Hume, David. "Of Public Credit." In *Political Essays*, edited by Knud Haakonssen, 166–78. Cambridge: Cambridge University Press, 1994.

Huyssen, Andreas. *The Great Divide: Modernism, Mass Culture, Postmodernism*. Bloomington: Indiana University Press, 1986.

Jameson, Fredric. *Postmodernism: or, The Cultural Logic of Late Capitalism*. Durham: Duke University Press, 1991.

Kazin, Alfred. *On Native Grounds: An Interpretation of Modern American Prose Literature*. New York: Harcourt, Brace, 1942.

Kroker, Arthur, and Marilouise Kroker, eds. *Panic Encyclopedia: The Definitive Guide to the Postmodern Scene*. New York: St. Martin's, 1989.

Kroker, Arthur, and Michael Weinstein. *Data Trash: The Theory of the Virtual Class*. New York: St. Martin's, 1994.

Kuchta, Todd. *Semi-Detached Empire: Suburbia and the Colonization of Britain, 1880 to the Present*. Charlottesville: University of Virginia Press, 2010.

Kupinse, William. "Wasted Value: The Serial Logic of H. G. Wells's *Tono-Bungay*." *Novel* 33, no. 1 (Fall, 1999): 51–72.

Laporte, Dominique. *History of Shit*. Translated by Nadia Benabid and Rodolphe el-Khoury. Cambridge, MA: MIT Press, 2000.

Locke, John. *Two Treatises of Government*. London: Dent, 1991.

Lyotard, Jean-François. *The Post-Modern Condition: A Report on Knowledge*. Minneapolis: University of Minnesota Press, 1984.

Malthus, Thomas Robert. *On Population*. New York: Random House, Modern Library, 1960.

Marx, Karl. *Capital*. 3 vols. New York and London: Penguin, 1981.

McCulloch, J. R. "Emigration." *Edinburgh Review* 45 (1826): 49–74.

McGowan, Todd. "The Obsolescence of Mystery and the Accumulation of Waste in Don DeLillo's *Underworld*." *Critique* 46, no. 2 (Winter 2005): 123–45.

Meštrović, Stjepan G. *The Barbarian Temperament: Toward a Postmodern Critical Theory*. New York: Routledge, 1993.

Michaels, Walter Benn. *The Gold Standard and the Logic of Naturalism*. Berkeley: University of California Press, 1987.

Morton, Peter. *The Vital Science: Biology and the Literary Imagination, 1860–1900*. London: George Allen and Unwin, 1984.

Osborne, Sidney Godolphin. "Immortal Sewerage." *Meliora; or, Better Times to Come* 1st ser. Edited by Viscount Ingestre. 1853. London: Frank Cass, 1971: 7–17.

Pearce, David W. *The MIT Dictionary of Modern Economics*. Cambridge, MA: MIT Press, 1995.

Richards, Thomas. *The Imperial Archive: Knowledge and the Fantasy of Empire*. London: Verso, 1993.

Sekora, John. *Luxury: The Concept in Western Thought, Eden to Smollett.* Baltimore: Johns Hopkins University Press, 1977.

Simmel, Georg. *The Philosophy of Money.* 2d ed. Translated by Tom Bottomore, David Frisby, and Kaethe Mengelberg. London and New York: Routledge, 1990.

Smiles, Samuel. *Thrift.* 1875. Chicago: Belford, Clarke, 1889.

Smith, Adam. *The Wealth of Nations.* New York: Random House, Modern Library, 1965.

Spindler, Michael. *Veblen and Modern America: Revolutionary Iconoclast.* London: Pluto Press, 2002.

Stallybrass, Peter, and Allon White. *The Politics and Poetics of Transgression.* Ithaca, NY: Cornell University Press, 1986.

Strasser, Susan. *Waste and Want: A Social History of Trash.* New York: Henry Holt, 1999.

Taiganides, E. P. "Wastes Are Resources out of Place." *Agricultural Wastes* 1 (1979): 1–9.

Thompson, Michael. *Rubbish Theory: The Creation and Destruction of Value.* Oxford: Oxford University Press, 1979.

Veblen, Thorstein. "The Captain of Industry." In *The Portable Veblen,* edited by Max Lerner, 377–94. New York: Viking, 1971.

——. *The Engineers and the Price System.* 1921. New York: Viking, 1940.

——. *The Place of Science in Modern Civilisation and Other Essays.* 1919. New York: Russell and Russell, 1961.

——. *The Theory of Business Enterprise.* 1904. New York: Augustus M. Kelley, 1975.

——. *The Theory of the Leisure Class.* 1899. New York and London: Penguin, 1979. Unless otherwise indicated, page numbers in parentheses refer to this text.

Wells, H. G. *Anticipations of the Reaction of Mechanical and Scientific Progress on Human Life and Thought.* 1901. New York: Harper, 1902.

——. *Experiment in Autobiography.* New York: The Macmillan Company, 1934.

——. *Tono-Bungay.* 1909. Oxford: Oxford University Press, 1996.

Wollen, Peter. *Raiding the Icebox: Reflections on Twentieth-Century Culture.* Bloomington: Indiana University Press, 1993.

Žižek, Slavoj. *Living in the End Times.* London: Verso, 2010.

7. Shopping on Red Alert: The Rhetorical Normalization of Terror

Bates, Kristin A., and Richelle S. Swan, eds. *Through the Eye of Katrina: Social Justice in the United States.* Durham, NC: Carolina Academic Press, 2007.

Burbach, Roger, and Jim Tarbell. *Imperial Overstretch: George W. Bush and the Hubris of Empire.* London: Zed Books, 2004.

Chomsky, Noam. *Failed States: The Abuse of Power and the Assault on Democracy.* New York: Henry Holt, 2006.

Davis, Mike. *In Praise of Barbarians: Essays against Empire.* Chicago: Haymarket Books, 2007.

Domke, David. *God Willing? Political Fundamentalism in the White House, the "War on Terror," and the Echoing Press.* London: Pluto Press, 2004.

Everest, Larry. *Oil, Power and Empire: Iraq and the U.S. Global Agenda.* Monroe, ME: Common Courage Press, 2004.

Falk, Richard. *The Great Terror War.* New York: Olive Branch Press, 2003.

Fukuyama, Francis. *State-Building: Governance and World Order in the 21st Century.* Ithaca, NY: Cornell University Press, 2004.

Gareau, Frederick. *State Terrorism and the United States.* Atlanta: Clarity Press, 2003.

Goodman, Amy, and David Goodman. *The Exception to the Rulers: Exposing Oily Politicians, War Profiteers, and the Media That Love Them.* New York: Hyperion, 2004.

Greenwald, Glenn. "Obama's Illegal Assaults." *In These Times,* September 2011, 24–25.

Hagopian, Elaine C. *Civil Rights in Peril: The Targeting of Arabs and Muslims.* Chicago: Haymarket Books, 2004.

Herbst, Philip. *Talking Terrorism: A Dictionary of the Loaded Language of Political Violence.* Westport, CT: Greenwood Press, 2003.

Herman, Edward S. *The Real Terror Network: Terrorism in Fact and Propaganda.* Boston: South End Press, 1982.

Hobbes, Thomas. *Leviathan.* London: Collier Macmillan, 1962.

Johnson, Chalmers. *Nemesis: The Last Days of the American Republic.* New York: Holt, 2006.

Juhasz, Antonia. *The Bush Agenda: Invading the World, One Economy at a Time.* New York: HarperCollins, 2006.

Kegley, Charles W., Jr., ed. *The New Global Terrorism: Characteristics, Causes, Controls.* Upper Saddle River, NJ: Prentice Hall, 2003.

Kellner, Douglas. *From 9/11 to Terror War: The Dangers of the Bush Legacy.* Lanham, MD: Rowman and Littlefield, 2003.

Klein, Naomi. *The Shock Doctrine: The Rise of Disaster Capitalism.* New York: Holt, 2007.

Laqueur, Walter. *No End to War: Terrorism in the Twenty-First Century.* New York: Continuum, 2004.

———. *Terrorism.* Boston: Little, Brown, 1977.

Marchak, Patricia. *Reigns of Terror.* Montreal: McGill-Queen's University Press, 2003.

Miller, Mark Crispin. *Cruel and Unusual: Bush/Cheney's New World Order.* New York: W.W. Norton, 2004.

Palast, Greg. *Armed Madhouse.* New York: Dutton, 2006.

Parenti, Michael. *The Terrorism Trap: September 11 and Beyond.* San Francisco: City Lights Books, 2002.

Parry, Albert. *Terrorism: From Robespierre to Arafat.* New York: Vanguard, 1976.

Phillips, Kevin. *American Theocracy: The Peril and Politics of Radical Religion, Oil, and Borrowed Money in the 21st Century.* New York: Penguin, 2006.

Robin, Corey. *Fear: The History of a Political Idea.* Oxford: Oxford University Press, 2004.

Scahill, Jeremy. *Blackwater: The Rise of the World's Most Powerful Mercenary Army.* New York: Nation Books, 2007.

Schmid, Alex. *Political Terrorism: A Research Guide.* New Brunswick, NJ: Transaction Books, 1984.

St. Clair, Jeffrey. *Grand-Theft Pentagon: Tales of Corruption and Profiteering in the War on Terror.* Monroe, ME: Common Courage Press, 2005.

Taussig, Mick. "Terror as Usual: Walter Benjamin's Theory of History as a State of Siege." *Social Text* 23 (Fall/Winter 1989): 3–20.

Weisberg, Jacob. "The Complete Bushisms: Updated Frequently." *Slate.* http://politics .slate.msn.com. Accessed October 9, 2012.

Zulaika, Joseba, and William A. Douglass. *Terror and Taboo: The Follies, Fables, and Faces of Terrorism.* New York: Routledge, 1996.

8. The State of Iraq

[No Works Cited]

9. On the Postmodernity of Being Aboriginal—and Australian

Aldred, Lisa. "Plastic Shamans and Astroturf Sun Dances: New Age Commercialization of Native American Spirituality." *The American Indian Quarterly* 24, no. 3 (2000): 329–52.

Anderson, Warwick. *The Cultivation of Whiteness: Science, Health and Racial Destiny in Australia.* Melbourne: Melbourne University Press, 2002.

Ashcroft, Bill. "Reading Carey Reading Malley." In *Who's Who?,* edited by Nolan and Dawson, 28–39.

Attwood, Bain. "Portrait of an Aboriginal as an Artist: Sally Morgan and the Construction of Aboriginality." *Australian Historical Studies* 99, no. 25 (October 1992): 302–18.

"Barrington, George." *Australian Dictionary of Biography.* Melbourne: Melbourne University Press, 1966: 1:62–3.

Behrendt, Larissa. "What Lies Beneath." *Meanjin* 65, no. 1 (2006): 4–12.

Bennett, Bruce, and Jennifer Strauss, eds. *The Oxford Literary History of Australia.* Melbourne: Oxford University Press, 1998.

Brantlinger, Patrick. "'Black Armband' versus 'White Blindfold' History in Australia: A Review Essay." *Victorian Studies* 46, no. 4 (Summer 2004): 655–74.

———. "Notes on the Postmodernity of 'Fake' (?) Aboriginal Literature." *Postcolonial Studies* 14, no. 4 (December 2011): 355–71.

Carey, Peter. *My Life as a Fake.* London: Faber and Faber, 2003.

Carter, Paul. *The Road to Botany Bay: An Exploration of Landscape and History.* Chicago: The University of Chicago Press, 1987.

Caterson, Simon. *Hoax Nation: Australian Fakes and Frauds, from Plato to Norma Khouri.* Melbourne: Arcade Publications, 2009.

Chatwin, Bruce. *The Songlines.* New York: Penguin, 1987.

Chow, Rey. "Where Have All the Natives Gone?" In *Writing Diaspora: Tactics of Intervention in Contemporary Cultural Studies,* 27–54. Bloomington: Indiana University Press, 1993.

Clark, Maureen. "Mudrooroo: Crafty Impostor or Rebel with a Cause?" In *Who's Who?,* edited by Nolan and Dawson, 101–110.

Davis, Jack, Stephen Muecke, Mudrooroo Narogin, and Adam Shoemaker, eds. *Paperbark: A Collection of Black Australian Writings.* St. Lucia, AU: University of Queensland Press, 1990.

Derrida, Jacques. *Of Grammatology.* Translated by G. C. Spivak. Baltimore: The Johns Hopkins University Press, 1976.

Egan, Susanna. "The Company She Keeps: Demidenko and the Problems of Imposture in Autobiography." In *Who's Who?,* edited by Nolan and Dawson, 14–27.

Elder, Catriona. *Being Australian: Narratives of National Identity.* Crow's Nest, NSW, AU: Allen and Unwin, 2007.

Errington, Shelly. *The Death of Authentic Primitive Art and Other Tales of Progress.* Berkeley: University of California Press, 1998.

Fesl, Eve. "Koorie Languages and Folk Speech." *The Oxford Companion to Australian Folklore,* edited by Davey, Gwenda Beed, and Graham Seal, 232–37. Melbourne: Oxford University Press, 1993.

Gelder, Ken, and Jane M. Jacobs. *Uncanny Australia: Sacredness and Identity in a Postco-lonial Nation*. Melbourne: Melbourne University Press, 1998.

Goldie, Terry. *Fear and Temptation: The Image of the Indigene in Canadian, Australian, and New Zealand Literatures*. Montreal: McGill-Queen's University Press, 1989.

———. "On Not Being Australian: Mudrooroo and Demidenko." In *Who's Who?*, edited by Nolan and Dawson, 89–100.

Griffiths, Gareth. "The Myth of Authenticity: Representation, Discourse and Social Practice." In *De-Scribing Empire: Post-Colonialism and Textuality*, edited by Chris Tiffin and Alan Lawson, 70–85. London and New York: Routledge, 1994.

Herbert, Xavier. *Capricornia*. 1938. North Ryde, NSW, AU: Angus and Robertson, 1989.

Hodge, Bob, and Vijay Mishra. *Dark Side of the Dream: Australian Literature and the Postcolonial Mind*. North Sydney, NSW, AU: Allen and Unwin, 1991.

Huggan, Graham. *Australian Literature: Postcolonialism, Racism, Transnationalism*. Oxford: Oxford University Press, 2007.

James, Clive. "Party Town." In *Best Australian Essays 2000*, edited by Peter Craven, 19–33. Melbourne: Black Inc, 2000.

Johnston, Anna, and Alan Lawson. "Settler Colonies." In *A Companion to Postcolonial Studies*, edited by Henry Schwarz and Sangeeta Ray, 360–76. Oxford: Blackwell, 2005.

Kamiya, Gary. "Already Gold." *Salon.com*, September 15, 2000. http://www.salon.com/2000/09/15/opening_2/. Accessed October 28, 2012.

Keneally, Thomas. *The Chant of Jimmie Blacksmith*. New York: Viking, 1972.

Klapporth, Danièle M. *Narrative as Social Practice: Anglo-Western and Australian Aboriginal Oral Traditions*. Berlin: Mouton de Gruyter, 2004.

Kurtzer, Sonja. "*Wandering Girl*: Who Defines 'Authenticity' in Aboriginal Literature?" In *Blacklines: Contemporary Critical Writing by Indigenous Australians*, edited by Michele Grossman, 181–88. Melbourne: Melbourne University Press, 2003.

Lindqvist, Sven. *Terra Nullius: A Journey through No One's Land*. London: Granta Books, 2007.

Manne, Robert, ed. *Whitewash: On Keith Windschuttle's Fabrication of Aboriginal History*. Melbourne: Black Inc. Agenda, 2003.

Martin, C. E. M. *The Incredible Journey*. London: Jonathan Cape, 1923.

Morgan, Sally. *My Place*. South Fremantle, WA, AU: Fremantle Arts Press, 1987.

Mountford, Charles P. *Brown Men and Red Sand: Journeyings in Wild Australia*. New York: Praeger, 1952.

Mudrooroo. *Doctor Wooreddy's Prescription for Enduring the Ending of the World*. Melbourne: Hyland House, 1983.

Nolan, Maggie. "In His Own Sweet Time: Carmen's Coming Out." In *Who's Who?*, edited by Nolan and Dawson, 134–48.

Nolan, Maggie, and Carrie Dawson, eds. *Who's Who? Hoaxes, Imposture and Identity Crises in Australian Literature*. Brisbane: University of Queensland Press, 2004.

Nolan, Marguerite. "The Demidenko Affair and Australian Hoaxes." In *A Companion to Australian Literature since 1900*, edited by Nicholas Birns and Rebecca McNeer, 127–38. Rochester, NY: Camden House, 2007.

Ong, Walter J. *Orality and Literacy: The Technologizing of the Word*. London: Methuen, 1982.

Phillips, A. A. *The Australian Tradition: Studies in a Colonial Culture*. Melbourne: F. W. Cheshire, 1958.

Pierce, Peter. *The Country of Lost Children: An Australian Anxiety.* Cambridge: Cambridge University Press, 1977.

Povinelli, Elizabeth A. "Consuming *Geist:* Popontology and the Spirit of Capital in Indigenous Australia." *Public Culture* 31 (2000): 501–28.

——. *The Cunning of Recognition: Indigenous Alterities and the Making of Australian Multiculturalism.* Durham, NC: Duke University Press, 2002.

Prichard, Katharine Susannah. *Coonardoo (The Well in the Shadow).* 1929. Sydney: Angus and Robertson, 1956.

Pybus, Cassandra. *Black Founders: The Unknown Story of Australia's First Black Settlers.* Sydney: The University of New South Wales Press, 2006.

Read, Peter. *A Rape of the Soul So Profound: The Return of the Stolen Generations.* St. Leonards, NSW, AU: Allen and Unwin, 1999.

Reynolds, Henry. *The Law of the Land.* Ringwood, VI, AU: Penguin Australia, 1992.

——. *Nowhere People.* Camberwell, VI, AU: Penguin, 2006.

Schaffer, Kay. *In the Wake of First Contact: The Eliza Fraser Stories.* Cambridge: Cambridge University Press, 1995.

Scott, Kim. *Benang: From the Heart.* North Fremantle, WA, AU: Femantle Arts Centre Press, 1999.

Shoemaker, Adam. *Black Words, White Page: Aboriginal Literature 1929–1988.* Brisbane: University of Queensland Press, 1989.

——. "Tracking Black Australian Stories: Contemporary Indigenous Literature." In *Oxford Literary History of Australia,* edited by Bennett and Srauss, 332–47.

——. "White on Black/Black on Black." In *Oxford Literary History of Australia,* edited by Bennett and Srauss, 9–20.

Sitka, Chris. "Mutant Message Down Under: Cultural Mutilation Uptop." *Leatherwood Trail.* http://wmuma.com/mutantmessage/mutantmessagebookcsitka.html. Accessed October 29, 2012.

Smith, William Ramsay. *Myths and Legends of the Australian Aborigines.* London: George G. Harrap, 1930.

Stanner, W. E. H. *White Man Got No Dreaming: Essays 1938–1973.* Canberra, AU: Australian National University Press, 1979.

Taggart, Stewart. "Aboriginal Culture Awakens Australia." *Wired,* September 19, 1997. http://www.wired.com/culture/lifestyle/news/1997/10/7394. Accessed October 29, 2012.

Trumpener, Katie. *Bardic Nationalism: The Romantic Novel and the British Empire.* Princeton, NJ: Princeton University Press, 1997.

Van Toorn, Penny. *Writing Never Arrives Naked: Early Aboriginal Cultures of Writing in Australia.* Canberra, AU: Aboriginal Studies Press, 2006.

Windschuttle, Keith. *The Fabrication of Aboriginal History, Volume I: Van Diemen's Land, 1803–1947.* Sidney: Macleay Press, 2002.

——. *The Fabrication of Aboriginal History, Volume II: The Stolen Generations, 1881–2008.* Paddington, QLD, AU: Macleay Press, 2009.

10. McLuhan, Crash Theory, and the Invasion of the Nanobots

Allenby, Braden, and Daniel Sarewitz. *The Techno-Human Condition.* Cambridge, MA: MIT Press, 2011.

Barney, Darin. *Prometheus Wired: The Hope for Democracy in the Age of Network Technology*. Chicago: University of Chicago Press, 2000.

Baudrillard, Jean. *In the Shadow of the Silent Majorities . . . or the End of the Social*. Translated by Paul Foss, Paul Patton, and John Johnson. New York: Semiotext(e), 1983.

———. "The Masses: The Implosion of the Social in the Media." In *Jean Baudrillard: Selected Writings*, edited by Mark Poster, 207–19. Stanford, CA: Stanford University Press, 1988.

———. *Simulations*. Translated by Paul Foss, Paul Patton, and Philip Beitchman. New York: Semiotext(e), 1983.

———. *The Spirit of Terrorism and Requiem for the Twin Towers*. Translated by Chris Turner. London: Verso, 2002.

Bauman, Zygmunt. *Globalization: The Human Consequences*. New York: Columbia University Press, 1998.

Bimber, Bruce. "Three Faces of Technological Determinism." In *Does Technology Drive History?*, edited by Smith and Marx, 79–100.

Brantlinger, Patrick. *Bread and Circuses: Theories of Mass Culture as Social Decay*. Ithaca, NY: Cornell University Press, 1983.

Buchanan, Allen. *Better Than Human: The Promise and Perils of Enhancing Ourselves*. Oxford: Oxford University Press, 2011.

Castells, Manuel. *The Informational City*. Oxford: Basil Blackwell, 1989.

Cavell, Richard. "Specters of McLuhan: Derrida, Media, and Materiality." In *Transforming McLuhan*, edited by Paul Grosswiler, 136–61.

Clark, Andrew. *Natural-Born Cyborgs: Minds, Technologies, and the Future of Human Intelligence*. Oxford: Oxford University Press, 2003.

Crichton, Michael. *Prey: A Novel*. New York: Harper Collins, 2002.

Deleuze, Gilles, and Félix Guattari. *Anti-Oedipus: Capitalism and Schizophrenia*. Translated by Robert Hurley, Mark Seem, and Helen R. Lane. Minneapolis: University of Minnesota Press, 1983.

———. *A Thousand Plateaus: Capitalism and Schizophrenia*. Translated by Brian Massumi. Minneapolis: University of Minnesota Press, 1987.

Der Derian, James. "Introduction." In *The Virilio Reader*, edited by James Der Derian, 1–15.

Drexler, K. Eric. *Engines of Creation*. Garden City, NY: Anchor Press/Doubleday, 1986.

Edwards, Steve Alan. "Surviving the Singularity." http://textfiles.meulie.net/russian/cyberlib.narod.ru/lib/critica/sing/singsurv.html. Accessed December 10, 2012.

Eisenstein, Elizabeth L. *The Printing Revolution in Early Modern Europe*. Cambridge: Cambridge University Press, Canto Edition, 1993.

Garrau, Joel. *Radical Evolution: The Promise and Peril of Enhancing Our Minds, Our Bodies—and What It Means to Be Human*. New York: Random House, 2005.

Grosswiler, Paul. *Method Is the Message: Rethinking McLuhan through Critical Theory*. Montreal: Black Rose Books, 1998.

———, ed. *Transforming McLuhan: Cultural, Critical, and Postmodern Perspectives*. New York: Peter Lang, 2010.

Habermas, Jürgen. *Toward a Rational Society: Student Protest, Science, and Politics*. Translated by Jeremy J. Shapiro. Boston: Beacon, 1971.

Hanke, Bob. "McLuhan, Virilio and Speed." In *Transforming McLuhan*, edited by Paul Grosswiler, 203–26.

Hayles, N. Katherine, ed. *Nanoculture: Implications of the New Technoscience*. Portland, OR: Intellect Books, 2004.

Hughes, Thomas P. "Technological Momentum." In *Does Technology Drive History?*, edited by Smith and Marx, 101–113.

Joy, Bill. "Why the Future Doesn't Need Us." *Wired*, April 2000, 238–46. http://www .wired.com/wired/archive/8.04/joy.html. Accessed October 31, 2012.

Kaku, Michio. *Visions: How Science Will Revolutionize the 21st Century*. New York: Random House, 1997.

Kellner, Douglas. *Jean Baudrillard: From Marxism to Postmodernism and Beyond*. Stanford, CA: Stanford University Press, 1989.

———. "Reflections on Modernity and Postmodernity in McLuhan and Baudrillard." In *Transforming McLuhan*, edited by Paul Grosswiler, 179–202.

Kroker, Arthur. *Technology and the Canadian Mind: Innis/McLuhan /Grant*. New York: St. Martin's, 1985.

Kroker, Arthur, and Marilouise Kroker, eds. *Digital Delirium*. New York: St. Martin's, 1997.

Kroker, Arthur, and Michael A. Weinstein. *Data Trash: The Theory of the Virtual Class*. New York: St. Martin's, 1994.

Kroker, Arthur, Marilouise Kroker, and David Cook, eds. *Panic Encyclopedia: The Definitive Guide to the Postmodern Scene*. New York: St. Martin's, 1989.

Kurzweil, Ray. *The Age of Spiritual Machines: When Computers Exceed Human Intelligence*. New York: Penguin, 2000.

———. *The Singularity Is Near: When Humans Transcend Biology*. New York: Penguin, 2005.

Landon, Brooks. "Less Is More: Much Less Is Much More: The Insistent Allure of Nanotechnology Narratives in Science Fiction." In *Nanoculture*, edited by N. Katherine Hayles, 131–46.

Levinson, Paul. *Digital McLuhan: A Guide to the Information Millennium*. New York: Routledge, 1999.

Marshall, Kate. "Future Present: Nanotechnology and the Scene of Risk." In *Nanoculture*, edited by N. Katherine Hayles, 147–59.

May, Christopher. *The Information Society: A Skeptical View*. Cambridge: Polity Press, 2002.

McKibben, Bill. *Enough: Staying Human in an Engineered Age*. New York: Times Books, 2003.

McLuhan, Marshall. *The Gutenberg Galaxy: The Making of Typographic Man*. University of Toronto Press, 1962.

———. *Understanding Media: The Extensions of Man*. New York: McGraw-Hill, 1965.

Milburn, Colin. "Nanotechnology in the Age of Posthuman Engineering: Science Fiction as Science." In *Nanoculture*, edited by N. Katherine Hayles, 109–29.

Moravec, Hans. *Mind Children: The Future of Robot and Human Intelligence*. Cambridge, MA: Harvard University Press, 1988.

Mulhall, Douglas. *Our Molecular Future: How Nanotechnology, Robotics, Genetics, and Artificial Intelligence Will Transform Our World*. Amherst, NY: Prometheus Books, 2002.

Postman, Neil. *Technopoly: The Surrender of Culture to Technology*. New York: Vintage Books, 1993.

Rosenthal, Raymond, ed. *McLuhan: Pro and Con*. Baltimore: Penguin, 1968.

Roszak, Theodore. *The Cult of Information: The Folklore of Information and the True Art of Thinking*. New York: Pantheon, 1996.

Smith, Merritt Roe, and Leo Marx, eds. *Does Technology Drive History? The Dilemma of Technological Determinism*. Cambridge, MA: MIT Press, 1994.

———. "Introduction." In *Does Technology Drive History?*, 1–35.

Stamps, Judith. *Unthinking Modernity: Innis, McLuhan, and the Frankfurt School*. Montreal: McGill-Queen's University Press, 1995.

Standage, Tom. *The Victorian Internet: The Remarkable Story of the Telegraph and the Nineteenth Century's On-Line Pioneers*. New York: Walker, 1998.

Theall, Donald. *The Virtual Marshall McLuhan*. Montreal: McGill-Queen's University Press, 2001.

Vinge, Vernor. "The Coming Technological Singularity: How to Survive in the Post-Human Era." Paper presented at the VISION-21 Symposium, March 30–31, 1993. http://www-rohan.sdsu.edu/faculty/vinge/misc/singularity.html. Accessed October 31, 2012.

Virilio, Paul. *The Art of the Motor*. Translated by Julie Rose. Minneapolis: University of Minnesota Press, 1995.

———. *Ground Zero*. Translated by Chris Turner. London: Verso, 2002.

———. *The Information Bomb*. Translated by Chris Turner. London: Verso, 2000.

———. *Open Sky*. Translated by Julie Rose. London: Verso, 1997.

———. *The Virilio Reader*. Edited by James Der Derian. London: Blackwell, 1998.

Webster, Frank. *Theories of the Information Society*. New York: Routledge, 1995.

Wiener, Norbert. *The Human Use of Human Beings: Cybernetics and Society*. 1950. New York: Avon, 1967.

11. Army Surplus: Notes on "Exterminism"

Adorno, Theodor. *Negative Dialectics*. Translated by E. B. Ashton. 1973. New York: Continuum, 1995.

Agamben, Giorgio. *Homo Sacer: Sovereign Power and Bare Life*. Translated by Daniel Heller-Roazen. Stanford, CA: Stanford University Press, 1998.

———. *Means without End: Notes on Politics*. Translated by Vincenzo Binitti and Caesare Casarino. Minneapolis: University of Minnesota Press, 2000.

Alexander, Michele. *The New Jim Crow: Mass Incarceration in the Age of Colorblindness*. New York: The New Press, 2010.

Arendt, Hanna. *Imperialism*. Part 2 of *The Origins of Totalitarianism*. 1951. New York: Harcourt, Brace and World, 1968.

Bauman, Zygmunt. *Modernity and the Holocaust*. Ithaca, NY: Cornell University Press, 1989.

Black, Edwin. *War against the Weak: Eugenics and America's Campaign to Create a Master Race*. New York: Four Walls Eight Windows, 2003.

Bloxham, Donald, and A. Dirk Moses, eds. *The Oxford Handbook of Genocide Studies*. Oxford: Oxford University Press, 2010.

Boner, Harold A. *Hungry Generations: The Nineteenth-Century Case against Malthusianism*. New York: King's Crown Press, Columbia University, 1955.

Bradshaw, David. "Eugenics: 'They Should Certainly Be Killed.'" In *A Concise Companion to Modernism*, edited by David Bradshaw, 34–55. Oxford: Blackwell, 2003.

Brantlinger, Patrick. *Bread and Circuses: Theories of Mass Culture as Social Decay*. Ithaca, NY: Cornell University Press, 1983.

———. *Dark Vanishings: Discourse on the Extinction of Primitive Races*. Ithaca, NY: Cornell University Press, 2003.

Carlyle, Thomas. *Chartism*. 1839. In *Essays: English and Other Critical Essays*. London and New York: J. M. Dent, 1964.

Clifton, Eli. "U.S.: Suicide Rate Surged among Veterans. *IPS News*. January 13, 2010. ipsnews.net/news.asp?idnews=49971. Accessed November 2, 2012.

Danner, Mark. "After September 11: Our State of Exception." *New York Review of Books* Oct. 13, 2011. http://www.nybooks.com/articles/archives/2011/oct/13/after -september-11-our-state-exception/?pagination=false. Accessed November 2, 2012.

Ehrlich, Paul. *The Population Bomb*. New York: Ballantine Books, 1968.

Fein, Helen. *Genocide: A Sociological Perspective*. London: Sage Publications, 1993.

Foucault, Michel. *History of Sexuality, Vol. 1: An Introduction*. Translated by Robert Hurley. New York: Vintage Books, 1980.

———. *"Society Must Be Defended": Lectures at the Collège de France 1975–1976*. Translated by Mauro Bertani and David Macey. New York: Picador, 2003.

Harman, Chris. *Zombie Capitalism: Global Crisis and the Relevance of Marx*. Chicago: Haymarket Books, 2009.

Harvey, David. *The Enigma of Capital and the Crises of Capitalism*. Oxford: Oxford University Press, 2010.

Himmelfarb, Gertrude. *The Idea of Poverty: England in the Early Industrial Age*. New York: Knopf, 1983.

Horkheimer, Max, and Theodor Adorno. *Dialectic of Enlightenment*. Translated by John Cumming. New York: Continuum, 1997.

Huffington, Ariana. *Third-World America: How Our Politicians Are Abandoning the Middle Class and Betraying the American Dream*. New York: Broadway, 2010.

Johnson, Chalmers. *Nemesis: The Last Days of the American Republic*. New York: Holt, 2006.

Jones, Adam. *Genocide: A Comprehensive Introduction*. New York: Routledge, 2006.

Kevles, Daniel J. *In the Name of Eugenics: Genetics and the Uses of Human Heredity*. Cambridge: Harvard University Press, 1995.

Le Bon, Gustave. *The Crowd: A Study of the Popular Mind*. 1895. New York: Viking, 1960.

Lombardo, Paul, ed. *A Century of Eugenics in America: From the Indiana Experiment to the Human Genome Era*. Bloomington: Indiana University Press, 2011.

Malthus, Thomas Robert. *On Population*. New York: Modern Library, 1960.

———. *An Essay on the Principle of Population*. 2d ed. London J. Johnson, 1803. (Book IV, Chap. VI, p. 531.)

"Marcus." *Book of Murder! Vade-Mecum for the Commissioners and Guardians of the New Poor Law throughout Great Britain and Ireland. . . .* 2 ed. London: John Hill, 1839.

Marx, Karl. *Capital*. 3 vols. New York: Penguin Books, 1990.

———. *Grundrisse*. New York: Penguin Books, 1993.

Maze, Rick. "Obama Unveils Major Jobs Initiative for Vets." *Army Times*. August 5, 2011. http://www.armytimes.com/news/2011/08/military-obama-unveils-major-jobs-plan -veterans-080511w/. Accessed November 2, 2012.

Meek, Ronald, ed. *Marx and Engels on the Population Bomb*. Berkeley, CA: Ramparts Press, 1971.

Moses, A. Dirk, ed. *Empire, Colony, Genocide: Conquest, Occupation, and Subaltern Resistance in World History*. New York: Bergahn Books, 2008.

Osborne, Rev. Sidney Godolphin. "Immortal Sewerage." In *Meliora; or, Better Times to Come* 7–17. Viscount Ingestre, ed. 1st series, 1853.

Pager, Devah. *Marked: Race, Crime, and Finding Work in an Era of Mass Incarceration*. Chicago: University of Chicago Press, 2007.

Pick, Daniel. *Faces of Degeneration: A European Disorder, c. 1848–c. 1918*. Cambridge: Cambridge University Press, 1989.

Rawson, Claude. *God, Gulliver, and Genocide: Barbarism and the European Imagination, 1492–1945*. Oxford: Oxford University Press, 2001.

Rubinstein, Richard L. *The Age of Triage: Fear and Hope in an Overcrowded World*. Boston: Beacon Press, 1983.

Rummel, R. J. *Death by Government*. New Brunswick, NJ: Transaction Publishers, 1994.

Shamsi, Hina. "The Legacy of 9/11: Endless War without Oversight." *The Guardian*, September 7, 2011. http://www.guardian.co.uk/commentisfree/cifamerica/2011/sep/07/us-constitution-and-civil-liberties-congress. Accessed Nov. 2, 2012.

Shuster, Martin. "Philosophy and Genocide." In *The Oxford Handbook of Genocide Studies*, edited by Donald Bloxham and A. Dirk Moses, 217–35.

Wells, H. G. *Anticipations of the Reaction of Mechanical and Scientific Progress on Human Life and Thought*. 1901. New York: Harper, 1902.

Žižek, Slavoj. *Welcome to the Desert of the Real*. London: Verso, 2002.

12. World Social Forum: Multitude versus Empire?

Amoore, Louise, ed. *The Global Resistance Reader*. New York: Routledge, 2005.

Anderson, Sarah, et al., *Field Guide to the Global Economy*. New York: The New Press, 2000.

Balakrishnan, Gopal, ed. *Debating Empire*. London and New York: Verso, 2003.

Bello, Walden. *Deglobalization: Ideas for a New World Economy*. London and New York: Zed Books, 2002.

Benjamin, Medea. "The Debate over Tactics." In *Globalize This!*, edited by Danaher and Burbach, 67–72.

Bennis, Phyllis. *Challenging Empire: How People, Governments, and the UN Defy US Power*. Northampton, MA: Olive Branch Press, 2006.

Blum, William. *Rogue State: A Guide to the World's Only Superpower*. Monroe, ME: Common Courage Press, 2000.

Boushey, Heather, and Christian Weller. "What the Numbers Tell Us." In *Inequality Matters: The Growing Economic Divide in America and Its Poisonous Consequences*, edited by James Lardner and David A. Smith, 27–40. New York and London: The New Press, 2005.

Bové, José, and F. Dufour. *The World Is Not for Sale: Farmers against Junk Food*. London: Verso Books, 2001.

Bruce, Iain, ed. *The Porto Alegre Alternative: Direct Democracy in Action*. London: Pluto Press, 2004.

Cassen, Bernard. "On the Attack." *New Left Review* 19 (2003): 41–60.

Cavanagh, John, and Jerry Mander, et al. *Alternatives to Economic Globalization: A Better World Is Possible*. San Francisco: Berrett-Koehler, 2002.

Chomsky, Noam. *Year 501: The Conquest Continues.* Boston: South End Press, 1993.

Collier, George. *Basta! Land and the Zapatista Rebellion in Chiapas.* 3d ed. Oakland, CA: Food First, 2005.

Condon, Garret. "Futurists Say World Is at a Turning Point." *Chicago Tribune,* April 9, 2003.

Danaher, Kevin, and Roger Burbach, eds. *Globalize This! The Battle against the World Trade Organization and Corporate Rule.* Monroe, ME: Common Courage Press, 2000.

Danaher, Kevin, and Jason Mark. *Insurrection: Citizen Challenges to Corporate Power.* New York: Routledge, 2003.

Davis, Mike. *Planet of Slums.* London and New York: Verso, 2006.

Eschle, Catherine. *Making Feminist Sense of the Global Justice Movement.* Lanham, MD: Rowman and Littlefield, 2010.

Fanon, Frantz. *The Wretched of the Earth.* Translated by Constance Farrington. New York: Grove Press, 1963.

Fisher, William, and Thomas Ponniah, eds. *Another World Is Possible: Popular Alternatives to Globalization at the World Social Forum.* London: Zed Books, 2003.

Foucault, Michel. *Discipline and Punish: The Birth of the Prison.* Translated by Alan Sheridan. New York: Vintage Books, 1979.

———. *Language, Counter-Memory, Practice: Selected Essays and Interviews.* Edited by Donald F. Bouchard. Translated by Donald F. Bouchard and Sherry Simon. Ithaca, NY: Cornell University Press, 1977.

George, Susan. *Another World Is Possible If. . . .* New York and London: Verso, 2004.

Gilber, John. *Mexico Unconquered: Chronicles of Power and Revolt.* San Francisco: City Lights, 2009.

Gret, Marion, and Yves Sintomer. *The Porto Alegre Experiment: Learning Lessons for Better Democracy.* London: Zed Books, 2005.

Hacker, Jacob, and Paul Pierson. *Winner-Take-All Politics: How Washington Made the Rich Richer—and Turned Its Back on the Middle Class.* New York: Simon and Schuster, 2010.

Hardt, Michael, and Antonio Negri. *Empire.* Cambridge, MA: Harvard University Press, 2000.

———. "Foreword." In *Another World Is Possible,* edited by Fisher and Ponniah, xvi–xix.

———. *Multitude: War and Democracy in the Age of Empire.* New York: Penguin, 2004.

Harvey, David. *The New Imperialism.* Oxford: Oxford University Press, 2003.

Hawken, Paul. "Skeleton Woman Visits Seattle." In *Globalize This!,* edited by Danaher and Burbach, 14–34.

Hedges, Chris. "Stand Still for the Apocalypse." *Truth-out.org,* Saturday, December 1, 2012. http://truth-out.org/news/item/12949-chris-hedges-stand-still-for-the-apocalypse. Accessed December 10, 2012.

Huffington, Ariana. *Third-World America: How Our Politicians Are Abandoning the Middle Class and Betraying the American Dream.* New York: Random House, 2010.

IFG (International Forum on Globalization). *Does Globalization Help the Poor?* San Francisco: IFG, 2001.

Johnson, Chalmers. *The Sorrows of Empire.* New York: Henry Holt, 2004.

Khasnabish, Alex. *Zapatismo beyond Borders: New Imaginations of Political Possibility.* Toronto: University of Toronto Press, 2008.

Klein, Naomi. *Fences and Windows: Dispatches from the Front Lines of the Globalization Debate*. New York: Picador, 2002.

Leite, José Corrêa. *The World Social Forum: Strategies of Resistance*. Chicago: Haymarket Books, 2005.

Lessig, Lawrence. *Republic, Lost: How Money Corrupts Congress—and a Plan to Stop It*. New York: Hachette Book Group, 2011.

Lowes, David. *The Anti-Capitalist Dictionary: Movements, Histories and Motivations*. Nova Scotia, CAN: Fernwood Press, 2011.

Madrick, Jeff. *Age of Greed: The Triumph of Finance and the Decline of America, 1970 to the Present*. New York: Knopf, 2011.

Maeckelbergh, Marianne. *The Will of the Many: How the Alterglobalisation Movement Is Changing the Face of Democracy*. London: Pluto Press, 2009.

Mander, Jerry, and Victoria Tauli-Corpuz, eds. *Paradigm Wars: Indigenous Peoples' Resistance to Economic Globalization*. San Francisco: International Forum on Globalization, 2006.

Marcos, Subcomandante. *The Speed of Dreams: Selected Writings 2001–2007*. Edited by Canek Peña-Vargas and Greg Ruggiero. San Francisco: City Lights Books, 2007.

Mertes, Tom, ed. *A Movement of Movements: Is Another World Really Possible?* London and New York: Verso, 2004.

Meyer, Lois, and Benjamin Maldonado Alvarado, eds. *New World of Indigenous Resistance: Noam Chomsky and Voices from North, South, and Central America*. San Francisco: City Lights Books, 2010.

Monbiot, George. *Manifesto for a New World Order*. New York and London: The New Press, 2003.

Munck, Ronaldo. *Globalization and Contestation: The New Great Counter-Movement*. London and New York: Routledge, 2007.

Navarro, Luis Hernandez. "The Revolt of the Globalized." In *Globalize This!*, edited by Kevin Danaher and Roger Burbach, 41–43.

Olesen, Thomas. *International Zapatismo: The Construction of Solidarity in the Age of Globalization*. London and New York: Zed Books, 2005.

Perkins, John. *Confessions of an Economic Hit Man*. San Francisco: Berrett-Koehler, 2004.

Pieterse, Jan Nederveen. *Globalization or Empire?* New York and London: Routledge, 2004.

Pleyers, Geoffrey. *Alter-Globalization: Becoming Actors in the Global Age*. Malden, MA: Polity, 2010.

Ponniah, Thomas, and William F. Fisher. "Introduction: The World Social Forum and the Reinvention of Democracy." In *Another World Is Possible*, edited by Fisher and Ponniah, 1–20.

Rees, John. *Imperialism and Resistance*. New York: Routledge, 2006.

Santos, Boaventura de Sousa, ed. *Voices of the World*. London: Verso, 2010.

Seyoum, Belay. *The State of the Global Economy 2001/2002: Trends: Data: Rankings: Charts*. Baldwin Place, NY: Encyclopedia Society, 2001.

Shiva, Vandana. "The Living Democracy Movement: Alternatives to the Bankruptcy of Globalization." In *Another World Is Possible*, edited by Fisher and Ponniah, 115–24.

Smith, Jackie, et al. *Global Democracy and the World Social Forums*. Boulder and London: Paradigm Publishers, 2008.

Starr, Amory. *Global Revolt: A Guide to the Movements against Globalization.* London and New York: Zed Books, 2005.

Stedile, João Pedro. "Brazil's Landless Battalions: The Sem Terra Movement." In *A Movement of Movements,* edited by Fisher and Ponniah, 17–48.

Stiglitz, Joseph. *Globalization and Its Discontents.* New York: W. W. Norton, 2003.

Stiglitz, Joseph, and Linda Bilmes. *The Three-Trillion Dollar War: The True Cost of the Iraq Conflict.* New York: W. W. Norton, 2008.

Thomas, Janet. *The Battle in Seattle: The Story behind and beyond the WTO Demonstrations.* Golden, CO: Fulcrum Publishing, 2000.

Turbulence Collective. *What Would It Mean to Win?* Oakland, CA: PM Press, 2010.

United States Social Forum Program, "Neoliberalism." http://www.ussf2007.org /program_neoliberalism. Accessed November 6, 2012.

Wolin, Sheldon. *Democracy Incorporated: Managed Democracy and the Specter of Inverted Totalitarianism.* Princeton, NJ: Princeton University Press, 2008.

Wright, Angus, and Wendy Wolford. *To Inherit the Earth: The Landless Movement and the Struggle for a New Brazil.* Oakland: Food First, 2008.

Žižek, Slavoj. *Living in the End Times.* London: Verso, 2010.

INDEX

PATRICK BRANTLINGER is James Rudy Professor of English (Emeritus) at Indiana University Bloomington. His books include *The Reading Lesson: The Threat of Mass Literacy in Nineteenth-Century British Fiction* (IUP, 1998); *Bread and Circuses: Theories of Mass Culture as Social Decay; Crusoe's Footprints: Cultural Studies in Britain and America; Who Killed Shakespeare? What's Happened to English since the Radical Sixties;* and *Taming Cannibals: Race and the Victorians.*